In the Chair

In the Chair

Interviews with Poets from the North of Ireland

JOHN BROWN

salmonpublishing

Published in 2002 by
Salmon Publishing Ltd.,
Cliffs of Moher, County Clare, Ireland
Website: www.salmonpoetry.com
email: info@salmonpoetry.com

A catalogue record for this book is available from the British Library.

Salmon Publishing gratefully acknowledges the financial assistance of The Arts
Council/An Chomhairle Ealaoin and The Arts Council of Northern Ireland

ISBN 1 903392 21 7

Cover artwork: 'Matter' by Fiona Murray
Cover design by Keith Connolly at Tonic Design, Belfast
Typeset by Siobhán Hutson, Salmon Publishing
Printed by Colour Books, Dublin

for Pamela Hunter

ACKNOWLEDGEMENTS

Acknowledgement is made to Frank Ormsby who suggested the title and whose *Poets from the North of Ireland* was an invaluable model and source. 'Roy McFadden Interviewed' was first published in *The Irish Review* (24, Autumn 1999). An early, shorter, draft of the 'Interview with Padraic Fiacc' (undertaken with Henry MacDonald and Martin Crawford) which first appeared in *Gown Literary Supplement* (1988) formed the basis for the current interview undertaken in September 1999. Grateful acknowledgement is also made to *The Paris Review*, Derek Mahon and Eamon Grennan for permission to reprint the 'Interview with Derek Mahon' which appeared in this publication (Spring 2000) as well as to Faber & Faber for permission to reprint the interview with Paul Muldoon from John Haffenden's *Viewpoints: Poets in Conversation* (1981). I am also indebted to Jamshid Mirfenderesky who read the introduction and made necessary changes and valuable suggestions, as well as to Ted Hickey who assisted with proofing an earlier draft of the text.

CONTENTS

INTRODUCTION

This book comprises twenty two interviews with poets from the North of Ireland. The poets were all born after 1920; each poet has published at least one book-length collection of poems. The interviews record the poets' perceptions of their work, describe the biographical and historical context of the poetry and offer commentary on the work of other poets or assimilated influences. Arranged chronologically, by each poet's date of birth, the sequence of interviews covers poems written in subsequent, if not always consecutive, decades. Familiar and less familiar voices are included. The collection attempts to gather as diverse and representative a range of poets as is possible within the scope and limitations of a single book. Given the number of practitioners and potential inclusions, however, one cannot claim to be exhaustively prescriptive. Inevitably there are 'absent qualifiers' [1]. In contour, chronology and title the book is greatly indebted to Frank Ormsby's anthology *Poets from the North of Ireland* (1979) although deaths, departures and the emergence of new voices in the period since that anthology was first published have modified the shape which this book takes.

Many of the poets interviewed have lived and written through a particularly troubled period of history in the North of Ireland, as well as a period of rapid change in Ireland and the wider world. Consequently interviews reflect (on) resulting tensions between 'place and displacement' (Seamus Heaney), between 'roots' and 'horizons' (to paraphrase John Hewitt's formulation) and between 'continuity and discontinuity' (as described by Seamus Deane). The book's subtitle takes its cue from the birthplace of the poets and the recurrence of northern subject matter as a shared concern in many poems but the interviews record divergent views and practices, individual preoccupations and mobility in the life and work. Many interviews record the impact of northern roots and Irish contexts as forcefields mapped or re-mapped in poems ; they do not point to any easy assumption of 'Ulsterkampf' as a prescribed theme or site in the work.

If the concept of home is central and recurrent, it is also recurrently interrogated as problematic when conceived of as purely fixed or real or discrete territory. The poets and poetry, inextricably linked with a native place, seem seldom to have been imaginatively or literally circumscribed by borders. Just as Stephen Dedalus's address encompasses Clongowes Wood College and 'the universe' so Paul Muldoon's 'Lefty' Clery in one poem outruns the 'leisurely pan' of the school camera to appear in the same photograph twice. The question of double-vision, of at least 'two thinks at a time', raised by Paul Muldoon in this poem — 'Two places at once, was it, or the same place twice?' — is revisited here [2]. Not only birthplace or place (where poems were written 'from', 'about' or 'for') but mobility (across internal, national or continental zones) seems to inform a complex dialectic in the poets' lives and works. Ratios between actual and imagined locations, between biography and the life of the poem, between the individual poet and the writing community, are neither simple nor stable in space or time. Indeed, given the pace of change in Northern Ireland and the mix of poets who have remained, relocated or who regularly commute between places, it is now also tempting to ask a variant of Paul Muldoon's question: 'One place twice, was it, or a different place once?' If interviews question the territory of poems — and the term 'northern poetry' is itself potentially reductive if it does not remain an open question — they do so to relish individual viewpoints, ambiguities, exemplary formal strategies, imaginative journeys and the 'possibility of (a) possible life' (Derek Mahon's phrase) which often seems inscribed in the poetry itself [3]. In recording the junctures poetry repeatedly encounters or negotiates — with biography, history, politics, religion, violence, myth, ecology, industrialism, place, culture, music, visual art and the work of other poets — these dialogues question the possible meanings, pleasures or values poems afford as 'places where a thought might grow'. [4]

The extent to which the creation of poems or subsequent interviews with poets makes possible, or even privileges, these values has been increasingly questioned. Randall Jarrell put it bluntly when he asserted that, for many critics, asking a poet about the work was akin to asking the pig to judge the bacon competition [5]. According to some theories, often loosely associated with post-modernism, the author has become de-centered and the text is interpreted "collectively". Poems and the poet's gloss are open to further critical testing which has increasingly tended to consider the function or comparative nature of literature as *language* or *discourse*, often in the light of extra-literary theories. While the interview process may appear to pose a different emphasis it is not one which, necessarily, excludes either critique or text being returned to the poet as 'reader' in the form of questions. Indeed some interviews may suggest that some poets consider themselves not only 'readers' but 'makers' of poems, responsible for determining key features of texts and their ideolects such as the selection and experimental arrangement of language within the given language(s) or the pushing of the envelope of inherited forms or genres. Given that poets from the North have written poems to, for and about, named friends and fellow poets or poems modifying those of predecessors and contemporaries as well as poems fusing imaginary and autobiographical elements, then it might be suggested that a total severance of text and author may suppress as well as reveal clues or currents within the poem. If a poet's subjectivity is constructed by language *in* poems this surely does not exclude the idea that a poet may also (de)construct subjectivity *through* poems. Indeed many of the poets interviewed might be seen as encoding or questioning subjectivity in poems which deploy multiple narratives or exploit the uniqueness or unreliability of singular perspectives or in poems which fruitfully exchange phrases or ideas from one context or consciousness into another. Surely critical self-awareness, openess to the ambiguities and implications, to the potential and limitations of language (to the ways it is spoken, spoken for, or speaks us) are often evoked in the very process or language of some poems? Seamus Heaney's 'Death of a Naturalist' is aware that 'all' that is known is a 'door into the dark'; Paul Muldoon's 'October 1950' knows that 'whatever it is' that is knowable about his own conception (or misconceptions?) still 'leaves me in the dark'.

These interviews, then, place a premium on the poet's voice while attempting to retain both critical scepticism and the empathy of a reader. A reflex 'reading response' or a 'willing suspension of disbelief' which happens when a poem is read, admired and soaked up (when it 'hits home' or reads us) is acknowledged as a part of the way poetry works to enact vital, though barely discernible, shifts in the consciousness. Poetry is accepted as reverberating at this deep, inter-peronal, inter-subjective level before one questions the way it is structured to that end. Gaston Bachelard's *Poetics of Space* refers to images which can 'posses us entirely' so that the space between reader and poet *appears* to be virtually annulled: 'The image offered us by reading the poem now ... becomes really our own. It takes root in us. It has been given us by another, but we begin to create the impression that we could have created it, that we should have created it. It becomes a new being in our language, expressing us by making us what it expresses and a becoming in our being. Here expression creates being.' [6] In one interview the poet Michael Longley refers to the art curator Jamshid Mirfenderesky whose essay *Light in Painting* refers to some of these issues: 'As Barthes argues, by interpreting art works as "collective texts", the author becomes de-centered. However, based on certain experiences of art works, the existence of authors and their responsibilty is immediately restored and vindicated. For example, our feeling of admiration and a sense of gratitude which we often experience in viewing an art work which we find fulfilling is never attributed to the work, its history, its sociological connotations or its cultural significance etc. but rather it is directed to the person who is responsible for its conception and execution.' [7]

The extent to which poems and our admiration of them as readers is explicable still remains questionable. If poetry is considered as a 'being' taking shape in language demarcated from everyday usage (by highly textured patterns, especially dense imagery, significant forms or the particularly heightened presence of the medium) then it is questionable whether poems either continually reveal or displace explication or conceptual understanding of their fulfilment purely as a message. The extent to which poetry's language is a realist medium simply geared to communicate information or reinforce shared understanding remains an open question. Can it be assumed, for instance, that either interrogating text or questioning the poet will yield a stable interpretation if the language of poetry not only works hard to heighten aspects of reality but also 'worklessly' (Maurice Blanchot's phrase) recedes or slips further sideways into language itself? [8] The poem's artifice or poet's gloss in interviews are, of course, open to further critical, detached or sceptical questioning of their finer print as they enter arenas of textual criticism, shared speech or political or cultural frameworks. Ciaran Carson, though, pithily anticipates and questions whether this critically distant decoding of the text, in itself, gaurantees more access to the text, if the text is treated as a secure source or bedrock of knowledge. He states: 'I'm amazed at the number of people — this includes many academics — who think they *know* something because they read it in a book.' Why then read books of poems or question poets? Perhaps because poetry seems especially capable as a concentrated, virtually unparaphrasable, medium of describing or inscribing (while experimentally testing) the limits of what it is, or may be, known and imagined in language. By inviting communication while receding in the face of categorical explanation much of the poetry from the North of Ireland remains rich in both encryption and specific realities, offering both concrete images and oblique slippages. The extent to which this poetry resists or assists a literal re-translation back into the world from which it emerges remains an open question. Whether, in general, poetry's language or formal procedures will ensure its longevity (in the memory) or militate against its communal survival (as a source of difficulty for the reader) is also likely to remain an on-going and, perhaps, related issue. [9]

In exploring poetic influences or intertextuality (complex, often subtle, processes) interviews hope for retrospective insight on poems or their process of making within the space and conventions of the interview format. Influences appear to register variously, often richly, in poems: as prolonged conversation; as direct or modified quotation; as loose affinity or sustained shared concerns; as subliminal or even half-conscious awareness; as reactions, inflections, paraphrases,deflections, ironic spins, renovations and red herrings. Further close reading and sifting of the poetic texts or the great number of critical writings, lectures, anthology selections and translations undertaken by northern poets may uncover more depths or echoes or possible currents; it is a modest hope that interviews might provide additional, useful pointers in passing.

In compiling this anthology of interviews the gender imbalance of the inclusions became apparent. Inherited historically it is, perhaps, accentuated by the chronological approach. One attempts to signal inclusive change in interviews with emerging poets who are women; one attempts to resist tokenism or condescension. In compiling this anthology it is hoped that students of a body of work (that increasingly attracts critical attention) will find this book of interest and use; it is also hoped that more readers will discover the mysterious, never totally explicable, presence of the poems and, perhaps, attempt to re-write them 'anew' for both others and themselves.

The interviews, in the chronological order in which they appear, were completed on/by the following dates: Robert Greacen (September 1999); Roy McFadden (May 1999); Padraic Fiacc (September 1999); John Montague (October 1999); James Simmons (August 1999); Seamus Heaney (July 2001); Michael Longley (September 2000); Seamus Deane (February 2000); Derek Mahon (Spring 1995); Frank Ormsby (July 2001); Ciaran Carson (September 2000); Tom Paulin (January 2000); Medbh McGuckian (April 2000); Paul Muldoon (1981); Gerald Dawe (June 2000); Cathal Ó'Searcaigh (June 2001); Jean Bleakney (January 2001); Moyra Donaldson (December 2000); Cherry Smyth (August 2001), Martin Mooney (November 2000) Conor O'Callaghan (May 2001), and Colette Bryce (June 2001).

NOTES

(1) Frank Ormsby, *Poets from the North of Ireland* (Blackstaff Press, 1979; revised edition 1990); Preface to first edition, p.11.

(2) Paul Muldoon, 'Twice', *The Annals of Chile* (Faber, 1994),p.12.

(3) Derek Mahon, 'Poetry in Northern Ireland', *20th Century Studies* No.4 (University of Kent, 1970), p.93.

(4) Derek Mahon, 'A Disused Shed in Co. Wexford', *Collected Poems*, (Gallery Press, 1999), p.89.

(5) Randall Jarrell, *Poetry and the Age* (Faber edition, London 1973), p.74.

(6) Gaston Bachelard, *The Poetics of Space* (Beacon Press edition, 1994), p.13.

(7) Jamshid Mirfenderesky, *Light in Painting* (Fenderesky Gallery, 1998), p.13.

(8) See Ullrich Haase & William Large, *Maurice Blanchot* (Routledge, 2001)

(9) See Edna Longley, *Poetry and Posterity* (Bloodaxe Books, 2000),

ROBERT GREACEN

You were born in 1920 in Derry but there are few Greacens in the British or Irish telephone directory. Where does your surname come from?
The origin of the surname is from the Scottish 'grieve' which means a farm bailiff or overseer; you may remember that the Scottish poet Hugh MacDiarmid's real surname was Grieve so, perhaps, I am related to him. I imagine that my ancestors who settled in County Monaghan were probably illiterate or else half-literate because the name changed through time to the written form I now use. My father came from poor farming people, he was born and brought up in County Monaghan near the Cavan border, and when I visited relatives there neighbours would mispronounce the name as Gracey. My father had a number of half-brothers and a sister — my grandfather married twice — and I would stay with my aunt, a Mrs Armstrong, or visit her half-brother George who had an adjoining farm near Castleblayney. In the 1930s, when I was growing up in Belfast, I visited Monaghan frequently in the summer and this gave me some insight into what life was like in the Free State as it was referred to at this time. My Monaghan ancestors must have emigrated to the United States because the surname is not uncommon there.

The first years were spent in Derry, though, and you re-visit the city in the poems. What is your view of Derry?
Once again there is ambivalence in the name and nobody knows whether the city is Derry or Londonderry. I very often call it 'Foyleville' or 'Stroke City' after Gerry Anderson. I spent my first four or five years there before I moved with my aunts and grandmother to Belfast; they would often talk about the idyllic time we had spent in Derry. They would speak of Derry in conversation but would probably have written the name of the city down on an official form as Londonderry. My aunts would tell me that if we had stayed in Derry I would have gone to Foyle College which they spoke of as *the* great educational institution there. I have gone back to Derry periodically but I feel that I was cheated of growing up there. I remember going back with my Aunt Tillie when I was fifteen or sixteen on the 12th of August which they very much celebrate there, not in terms of killing a grouse but in terms of re-living a grouse. I knew Derry as a lovely

city with a long history and although parts of the city were very run down it is becoming more prosperous again now. Of course, if I had grown up there I would have been a member of the minority Protestant community. While there was much ill-feeling between the two communities — after all, the "Troubles" really started in Derry — I have heard that for long periods the two sides got on better there than they did in Belfast.

Poets like Padraic Fiacc and John Montague experienced dislocation in childhood which often emerges in poems as a search for a lost Eden. Is this applicable to you?
Absolutely. I agree to that. I never really took to Belfast. I was brought there at four or five and I left in my early twenties. I was left in Derry by my parents with my maternal grandmother and two aunts when my father went off to open a business in Belfast. He was a heavy drinker — I can never really decide whether he was an alcoholic or heavy drinker — and the business failed like every succeeding business he tried. When my aunts and grandmother moved to west Belfast to open a grocery shop — which developed successfully into a newsagency — I followed my parents to Belfast. I looked on them as strangers. I never really felt that my mother was my mother because I had transferred my affections to my Aunt Tillie; she really seemed to be my mother. Aunt Tillie had great strength of character and intelligence and so it is to her that I dedicate my *Collected Poems*.

Parental conflicts in Belfast — a father who drank and gambled and a mother who had more genteel aspirations for you — read like D.H. Lawrence's Sons and Lovers. *Did these conflicts manifest themselves in the poems?*
I never got on with my father: he seemed to resent me; he put me down; he denigrated me; he did not seem to want me to have an education. It was my Aunt Tillie who bought my school clothes when I went to Methody; she impressed on me the need to have an education and a career, to mix with people who behaved well. Perhaps her aspirations — both educational and social — were due to the fact that she had known difficult times. My maternal grandmother, who had been brought up in Tyrone and left a widow with four children — I'll never know how she managed to bring them all up — did not want my father to marry my mother. She expressed this in two words: 'he drank'. She probably foresaw trouble. In Derry and in Belfast I lived with my aunts. I only stayed with my parents briefly when I went to Templemore Avenue School in Belfast and I returned to my aunts when I went to school at Methody. The excuse was that the school was nearer to their house but the real reason was that I did not want to stay at my parents, nor did they want me there. Although I visited my parents at weekends I hated it; on Sundays I was pleased to be standing at the tram stop outside the Brittanic pub, bound

for my aunts in Donegall Road and thinking 'it's over'. My mother was always nice to me but there was too much quarrelling in the house. In later life, as my mother grew older, I came to know her better and I warmed to her. She outlived the others and she remained with my father only leaving eventually, quite late in life, to live with her sisters. Occasionally, there were times when I did get on with my father but these never seemed to last. He said on numerous occasions that I was the cause of the trouble which always seemed odd to me as a child. The relationship features in the poem 'Father' and in 'Father and Son' where 'hatred seeded and grew rank' — 'Yet that isn't the whole story./ I remember evenings when, father and son,/ We walked the velvety spring streets/ And greeted the blossoms one by one.'

Was east Belfast with its trams, newsagents, comics, football matches and penny cinemas as important as any specifically literary influences on the writing?
I suppose that this is the case and it is odd that I have written more about east Belfast when I spent at least as much time, if not more, in west Belfast. My early life though was full of numerous places: my aunts moved house in Belfast; I spent a year with my parents in Monaghan when my father went there to be a farmer (at which he failed as he failed at everything); later I lived in many places in London; since moving back to Dublin I have moved twice. I'm happy now in Sandymount and this is my last address but one. My early life though was good training for moving and I have never settled too long in one place.

You sent out poems as an adolescent. Were these adolescent poems?
These poems were mainly descriptive. I remember one was about old fishermen mending their nets while others were based on leftist propaganda about the Spanish Civil War and the struggle to defeat Franco and Fascism. My first piece of writing published outside the school magazine was an article, 'A Youth's View of Education', which appeared in *The Irish Democrat* in 1937. I had got to know the writer John Boyd in Belfast, a strong left-winger who called himself a Communist, and even though he was eight years older than me he helped me a great deal and he sent out the article on my behalf. This had a major impact on me. Boyd also lent me books and introduced me to recent literature — to D.H. Lawrence and James Joyce. A teacher at Methody told me that Lawrence was not healthy reading for a boy but I developed a high regard for *Sons and Lovers*; I still do rate Lawrence even though he has dipped in fashion. The article impressed some — not all — of my school friends; I was not quite seventeen and the youngest contributor when it was published and I felt I would soon take my place in the adult world as a writer.

At Methody you read Left Wing Book Club titles and informed your mother that your ambition was 'to be the next Socialist Prime Minister or Poet Laureate'. Over fifty years later you attack Margaret Thatcher in the poem 'Queen of the Bucket Shop'. Is radical politics a continuing theme in the poems?

Yes. This was under the influence of John Boyd. Until I met Boyd I was barely aware of the existence of the Soviet Union. I would have been a moderate Unionist — a boy with liberal instincts and a feeling for the underdog — who felt that exploiting people irrespective of religion was wrong. Boyd influenced me deeply. Up to the Soviet-Hitler Pact in 1939 I was as sympathetic to Marxism as it was possible to be without being a member of the Communist Party. The Pact ended for me, though, both Marxism and Communism and I became an Orwellite (even though I had not read Orwell at this time). So, I remained on the moderate left while Huxley's *Ends and Means* hastened my conversion to pacifism. After reading *Assignment in Utopia* by the American journalist Eugene Lyons — Lyons had lived in Russia and described the reality of a place where the workers were not allowed to strike — I became a strong critic of the Soviet Union and Communism, like Orwell, while remaining a Socialist. I'm not sure if I would call myself a socialist now. I no longer believe to any great extent in wholesale nationalisation — perhaps *some* industries should remain nationalised — and Britain seems to have a fairly healthy mixture of capitalism and state-run organisations. I'm in two minds though about Blair. I would be more to the left than Blair but not as far to the left as Tony Benn.

Your autobiography EVEN WITHOUT IRENE *(1969) images Northern Irish history and politics as '(hanging) round people's necks like a gigantic albatross'. When did you become aware of a divided community here?*

I think that I was aware of this very early on. In County Monaghan I went to the local school where I was the only Protestant and I was left to play outside in the playground while the others prayed inside. I was the only Protestant at the school and had there been a dozen of us one does not know what would have happened. My aunt and my uncle socialised with Catholic neighbours and yet there was a sense of difference; I remember wanting to go to a Gaelic football match and being told that we Protestants did not do this on a Sunday. In Belfast too when I went — briefly and reluctantly — to live with my parents on the Newtownards Road I remember being told that I was not to go to a Catholic enclave on the Short Strand because I would get into trouble. I went there once or twice and, fortunately, nothing happened. I remember rioting in the 1930s and barricades being erected on Seaford Street where you had to go though a narrow opening. Near my Aunts' house on the Donegal Road I recall a line of soldiers being drawn up and a young lieutenant, fresh from Sandhurst, shouting orders to the squaddies: 'Right Turn'.

You met the Belfast poet Roy McFadden in 1939; you both date poems in that pivotal year. McFadden was a militant pacifist then and his poem celebrating your seventieth birthday in POETRY IRELAND *(1990) reflects on your conversations as a 'strut through familiar themes'. How would you describe your relative positions at this time?*

The outbreak of what we feared was on us in 1939. I was in McFadden's camp although I was probably less militant. His pacifism came partly from within his family — especially from his mother — whereas my family supported the war and believed in Churchill. Like Roy, I had no sympathy whatsoever for Nazism. The poems of this time share themes like the threat or fear of what was to come, the hatred of violence, the hope that nations could live amicably despite their differences — the fear that war would lead, pretty much, to what it did lead to.

EVEN WITHOUT IRENE *sees McFadden as influenced by Keats but states that you were searching for a more modern, contemporary influence. Would you include Yeats as a modern influence?*

I would have been reading MacNeice, Auden, Spender and Day Lewis; these poets represented the contemporary world for me. At this time McFadden would have been influenced by the Romantics. I was not influenced by Yeats although I very much admired him and thought he was a great poet; I did not know his west of Ireland though and his politics did not please me. Yeats had written songs for the Blueshirts and as far as I am concerned he was absolutely wrong there. So Yeats was, and remains, a great poet without being an influence. MacNeice, on the other hand, wrote about the North, about art in general and about England; for many years I had been going over to an uncle in Birmingham and I had visited London and Stratford and my education at Methody had been very much English-centered. I knew much more about British politics and about what was going on in England than I did about politics or events in the South of Ireland; MacNeice rather than Yeats was the more important influence.

MacNeice is surely the great poet of flux — of change and shifting sunlight — and he does work the modern landscape. What did you find in MacNeice?

I found much of what you are suggesting. I mention visiting Birmingham. MacNeice had been a lecturer in classics in Birmingham and so his world was Belfast, Birmingham and Carrickfergus and London — the contemporary world and personal relationships; these were the kinds of things I wanted to write about. In *Autumn Journal* he explored this world as well as the world of contemporary politics. Just after the outbreak of the war I began editing *The Northman* at Queen's University. We hoped to 'act as the bridgehead between Ireland and Great Britain, and to seek the best out of the English, the Gaelic and the Anglo-Irish culture' as an editorial in

1941-42 put it. Perhaps that would have appealed to MacNeice. I am not sure though that we achieved this or that I have achieved this in my own writing but you do want to take the best from everywhere.

In the magazine RANN (No 14) you state that: 'Since the generation of Joseph Campbell and AE, until the late thirties there was an almost complete blank in poetic utterance...' Your retrospective account of the Ulster literary scene in the early '40s though points out that writers gathered around Michael McLaverty and Sam Hanna Bell and in Campbells' Coffee House, Belfast. Did these groups amount to a literary renaissance in Ulster and, if so, was there a shared theme or northern pre-occupation?
I'm not sure that this did amount to a renaissance, although at the time I would have wanted it to be and I probably thought that it was. Possibly that was wishful thinking. We would have shared concerns about living in a divided community and exploring how this could be resolved in terms of decent human relationships.

Did you know Fiacc at this time in Belfast? 'The Bird' (1941) with its 'black, unknowing face of death' at the window registers like an omen; Fiacc would set store by this Irish tradition of birds as omens. Do you?
I did not know Fiacc then. I left Belfast in my early twenties and when I went back I would see Roy McFadden, John Boyd, John Hewitt and Sam Hanna Bell. This poem proved popular amongst my earlier work; it was reprinted in a lot of anthologies but I think that it was untypical of my work then. The person in the poem was imagined and the poem did not come from any overt Gaelic influence. I may have picked up on something subconsciously — my Uncle George's death for instance — but, like a lot of work, it largely came from the subconscious.

Your first volume ONE RECENT EVENING (1944) appeared when you were twenty four. Was the influence of the New Apocalypse and New Romantic movement in this volume manifest in subject matter — 'pylons not daisies' as you put it — or in style?
The New Romantic movement influenced both style and subject matter but the style probably owes more to it. That movement is now almost universally reviled for the kinds of overwriting associated with Dylan Thomas — although he was really only on the fringes of it. At this time I would have read Auden and I picked up on writers from the '30s generation like Alex Comfort or Nicholas Moore (who are largely forgotten) and Norman MacCaig (who has survived in the literary sense). I've heard that the best way to anger MacCaig in later life was to bring up the influence of the New Apocalypse on his writing. I was not in the movement sufficiently long enough for its influence to bother me; I came in at the tail

end when its last two anthologies were being published and it was the earlier anthologies such as *The White Horseman* which really got the publicity. George Fraser, a very able man who became a good literary critic, was also associated with the movement but I only got to know him later on in London and he died early, at the age of sixty. I did come to feel though that these writers were of an older generation; I realised that you could not write like them. Later I changed my own writing so that it was not geared to the extreme romanticism of these influences.

You edited two anthologies, NORTHERN HARVEST *and* IRISH HARVEST, *in the 1940s and contributed (with Val Iremonger and Bruce Williamson) to* ON THE BARRICADES *(1944) where the introduction talks of raising and defending 'the first barricades against the low standards, facile half-truths and lack of integrity that have for too long rotted the Anglo-Irish spirit.' What were you identifying and attacking?*
At that time Val was very much on the left. We thought that there were a great many poets in Dublin who were simply living in the past and not engaging with the contemporary world or modern issues. They were simply picking up the fag end of the great Anglo-Irish tradition left by Yeats, Synge and Lady Gregory — they were with O'Leary in the grave. I felt we had to write about more than wolfhounds and round towers and engage with the new. *Northern Harvest* was published in Belfast in 1944 and drew only on Ulster contributors whereas *Irish Harvest* — published in Dublin in 1946 — had contributors from north and south. For instance, the latter included Mary Lavin, Sean O'Faolain, Lennox Robinson and Elizabeth Bowen. I was trying to point to the continuity of a tradition. In *Northern Harvest* I included both my younger contemporaries like McFadden and Iremonger as well as the older generation like Forrest Reid, Helen Waddell and Robert Lynd who wrote the introduction. While I was in rebellion against many of the older generation I did also feel that they had something to offer.

Did Yeats (in the recurring use of masks) and T. S. Eliot (in the withheld lyrical possibilities of some poems) offer options? Why so many masks?
I would see masks as a symbol of not revealing oneself and of other people not revealing themselves. I admired Eliot's work and I was certainly very impressed with 'Prufrock' and *The Waste Land* — possibly a bit less by *The Four Quartets*. I corresponded with Eliot in 1949, when Iremonger and I were putting together the anthology of *Contemporary Irish Poetry*, and I went along to see him, rather nervously, to the offices of Faber and Faber in Russell Square. If I remember correctly we talked about Regionalism in poetry — Robert Frost in America, John Hewitt in Ulster and Scottish poets. Captain Fox quotes Eliot. 'At Night in London' parodies Eliot —

'Flow on dark, cool and uncommitted Thames'. In 'Life Without the Captain', 'Time then dissolves into time now. Time future seems almost bearable'. Eliot's work certainly often comes to mind but I see his influence as largely subconscious rather than direct; MacNeice would have been the stronger influence. A favourite quotation is Eliot's 'Teach us to care and not to care. Teach us to sit still.' That's very often in my mind. Muriel Spark and Derek Standford, as friends of mine in London, would have admired and talked of Eliot and, perhaps, his words stayed in the mind. His politics would have been a bit of a problem for me though.

You spent time in neutral Dublin in the 1940s and it's 'carnival' atmosphere, its 'expansiveness', contrasts with your view of Belfast as an industrial, puritanical city with its 'northern drizzle... its black out and khaki and drab rationing.' Does this contrast still hold?
This probably has remained but the feeling of difference is not as intense. I have some happy memories of Belfast but having been brainwashed by my aunts into seeing Derry as much more attractive and having had so much trouble with my father — largely in Belfast — I may have transferred personal dislikes on to the place. If I had been brought up in County Monaghan with my father, I would probably not have wanted to visit Monaghan very readily. The sectarianism that one found in Belfast though was pretty repulsive.

You met Patrick Kavanagh in Dublin in the 1940s. Did this influence you?
When I was in Donnybrook on Raglan Road Kavanagh came to stay at the Guest House and I saw him frequently. When I stayed in London with Stephen Spender for a short time — he was extremely kind — he introduced me to Cyril Connolly who asked me to review *The Great Hunger* in *Horizon*. I wrote a favourable review with a few minor criticisms; Kavanagh never ever mentioned it. He was disturbed personally and very ill-mannered and he could be extremely unpleasant — most people in the guest house disliked him — so I ended up defending him because I knew that he was a fine poet. Kavanagh was a great writer but he came from a rural Catholic community and this influenced his themes; I do not think that he did have an influence on me. The writers who left the strongest marks were MacNeice, Auden and John Hewitt.

Between 1948 (when you left Dublin for London) and A GARLAND FOR CAPTAIN FOX *(1975) there is a hole in the centre, a big poetic gap. Why?*
I have been asked that question dozens of times. I am not sure if I always give the same answers. After I had written *The Undying Day*, I simply felt less pressure to write. Many of the places I had written in closed down; new editors came who were simply less interested in my work; I ran into

personal and financial problems; I had to earn a living; I began to feel that I was more a prose writer, a literary editor or political journalist or the like; I simply felt less creative than I had been. I wrote a few poems which were published here and there but I did not seem to be getting anywhere as a poet. So, for some years, I worked with the United Nations Association as Assistant Editor writing about International Affairs.

Is it fair to see this tension between the creative poet (the intimate voice) and the public speaker (the rhetorical/political or journalistic voice) as already existing in the second volume THE UNDYING DAY *(1948). Did the rhetoric swamp the poetry? Was the combination a good or bad idea?*
I was absolutely set on going to London University to take up a course in professional journalism just before the Second World War broke out and the course was abandoned. I wanted to become a qualified journalist who also wrote short stories and poems and reviewed books — a bit like Robert Lynd (who left Belfast early on to do this in London) or St. John Ervine (who left to write a combination of journalism and plays). It was not uncommon; even Stephen Spender, for instance, combined poetry with writing articles about public affairs. I certainly did not think of the two voices as mutually exclusive and I was, and remain, interested in public affairs. In so far as I have become a poet in later years the combination was probably a bad thing. At the time I wrote that book I had vain political ambitions and I saw myself as having a role as an MP. Later I realised that this would not be a role I would play or even a role I would want. Still, I did remain interested in political journalism and, to some extent, I still am.

Did London give a different perspective on Irish politics? Do you think there is a political solution to the current problems in Ireland/Ulster? Do you vote?
I suppose that London did give me a different perspective. In London I wrote political articles for the *Tribune* which was associated with Aneurin Bevan, after having submitted poems during the war years which George Orwell as literary editor must have sanctioned for publication. In Ulster I would like to think that there is an answer but I'm not sure what this is. I would like to see an end to the violence; I would like to see accommodation for both sides. I am not sure if a settlement is possible; in fact, it may be further off than it was when I was in my twenties and thirties in view of what has happened in the last thirty years. The violence has now caused so many deaths, so many victims and injuries and so much destruction; the bitterness is probably greater now than it was when I was growing up in the '30s. So many people are mourning brothers, sisters and uncles and so many have served prison sentences. There are hopeful signs but I am as confused as anyone as to what the answer is. You ask how I vote; here, in the South, I vote for the Labour Party.

In THE SASH MY FATHER WORE *(1997) you describe your experience of LSD before it became widely used as a recreational drug of the 1960s.*
Towards the end of the 1950s I began to feel depressed. My marriage was no longer going well, I had financial worries and was generally unhappy with the direction of my life. Where was the zest and energy I could draw on in my twenties? I sought help from a psychiatrist in London called Dr Joshua Bierer, a Viennese. He believed in the use of LSD, a drug at that time largely unknown to the lay public. None of my friends had ever heard of it. I had a series of treatments which sometimes induced painful hallucinations but these provided insight into my somewhat troubled childhood. The benefit was very considerable and soon I began to write creatively and undertake some teaching work.

In the North in the 1960s new poets emerged. What is your view of northern poetry in this period?
I like and admire the Nobel Prize winner Seamus Heaney. I'm glad that poets emerged in the North in the 1960s; the '50s were a wilderness. On repeated visits home I would ask McFadden about new writers and he would tell me that few new voices had emerged. With the emergence of Longley, Mahon and subsequently Paul Muldoon and Frank Ormsby the North does have a continuing literary tradition: all of these writers have written poems which I have enjoyed. Heaney is a significant poet *and* literary critic. Many poets have left as have novelists like Brian Moore and Bernard MacLaverty.

Your wife is largely an absent presence in the autobiographical writing and the poems? Did this relationship feed into the poems?
This relationship was, initially, a good thing for the work because my wife was a writer; she published critical books about Joyce and Ezra Pound. I have written three poems about my wife and one of these is about her funeral — 'St. Andrew's Day'. It's been on the Dart in Dublin. I have just completed another poem about her and she has come more into my writing in recent years. My wife's father was from an Anglo-Irish background and her mother was from a London business family. She was brought up partly in Co. Cork and partly in England. She shared much of my own fairly radical political views — which both our families did not — and we would have shared a similar taste in literature.

Was the poet who emerged in his fifties in the 1970s different from the poet who wrote in his twenties?
Yes. I had a totally different style, totally different themes. An earlier version of *Even without Irene* came out in 1969, published by Dolmen. The book was Roy McFadden's idea and he encouraged me to write it

although it was with the publisher for years before it came out. When that book was published I remember deciding quite strangely and emphatically that I was going back to writing poetry again. I had the feeling that I was really going to write again. This poetry was different; so many of the early poems were over-written — too exaggerated, too full-blown and uncontrolled. I feel that I only really achieved my poetic voice in the 70s when I was in my fifties.

Voyage and exile are important themes in early Irish narratives and modern Irish poetry; these surely also run through your own writing from 'The Undiscovered Island' and Captain Fox poems to Columcille, the traveller and monk who also left Derry.

Yes, I think there is a sense of journey. The Fox theme emerged from correspondence with a dear friend of fifty years, Derek Standford, who left London to live in Sussex; in one letter I invented Captain Fox. Derek took up this private joke and he would write back telling me he had seen Fox in Brighton or places he visited. Fox then took life in three or four poems published by Robert Nye in *The Scotsman*. In the fourth poem I killed Fox off but when I visited Nye in Edinburgh he told me that I *had* to bring Fox back to life and write a sequence. On the train, on the way home, I thought: 'What a good idea!' And so I wrote a poem in which Fox's death was presented as rumour and I suggested that he was living in Montevideo. I've probably written forty or so Fox poems now; Peter Fallon at Gallery Press published twenty or so in *A Garland For Captain Fox* in 1975. After that book I began to think about what I might do when the Fox series ran out; it was then that my childhood and the North came back as material I had still not fully tapped. One of the poems about Fox, 'The Captain in Spain', is about the journey from the airport into the centre of Madrid, and then a journey to Toledo and to El Pardo, the residence of General Franco. Fox travels all over the world. He was in Montevideo for a time though I have never been there, but of course I've visited many of the places, such as the Black Forest in Germany, where Fox has been. The idea of a journey is symbolic as well as factual.

What does Fox symbolise?

Rory Brennan answers that question well. Let me quote his critique in *The Irish Independent*: 'Fox is a gunrunner, a bon vivant, an informed amateur philosopher, a user of women, a world traveller, a holder of numbered bank accounts, a spy, most likely a murderer. But behind the tales of deeds and plots hangs a tapestry tinged with metaphysical doom. The Captain with his tales of debonair betrayals seduced us into a shoddy admiration of evil. Thus Greacen exposes the fellow traveller in all of us for Fox is a figure that underwrites the glib codes of the late twentieth century capitalism or what you will. Though it smacks of the barracks and gaming table and not at all of the pulpit here, in fact, is poetry of a high moral order.' I add: 'Imagine Fox had been a real character as indeed he is to me and not a creature I invented, how would his death have been recorded in one of the broadsheets.' I go on to give him a glowing European career and a dubious obituary.

You also suggest though, in one poem that Fox finds his roots in Ulster Non-Conformity and English Methodism.
Fox's mother came from Banbridge in Co. Down and it's through his mother and, in a sense, through me that this tradition comes out in Fox. He is linked with the once Protestant city of Zurich too, but Fox has been all over the world; he lives in numerous worlds and I do not want to pin him down. In a later poem 'Across the Rhine', a professor tries to trace Fox's origins and I suggest that he has Polish-Jewish parents and provide supporting evidence by setting the poem in a German town where I often visited friends — Waldshut, near the Swiss border.

The creation of gaps, ambiguity and deliberate sensationalism are part of the strategy in inventing Fox. Did thriller writing influence this?
No. I do not read thrillers. Graham Greene though may have been an influence.

YOUNG MR GIBBON *(1979) features Fox, the North and poems about writers. Is there an over-arching theme?*
No. I simply returned to childhood and boyhood material I had not tapped.

You have written about Jesus, ironically re-written the Ten Commandments and virtually every Old Testament prophet appears in the poems. Is Protestantism and the Bible a positive or negative influence? In what way does religion enter the poems?
I was brought up in the Presbyterian tradition by my Aunts and my mother's side of my family were very aware of this heritage; on my father's side the influence seemed less strong or, perhaps, I was just less aware of it. There were certain ideals — honesty and integrity seemed to be important; on the negative side there was a narrowness and an unwillingness to explore other religions — not only Catholicism, but Buddhism, Hinduism or Islam. I rebelled against this at one time, but the Bible is something I grew up with — part of my mental furniture — in the same way that it was for W.R. Rodgers, though I imagine that his family was even more strict. His poem about Mary Magdalene is a great poem which could not have been written without this influence. I'm more interested in spirituality than organised religion or religiosity. I am not sure how this manifests

itself in my work. Certainly I have a feeling that something exists beyond this mortal existence; what exactly that is and at what point you call it God or spirit I do not know. I have met Buddhists who accept re-incarnation — and this would explain much in life and I do not discount this belief either. I think that we would be wrong to think that the evidence of our senses is all there is.

'One Day in August' records an Ulster journey to Annalong, through 'fields brown-pimpled with haycocks', while 'John Hewitt' in CARNIVAL AT THE RIVER *(1990) commends the poet and McFadden for trying 'to break the mould of bigotry'. Surely this volume is a move back to nature away from the early aesthetic of pylons? Were you influenced by Hewitt and Regionalism?*
It is quite possible that if I had stayed in Belfast I would have been influenced even more by Hewitt than I was. I might have become a disciple — as McFadden did for a time — but from early on I wanted to explore a wider world and to go to London. I appreciated Hewitt's poems for their relevance to Belfast and the province of Ulster. A city man by birth and upbringing he tried to come to terms with country life and concerns, especially in the Glens of Antrim. But he admits that in this he didn't wholly succeed. I disagreed with Hewitt's extreme Socialist stance and his sympathy for the Soviet Union and its satellites in Eastern Europe. At the same time I admired the way he championed unpopular causes in the face of hostility. I found him stimulating though I rarely argued with him. He had a profound knowledge of Irish poetry and particularly northern poetry. As a poet, a critic of literature and art, curator of the Coventry Art Gallery and political spokesman for Marxism he was an outstanding man, and deserves to be remembered and honoured. In fact he did get a singular honour for a poet, the Freedom of his native Belfast. His wife Roberta was a great support to him, and I spent many evenings in their flat in Mount Charles near Queen's University. I wrote the poem 'Carnival at the River' after visiting London from Dublin. I remember drifting asleep in a flat near where I once lived in Notting Hill Gate and these images from boyhood drifted back through my mind. I suppose it is the kind of thing you conjure up before you die or fall asleep. My grandfather appears and quotes Beckett as we travel towards the river but that's poetic license because that piece of writing came after he was gone.

Visual art features periodically in your work: Toulouse-Lautrec, Beatrice Behan's 'Mona Lisa smile', Fox's admiration for Goya. The White Stag Group of Dublin painters are mentioned in the Introduction to AN IRISH HARVEST *and there is a poem about Nano Reid who lived with your wife. In 'Words' you even contemplate going 'totally bananas, thinking I'm Dali or Picasso,/ ... making love to a piece of canvas or a blank wall.'*

I certainly enjoy painting but I cannot claim to be informed from other than an amateur position. I enjoy pictorial narratives and, to some extent, abstraction. On the walls I have a couple of Japanese prints and a 'Buddha' — a painting by a Buddhist monk from Tibet who was a pupil of mine when I taught English as a foreign language; I've a delightful little sketch by the Belfast painter Markey Robinson which tells you so much, without words, in a minimum number of lines. I like to visit galleries and look at paintings. I remember Colin Middleton (an interesting and experimental painter) who probably had too many styles and Daniel O'Neill and George Campbell. A couple of years ago, talking at the John Hewitt Summer School, T.P. Flanagan pointed out that there have been many Ulster painters like J. Humbert Craig who are interesting in the Ulster context but minor in the context of British or European art. Jack B. Yeats is the outstanding Irish painter and his father was pretty good too; from a contemporary perspective Louis Le Brocquy's images of writers are extremely evocative. After I saw Lavery's 'Twelfth of July Procession, Portadown, 1928' it remained with me so I simply had to use the painting for the book jacket of *The Sash My Father Wore*.

Roy McFadden has written of 'the sullen masturbation' of Orange drums; you have described your father's annual walk to the field. What is your attitude to Orangeism?
I have always been absolutely outside the Orange Order. Some Orange men are good people and Christians; on the whole the Order seems too politicised and there is a hard core who are extremely intolerant or very bigoted. I simply don't like parades or marches; they are too militaristic.

In Protestant Without A Horse *(1997) Anglo-Ireland is resurrected via the ironic reference to Behan; the introduction to* Irish Harvest *reveals an awareness of the slum dwellers behind the fan light. Has Anglo-Ireland totally disappeared with the rise of the Celtic Tiger in the 1990s?*
I came in contact with Anglo-Ireland through my wife who came from an Anglo-Irish family in Co. Cork. She had been brought up there and in England. I became friendly with her friend Hubert Butler (a cousin of Elizabeth Bowen), a remarkable man who spoke his mind fearlessly and reminded me that Yeats had said the Anglo-Irish were 'no petty people'. Recently I've written poems about my wife Patricia (nee Hutchins), how we met in Dublin and how I went to visit her at the ancestral home, Ardnagashel. Dublin is currently a liberated city. You can say what you like here; there's tolerance to the point of indifference. Dublin has become remarkably like London. On the other hand there's a new materialism: house prices have rocketed; money rules O.K.; people are interested in a fast buck; I've had my wallet stolen twice; a friend in posh Foxrock has

been burgled five times. Robbery with that frequency was unheard of when I was living in Dublin in my twenties.

Places, people, specific dates or days feature large in the poems. Do you have a favourite poem?
'St. Andrew's Day'. You mention that my wife is a missing presence in the writing but I have written three poems about her and she is in a recent Lapwing Press collection and this poem is very much about her. She was buried on St. Andrew's Day. On the day of her funeral I simply could not go; I was too upset. Although we had divorced we had become good friends again; she was coming to my flat to stay before she became ill and died of a stroke. The fact that we had become friends is important to me.

You say in EVEN WITHOUT IRENE *that 'Poetry is the antidote for hurt and frustration'. The preface to your* COLLECTED POEMS *quotes Spender's hope that the 'created poem' can achieve 'some final innocence exempt from dust' but the final poem states that 'Things are not what I expected'. Has poetry disappointed or provided resolutions?*
You mentioned a journey earlier: it has been a poetic and a human journey. I think I have arrived at resolutions but you do keep looking back too. In a recent poem 'Ardnagashel' I revisit the ancestral Anglo-Irish home of my wife Patricia and the Hutchins family, near Bantry in County Cork, with my friend Freddie Vine from Belfast. The poem is set in 1939 and written in short lines; it describes the 'small big house', 'Anglo yet untouched' by torches because the Hutchins family had good relations with the locals. At that time Collins was very much within living memory and the ports had just been given back; the house belonged to a family where a brother served in the army and my wife's sister was in the Women's Auxiliary Air Force. 'Shadowed Ireland/Croziers ruling OK,/Censors at work... /Big houses torched,/Drunk black and tans/On murder sprees, /Michael Collins towering/Over the rebel county/Then falling down dead... I took her hand/Strode into the future. /Coiled in the grass/The serpent slept.' Auden said that poetry makes nothing happen; perhaps it doesn't but it can help to make sense of life. Things often have not turned out as I expected: I did not expect my marriage to break up; I did not expect such a long gap in the writing; there were frustrations and disappointments I had not forseen. Things have often not been what I expected. At the same time positive things have happened and poetry helps to come to terms with hurts and disappointments.

ROY McFADDEN

Was your family background an important influence in your life and in the poems?
I think that goes without saying. However, my mother's side of the family
had an additional attraction in that she had been born in County Durham
— 'the English North' — of a Scottish father and an English mother with
(I like to think) the Welsh maiden name of Williams. My grandfather
Steel came with his family to Belfast in 1904 as chief draughtsman to
Workman Clark, the second shipyard there. He was also a relief preacher
for the Unitarian church and my mother as a young girl often accompa-
nied him to the provincial churches. My father's mothers' people, Quail,
had been cabinet makers, among other callings, in Downpatrick for over
two hundred years. The connection between the two families is explored
in my poem 'The Lay Preacher'.

As a youth alone in Downpatrick after his father's early death and the
departure of his mother and the other children, my father worked in a
solicitor's office until, aged eighteen, he entered the legal department of
a Belfast bank. As a young man he played hockey and cricket, and
reported matches for the local papers. He became the bank's librarian,
and was one of the founders and secretary of the Botanic Literary Club.
He inherited a love for wood and craftsmanship and made many items of
furniture for the home. His politics and religion were more conservative
than my mother's, and helped to create a balance in the family.

My grandfather Steel collected books and 'curios'; and he was a week-
end painter. He published at least one poem in a Scottish newspaper. My
mother inherited that cultural background. She was a pianist; she sang in
choirs; she was involved with theosophy and attended weekly meetings of the
Adult School; and she was an active member of the Peace Pledge Union.

Your parents directly influenced your own personality?
Yes: stability and mobility in something like equal measure.

You moved to Dundonald. Why? What is your earliest recollection of place there?
When my father followed his mother to Belfast in 1905 he lived in a house
in the Albertbridge Road; he subsequently married my mother and
moved into a nearby house in Mountpottinger where I was born. It was

the '20s and the 'real Troubles' as I call them were on. I've a poem recounting how I was born behind a barricaded window with soldiers in the front garden and snipers on the roof. We were victimised by activists and told to get out or be burned out so we moved to Dundonald, to a damp bungalow in Daisymount Terrace, where I got double pneumonia. I do not remember much about the Dundonald experience apart from the smell of paraffin oil and the sight of potato bread oozing butter at the side of the fire. My father made friends there and played cricket for the local eleven, so there were subsequent periodic return visits.

Sean McMahon's entry in the DICTIONARY OF IRISH LITERTAURE *edited by Robert Hogan (1979) sees 'gnomic significance' in your birth date coinciding with the birth of Northern Ireland. One poem states that you 'began in violence' and your 'age coincided with murder'. How aware of the early "Troubles" were you? Is there a parallel in your life with Padraic Fiacc's as writers born into the early "Troubles"?*
What is the significance in a birthdate? I also share this birthdate with Tom Caldwell, as someone once pointed out, and he sells furniture in Bradbury Place; Fiacc is two and half years younger than I am and I did not know Joe, as I call him, in the early years. When I was Chairman of the Belfast PEN Centre for one unfortunate year he was night porter in the hotel where we met although he was never involved as a writer. In the 1960s I did meet Fiacc when Michael McLaverty invited him with Heaney to his house in Deramore Drive. I suppose there is a parallel in our beginnings here — although in the '20s Fiacc would have been in America while I was here. In 'Evictions', a poem dedicated to Fiacc, there is a bit of fiction with the two children leaving their different ghettos and the child in the pram exchanging his flag for the other child's wooden tomahawk. Certainly I was thinking of Fiacc and myself when I wrote that poem.

When did you write your first poem? Were you interested in poetry at secondary school?
I wrote my first poem called 'Ode to a Daisy' when I was seven and I gave it to my grandfather Steel who framed it and hung it over his bed. I have no idea about why I began to write although my interest was well developed even before I went to secondary school. I had already published a poem before I was thirteen and received half a guinea for it. My father was always bringing home magazines and books; my mother copied out poems from periodicals although she was more interested in music. Words and music were always in the background at home. My main source for poetry was Palgrave's *Golden Treasury* and I was attracted to the lyrical rather than the narrative poems in Palgrave: it was the Bible, the holy book, the main influence. I did not really discover Yeats, apart from his early lyric poems in Palgrave, until I was about to leave secondary school.

Is there a conflict in your first volume of poems Swords and Ploughshares *(1943) between poetry as inner world and public commitment: the war with its 'hunted echo' in the local whin?*
Yes. This conflict was very much of that time and I did feel that it was incumbent on me to make a stand against the war. I was under the influence of Gandhi, amongst others. Like many in my group of peers, gathered around the *Northman* at Queen's University, the poetry welled up and we were not averse to sending out poems for publication although I did feel that my primary duty was to involvement with society and with what was happening to people at that time. While I felt that not every poem need necessarily be committed, I felt that *I* should be and, inevitably, that comes out in the poems. It was hard to escape the war. We were not quite as brutalised as we are now. I do realise that poetry which is pure propaganda is virtually artless. Increasingly my favourite poet of those years was Alex Comfort who was an active pacifist and he wrote to me saying that while 'poets can carry banners, poems shouldn't': that's impressive because Comfort was up to his eyebrows in anti-war propaganda and campaigning for various causes that were not official policy. Comfort's poetry is unjustly excluded from most war anthologies: he wrote many fine poems about the impact of the war on civilians such as 'Firewatching'. In the Easter Tuesday Blitz of 1941 we were bombed out and lost our house in an air raid. Perhaps the Luftwaffe bomber (if a poet) had a greater claim to inclusion in such an anthology than I had.

Many poems in this early volume use apostrophes and rhetorical devices to directly address the reader: — 'You, sitting in silent rooms...' Is this a weakness?
Yes, I think so. In the early poems, perhaps, there was too much of myself involved but you do become more sophisticated in addressing the reader and you get away from the strictly autobiographical 'I' and sometimes it's 'he' or another person entirely that voices the poem.

Cuchulainn recurs in the poems. Why? What is your sense of him?
Cuchulainn largely came from W.B. Yeats but I did get involved personally, not so much with Cuchulainn as the heroic figure but with the tragic element. For folk here Cuchulainn is an Ulster figure: this would have been less true for Yeats. These days, when every second word in the North is identity, Cuchulainn is used in all sorts of ways; but back in the '40s, with the war on and the overwhelming sense of Britishness, an Ulster figure on a grand scale, with a mythology spun around him was exceptional. In a later poem, 'Smith' — Cuchulainn was the hound of the Smith — there is the tragic refrain: *'Men of Ulster, Behold I bring you my son'*. There is also another poem about the killing of Ferdia at the ford. In these poems there is a sense of a contemporary war going on with its blood and vio-

lence and there is also that vague feeling of a local figure rising up from our midst, from a local landscape. John Hewitt called Cuchulainn, whose weapon was the Gae Bulga, a 'dirty fighter'; as a figure Cuchulainn tied in with my feeling about the absolute futility of violence. Cuchulainn kills the boy, who turns out to be his son, before he knows who the boy is, and in later poems I repeatedly refer to faceless people and those who wear masks, to make the point that involvement with violence dehumanises and corrupts.

In FLOWERS FOR A LADY *(1945) the elegiac note prevails. To what extent is this volume an exorcism of deep personal loss on the death of your mother?*
These elegies are central to my work. My mother died at the end of 1943. We had moved from Knock, where I had been brought up for eighteen years, to Cliftonville and then, when that house was bombed eleven months later, we lived briefly in Downpatrick until we moved to Lisburn. Beyond the house, which was surrounded by trees, was the headquarters of the British Army whose vehicles charged up and down the lovely country roads. I was studying for law exams and I was in the house on my own for much of the time. My constant companion was a young spaniel, who was killed by a vehicle on one of our walks. Those elegies are full of walks in the Antrim countryside with the trees and their supplicating hands. I was indeed Cuchulainn fighting the waves. Those poems go very deep and, whatever else, they are central to my feelings as a poet.

Do these poems move towards questioning conventional religion and accepting a sense of immortality?
I had questioned conventional religion from an early age. It was bad enough that my mother was a Unitarian, but she became interested in theosophy allied to Buddhism and spiritualism, with occasional sceptical visits to seances; and I had a nodding acquaintance with Krishnamurti. My mother spoke of Christianity as the youngest of the living religions. She gave me a very broad religious background. As part of my upbringing I half-believed in the idea of re-incarnation, and in that sense the skulls burgeoning with flowers in the earlier verse express a hope for some kind of continuity or immortality. I am less sure now. I was young then and the burgeoning was happening. Around that time I was confirmed in the Church of Ireland by Louis MacNeice's father, the Bishop of Down and Connor, and fifteen months later I took my first communion in London, at a high church ceremony exotic with incense and genuflections. The preceding three months had been ones of near religious mania — although I had questioned the curate — but, strangely, the whole thing suddenly fell from me as I was going to take that first communion. I'm now an agnostic which means that I keep an open mind. I have never

really been entirely convinced by the Christian myth though; it has been given to us by poets and artists. The Bible is literature.

To what extent do poetry and politics mix? In the poem 'Sixes and Sevens' you state that to separate art and politics is to become 'oblivious of the rats beneath the floor'.
Yes. While Comfort's comment on the difference between poems and banners seems right, it is also true that the poets I admire are politically educated although they do not necessarily have a party political outlook. Less and less of the Yeatsian attitude towards politics or Eliot's view of the world as 'wormeaten with liberalism' seems sensible. There has been such a growth of political cynicism these days though, that it is very difficult to embrace any political creed to which poetry might give shelter. Having spent forty years as a lawyer, I have been trained to think straight and that has not interfered with the lyrical quality of my writing, which is my essential contribution to poetry. In that sense a political consciousness or the ability to think about how a country should be governed equitably does a poet no harm. Reginald Reynolds, a Quaker involved in the peace movement, described himself as a 'Quaker Oat run to seed'; perhaps I am a Socialist run to seed. I used to use the word 'anarchist' to describe myself, but that's frightening for people these days. I suppose, you could call me an unorthodox Socialist. I am totally disillusioned with Nationalism of any description: flags and national anthems are certainly out as far as I am concerned. While human beings are not necessarily that attractive either we do hang on to the dregs of some kind of Socialist philosophy.

In the poem 'Saints and Scholars' you state: 'And now the orange and green/ are prostituted to the cant/ of candidates for parliament'. In terms of the Irish/ Northern Irish situation do you have a political position?
Yes. I would never have objected to Ireland being one undivided country and it seems to me that objections to this are increasingly ridiculous compared with what could be gained. The whole talk of Irish culture, though, also appears increasingly ridiculous and I'm cynical about that too — given that, at seven o'clock of an evening, they all sit down and watch *Coronation Street* or whatever. What is Irish culture as distinct from Northern Irish culture these days? During the war years there were differences: Dublin's second hand bookshops; steak and cream; no Black Out; lunch with Mrs W.B. Yeats in the Gresham. That world, Romantic Ireland is dead and gone now, it's with O'Leary in the grave. The six counties — Northern Ireland or whatever you want to call it — is perking up now after a terrible thirty years but, if the dregs of my theosophy tell me anything, the karma for the last thirty years here is going to be bloody awful. It is human beings and notions of life and death that concern me. I do vote but the unification of Ireland will be a drab affair, an economic

alliance without passion, and so my feelings for Ireland are virtually nil. At local elections I vote for Niall Cusack, an Old Labour candidate; and at national elections I vote for small opposition parties like the Women's Coalition or the Green Party; in one election I changed my vote from the Workers' Party to the SDLP, when the visiting candidate told me he had one of my poster poems on his wall.

In one poem '2 September 1939', you celebrate the last day of peace. In another, 'Kew Gardens', you say that the killer and the victims stay the same. Is there a connection between the Second War and the "Troubles" here?
Yes, definitely: these are both very close indeed; I'm glad that you see that. Julian Symons reviewed my 1977 collection *Verifications* in the *Sunday Times* and he made the point that I made the "Troubles" sound like the Second World War. The connection is the violence. The Kew Gardens poem is somewhat ironic. The German widow would have been oblivious of the provincial quarrel here, 'behind the trees'; I equate the two in the poem. When I was eleven months old I was evicted from my birthplace due to the "Troubles", and then when I was nineteen I was evicted by German bombs. The effects of violence are the same.

What is your attitude to Regionalism? In 'The Heart's Townland' you talk of the townland as 'a desert' and the poem appears to pay Hewitt a double-edged, backhanded compliment.
I initially endorsed Hewitt's attitude to 'Regionalism' to a large extent. I met him around 1943-44 when he referred to Belfast and Northern Ireland as 'the Sahara of the arts'. At that time Robert Greacen, my contemporary, had gone to Dublin and Bertie Rodgers had gone to London, to work for the BBC. Quite literally, Hewitt and myself were the only two poets writing here and we were virtually alone in having kept up the habit of writing poetry. By 1948 when I had published four collections, I came to realise that my mixed ancestry of Scottish grandfather, English grandmother, and a mother born in England, rather queered the pitch for talking in terms of an exclusively Ulster credo. Hewitt's Regionalism struck a chord with my own reading and thinking during the war years about decentralisation and it fitted in with with my longstanding belief in localising a subject, writing about the immediate environment. It's a rather obvious thing to do. There was common ground there, but I feel that Hewitt made a dogma of Regionalism to the extent of dishing up minor poets for consideration on the basis of their birth in Ahoghill, or their qualifications in lint-pulling. I stayed with Hewitt at Tiveragh in the Glens but, with the war raging around us, I felt that I should be in Belfast on Royal Avenue holding a placard instead of looking for an Ulster identity around Tiveragh. I was also more attracted to Dublin and to notions of

Ireland than Hewitt admitted. I felt that his Regionalism was too narrow, too close to being a cultural mask for Unionism, or, paradoxically, a mini-nationalism. It is possible that I was more romantic than Hewitt — he was fourteen years my senior — but I did feel that the regional idea carried the danger of running into a cul-de-sac.

Is there an 'Irish tradition' in poetry? Are there poets from Ireland you admire?
I am not fond of labels. When you talk of an Irish tradition in poetry do you mean poetry written in the Irish language? I cannot read Irish. There is also Anglo-Irish poetry, Irish poetry written in English. It is easier to talk specifically of American, French, German or English poetry in terms of the language they are written in. Yeats dominates Irish poetry written in English; the others, like Val Iremonger, are minor. Austin Clarke is a good technician; Kavanagh I never really took to, although he is in vogue now. I'm amused by one critic's notion that Hewitt and myself provide the link between Kavanagh and Heaney: a conduit between Shancoduff and Mossbawn. Apart from *The Great Hunger*, which I like, Kavanagh's *Collected Poems* do not make compelling reading.

Is there a dichotomy between poetry as responsibility and poetry as vision? In your work you refer to D.H. Lawrence and Blake, (in THE HEART'S TOWNLAND*), as poets one might associate with vision, but you also talk of Hewitt and sensible ancestors, who evoke an association between poetry and responsibility?*
There is a healthy tension. I admired Lawrence's *Sons and Lovers* but I've said: 'I don't read Lawrence any more, my favourite book a street direc-tory, that pages streets forever running home'. Lawrence's notions of blood and sex are largely discredited now. I identify with Blake's visionary qualities, and one poem has the repeated refrain, 'William Blake died singing'. I think that Blake attempted a poetry of praise which also often borders, paradoxically, on a poetry of condemnation.

I would like to test two influences in the poems: Hopkins and Dylan Thomas. In 'Heartholder' (published in the 1940s) you talk of 'salmon-shimmering things' and 'Heartholding-folding all things, furled wings, fast'.
I read Hopkins and he had a direct influence on lyrics like 'Heartholder'. I don't think I was influenced by Thomas though and at that date I don't think I knew much of his work. I heard him reading poetry some time later in London and, although I don't like poetry readings, I was enthralled by his declamation of 'Poem in October'. Mahon is alone among the local poets in reading well. I am not totally convinced by poetry readings though. A good voice can make 'Wee Willie Winkie' sound magnificent but you do need to see a poem on the page to judge its technique and its quality.

Technical construction, then, is important in your work?
Yes. I often engage and flirt with the conventional pentameter which is, as
Hewitt claimed, a conversational rhythm. He had a good ear for these five
beat lines; and, as he pointed out, a line like 'For definition means com-
parison' has both the stress of pentameter and the feel of a conversational
phrase you might hear on the bus. I am fond of counterpoint tied up with
pentameter, which also endorses the verse with conversational rhythms. I'm
fond of trimeter, the three beat line. I constantly experiment with rhythms
and rhymes and conventional scansion — as Yeats, not always successfully,
did — and I need this discipline, this skeletal rib structure, if only to pull
against. The fashion today is for prose — jottings, of the sort which
prompted Larkin to say, 'Now write the poem'. You have to work hard,
sometimes with six or seven drafts, to get the stresses and strains and a sense
of completion right in a poem. As Johnny Hewitt said: 'The completion of
a poem in itself is an achievement, and if it gets published that is a bonus'.

*Is there one poem you have written where you feel you reached a pinnacle of tech-
nical achievement?*
Yeats grew to hate 'The Lake Isle of Innisfree'. I continue to be friends
with most of my poems; but I regret that some have been repeatedly
anthologised to the neglect of others, perhaps their betters. If not quite
at random, then partly for personal reasons, from a large body of work I
pick 'The Dancers'. One of two poems dedicated to my wife, it combines
short and long lines and is, technically, one of my better poems. The three
half-rhymes in each stanza keep the bell ringing just loudly enough for it
to register sufficiently without this being too obvious and the longer lines
come in to clinch the stanzas. Strangely, though, it is the free verse with-
out strict metrical schemes, like 'Elegy for the Dead of the Princess
Victoria', which prove most popular with younger people while antholo-
gists also tend to favour the looser limbed verse.

In a 1946 essay in THE NORTHMAN *you commend Hewitt's 'Conacre' and
W. R. Rodgers's poetry but you see Ulster poetry as 'generally superficial or
exact, with no loose strings to entice the reader underground'. What did you
mean by this? Surely MacNeice is exempt from this critique?*
The dominant poets here in 1946 would have been Hewitt and Rodgers
and both were largely concerned with landscape whereas in England the
New Apocalypse poets often attempted 'sub-edited Surrealism' or neo-
Surrealism, like Comfort. The English writers of the time seemed more
varied and, perhaps, they reached deeper into areas of the personality in
being less concerned with appearances. 'Nature poetry' is something
which I never found exciting. Maurice Craig I admired, but he could also
seem packaged or derivative. Rodgers was capable of providing a lighter

touch than Hewitt in turning clichés around. On giving up the church, for instance, he found that 'too many books spoil the cloth'. I think MacNeice was technically a superb craftsman and poet. 'March gave clear days and unaccustomed sunshine,/Prelude to who knows/What dead end or downfall'. He is second only to Yeats and in some ways the more interesting poet because, as Auden pointed out, Yeats sometimes told lies. Yeats fed the notion of himself as a thoroughly modern poet engaged in creating the new, but in many ways he built the world, not as it was, but as he wished it and he coloured it with esoteric thought. He invented Anglo-Ireland in literature and spun a personal fantasy around writers like Swift. MacNeice saw Ireland clearsightedly; there is little in its culture or religion which he does not assess. In many ways he was also more politically educated than Yeats. His schooling in England, his familiarity with English contemporaries and his repeated journeys to and from Ireland gave him width and a worldly wisdom, and he really knew the contemporary world in a way that Yeats disdained. MacNeice came over to Dublin regularly for rugby matches but he also knew the hinterland of the west of Ireland.

Between 1948 and 1953 you co-edited RANN *with Barbara Hunter. What contribution do you feel that this magazine made to literature here?*
Rann made an important contribution as the first poetry magazine to appear in Northern Ireland although this has not been generally acknowledged and it is referred to in passing in the academic books. *Rann* was published at a time when this place was, as Hewitt described it, a 'Sahara of the arts' and at that time there were no Arts Council subsidies for these kinds of ventures. In the first issue, Rowel Friers designed the cover and we solicited material from writers who would not normally have written poetry, such as John Boyd and Michael McLaverty. McLaverty's only published poem appeared in *Rann*; we also published a short piece by John Butler Yeats which strangely anticipated Rodgers's interest in the hare and its mythology. I was in touch with other editors, welcoming work from other regions. We published a Welsh issue. But, most importantly, our pages were open to local poets. With increasing subscriptions, *Rann*, in its modest way, travelled the world for five years until we concluded with the publication of the first comprehensive bibliography of Ulster writers since 1900.

You have lived most of your life in Belfast? Has it, or your attitude to it, changed?
Yes. Old age has laid its hand upon me but the city has physically changed and that's not just a matter of nostalgia for youth in old age. Having been reared in Belmont I was conscious that you could walk into the countryside in half-an-hour and there was the intimacy of neighbours, the street games and skipping songs and the trams which have all gone. Belfast is

now just another city with cars, car parks, taxis and multi-storey hotels, and these days children seem to travel in cars to school and then return home to watch television. Belfast, like many cities, has lost its individual spirit. Just as I feel little warmth for this country in general, I feel little affection for Belfast in particular. The poison of the "Troubles" though would also erupt in my younger days. The poison still exists.

You talk of the 'sullen masturbation' of Orange drums which taint the evening in 'Those Glorious Twelfths' and in poems you have written repeatedly about the 12th of July. Are you a critic of Orangeism?
When I was a child my family left Belfast around the 12th July for holidays in Portrush or elsewhere so as to get away from it. It seems mild enough now but you would hear stories about people being questioned about their religion at that time of the year. I'm largely uninformed about the philosophy or beliefs of the Orangemen but I did feel a threat of latent violence in the noisy Lambeg drums summoning the tribe and in encounters with rough or drunk men. My father was not interested; my mother was in part English; and my roots were everywhere.

In poems such as 'The Song Creates All' are you stating, through Blake, a preference for poetry which recreates, rather than purely records, reality? In 'Doctor Serafico' you also talk of Rilke returning to 'the untransmuted scene'.
The recording of appearances is, I suppose, verse. Poetry is concerned with recall, recreation and recognition. With Blake celebration and condemnation share the same pew and like Hopkins he looked for God in a tree. I'm not attracted to landscape verse as I am to Rilke when he insinuates himself beneath the natural scene into his own domain and beyond to his personal hinterland. After the turmoil in composing the *Duino Elegies*, 'He marvelled that the untransmuted scene/ Could still seem probable.'

Why in your own writing was there such a big gap between THE HEART'S TOWNLAND *(1947) and* THE GARRYOWEN *(1971)?*
The gap is between volumes. During that period I continued to write and contribute to periodicals. (I have recently counted a total of sixty poems published in *The Irish Times*, many of them in those years.) I published *Elegy for the Dead of the Princess Victoria* in 1952 and my verse play about Cuchulain, *The Angry Hound*, was broadcast by the BBC. Over the years I was a frequent broadcaster and radio scriptwriter. I was also busy building a law practice and rearing a family.

Why in THE GARRYOWEN *is the poem which gives this volume its title based on rugby?*

I played rugby at school and, like Louis MacNeice, I attended interna-
tional games. As others have pointed out these were an opportunity for
celebrating being Irish and 'buying nationality with a pint'. Very few of my
poems are entirely limited in theme. In this poem there is the added
implication of the threat of nuclear war in the image of the ball as a
bomb. 'Ponder an Irish remedy for rout: *The Garryowen and the game set
free.*' The Garryowen was a rugby tactic of launching the ball high into the
air, when you were being pressed back, to buy your forwards time to rush
into the attack and set a countermove going. I am saying in the poem:
'don't lose yourself entirely in shouting for your side and being Irish but
remember overall that there is this threat of nuclear destruction'. In that
sense *The Garryowen* is about freeing yourself from the orthodoxies and
conventions which lead to war: that's the task of freedom, real freedom.

To what extent did the "Troubles" post-1968 have an impact on your writing?
The "Troubles" did of course have an impact on my life and work: I
equated the killing with the Second War. You saw the gap widening as
close acquaintances drew apart or said things which they would not nor-
mally have said. There was the absurdity of the violence which, from a
Republican point of view, drove the idea of a United Ireland further and
further into the distance, and, on the Unionist side, there was increasing
bitterness, dislike and hatred. One really despaired as atrocity followed
atrocity. We all became brutalised, and we forgot the names of the victims
after a week . I've made this point in a poem about one of the first victims
shot in the flats. Certainly, the "Troubles" added to my disenchantment
with this country and patriots of every colour or allegiance.

*Surely you are more optimistic about the future now, after the Good Friday
Agreement?*
I think so. In 'Those Glorious Twelfths' I wrote: 'Project an image for this
place and time -/Aloof from cheers and flags, the maddened gun -/Of
one embarrassed, guilty monument/Leaving its plinth in the establish-
ment /To smuggle flowers to graves it can't disown.'

*Women feature prominently in the poems. There is the mythic Eurydice and
'Contemplations of Mary'. How important are women in your life and work?*
From time to time my childhood was darkened by sickness and dying.
When I was four or five I was taken upstairs by a well-intentioned aunt to
view the corpse of my grandmother. In the same year my mother's
youngest sister died at the age of twenty-three, and her baby died shortly
afterwards. The women in my poems derive in some instances directly
from life, others from mythology. Frequently life and mythology inter-
twine. 'The Invisible Menders' is a direct account of a pretty young girl

who worked as an invisible mender in my office building. She contracted tuberculosis and was absent for some months: 'When, after winter, she appeared, /McKelvey, hand on heart, behind the door, /Cried out Persephone; but softly said/The flush, the lowered look, implied/No one would make a job of mending her.'

In A WATCHING BRIEF (1979) the poem 'The Law Courts Revisited' implies that poetry and the law are compatible; surely the law involves linear or rhetorical thinking (in clause and sub-clause) and poetry involves thinking sideways (in images and metaphors)? Did you see yourself as a radical or conservative critic of the law?

A good mind contains both types of thinking. Many of my metaphors derive from my experiences as a lawyer. I was a conveyancer and that, in the main, meant dealing with people and language. Where there was conflict I saw my function as defending human beings against impersonal authority. I did little court work or litigation, and then, only when it was unavoidable. I never sought it out.

In the 1980s volumes earlier ideas of 'the hinterland' increasingly gather momentum and you wrote NOTES TO THE HINTERLAND in 1983 and LETTERS FROM THE HINTERLAND in 1986. What is the hinterland?

The hinterland for me immediately embraces counties Down, Antrim and Durham, in particular Dundonald and Ballyhackamore, Downpatrick and Lisburn and their inhabitants. Portrush, which I visited when I was young and sensitive to its impact, became part of the hinterland; I remember revisiting Portrush on one of the few excursion trains during the war when they were fencing off the beaches and childhood with barbed wire. The hinterland involves an inheritance of vanished landscapes, buildings and people, still active in the imagination, to which and to whom one owes allegiance in return for a continuing relationship.

You see poetry as offering a better model than political reality?

'Art is not life and cannot be a midwife to society'. Poets are not the 'unacknowledged legislators' of the world. It is difficult to see how you could legislate with poetry; and so, reluctantly, I'd say, in the short term, that poems have little impact although they may influence people who read them over a long period.

How important is music as an influence on your work. Do you like modern music by groups like the Beatles?

I would not put the Beatles top of the list but there is an apparent influence of Paul McCartney's 'Yesterday' in a poem, which I am fond of, 'Sancto's Dog'. I talk of the trees being chopped down, and the song's dying fall is in: 'The cornered field before/They folded it and carried it away, With all the picnic things/Of childhood, adolescence; yesterday.' When I was a child I was taken to symphony concerts in the Ulster and Wellington Halls and my mother, who sang in various choirs, made a record which was lost in the Blitz. There was a piano in the house; music was always in the background and it often has an associative power to take you back and evoke the specific time or emotion when you first heard it. I would say that music has worked as a general influence on the work, surfacing occasionally as a more specific and direct influence. Yeats (who was tone-deaf) was said to hum some unintelligible tune while he worked at a poem and one reviewer described my earliest work as 'muted lyricism'. I have always liked to think that my poetry is distinguished by a degree of musicality. In later years folksong has been a major influence; and I owe much to Ewan MacColl.

Have you been influenced by painters? Cecil Salkeld was involved with the early pamphlet RUSSIAN SUMMER *and you mention painters like John Luke, Paul Nietsche and William Conor.*
The painter I was probably closest to was Colin Middleton although I don't mention him in the work. I met Middleton when he lived in Ardglass and then when he moved to Bangor. In commending something, he was fond of saying 'That's a piece of the true Cross'. John Luke was unassuming and ascetic, with a wry humour; I housed one of his paintings in my office strongroom for several weeks. Paul Nietzsche had a studio on the Dublin Road, where he flaunted a huge ceramic penis on the wall. He learnt his English from the Sunday papers. He wanted to paint my portrait when I was twenty-four; but I felt unworthy. Cover illustrations for *Rann* were provided by Rowel Friers, Anne Yeats, Paul Nietzsche, Raymond Piper, William Conor, Catherine Wilson and H.E. Broderick.

In AFTER SEYMOUR'S FUNERAL *were you breaking new territory or sustaining established themes?*
I don't choose themes. They choose me.

How would you like to be remembered?
Not particularly.

PADRAIC FIACC

You were born in Belfast in 1924. Was your family background an important influence?

My family were a big influence. My mother and father were mad rebels in the 1920s. My grandmother was madder. She kept a gun in her apron; she ruled the whole of East Street in Belfast. She would tell the military, 'Don't you dare come through that door, I've just washed the floor.' I come from folks who are not terribly sane. My grandmother would march you up and down East Street shouting, 'You wee hussies! Get in and wash your hair! Go in and mind the wains!' I still don't know who my father was. He went off early to America and became a barman. He had to get out because they were killing Catholic barmen in Belfast whether they were involved in the "Troubles" or not. My mother was a fierce Republican but there was no way she was going to be sent out of her own country. I was the oldest, the first born alive. As the eldest I was conscious of my father not being there from an early age although he sent my mother home costumes from America — she was a flapper — and after he left in 1927-28 we moved to East Street. Even though we all called our grandfather 'da' I knew he wasn't. In the very early years I grew up on Elizabeth Street on the Falls. ELIZABETH Street? Now how's about that? I've only the briefest memories of my father: he used to come home from work and kiss me and I'd run my fingers through his black, curly hair and I remember — like all children I was conniving — asking him one day to hold me up to look over the big blind wall at the back of the house. And what was on the other side of the wall? Just a hungry dog gnawing into the bin. The poetry in life, eh?

Why did your father leave?

He had to get out. He left in 1927 just in time for the American depression. At a joint reading with John Montague he pointed out that we shared a liking for Patric Collins; I pointed out that we shared fathers who had sweated working in the New York subways. After my father left we moved from Elizabeth Street to East Street to live with my grandmother.

You left Belfast at an early age for New York. What were your first impressions of New York?

I was five when we went to New York. People in Belfast all came down to say their goodbyes at the docks and 'Auld Lang Syne' was sung. Leaving seemed permanent, forever. We landed at Halifax. We had such a good time on the boat but on arriving we would have gone back in an instant. We'd been told so much about New York — and I really wanted to see it — but at Halifax there was another brick wall, an even bigger one; my stupid father had missed the train to the boat to meet us, so we sat disappointed beside our bags waiting until some fireman or policeman — somebody or other — came to help us. Joyce calls the Atlantic an 'abyss of tears'; it is for any one who crosses it as an Irish immigrant. There is that sense of loss. Recently I wrote a poem about the flight from Toronto to London; it's now just a single night flight and I needed St. Augustine in the poem to slow the flight down but in my mother's day America was exile. My first impressions of New York were that it was full of bright light and yellow taxis and movement. I loved the brightness. I was excited. I was very close to my mother and I knew instinctively that she did not want to go to America. I came to hate every part of New York — even the brightness — for no matter how glittery it was I was determined to hate it because my mother hated it. I went to Commerce High School and there was all that standing up everyday to do 'God Bliss A-mer-ic-a' — awful, hypocritical — and it left you, as it probably did many immigrant children, trapped somewhere. Everyone in America in the '30s was fighting the Spanish Civil War in the kitchen, even at Thanksgiving Dinners, but I'd just do wash up with my mother and she'd listen to them talking and she'd say, 'Shit, shit, and more shit — and sugar on the top of it.' We'd do the washing up and let them fight in the Spanish Civil War.

When did you start writing?

I started writing in the late '30s, the early '40s, in New York. I had this teacher — a Jewish, forcefully leftist Communist — who encouraged me; he thought I had a flair in words. Of course he was up against it, with Franco being a Fascist and me being a Catholic, but he needed someone to argue with so I cut my teeth on him as a writer. I'd get up in class and ask him to 'forgive me' just before I'd set off to wind him up. My first real poem was 'Der Bomben Poet' from 1941; it is the first poem in *Ruined Pages*. 'This is my birthday. I have just turned seventeen. My home town has just been blown up.' I was riding a bus through Hell's Kitchen and I saw this newspaper headline: 'Belfast Bomb'. Ah, I couldn't believe it. It's a good poem though: 'Dead feet in dead faces'. It's therapeutic, mad. I remember thinking about my home town and family. I was frightened for them.

You studied for the priesthood and your early poems repeatedly refer to 'sanctuary', *'monastery' and 'psalm'. What is your attitude to Catholicism? Why didn't you* *become a priest?*

Who are you talking to? Of course, I fucked that up. I'm a Catholic, but I was never totally interested in becoming a priest. The nuns at my first school told me not to go to Haaren High School because it was in Hell's Kitchen. The nuns also said to 'Go to any school that teaches Latin' and with Haaren being the only school nearby to teach Latin I wrote and applied when I was thirteen or fourteen. 'Ah, Te-Tum, hum-ah-hum-ah-hum.' 'E-TAL-E-AN?' 'LATIN?' About as good as getting yourself an alsatian dog! My mother's side of the family were not that religious, but on my father's side I'd my Aunt Mary who took me to do the Stations of the Cross. I could never understand, though, how Christ as the Son of God could allow those bastards to torture him. And, yet, that's complicated for the image came with my awareness of sex and death; I'd look at the soldiers, at those centurions with their muscular legs, and at the time — I was thirteen — I had just started reading Dostoevsky's *The Brothers Karamazov* where Father Zosimas's body gives off a smell when he dies. He was supposed to be a saint but he gives off a foul odour. Dostoevsky talks truth and faces reality. God, even a big horsefly came out of the saint's body.

The suggestion though has been made that you parted company with the seminary and a vocation because you wrote morbid poetry?

Sometimes I felt trapped in the monastery. I used to jump up and down on my glasses and smash them to get home. I remember an old priest who was sympathetic to the Irish climbing the hill to the monastery, and meeting me in a yellow shirt and black jacket and tan boots, and he stops me and asks: 'What are you doing in that get-up?' And so I told him I didn't want to end up looking like a penguin but, of course, he made me climb the hill and put on a black suit. They were strict. The story is that I left the monastery because of the morbidity of my writing, but I remember writing a play called *Fire* about St. Patrick where he was supposed to meet the King of Ireland's wife. Mickey Maloney, a real arm-wrestler from the Bronx, insisted on playing the Queen in high heels — he wasn't too hot on historical accuracy — and came in *click, click, clicking* across the stage and he says he 'do believe in St. Patrick'. Of course the priests were outraged and laughing into their sleeves. The corpse that was supposed to be dead on the stage came awake; it was tragedy gone into a farce. You see, I just didn't have the habits of a monk. I had to leave the regimental orders. I left in 1945.

You submitted an early volume of poems, INISFAIL LOST *to Padraic Colum at* *Macmillans. What influence did he have on your subsequent work?*

Colum was a little old priest. He got hold of the New York poems like 'Inisfail Lost'. Although he thought poems like 'Master Clay' were nasty he did see something in the poems and he helped me move from verse that was sweet and twee into a new phase. The poems I wrote at this time were nasty, wonderful and full of terrible longing. Padraic advised me: 'Write of your own people. Dig in the garden of Ireland.' He gave me Gaelic literature and folklore and myth and that became important in my work. And, of course, the more I dug, the more I was horrified. Colum was trying to take me off the streets of New York and I guess I was flattered that an older, established poet was interested. In New York even if you want to escape reality you have got to face it for it just keeps coming and coming at you — there might be five or six murders a night every night in Manhattan. You see, I had this terrible longing for Ireland — and Padraic nursed that in me; there are the translations of early Irish literature but these poems are not about escape. Look at Deirdre who 'pitched herself into the sea. *Turn the page. Turn the page.*' She's the Deirdre who is the 'gold albino' who would 'eat the spokes out of the wheel' . You might say I was trying to escape the niceties of my early verse. This early Irish literature is supposed to be about men — I was trying to write about men — but I came to realise that all those women are ferocious and they take over so the men don't get a look in. 'And great King Conor of himself said/Did you ever see a bottomless bucket/In the muck discarded?' How New York *can* you get? The link between early Irish poetry and New York is that both force you to face reality.

Does Cuchulainn interest you as mythic character?
Cuchulainn does interest me as a mythic character. He's masculine, an Irish King Kong, a pampered, rugged, destructive little shit — the opposite of Deirdre, who was also cursed in the womb from birth, but at least she spent her early years in a garden like the Buddha; she did not experience violence early, unlike Cuchulainn who was trained in arms early on. Cuchulainn is stubborn and macho, and having been around men all my life I know how they behave like children, so there is a link in my head between Cuchulainn and men in twentieth century Ireland. Conor fell in love with Cuchulainn and made him his Hound of Ulster so he defends Ulster against Medbh all over the head of a lousy cow and he kills his own son and falls into a depression — and so he should. He's a man who never grew up.

'Gloss': that sense of poetry as re-translation, a re-injection of old truth in new language, implies that poetry is trans-cultural, that it can translate. Is that important in your work?
Yes. The Benedictine monks who came to Ireland were influenced by

post-Reformation thinking when they came over here. Like the Jesuits they had a lot up top. And they dug into and dug up Irish mythology. I know this Irish literature like a Benedictine monk. The Scots and Welsh know these stories too and the Scottish are Celts and the Welsh are Celts and the northern English are Celts. This place should not be called the British Isles but the Celtic Isles.

Religion, though, in its contemporary Ulster variety, is surely a barrier against 'gloss' or translation. Look at Seamus Heaney's poem 'The Other Side'. The rosary goes on inside a Catholic farmhouse and the Biblical Protestant farmer stands outside; the poet is uncertain whether he can talk to the man about every-day things like the 'weather' or 'the price of grass seed'.

Yes, but I'm not an orthodox Catholic. French Catholicism and Jansensism has always had a big influence in Ireland and a lot of priests here trained in France. Spain would have been better. Here in Ulster you get Protestantised. In the monastery in America they taught us that Protestants wanted individuality and Catholics were for a universal conscience. I wanted, of course, to be more individualistic than Protestants. You know I even think Paisley has a sense of humour and I think I've probably more in common with him than I have with many middle-class Catholics. Recently when I was in hospital, after I was beaten up, this guy, who was lying across from me, says: 'You're that poet fellow who writes about killing Catholic babies.' And that's sad. Just *Catholic* babies? I include every baby, every single one. I love kids. I'm a good baby sitter and I've written poems about, and for, kids. Did he not know I'd written poems for the Protestant minister, James Parker, who kept a toll of the dead in Belfast? Did he not know that poem about those wee Protestant girls who meet the nuns and ask them when they are 'gonna get morried'?

You left New York for Ireland in 1946 and returned to New York in the early '50s. Why?

Well, the move back to Ireland from New York was a choice between enlisting in the American army and going back to Belfast. I found a man who could get me a passport back. Padraic's wife Mary told me I was mad: 'What do you wanna be going back to Ireland for?' she asked. 'There's no work there.' I boarded a Swedish liner though, the Gripsholm, and got to the far end of the boat to get away from everybody waving bye-bye to The Statue of Liberty. I met this woman who lived in a studio in Paris that Verlaine and Rimbaud had lived in — they were both lovers and I loved Rimbaud — so I didn't need to be down the far end of the boat when I could talk Rimbaud with her. In Belfast I wrote poems for magazines here. I was included in *New Irish Poets* in the late '40s. I gave them poems and my Aunt Mary took me down to the photographer and stood behind him shouting, 'Stop grinning! Only fools grin.' And so I was included — grinning — as the youngest poet and it was those poems that Nancy read ten years later when she was working in a bookshop in America. She began to write; she fell for those poems, their innocence, hook, line and sinker, and I was amazed. I guess we were both religious and romantic, even if I was a manic depressive. Nancy linked in with the religious element in the poems. Look at 'chaunt rann of a singer', such innocence. I don't think I could write that kind of poem now. I went back to New York in the early '50s, even though I hated it, to look after my kid sister when my mother died. My mother was dark, tempestuous, Spanish, beautiful. I loved her. My brother had come back from World War II permanently damaged, unrecognisable, and even my father (who was far gone on whiskey) recognised that something was wrong. There was no alternative but to stay and look after my sister and father. I did his washing and ironing and tried to be my mother to him. I got a job as a typist with IBM on forty two dollars a week. In the evening, when I was playing mother, I wrote those tough guy poems of the early '50s — the sort of poems you would write if you never took a cigarette out of your mouth.

New York in the '50s was different from New York in the '20s?
Yes. New York had become an American city. It was now full of immigrants and black people and Puerta Ricans and people with different sexual preferences. They were all hated, especially if they were suspected of sexual perversity or Communism. I'd a German friend and I'd use my finger as a make-belief moustache to pretend I was Hitler until I found out later that Hitler really was a madman who didn't know his arse from his elbow. I'd a Jewish teacher who, like many Jews, gave himself a simpler name when he arrived in America. He chose Maidman. He was asking for trouble and my friend Bubbles changed one syllable on the blackboard to make him a madman too. America paid for freedom and its many races in paranoia and materialism. You know, I remember helping the mothers undress the kids to go to the wading pool in the little green oasis that was Central Park — I love kids — and my own father even accused me of sexual perversity. Ah, that's terribly sad.

Your sexuality, though, is a subject for speculation and dirty gossip in Belfast.
Well, folk want me out of the cave and into some other closet. I know they say I'm homosexual but *naturally* I love both men and women and that's what you are supposed to do. Edna O'Brien says that 'Women are the valleys and men are the fountains.' And she's right. That's the way God made us. I was conscious of that in Swansea recently, the valley of the swan. I am fond of men. I have had five or six close physical relationships with men; I love their bodies but I'm vulnerable because men pick on my feminine

side; whilst I try to accommodate everybody I'm only a human being. I'd gladly give in to a man but I'm Catholic so I would have to make confession to the priest; there would be a hell of a lot of Hail Marys. As a priest once said to me, 'You have always got to think of the other guy.'

You were in Belfast in the early and late '50s? How would you describe that time?
The '50s were a kind of natal depression; I've written about this. W.R. Rodgers, like MacNeice, left for the BBC in London; Robert Greacen left too — although he continued to write letters — and I left in the middle of the decade for New York. W.R. Rodgers's second poetry collection *Europa and the Bull* came out in the early '50s and there was John Montague's *Poisoned Lands*, which was well named. There was McFadden's long and chilling poem, *Elegy for the Dead of the Princess Victoria*. To my mind Brian Moore's *Judith Hearne* was the great novel of the '50s; it testifies to the depression found in the North of Ireland. In Belfast PEN meetings took place in the Union Hotel at the back of the City Hall after the American troops, who had been stationed there during the war, had gone. I worked as a night porter in the dump. I would see writers, like John Hewitt, ensconced between the palm trees before their meetings. In Cork, *Poetry Ireland* was edited by David Marcus. John Hewitt was a guest editor of an Ulster edition; although he found my poems disconcerting (with their Gaelic words like 'leifer' or 'chaunt-rann') he wrote from Coventry later asking for poems to print in Mary O'Malley's *Threshold* and he used a long one. I dedicated 'Jackdaw' to him, because of his love of the Glens of Antrim, and he dedicated 'The Scar' to me. I didn't know McFadden until the '70s when we met in Michael McLaverty's home where I also met Seamus Heaney.

Let's talk about specific literary influences in the writing. You preface poems with quotations from Mauriac and Baudelaire. Critics such as James Liddy and Terence Brown suggest that your poems use syntactical disruptions, internal rhymes and sentences that spill over the line so that technique encounters the shock of real life. Were you influenced by French literature in this?
Ah oui. And si. Terence Brown understands me, my work. French and Spanish writers influenced me to a very bad degree and American poetry with its new freedom. I use words broken by hyphens, sentences that brake and swerve in the middle. Padraic Colum's wife Mary gave me a copy of Rimbaud, a beautiful translation of *The Drunken Boat* (*Le Bateau ivre*). Rimbaud was the nasty wee boy I wasn't allowed to be. I was the oldest; I ended up looking after my father and taking the kids to Central Park. There's darkness in Rimbaud, the ability to make real life more real. He's *dangereus*. Internal rhymes? I'm a poet and it's just a matter of giving myself license; while this is in French literature (and in Irish literature

too) it doesn't mean that there is no composition. John Hewitt said that in my poems 'even the very syllables count' and they do. That's oriental. The Japanese and Chinese wrote poems on rice paper, hung them on trees, and let the wind blow them where it would; I think that's beautiful. Li Po says that when he woke up in the morning to a whole lot of noisy people and commotion it was 'only the lamentation of monkeys'. He could compress a lot. Chinese and Japanese poets attract me because they are saying less is more. Of course this means that the more poems I've written, the less I've written.

Which American poets do you admire?
Robert Lowell. Lowell refused to serve in the army and I admired that. 'Why do you love me if I am not a man?' Lowell wrote in one poem. 'I am bleak bone with survival.' I understand that too. Walt Whitman who was homesexual and went around kissing everyone. Emily Dickinson, too, wrote the most beautiful poems: she was enclosed but wrote wonderfully; she had no social occasions to shine in. I like Hemingway too, his great style. I identify with the Americans because of their individualism and materialism.

Have English language poets from England influenced you?
Only in so far as you write in the English language are they an influence. There are the Romantics like Shelley, Keats, Wordsworth and Coleridge — I like his nasty habits — but they are not a direct influence. Poetry is not a rigged card game anyway, a case of knowing all the cards or literary influences. The bad social vibes, the violence that happened on the streets of Hell's Kitchen, and my own way of making it up out of cheese-cloth break in. Shostakovich did the same in music. I'm a manic depressive, perhaps even schizophrenic, and that is important in my poems and there is also the unpredictable in life and what happens there.

Surely there is also fatalism in your work, a determinism which closes off doors, which makes the womb a prison that ejects us forcibly into what Hopkins called 'the blight that man was born for' ?
The fatalism — I am fatalistic — comes from French writing. I do believe in destiny. There's that Arab way of seeing which knows that 'the desert is the garden of Allah'; that's understood by the French and Spanish and it came into Europe from North Africa for the Mediterranean is not a sea — it's only a wee river between north and south Europe — so that the desert enters French thinking from the Arabs. What it amounts to is that suffering is part of my vision. Some people tell me that not everyone suffers but I do not believe that; I think everybody does.

You returned with Nancy to live in Belfast in 1956. How important was your relationship with Nancy for the poems?

The secret of my work is my wife Nancy, her leaving me — it's loss. I was left on the ground when she left with our beautiful baby daughter; even the dog she left chewed up my shoes when I was upstairs watching T.V. I suppose that coming back to the North brought back my childhood which I'd tried to avoid. I had been born into the Civil War here when they were just making Northern Ireland. Although I was only a child I knew there was something wrong. My grandmother was burned out of Lisburn and she ended up mad and even in childhood I could tell she was paranoid about me wandering. I remember wandering off into Lagan Street one day and seeing these two kids blurtin' and pointing to a man who was whipping a horse. I went over to ask him not to whip the horse and called him a 'bad baste' and he turned and asked, 'Do you want me to whip you?' He *meant* it. So when I came back in the '50s, and tried to live in the suburbs in Glengormley, I guess we were trying to get out of a ghetto mentality. Even in the '60s there was still a certain amount of hope — we planned kids, O'Neill met Lemass, all that kind of thing. Nancy and I were very much in love. There were bad omens though. I remember two wee blackbirds getting trapped between the nylon drape and the window and fluttering madly, not able to get out; as I released them the sky darkened, a shadow came across the window just as they escaped. I'm a poet who believes in omens. There was news that Nancy's brother who was schizophrenic had killed himself; there was the "Troubles". Things conspired against us. I started getting migraines. Nancy got ill too. All that medical stuff is in the poems — haemorrhage and migraine. The doctors told Nancy that my problem was not physical — so it had to be mental; they put me away for ten days or so in the hospital. Of course, I told all the people in there to 'get up out of their beds and get on with it, for this was all just a conspiracy by the lunatics against us' until they had to let me out.

Belfast is central in the poems. BY THE BLACK STREAM *(1969) and* ODOUR OF BLOOD *(1973) capture a black, bleak, rainy, sectarian and violent town. Why did you leave New York and choose Belfast?*

I call it Hellfast. I was asked by a journalist from Dublin about leaving New York and I told her, 'I couldn't breathe in New York. Next question.' She asked why I'd come to Belfast and I told her, 'I like it O.K., but it's Hellfast.' She wrote about what would he not call it if he *didn't* like it! Belfast is not love-hate though, for I do love the place and I couldn't tell you why. It smells of tar, chimneys, cooking grub and the boneyards. There's that poem from the bad days in the '70s where I call it a 'beaten, sexless dog'. You'll get what I feel about its suffering in 'Glass Grass'. Why do I love it? God knows? In my darkest and bleakest book, *Nights in a Bad*

Place, it's a place where the 'dead stick in your gut'; you can't live here without being poisoned. There is something else here too though. I remember coming down over the mountain one evening in a car with John Hewitt and Roberta and driving back home and thinking about the street names — gorgeous names like Violet Street — and about how beautiful the place seemed. I love flowers — my grandfather was a gardener for the Quaker School in Lisburn — and even in Wellesley Avenue I could grow geraniums in the window box. But look at the place now. I can understand them wanting to kill a taxi driver the odd time — I've even wanted to myself — but not literally, not one or two every night. God, what a sweetheart of a place.

Is your poetry political? Should poetry be political in the context of Northern Ireland?
No. In America it was all politics and politics there is religion: you have to take one side or another. I don't like taking sides. Here I try to keep my mouth shut, difficult though that is. I suppose we could have Northern Ireland and that other shitbag of a neighbour together — a bit like England and Scotland and Wales — but the whole question of a united Ireland depends on people. Even Jimmy Connolly knew there was no point in having a united Ireland unless the people were united in wanting it. Connolly talked of a unity of Catholic, Protestant and Dissenter. I guess that whatever the answer I'd be a dissenter.

ODOUR OF BLOOD *was published in 1973. How would you describe that volume?*
'Odour of blood when Christ was slain / Made all Platonic tolerance vain / And vain all Doric discipline.' I put Yeats and Lawrence at the front of the book talking about blood and Joyce talks about 'bleeding for his torn bough... by the black stream' inside the book which takes you back to the crucifixion. That Yeats' quote is one of his deepest and darkest perceptions. It's a bloody book. Don't leave that book on the coffee table. Tolerance and just about everything else, including philosophy, goes out the window when crucifixions start happening. Christ is the enemy in the book and in a century as dark as this one is he is the enemy. Do you know that the colour of red appears in all my books. I was anaemic as a child, I could hardly look at a bowl of tomato juice without fainting (let alone blood), so I'm facing up to a deep fear — the fear of death — in the book. I remember, when I went to school in New York, they gave us red ties as part of the uniform and when I asked why they said it was because we were all now martyrs for Christ. I don't want to be a martyr. Do you know that early poem 'Trying to Study Philosophy' ? I wrote it in New York; it's about a blackbird singing down Belfast Lough, its song from its lovely 'black

bell' singing from the twelfth century when Finn McCool brought the blackbirds here from Norway. The last two lines ask: 'What is true?/ What is beautiful?' And the only thing that is... is the bird's song; I'm saying you can experience and imagine that but you can't build philosophy out of it. The bird song is the only concrete thing in the poem and the abstracts give way to that. In *Odour of Blood* I'm saying that poetry is the enemy of philosophy. 'I can't love the furled flag on the responsible street'.

If poetry is not philosophy is 'a poem a prayer'? You quote Samuel Beckett saying this in the introduction to one poem. And yet you say, in another poem, that you want 'pagan words'. Surely there is a contradiction? You also admire the painter Francis Bacon who thought, like Beckett, that man's existence was an accidental act, a 'game without reason'. Bacon would probably have gone as far as saying that God was dead. Would you agree?

No. I don't agree with that. Bacon and Beckett could get carried away sometimes. Beckett, though, is right in saying that 'a poem is a prayer'. The only problem is that I need 'pagan words' sometimes. I'm contrary — but this has been a brutal century and the poems are about human beings and experience and that is contradictory in itself. Poetry, painting and music are all pagan. Beckett, though, is so deadly serious. He picked up Socrates's notion of life as a tragic joke, a black farce, and I'd say too that the loneliness in life is the wildness in life. Yes, the loneliness in life is the wildness in life! Let the poets explore that. You know I was supposed to go and meet Beckett once. I went along to this café in Paris but he just up and died so he didn't turn up. Now what a contrary thing to do. Ain't life 'just one big bowl of cherries'.

In the mid-'70s you edited an anthology called THE WEARING OF THE BLACK *which attracted a storm of criticism. What motivated you to do this anthology? Would you still defend it?*

I met a student after doing *The Wearing of the Black* and he asked if I was the poet Pad-rage Fiasco or Out-raged Franco or something and I told him, 'Sure, you're getting warm.' The anthology drove folks mad and I loved every minute of it. I must have been a sadist and a masochist to do an anthology of "Troubles" writing. I'm an American and an outsider. The critics wanted to crucify me. Even the funders were annoyed. I was motivated by my own sense of outrage. I watched a Canadian interviewer talking to poets from here and commending them for their 'lovely cadences from such a troubled place' but I wanted to tell how raw this place really was. The Europeans loved this book; it was taken up by a European underground. Of course I was producing a book that went right in the teeth of the funders and good taste. All the bards have had sharp tongues.

NIGHTS IN A BAD PLACE *is also no picnic. In poems like 'Christ Goodbye' a man's genitals are 'roasted with a ship/-yard worker's blow lamp'. Has the poetry been 'swamped by brutality'? How do you react to the criticism that in being too close to experience you forget to analyse it?*

Experience in good poems is analysis. This book came in the wake of Nancy leaving and in the face of the "Troubles" and, even more than *Missa Terrablis*, it is my bleakest and blackest and darkest book. The poet is alone, the 'wolf outside munching the leopards head'. 'Christ Goodbye' was a harder poem to write than 'Glass Grass' and I don't understand — I still can't understand — why they would want to torture some one like the innocent old Protestant man I had dinner with in Rathcoole. Ratcool! I often wonder what happened to him. I tried to get near to the killer mentality in this book and Father Des Wilson says he still can't understand the sentiments in it. Behind the book is the murder of Gerry McLaughlin, a poor innocent boy, who used to come visit me in Glengormley and bring some chips and beer and keep me company while we weeded the garden. God, we didn't even use weedkiller. One day you switch from classical music to Radio Ulster and you just find out they murdered him. I'd seen too much when I came to write that book. I was, I still am bitter. I just can't understand — I just can't understand — why people would kill each other over religion and politics here.

Is there a difference between the poem that is crafted and the poem that is given? The poet is born, not made? Or the poem made, not born?

Only academics make these kind of distinctions. I think poems are spontaneous; there is a great deal of luck in writing. Even if poets are born, poems still need revision and I remember Nancy asking me why I'd go over and over poems but you have to work at it. Take 'First Movement' which dreams itself over from America to Ireland on drifting clouds — I loved watching clouds when I was a kid — where there's the yellow of the poem's opening before your expectation darkens suddenly as you experience coming home. It appears spontaneous, and it is, but there's also composition.

What is the relationship between painting and your work?

I understood painting long before I understood poetry. I started off painting like the Surrealists in the monastery and it frightened the priests. When I did an art class in Hell's Kitchen I did everything that was bright in pastels. Yellow is my favourite colour. I didn't have the discipline for it though. I remember doing a 'Madonna with the Child Teething'. It was beautiful. I myself know (*laughs*). I was influenced by religious art even if you can't imagine me with Da Vinci. There was a time when I was knocking Madonnas out all over the place. Raphael's are best of all. During the

Second World War the treasures of European painting went over to New York and I used to go to the galleries and museums there. I loved El Greco; he's in one poem. I remember winding up Padraic Colum's circle of admiring young girls when he gave me colour plates of El Greco by telling them the artist had only elongated everybody and should not be allowed to get away with that. Picasso was influenced by El Greco and I love Picasso. I love him saying that 'soldiers are donkeys' and I agree with him in the poems I've written about soldiers. 'Guernica' was an important painting in my day (even if we fought the Spanish Civil War sitting on our asses) and the Second World War darkened my writing; it permanently damaged my brother and I knew many Jews as humorous and lovable people in New York. Hiroshima? It's in that poem where the child asks its mother why it is so dark. Picasso is the war artist. It was terribly *à propos* that I used his 'Guernica' on the cover of my *Missa Terrablis* because he's organic and so are my poems. If Picasso found a seashell — or something that he needed for his art — on the beach, the girlfriend went out the window. Both Picasso and Klee do everything in fragments, and so do I. I believe our century is in fragments, or smithereens as the Irish call it — fragments resulting from blows. Wars, though, throw up strange twists that neither poets nor painters bargain for. The BBC reporter I wrote about, who broke down on the screen when the bomb went off on Corn Market? I met him later when I was shopping in Marks & Spencers but he would not forgive me for the poem I wrote about this even when I asked. The soldier who saved the woman and children in another poem? I found out later that his wife had sold the V.C. because he had left her poor. Wars use soldiers who are poor and women and children suffer — my mother knew that.

In your last poem in RED EARTH *(1998) you tear up an image of yourself in a poem and a painting.*
The first painting Nancy made of me was of this very suave, sophisticated, guy smoking a cigarette in a Picasso mood. In a second painting, which she did after we split up, the whole jawline had changed. I could hardly bear looking at myself. She had captured me in a totally disruptive image; I nearly had to give up babysitting when a child looked at the painting and pointed at me and said, 'da, da'. The poem and picture are made from torn strips; the romance has gone.

Modernism's 'fragments... shored against... ruin'. Does Eliot's 'The Waste Land' strike you as an important poem?
Eliot, Klee and Stravinsky were all interested in working with the kinds of fragments I work with. I understood Eliot. I came across his work early on and read it again in the '70s. I think he is, perhaps, one of the greatest

poets of the century. He's certainly more highly educated than I am. Education does not necessarily make for good poems although in Eliot's case it did. With all his learning he spoke out for the lonely, the lost, the sick, for those on the operating table and I can't help but admire that. Eliot talks sense about the deadliness of existence; in the most perfect way he was a true existentialist.

Your last volume of the twentieth century was SEMPER VACARE *(1999). What are you saying in this volume?*
The volume goes back to my relationship with Nancy of twenty years. She would have been a Benedictine nun had she not met and married me; having left the order to be with me, I came to St. Benedict and the order through her. Benedict is everybody's saint, a Catholic-Protestant monk who is accepted by Anglicans, and he insisted that the monks drank wine with their dinner — which is civilised. Nancy was fond of saying the Benedictine Latin phrase 'Semper Vacare' — always make space, make room, make distance. It was something that happened in our relationship — our marriage fell apart — but it is also a deep spiritual saying about how to relate to the world. I'm trying, too, to give each poem space in this book and to still allow the mind 'to protect itself' in the face of 'pathos' (as Hugh Buckingham says in the preface to 'Your Man'); so there are poems about loving the blackbirds and poems about torture and you try to keep your mind intact by trying to write about both. I visited my cousin's son in the Royal Victoria Hospital, after he was injured by a bomb in Armagh, and in 'Your Man' I'm looking at his injuries and bringing him toys, 'Making him/ Unwrap the paper bags himself/To gauge the amount of brain damage'. It's a book about toys in the hospital, about the fact that even though suicide is deeply attractive we must go on to bring toys to the hospital because there is no other alternative.

The 'spoiled' book is recurrent in the work. There is the 'gold' that runs from the 'ruined pages' in the book found at the bottom of the lake and the cuckoo that shits lime on the page.
Birdshit on the page? Why not? In France there were two writers and one of them, Jacques Maritain, found himself and his book under attack from the other and he had to fight for his life in defending his book. I loved what he said in his defence: 'It's only a book'. How many books have I written? Nine? It's all rien. And that's all there is to it. Rien. You'd think by the cover on some books that the writer is supposed to be God. Does it mean the writer is God? Rien. Rien. Rien. Rien. Rien.

JOHN MONTAGUE

You were born in Brooklyn, New York, in 1929 and returned to Garvaghey in Tyrone in 1933 as a foster child in the care of two elderly aunts. Did this 'primal hurt' and the separation from kin and country produce the claiming of these later as themes in the poems?

The whole business of fosterage was endemic in Gaelic society, especially in the case of the Tyrone O'Neills; the position of Hugh O'Neill in particular was marvellously ambivalent with his fosterage in England. It may seem grandiose to link myself with that historical tradition but it lay behind me and 'fostering out' with nearby neighbours or within families remained fairly common in Tyrone. As a member of a family of the northern Nationalist diaspora in America my own fosterage felt particularly drastic. A door closed when I was four. With my Uncle John's death I lost my immediate natural family in Brooklyn. I returned to Derry with my two brothers, then found myself alone in the care of two elderly aunts in Tyrone. Like many children you see your own experience as normal but Austin Lynch, a neighbour's son, recalls that I woke screaming in the night; at a subconscious level I may even have felt I was to blame for the loss.

Arriving back in Ireland in knickerbockers with an American accent is not a good move. Of course, I soon became a little Ulster country boy, but the sense of another life in America remained. In *Smashing the Piano* one poem recalls being sent Dick Tracey and The Funnies. Periodically I was sent cowboy and Indian outfits which intrigued the little boys in Garvaghy no end. It was a healing, animal, Wordsworthian, childhood — that of a little boy who played in the fields while his dog chased rabbits. Two or three years after I was returned I was called in to meet a rather plump, pale woman dressed in black who I did not recognise. I was told she was my mother. She returned to nearby Fintona. My father only arrived back eighteen years later in the 1950s when my second eldest brother married. Having resigned his job and pension in America to rejoin his wife, he came off the boat a rather small, drunk man determined to fight a good Catholic Christian fight. I had not seen my father between the age of four and twenty two but I was disposed to like him despite his many faults. The 'primal hurt' you refer to from 'A Flowering Absence' is, metaphorically and emotionally, the loss of my whole early world. It is in the poems.

45

'History Walk' registers the gap between your story (growing up in Tyrone and Armagh) and taught 'history' (English, recent and remote). As a pupil at Garvaghy and Glencull Primary Schools (1935-41) were you also aware early of a gap between speech and writing?

Ulster and Irish history is complicated. It is one of the major themes in the poems; I interpret history mainly as 'his-story'. You sensed or felt the history that was in the family bones. The experience of my type of family, typified that of many Catholic families where the males were involved in the northern Nationalist struggle; you sensed that they found themselves in relation to employment in the same position as the American blacks. And so they remain hidden away in the poems, having no public function. Postmen in Tyrone were mainly ex-servicemen from the first war. Bleming, the big postman from Dungannon, would arrive and park his van in the shed and compare his great General Ludendorff to the poor British Generals just before the poorer Catholics in Tyrone enlisted at the beginning of the Second War. The family house doubled as a country post-office, as a news HQ: the local postman would arrive on his bicycle with news; we were a lending library; we were the site of the first telephone in the area; on pension day you would meet those extraordinary old people who are glimpsed in later poems such as 'Like Dolmens Round My Childhood'.

I don't quite see the point about a gap between speech and writing. Having been artificially made into an only child I led a rich fantasy life. The imagination superimposes many layers. The life and speech of the older people, the stones of the nearby Giant's Grave or the passage graves at Seskilgreen lay around me but this life was also caught up into the world of the wireless and books. After listening to the sport's commentary on the wireless you whittled out your first cricket bat and compelled the Lynchs to bowl; you might imagine yourself as a Wimbledon hero, Fred Perry or Bunny Austin, banging a ball against the gable end wall; *Boy's Own* style adventure stories, which mainly came from England, brought the world of Greyfriars. In the last year at Primary School one became increasingly aware of the war: voices like Churchill or Lord Haw-Haw came on the wireless; de Valera's declaration against conscription produced a sense of relief among Protestant neighbours. There was little formal history at Primary School but later, in Armagh, a young priest taught us Celtic Civilisation and took us on history walks to Navan. And so you did become aware of the history that lay around you.

World War II framed the 'Irish dimension' of your childhood between ten and sixteen in a 'drama of unevent'. The war virtually coincided with schooling at St. Patrick's in Armagh (1941-46). Was your experience of the war as a boy different from your evaluation and memory of the war as a poet?

The war was exciting. I remember a big barrage balloon over Belfast, strange and rather beautiful. It seemed connected to the world of Zeppelins and Jules Verne. My first ambition was to be a fighter pilot in the R.A.F. With American and British troops in the towns the war increasingly impinged on us in Tyrone. I remember the excitement of seeing a big Sherman tank in the fields. While a big allied invasion force was stationed in the North of Ireland this was training off-stage for the main theatre of war which lay elsewhere. That's in *Time in Armagh.* On visits South you were aware of an entirely different war and the 'Emergency'. The LDF trained in the fields. For the first time I saw Catholics with guns. I learned how to drill, how to handle a Lee Enfield rifle. I wrote letters to my Longford cousins in the South as Field Marshall Montague, in imitation of Montgomery. I plotted the army campaigns across a map of Europe.

There was less direct experience of the war in Armagh — the Luftwaffe only occasionally penetrated this far west from the main targets in Belfast — but we would visit the air raid shelters or go down to the Food Office for coupons. I remember us being taken down to hear John Snagge announcing the Normandy landings. I suspect now that much of the drama of war in the newspapers was kept from us and I have come to resent this. It meant that when I first encountered Wilfred Owen's 'Strange Meeting' at school I was impressed but I could not tell the difference between Owen and Rupert Brooke. There was that strange incident (described in 'A Welcoming Party') of being taken to see news reels of the full horror of the concentration camps. That left a mark. Who decided that we should be allowed to see that? I still do not know. The school was in a Nationalist area with pupils drawn from Louth and south Armagh, so my own fascination with the war and sympathy with the Allied side in school debate was was not generally shared by the other boys. The monarchy, after all, had been nicknamed by one pupil from Keady as 'Stuttering George and Bandy-Legged Lizzie'. Of course the American involvement and Roosevelt's death confirmed my sympathies with the allies, as a little Ulster American.

You studied English and History at UCD from 1945, publishing articles on Irish writers in THE BELL, *and a 1951 essay describes you as 'a young man reared on Keats and* KING LEAR *in secondary school and university'. As the first northern poet in the twentieth century to write about the rural community from which you emerged — this suggestion is in Frank Ormsby's Introduction to* POETS FROM THE NORTH OF IRELAND — *was there a writer who gave you 'permission'? Seamus Heaney, for instance, acknowledges Kavanagh's singular importance in shaping his confidence to walk over the 'fine lawns of elocution' with the 'hob-nail boots' from the parish.*

A discussion with the President of Armagh College in my final year pointed towards a career as a journalist or novelist; a family discussion in Fintona with my eldest brother (who had been to UCD) and my other brother (who was at Queen's University) confirmed my decision to go to UCD. I had written to Queen's and the syllabus seemed even more antiquated than those at UCD. I also have the feeling that much of the literary impulse in Belfast died after the war. There was John Hewitt's rather programmatic Regionalism in the '40s and Roy McFadden, who subscribed to Hewitt's ideas for a time, continued to edit *Rann* before Hewitt went to Coventry in the '50s. There seemed to be little else. English poets like Drummond Allison and Alun Lewis had come to Belfast during the war; others came south in the '40s like Robert Greacen. I too opted for Dublin.

I did meet Kavanagh in Dublin. I think the difference between Seamus Heaney and myself in relation to Kavanagh is that I encountered the poet in his middle urban phase (in which his relationship with the parish was extremely ambivalent and lay behind him) whereas Heaney would read the *Collected Kavanagh* which I helped to produce from behind the scenes. Kavanagh in Dublin was a city dweller trying to write urban poems. He talks in 'Innocence' of them 'laughing at the one I loved': 'Ashamed of what I loved/ I flung her from me and called her a ditch/ Although she was smiling at me with violets.' Kavanagh was also outside Dublin's literary circles; when I found his beautiful book *A Soul For Sale* in 1947 it was remaindered in a Dublin bookshop. I was also sure that the main influence on *The Great Hunger* was *The Waste Land*.

Dublin in the '40s and '50s was full of stops and starts, a fragmentary rather than hopeful world. De Valera was cuter than Franco; he ruled without the military while the hierarchy secured the votes of an obedient flock. Partition seemed to suit both the conservative South and the Unionist North as virtual mirror images of each other. Joyce and Yeats had died. *The Bell* was fitful. *The Dublin Magazine*, in which I first published poems, would have been seen by many as 'old hat'. Writers like Anthony Cronin published in *Poetry Ireland* or down in Cork, where David Marcus had also started an exciting magazine called *Irish Writing*. In Dublin though I did gradually become aware of creatures called poets. Cocky, liked by women (and sometimes by men), they dared to write what I had come to study: poetry. So, I became aware of a fuss being made around poetry and I began to dabble in verse.

Northern Protestant backgrounds sometimes register in poems linguistically (in Biblical irony or rhetoric) or psychologically (as guilt or individual struggles with conscience). In what ways did northern Catholicism shape your poetry? Is it a more visual or liturgical or 'shared' inheritance?

I'm a slightly different case. My grandfather, who was a ghostly presence in our house, was a real Old Testament man. He had a Family Bible, big as a flagstone. I read those extraordinary stories from the Old Testament early on. I brought my grandfather's books and Bible to Armagh College but they were taken from me because they were the 'wrong versions'. On Sundays Protestant neighbours like the Clarkes attended the meeting house but they quoted surprisingly little from the Scriptures. For a Catholic boy the big events of the week were Confession, Sunday Mass and the Benediction. It was quite a show, our theatre. As an altar boy I learned to recite in Latin, no mean feat for a boy with with a stammer. Priests at the altar seemed as if they were surrounded with such extraordinary power, a sacred silence. No one dared defy them when I was younger. I remember being told a story about a B-Special who had dared to insult a priest only to find his hair had turned white. I suspect that there is a more submissive 'we' in Catholicism as compared with the Protestant consciousness of an 'I'; there is probably also more ritual going on in the background. 'To the Hillmother' transforms the Benediction which I love into a pagan prayer. I do suspect there is what Seamus Heaney calls a 'slow papish burn' in the work. Early on though I became suspicious of the power priests had — in allocating scholarships to Armagh College — and reading Joyce's *Portrait of the Artist* as a student confirmed my rebellion. I gave up going to mass; I failed to consult a priest before I married for the first time and, perhaps, surprisingly it caused few problems within the family.

FORMS OF EXILE *(1958) was published after you had studied or taught at four American Universities (1953-55) and returned to Ireland (having met Madeleine de Brauer in Iowa and married in France). In this volume, which moves between Dingle monasticism and American bus stops, did 'alienation' and 'roots' inform style as well as location? Thomas Parkinson in* HILLFIELD: POEMS AND MEMOIRS FOR JOHN MONTAGUE *(1989) sees this volume as 'Audeny'. Is it?*

I was born into the twentieth century, dropped back into the nineteenth century, and I attempted to regain the world I had left. I went to America and travelled to Yale, Indiana, Iowa and San Francisco — trying to write about and discover what would have been my country had I grown up there. Had I grown up in America I would probably have travelled less widely with less curiosity. Behind *Forms of Exile* is a writer who had experienced the differences between the North and South of Ireland and who left and then returned to the literary paralysis of Dublin. Auden did greatly influence the style of this book; for my generation he was simply the best craftsmen around. Alec Reid, a virtually blind albino, had given a brilliant lecture on Louis MacNeice at University College Dublin — but it was Auden, with his great variety of verse forms, who impressed us most. Cronin quoted Auden endlessly; Kinsella learned from Auden; I sensed, in poems like his 'Elegy on the Death of Yeats', a poet who might mediate Yeats for us. Yeats was a big presence for my generation but his death in the '40s seemed so recent. He was too big a presence to tackle head on and more scholarship was needed before the relationship between Yeats's world of the Celtic Twilight and our world of cinema and the recent war could be uncovered. In Auden we sensed a mediator.

If POISONED LANDS *(1961) emerged from Dublin's 'stagnant fen of waters' (as you state in the Introduction to the revised edition) did Pound's Modernism, his experimental injunction to 'make it new', or Eliot's* WASTE LAND *offer other possibilities? Do modernist strategies still excite you?*
Modernist strategies certainly did excite me. Seamus Heaney once said that my trouble was that I had saddled myself with Modernism: Kinsella and myself were both great Poundians. The *Pisan Cantos* felt like great post-war poems, with their use of so many languages, their ransacking of world literature and their beautiful music which hides such pain: 'What thou lovest well remains/ The rest is dross./ What thou lovest well shall not be reft from thee/ What thou lovest well is thy true heritage. Whose world, or mine or theirs/ Or is of none.' If Auden was a master of many forms, Pound had music. My admiration for Pound, though, has dimmed. His Chinese came through a Japanese translator and the broadcasts would reveal just how mad he was. Still, there was that initial excitement in uncovering Pound's poems. Eliot's *Waste Land* I first encountered at a conference in Salzburg in 1950. Unlike now, it was not a text you studied at school. Like many contemporaries I had read his 'Prufrock' and we had 'measured out our lives with coffee spoons'; we had come 'Under the Bam/Under the Boo/Under the Bam-boo tree' in a marvellous Abbey Theatre production of *Sweeney Agonistes*. I was still not prepared for that first reading of *The Waste Land* with its 'falling towers' in Jerusalem and Athens and the earth literally did move for me. *The Waste Land* is full of such austerity and asceticism; I had tried to escape these as a young man; I had sought out Auden rather than Eliot. With its many voices and collage technique though *The Waste Land* is a great poem to teach and it is bound to have had an influence on a long poem like *The Rough Field.*

In the mid '50s and, again, in the mid '60s you met contemporary east and west coast American writers. What, technically, did these varied writers offer a writer from an Irish background?
The American influence on Irish writers is complicated. Richard Ellmann contends that the early Yeats was influenced by American poetry. Kavanagh collected American poets, read Gertrude Stein, and saw modern poetry as having been kick-started by Eliot and the Americans. A friend once nicked Conrad Aiken's *Anthology of American Poetry: Modern Library* from Kavanagh's flat and it became our Bible; we'd quote Pound's 'Marriage at Canan' endlessly. In *The Green Fool* you catch a glimpse of the

American influence when Kavanagh asks for a copy of *The Waste Land* in the library; the assistant thinks he is after a book on agricultural drainage. Austin Clarke, was influenced to a lesser degree, but he still visited Whitman and Poe's homes in America. To some extent this tradition has been tempered by more recent poetry from the North. I know both Edna and Michael Longley would trace a different line of descent there, through the English war poets or Edward Thomas or MacNeice especially, in verse written in the North. In America I met Lowell, groomed as the 'King Poet' after Eliot, on the east coast. I was impressed by his rhetoric, his combination of a New England Protestant background with Catholic imagery. I met Richard Wilbur and initially attempted to imitate both Lowell's rhetoric and Wilbur's elegance but neither would come quite right for me. I met and liked Penn Warren who was seen as a redneck with his Kentucky mountain background; he wrote novels and then curved back into poetry late in life but his long lines about hawks and poems, roughly shaped like like Robinson Jeffers, were not a specific influence. Snodgrass, Robert Bly and Donal Justice were all poets who had good, workmanlike standards and I met them in the context of workshops where we wrote and discussed poems. Initially resistant to this idea I came to enjoy these sessions. Iowa, though, had such climatic extremes: you could boil an egg on the road in summer when they cooled the swimming pools with blocks of ice; in the winter you could freeze to death. At the invitation of Tom Parkinson, a poet himself, and someone who was sympathetic to the new wave of poets, I went on to Berkeley.

Parkinson was Ginsberg's friend and academic mentor and so, in Berkeley, I heard the first reading of 'Howl'. Ginsberg had all the qualities of letting rip that were so far removed from the east coast. An ambitious young man with thick black glasses, he roused the audience with lines like 'let themselves be fucked in the ass by saintly motorcyclists' while Kerouac collected quarters and big jugs of mountain red went round. That psychic orgasm over, Gary Snyder read quieter poems about physical work, the first poems I had encountered on the subject since Kavanagh and these impressed me. I liked Synder. I read his *Earth House Hold* which is full of visionary mysticism but, with hindsight and distance, I can see now that these poems reduced the full emotional range of poetry into something dangerously close to a Scouts' manual of Buddhism. We taught together later and engaged in friendly competition in writing longer poems. Snyder's aesthetic though was not quite right for me. He would have resisted the very idea of a completed poem for instance whereas, like Yeats, I felt that a good lyric should be clicked shut like a box.

After working for Bord Fáilte Éireann in Dublin (1956-59) you helped found Claddagh Records and 'The Chieftains' were named after one short story. There is the symphonic structure of THE ROUGH FIELD *and the acknowledged debate with Sean O'Riada about traditional music. Does modern music — blues or jazz seems to have influenced poets like Jimmy Simmons or Paul Muldoon — influence you?*

I encountered cool jazz in America, in San Francisco. I would ride across the Bay Bridge from Berkeley to The Black Hawk Club. Musicians like Charlie Mingus or David Brubeck or Paul Desmond on alto sax started out there whereas, earlier, cool jazz had been closely allied to strip tease as in Chicago. Unlike other writers, though, there is no direct quotation or direct influence from jazz or blues in the poems (apart from the small prefatory quotation from Muddy Waters in 'Border Sick Call'). Perhaps I feel, with Toni Morrison, that the felt life of this music is essentially black. I have heard Van Morrison play with John Lee Hooker; I know poets like Muldoon go to concerts but it's not in my work. Should I relax an element of snobbery where modern popular music is concerned?

In my boyhood the great popular artist in Ireland was not James Joyce but Count John McCormack. An authentic tradition of Irish music in which songs had been sung in Irish had gone underground. It was MacCormack's music, so full of the weight of hopeless emotion, that was cranked up on the gramophone at home. I have used the felt life of this type of song in *The Dead Kingdom* often in ironic quotation. When I was younger I could sing until my voice broke and someone once suggested that my poems are spoken songs. My Uncle John's fiddle rotted in the rafters in Tyrone; my father sang poor imitations of older airs that would have originally been in Irish, like 'Slievenamonn' or 'Follow me up to Carlow'. It was not until the '60s when I met Garech Browne and Sean O'Riada that I became fully aware of just how dynamic a tradition Ireland had and working with Claddagh records I tried to recover and make it available.

You 'chose' France for an early holiday and worked in Paris as correspondent for THE IRISH TIMES *(1961-63). Like Derek Mahon you 'translate' modern French poetry.*

I have always been attracted to France. There was the example of Joyce and Beckett; it was one country to which gifted Irish writers could apply. I have been married twice to French women who seem to move easily in the world of men and drive cars as easily as they cook. Having lived and worked in France for twelve years I suppose it was natural that I should begin translating the work of French writers. I've translated Jouve, Char, Ponge, Guillevic and others. I'm fascinated by the adventure of modern French poetry: it is intelligent, it is highly trained and it is steeped in philosophy. So much remains to be translated. For better or worse I've committed myself to this task.

In the short story collections DEATH OF A CHIEFTAIN & OTHER STORIES *(1964) and* A LOVE PRESENT & OTHER STORIES *(1997) individuals struggle with oppressive forces: the Catholic Church, the B Specials, the class system. The black hackney in 'Sugarbush, I Love You So' is 'as dense with class consciousness as a Proustian salon...' Are class structures also important in the poems?*

Class is in the poems. Perhaps it's less rarely defined or less deeply embedded than it is in the short stories. Class structures are often sensed but rarely talked of in Ireland. As a boy I sensed class structures behind family prohibitions about which neighbours' children I was supposed to play with (which I ignored) or you sensed class consciousness behind the sorts of comments made when a council worker's daughter got pregnant. I'm probably even more deeply suspicious of the middle classes than I am of the Catholic Church. 'Clear the Way', for instance, is a fairly blatant class poem as is 'Winifred Montague'. I hope the element of social compassion in the poems comes across.

Many poems in A CHOSEN LIGHT *(1967) register a wonderfully 'exact', yet magical awareness of physical objects: the clock ('ticking in a fierce delight/ of so, and so, and so') or a lover's face above the negro's lamp in the 'hissing drift of winter rain'. Derek Mahon praises Nabokov's 'readiness to discern the halo round the frying pan'. In what way does your imagination work around inanimate objects?*

There is a certain kind of light falling on objects in that book: it's mainly French. I am intrigued by many objects like radiometers just as Auden was fascinated by mines and machinery. I'm especially interested in old agricultural implements like turf spades or ploughs and old tractors fascinate me. There is something beyond sentimentality in Rilke's assertion that real objects have been substituted with imitations in the twentieth century. I like objects with a handled, physical feel like pitchforks. Until recently I could help with hay-making but the big combines have put paid to the shared social and physical pleasure that lie behind objects like a pitchfork.

Is there a sense of 'neutral' energy and discrete eroticism in A CHOSEN LIGHT *which contrasts with the given electrical charge in* A SLOW DANCE *(1975)?*

A Chosen Light moves through French light and it's a French book in which there is a controlled use of the senses; *A Slow Dance* is an embrace of the earth, a return to the Ireland of my boyhood.

You also met Beckett in Paris and 'Salute, in passing, for Sam' acknowledges his 'icy human mathematics'. Are you suggesting that your imagination is warmer and your thought pattern less philosophically severe than Beckett's?

Beckett was a fierce devotee of both whiskey and philosophy. He was at ease in France. Although he had not studied philosophy at Trinity he was, in many respects, even more philsophically severe than the French. I think Beckett was wary of language and prone to silence because he saw life as an always changing subject perceived by an always changing object. Silence and language come into my own work but most poetry tends towards praise which was not Sam's forte.

TIDES *(1971) uses Hayter's sea engravings;* THE ROUGH FIELD *(1972) deploys sixteenth century wood cuts by John Derricke;* THE LOST NOTEBOOK *(1987) refers to many painters;* THE DEAD KINGDOM *looks to ancient sculpture. Have any of your poems come from paintings? Which painters do you admire?*
If you use adjectives you often feel closer to painters than fellow poets. I have been close to the Irish painter Barrie Cooke, an instinctive painter and a man who loves the countryside; I wrote 'Trout' with his watercolour painting behind my desk. I admire Louis le Brocquy's work too; it is more spiritual or cerebral and he prepares those wonderful white backgrounds into which the portraits float. Hayter, like Snyder, saw the world as a net of energies and as an engraver there was a great deal of physical work and effort behind what he produced. In *The Lost Notebook*, a fictional autobiography, I'm trying to learn more about Italian painting; perhaps the immense gap between two people in the idyllic circumstances of Florence finds an analogy in their different tastes in painting.

You have referred to the circular structure of TIDES *and* MOUNT EAGLE *and to 'the circular aesthetic of Irish art' in* THE FIGURE IN THE CAVE. *Writers like Joyce, Hewitt and Heaney have imaged experience as widening concentric ripples from a fixed point; you also seem to journey across landscapes along lines of energy — 'lines of departure and return' — where circling is also 'a failure to return'. A triangle between Ireland, America and France surely intersects the circle in the life and work. Is the idea of the poet as traveller or nomad important to you?*
Very few writers stay put. Joyce went to the continent and yet his work points downwards to a continual excavation of Ireland. There are two types of writer: centripetal and centrifugal. Keats one might take as representing a centripetal force — it is the poem he is doing which gets the attention — and he loads every rift with ore and draws a tight concentric circle around the poem; Shelley spins a net out into the world of politics and history that is beyond the immediate terrain of the poem. Ideally, like Dante, you try to gather this entire network and both energies up into one poem. Is the pattern or geometry, though, of any work of art necessarily in nature or the universe? Perhaps not. You ask about 'circling to return'? Who really returns anywhere? When I return to Garvaghy now, for instance, I often have Gertrude Stein's feeling that 'there is no there there' any longer and so you have the image of the broken circle in *The Rough Field.* What stays

or remains permanent? Even a bird, as it returns, changes its nest. I recently visited my family graveyard, which is close to the main Omagh Road described in *The Rough Field*, and one day the JCB, which has changed — altered — the rural landscape in that poem, may go on to widen the road. One can no longer assume that even the dead will sleep undisturbed or remain stationary.

MacDiarmid is listed as one of your four 'local masters' (THE FIGURE IN THE CAVE) and in your poem dedicated to him you both walk in search of the 'vairy inter-resting'. Surely MacDiarmid is the antithesis of Modernism in style and content, the poet as balladeer and storyteller?
Away with you! MacDiarmid in books like *Stony Limits*, like Neruda in his most important works, is *the* great poet of stones. He transcends Neruda's vision and Guillevic's stones in *Carnac*. MacDiarmid's 'On A Raised Beach' is simply the best poem about stones in existence, a hard vision of the universe concretised in stone: 'All is lithogenesis, all is lochia'. In search of that vision MacDiarmid brought poetry as close to prose as it could possibly go. I know he wrote Scots ballads and dipped back into a Scottish tradition but there is a harsh modern vision in MacDiarmid that has links with Modernism.

Between 1967-71 you taught Anglo-Irish literature at UCD. Teaching has been recurrent in your life. Are writing and teaching different crafts?
Teaching is an act of generosity mixed with selfishness which you do to create an audience for work you or others have already done; writing is a lonely act done when you want to develop that tension further.

After ten years' gestation THE ROUGH FIELD appeared in 1972. What crucible shaped old and new lyrics into this long poem sequence? Is it possible to assign THE ROUGH FIELD to any one genre?
A writer learns his craft, then discovers his subject; sometimes the pressure of the subject is so great that it works the other way round. Tyrone had a whole population which Frank O'Connor would call 'submerged', a people and place which had not been spoken for since the eighteenth century and Carleton. As the pressure of the material and subject built through the '60s I had to search far and wide for techniques to master the material and to frame it into a structure. There are eleven sections in the poem which is one short of the number of calendar months in the old agricultural year; I am looking at a rural world subjected to, truncated by, the JCB. In terms of genre I was looking for a tension between shorter lyrics and a larger, more epic, pattern; that tension also underlies the three long poems I have written.

Are there visual as well as rhythmic reasons for the tight structural columns of the 'New Seige' section of the poem?
It is based on the Anglo-Saxon metre which is chanted by the scop, a four beat line with a break in the middle, which is a great line for incantation or public speaking. David Jones, the Welsh poet, with whose ghost I am writing another long poem, loved the Anglo-Saxon, Langland and Hopkins.

THE ROUGH FIELD *carries the scars and suffering inflicted by history into the charred, bleak landscape of the Ulster '70s with its destructive political fissures, tribal hatreds and new road building. The landscape is instantly recognisable but is the 'our' in the poem inclusive or objective or meant to be or does* THE ROUGH FIELD *have a boundary? Do the personal scars and the retrieval of broken shards lead to a position of cultural or political Nationalism, which is surely more problematic in terms of poetry's function? I'm thinking of Joyce's image of nationality as an entrapping 'net' flung to 'hold the soul back from flight'.*
It is question of who is speaking and at what stage in the poem. As the French say: 'Tout proportion garde!' In 'The Fault', the fifth section of the poem, I acknowledge that I inherit — and share — a certain bitterness from my father; I'm looking at a broken man shaped by historical forces and I find that sad. My father said that he would live on bread and water for the rest of his days if he could see England brought to her knees. His world was shaped by a vision of Ireland which emerged after 1916 and took root in the '20s. Now that vision has been largely set aside. Most people in the South of Ireland are looking towards a new Europe without borders and to an integration of the two telephone systems to facilitate business. The Nationalist button in the South is seldom pressed now — virtually only when Ireland play football or at a time of violent outrage in the North and even then the Omagh bomb had further confused responses here. The 'Ulster Prophecy' section of the poem imagines a United Ireland, from the perspective of the 1960s, as an impossibility. Nationality and the nation state are nineteenth century phenomenon. If Germany, for instance, had remained a set of principalities we would probably not have had two World Wars; historically, though, I also happen to think that if Ireland had been united in Gladstone's time then many of the problems explored in the poem might have been avoided. I also happen to think that both myself and Kinsella are not as well know in England as we should be perhaps because the fault line of history shows in our poetry. If you look at the blessing in 'The Epilogue' it is inclusive: 'Acknowledged when the priest blessed/ the green tipped corn, or Protestant/ lugged thick turnip, swollen marrow/ to robe the kirk for Thanksgiving.' Even that blessing though is subject to a bigger economic pattern underlying the poem: the whole of this rural world will shortly fall prey to the JCB.

You wrote as a film critic for THE STANDARD *in 1949 and 'The Oklahoma Kid' records the impact of the first cinemas on Ulster. Is* THE ROUGH FIELD *cinematic?*
There is a cinematic imagination in *The Rough Field*. There are long shots and close ups, collages and edits — many of the techniques used in the cinema.

Is THE ROUGH FIELD *anti-clerical?*
I feel the same way about priests as a dog feels when a cat comes into the room. I'm wary of anyone who wants to try to control my mind. Look at 'A New Seige': 'RELIGION POISONS US NORTH AND SOUTH./ A SPECIAL FORCE OF/ ANGELS WE'D NEED TO PUT MANNERS ON US...'

Do poems like 'The Errigal Road', where you walk the shared Tyrone landscape with a Protestant neighbour, and 'A Real Irishman' and 'Foreign Field', which includes the shot British soldier and Protestant neighbour, in MOUNT EAGLE *(1988) offer a critique of* THE ROUGH FIELD*: the poet as 'mediator' between two tribes — as well as medium or shaman — Heaney's position in 'The Other Side'?*
The position of mediator happens in *The Dead Kingdom*; there are poems of conciliation like 'The Red Branch', which I interpret as a bleeding bough. The poem is a blessing for all those who have suffered within 'the iron circle of retaliation': 'Sing an end to sectarianism,/ Fenian and Free Presbyterian.' Having visited the Somme battlefields I am aware that European as well as Irish events can claim the dead on both sides: there are more O's and Macs on the roll call than people realise. There's also a poem like 'What a View' in *Tides* which is partly about Eustace Bullock, a coffin maker, who would come and chat to me in Fintona in the little bar where I worked with my mother. He was in a tank regiment and had been in North Africa. He had no respect for either side's orthodoxies.

If you edited THE FABER BOOK OF IRISH VERSE *(1974) now would selection or shape alter?*
You have to remember that in this book I'm dealing with a thousand years of Irish verse in under four hundred pages. I needed a thousand pages. There would be more translations now, especially of modern Irish poetry in Irish, and, of course, the younger poets like Paul Muldoon and Ciaran Carson and Medbh McGuckian, Tom MacCarthy and Peter Sirr would claim more space. (I pride myself that Ciaran and Paul were already chosen so early!) I would like to do an anthology of Modern Irish Verse as I think I am truly catholic in my tastes.

A SLOW DANCE *(1975) and* THE GREAT CLOAK *(1978) craft extraordinary fine love poems; these volumes appeared after marrying Evelyn Robson in*

*America and taking up a lectureship in Cork (1972). Can the private, inti-
mate, shared 'we' of love or sensuous experience obstruct writing which is, after
all, post-coital, structured and public? Which Irish love poets do you admire?*
The love poem as passion recollected in tranquility? I'm fascinated by the
whole idea of love, taken away from the context of the church; it's a pri-
mal force. I've contemplated love in poems in many guises, its many
allotropes. I'm fascinated by its intimacy, its harshness, its tenderness; I'm
fascinated by its variations from the love between father and daughter to
the love between adults and I've tried to keep love as part of my instinc-
tive learning. The whole tradition of courtly love is virtually impossible
now in poetry. You cannot go tripping over your heels after the muse as
Yeats once did; if you invoked women as Athene or some classical goddess
would they now accept the offering? Robert Graves is the last kick of this
tradition. I think love is central to creativity and there's the love of objects
in poets like Neruda and Derek Mahon (I too love rocks and trees and
women and I hug all three); in Simmons there is a cavalier poet like
Lovelace; Seamus Heaney is a domestic love poet.

*Woman as wife/mother, as femme fatale (Sheela na Gig) and as old, lonely
crone recur, as Antoinette Quinn points out, in 'Montague and the Muse' in
the* IRISH UNIVERSITY REVIEW *(1989). To what extent are women symbolic
or real or both in your love poems?*
Both. That triad — daughter, lover, hag — is a part of mythology, like the
three stages of man. There was a sculpture of them inset in the walls of a
building near my Paris home. As I grow older I would be less inclined to
mythologise, especially since I have daughters myself, but the shorthand
of archetypes is there. The 'Well Beloved' deconstructs the Muse, like the
Hardy novel of that name.

*Myth also recurs in your work; Cuchulainn shadows the movement north and
the darker mood of the third section of* THE DEAD KINGDOM. *What is your
sense of Cuchulainn?*
Kinsella was translating *The Tain*, Ulster's old epic cycle, at the same time
as I was writing *The Rough Field* and I greatly admire the energy he put into
it. Yeats created a romantic Cuchulainn which Kinsella's texts could not
sustain. My sense of Cuchulainn is of an ambiguous, treacherous warrior.
He pledges his vows to Emer and then sleeps with her best friend; he kills
his own son and uses that extraordinary weapon the Gae Bulgae which
disappears up arse-holes; when the armies of the South are approaching
Ulster he is in bed with his neighbour's wife. A right bastard you might
say. He is a small dark man (not an Ulsterman and therefore free of the
curse) who can blow himself up, literally, like a bullfrog or a Samurai or
Ian Paisley.

In 1988 you left University College, Cork, after sixteen years teaching. Do your 1990s volumes and 'Border Sick Call' tilt the buckets, first carried by 'The Water Carrier', away from the literal towards the metaphorical and memoried, in a poetry less directed towards physical encounters but more concerned with the 'fluid sensual dream' of 'Trout'?

'Border Sick Call', alas, is not a volume, though I meant it to be. Writing about the past is always 'memoried' but surely the snow in the 'Border Sick Call' poem is chill enough for anyone south of the Arctic: I completed it in upstate New York during blizzards. Growing older you might be more reflective but 'The Current' in my new book *Smashing the Piano* is my most sensual dream so far.

Does the non-chronological running order of volumes in the COLLECTED POEMS *(1995) reflect your view of their ranking in importance?*

Absolutely not. I wanted the three long poems to follow each other and, ideally, that would have been one volume while the individual lyrics, restored to their original volumes, would have comprised Volume II. But, ecomomics! I look forward to a chronological complete poems in due course.

As Professor of the Chair of Poetry for Ireland you have travelled between Cork, Belfast and Dublin in 1999. Do you feel there is convergence or divergence between these three cities? Having just completed SMASHING THE PIANO *in 1999 have you witnessed changes in Ireland over the fifty years which have altered the writer's role?*

The three cities have very different atmospheres. The most marvellous thing about Ireland is that we resemble each other, in different ways, like a real family; yet put us down in England and we are all Paddys! Ireland is a most varied little country with only whiskey and the pint as common denominators.

In the last fifty years there has been the erosion of the border as a concrete division. There has been a plethora of grants and Artists-in-Residence schemes — things that Kavanagh or Clarke never had. The consequent tendency is to conform, to believe that all is for the best which brings out the Voltaire in me. We, even the Unionist who travels to London or Brussels, are part of an international world which is both good and bad. The travel I undertook so intrepidly is now commonplace. *Smashing the Piano* closes the century with a discordance, like contemporary music. We cannot control our humanity, but we can change our attitudes. Super Taigues and Mega Prods can milk the system and success may be the only criterion as compared to the old parish or local system but I'm asking if they will they do as well as the doctor or the priest, morally speaking?

JAMES SIMMONS

You were born in Derry in 1933 and grew up there. 'They fuck you up your mum and dad', Larkin said in one poem. In two late-1960s poems, 'The Prodigal Thinks of His Mother' and 'A Reformer to His Father', are you suggesting that you had similar difficulties with your parents?

Larkin's is a good, funny but very extreme poem. I didn't have that sort of difficulty with my parents, except in the sense that most children have to fight free of their parents at some point in their lives, hopefully only to come back. Mine were loving, funny and unviolent. The amount of freedom they gave me was amazing. I was able to come or go as I pleased from the age of sixteen. Always enough money for a dance but none to show off. My only clash with them was that they didn't think of writing or show business as a proper career, especially as I didn't have a clear plan in my head. I was confused and stubborn. Having failed at school my father offered to pay for my education if I would study economics and go into his stockbroking office. This I refused. I had no desire to talk to my mother of my adventures in love and sex. Does any child? So one poem is trying to convince my mother that pre-marital sex is O.K. The other is trying to express my love for an admirable, clever and funny father who had no interest in my left-wing ambitions for society, and never talked intimately. Baffled love in both cases but nothing as sad as Larkin. In neither case did I expect my parents to read the poems. Both poems are stories addressed to the world at large.

You were six when World War II broke out. Is it fair to suggest that excitement rather than horror lies behind your recollections of the war?

Absolutely... and I think it would be true of the whole population. It brought money and work and glamorous sailors with English and American accents and smart uniforms into our homes and dance halls. Thousands of Derry girls married 'Yanks', including two of my sisters. They were good to youngsters too. We could explore their warships and wave to them as they sailed out to battle. A relatively depressed city came alive. They thought us glamorous in our own way, so that we became conscious that we had Irish accents.

You went to Campbell College in Belfast between the ages of eleven and seventeen. Did you write then? Which novelists or poets interested you?
Shakespeare I appreciated early. He is the anchor for me in all my work in all his variety and passion and humour and compassion and intelligence and use of language. But other writers touched me in various ways — at first Rupert Brooke and Omar Khayaam but also Keats and Wordsworth and Yeats and Owen and Sassoon, then Auden and MacNeice. Once you start they flow in. Day Lewis impressed for a while, especially the narrative poems like 'The Nabarra' which still stand up, though his political poems seem corny now. Posturing.

You studied at Leeds University (1955-58) where you met Wole Soyinka and Tony Harrison. How did this affect your writing? Behind the question is the implication that English poets and folk singers influenced you more than Irish poets?
All poets in the English language are influenced by English poets. They are the tradition. There is no great Irish poetry in English before Yeats, except for people like Goldsmith who are part of English poetry. I wouldn't have much time for any Irish or American poet who hadn't read Shakespeare, Donne, Wordsworth etc. Who would? Heaney has Hopkins and Keats written all over him — rightly so.

But, in fact, Leeds was a nest of poets, as good as those in Belfast in the '60s. The great Professor Bonamy Dobree had hired good teachers like Geoffrey Hill, established the Gregory Fellowship — which was the first writer-in-residence job in England. Tom Blackburn held it and Heath Stubbs and Pearse Hutchinson and Jon Silkin. Dobree had read my work and encouraged me to come to Leeds when I was hanging about England. There was so much good poetry being written in Leeds by students and published in their weekly magazine, although only Harrison, Soyinka and I seem to have kept it up after university. Larkin and Lowell were very much in the air. I looked forward to each Larkin volume. I took to his dexterity with forms, his way with rhyming and his use of the colloquial which can leap into exaltation. Meeting the northern poets in the '60s was a similar excitement nearer home.

You returned to the North of Ireland to teach at Friends' School in Lisburn (1958-63), to publish poetry and sing on radio and television. Was there a thematic core in this work?
Not really. It was a continuation of my work at Leeds. I bought my first guitar at Leeds, which had a fair share of folk singers and guitarists; but even in my last year at school I remember Terence McCaughey playing me 78s of Ewan MacColl singing Scottish ballads. Arnold Kettle at Leeds played us Patrick Galvin singing rebel songs. Belfast was also in the grip of the folk revival. Folk clubs were springing up and people were rediscovering Irish

and English and American folk music. I think it began with Burl Ives (who visited Belfast in the '50s and gave a guitar to a local singer who made some records) and then The Clancy Brothers made the old songs "cool".

Blues singers like Josh White and Bill Broonzy came over under the folk banner, so there was a greater emphasis on good words. I was very conscious of this sort of "poetry" being close to my own verse, close to the border ballads and close to the Shakespeare of 'Hey ho the wind and the rain' and 'Take, oh take those lips away', rough hewn and beautiful. When Elvis Presley and Rock'n' Roll came along it seemed a terrible vulgarisation of an important song tradition.

At first I sang the songs of other people, and then got restive that the subjects were all of time past or rural; I began to adapt, and then to create my own. The poem 'Didn't He Ramble' mythologises and philosophises all this, using some of Eliot's critical terms to praise a poetry outside 'court and bourgeois modes', suggesting it was a sort of bloodless revolution when an orphan like Louis Armstrong could make himself into the world's trumpet virtuoso.

Belfast was humming then. Sam Hanna Bell was introducing the local accent to radio, writing his fine *December Bride*, encouraging Sam Thompson and Joe Tomelty and me. Sean O'Riada was getting a bit of shape and modernity into Irish traditional music, and he came north with The Chieftains. Michael Emerson was producing plays and working up to The Belfast Festival, and the pamphlets that would introduce all the local poets to the world. I was restive with academe, its pomposity and obfuscation, and the Modernist poets who were too full of references and symbols, too far from the spoken word (at their worst, which was mostly). So perhaps that is the large theme of my writing then and now. Of course it's all relative. My family claim not to understand a lot of my poems. To them I'm too intellectual! The trouble with interviews is that I think time would be better spent listening to the songs and poems rather than trying to place them in history.

In 'Seasonal Greeting' you make a distinction between the language of poetry and the language of the 'common man'.
I know: 'If I was not so brainy, friends, I wouldn't give a damn;/but the common man's so common that I'm bloody well glad I am.' That poem is a squib, a joke, not characteristic, not important, though vivid and good fun. It's like questioning Heaney about an early poem like 'Docker' which is worse. No, just as most folk songs are rubbish you still cherish the good ones as a dream of paradise or just a better world. Most blues are rubbish but you get a line like: 'She stood on the corner with her feet all soaking wet'. Actually when I was doing radio-ballads, where you record hours of conversation with people and then pick out the gems, I saw that by sifting

and juxtaposing you could present magnificently vital speech. That is a sort of paradigm for writing poetry. You sift and sift until you create something wonderful and lucid from your dull notes but, as Yeats says, it has to seem 'but a moment's thought'.

You spent between 1963 and 1967 at Ahmadu Bella University in Nigeria. Is there an African James Simmons?
No, but there is a James Simmons in Africa. Most of my African poems are collected at the end of *Mainstream*. 'Letter to a Jealous Friend' is from the African period, but you wouldn't notice. Africa was a tremendous experience. Philadephia on a wet morning is just like Belfast, but Nigeria was totally different: blazing sun all winter, torrential rain in the summer. It has ferocious growth and brilliant colours; it is full of poverty and pain and vast class differences. The humblest lecturer could afford a cook and a garden boy. The old city had an Emir living in a mud castle with his concubines and on his birthday tribesmen would come in from the desert and rear their horses before his balcony, and there was a medieval jester running through the crowd with a bladder. In the new town poor Nigerian men in ragged shorts would pull huge loads by hand; in the open air market there were dead goats hanging, covered in flies. And when the market was over in the area where they sold onions — (hundreds of old women with little piles of purple onions)— there would be this silver purple carpet of onion skins. Out in the bush people lived in straw huts and hoed the soil with mattocks, as they must have been doing for a thousand years. Outside the grocery shops there were little mutilated boys, lepers, who would hobble towards you, smiling and joking, looking for tips. In the open air bars the High Life music was joyous, five drummers and one guitar coming through a rickety p.a. and everyone singing in subtle harmonies. Old people danced at ease with the young in their gorgeous costumes, so unlike the High School dance in Derry.

Then the civil war broke out and mobs raged through the campus, Hausas wanting to kill Ibos; the schools were closed and my wife and children went home.

I wrote my first play there with Tony Harrison which we put on with student actors. It was a version of *Lysistrata*, *Aitken Mata*, and the Christian element tried to have it cancelled (of course); but it went on in the great hall with great success. I also did the music for Brecht's *The Chalk Circle* and played primitive piano for a little jazz group. Later I did a one man show at The Edinburgh Festival called *Doilly McCartney's Africa*. One of the many good things that never took off.

You lectured in drama and Anglo-Irish literature at the University of Ulster in Coleraine from 1968 to 1984. 'Christ didn't court hard nails and fetters/to get

on well with men of letters', you state in 'To Certain Communist Friends'. How did you get on as an academic and teacher?
You keep bringing up untypical poems with strong opinions but I suppose that is an important one in the Blakean style. I suppose in all my teaching I have seen more of the students than my fellow lecturers. Teaching is a hard nut to crack but I have a go at in 'For and Against'. Self-destruction is not a good form of revolution, and working from within is very difficult. University education can be terrific when you are in a seminar room with people who want to learn, who have ideas of their own. It can also atrophy your enthusiasm if you are obliged to read authors you aren't ready for.

In Leeds I met my first bona fide Communists, and they seemed more inspired by hate than altruism. 'The best lack all conviction, the worst are full of passionate intensity.' It was magical, after hanging on to a vaguely Liberal/Christian ethos for thirty years, to find the Communist world collapsing from excess of its own cruelty and corruption. *Judy Garland and the Cold War* is a further exploration of such ideas.

In a festschrift for my sixtieth birthday, 'At Six O'Clock in the Silence of Things' published by Lapwing Press, Michael Dibdin the crime novelist, who was a pupil of mine in Lisburn describes my teaching methods nicely. Just to be open and frank and tender can seem subversive to those in authority. I remember when the headmaster was discussing the pupils' desire to have their own uncensored magazine with me, he warned me, 'Mr Simmons, we're sitting on a volcano!' I couldn't help laughing. The older pupils would come round to our house in Batchelor's Walk to watch *That Was the Week that Was* on TV.

At Coleraine too I saw much more of the students than I saw of the staff, although I always had one or two good friends among the staff both there and at Lisburn. I like doing things, putting on plays, forming groups and such. I've always thought putting on plays was a superior form of education to lecturing about them from a podium. That's why our present work in the Poets' House is so satisfying. You are in a room with younger fellow poets talking about their recent poems. At the same time it was very exciting working out a list of set plays for a new drama course. Which plays by Chekov, Brecht, and Ibsen and Arthur Miller would you cover?

In your first pamphlet 'Ballad of a Marriage' (1966) did you find a voice or break into new territory? How do you see this volume now?
I had been publishing since the '50s so it was far more a matter of picking a bunch of poems that excited me. It is a pretty eclectic mix. This must be the case for most poets who are a bit late in publishing their first volume. I think all the poems there might find their way into a Collected Poems. It was so exciting to have a nice little book out which you could hand to people — part of that energy of Belfast in the '60s. Then there's

the disappointment of not making quite the impact one hoped for. So many of us live under the shadow of Heaney's success, thinking our work more interesting but finding that critics don't find it so. Still the more positive feeling was in the air then, that we were all being heard. I have had a difficult period in the last ten years when it seemed that I was being written out of Irish literature. Sentences that would have included Simmons, Mahon, Longley and Heaney began to leave out my name, although I think my books get better and better. John Jordan, in one of his last essays, wrote: 'his work since 1980... is profoundly serious... The dazzle is becoming a sustained and impassioned glow'. You can't ask for better than that. He was reviewing *From the Irish* and thinking of *Constantly Singing* but there's *Mainstream*, a good many years later, and *The Company of Children*. These are the books I'd be more interested in talking about, although I don't disown any of the earlier books.

Sex is a recurrent theme as it is in the early John Donne and D.H. Lawrence. Did these writers influence you in creating 'the free hygenic mind' which you mention in 'Marital Sonnets'? There is surely a recurrent Simmons/Othello triangle in which ' your jealousy (is) as natural as our lust' as you put it in 'Letter to a Jealous Friend'.

Yes, sex and love and marriage are central themes in my work. Marriage is the central arena in most people's lives. The early Donne and D.H. Lawrence are poets who have written poems I admire tremendously, and I even wrote a poem addressed to Donne upbraiding him for giving in to pressure and becoming a churchman. There are several poems addressed to D.H.L. and I have set one of his poems for singing, 'Courage', which was vital to me in early years. 'What makes people dissatisfied is that they accept lies'. Having come out of a Christian phase I was deeply interested in Lawrence as a sort of secular preacher. I don't know anything that still turns me on so much as Donne lines like, 'And now goodmorrow to our waking soules, /Which watch not one another out of feare'. And there's many, many lines like this in his earlier poems! When I finally found girls who wanted to go to bed with me, after the first orgasm, I wondered what to do next. I wanted to read a book or go to sleep, if I didn't have much to say to my partner. Is this common? It has certainly taken me a lot of trial and error to find a happy exciting partner that I can cleave to. But sex is never separable from other matters: a romantic lust for beauty can be treacherous and it can keep you running around after the wrong thing, jumping into bed with the wrong person only to find that desire is a betrayal of yourself or other people. If only. If only. And yet no regrets.

Have you resolved these contrary 'natural forces': the pull of fidelity, love and 'marriages' and the contrary pull of lust and the joy of sex that can end in 'divorces'?

Yes. I seem to have solved most of my hang-ups. I have a very happy marriage now with Janice. She is a poet of different style and technique, but equal seriousness. We work together from home and share a deep love of our children, so many of the newer poems are a celebration of felicity; but earlier poems of infelicity are equally important because they perhaps share difficulties with other people. I don't know if the newer poems get a depth of seriousness from the pain we have suffered together with sick children and betraying friends.

I enjoyed a wonderful false dawn with my second wife, and I would stand over all the poems it produced from 'Honeymoon' to one of my favourite long meditations, 'Meditations in Time of Divorce'. In that poem I got on to a longer form, new to me, perhaps closer to Shakespeare in that it has a sort of narrative or dramatic drive, and produced a key couplet: 'I sing of natural forces,/ marriages, divorces...' — which, in a way, takes a new turn from that line you quoted from 'Letter to a Jealous Friend': 'Your jealousy's as natural as our lust.' I like pithy lines that are earned in a dramatic context. But the divorce poem brings in the town of Coleraine, the house I lived in, the house I left, the wife, the children, the new lover. It is more symphonic than anything that went before. There are five long poems like that in *The Company of Children* and 'Elegy for a Deadborn Child' from *Mainstream* has the same rich mixture of themes and narratives.

I feel ambivalent about the poems you write about sex: in some there's an energy and honesty, the shift and sheer 'chancy-ness' of life; in others you may be exposing another human being's private experience to possible humiliation without the contraceptive of a third person narrative: 'Last night my wife was fucked into the ground by a rugby player'.

Yes. I sometimes regret that first line but if you only read the poem to the end it all comes together. Such things do, *did*, happen, and isn't the husband the more humiliated that the wife rejects him and goes off? Perhaps it is the phrase 'fucked into the ground'; but I'm sure you understand from your own experience that that is what a woman sometimes wants of her beloved. That is all the phrase means... prolonged, passionate, intercourse. Lovers often use such coarse terms with each other; so it is no shame to the wife to relish this.

Now whether this ever occured in life (as it must often) is hardly the reader's business. The reader's only duty (and right) is to live through the poem to its conclusion. I read my poem 'Elegy for a Deadborn Child' to a workshop recently, and one or two of the other poets expressed shock at what they saw as the brutal realism of the poem... and I suddenly thought, 'That's what Shakespeare does. When Gloucester has his eyes put out, he rams it home — "out vile jelly"'. When Macbeth kills his king his wife wonders, 'Who would have thought the old man to have had so much blood in him?' That's where I come from. It's not gratuitous but it's powerful, and I'm proud of it. So let the offending line stand: 'Last night my wife was fucked into the ground'. And let them not consult my wife or ex-wife. It is none of their business. They are poems. Dramas. Isn't it a mistake to turn away from *Sons and Lovers* and try to work out how it relates to Lawrence's actual life? It is a novel, and of course his mother was probably like the mother in the book, but that distracts you from what the novel makes you experience in your own life.

I treat this subject in a new, long poem 'Winter Wedding' where the protagonist suddenly makes himself, as a poet with his art, into Cuchulainn with his dirty trick the gae bolga exposing his friend's weakness; but, unlike Cuchulainn, 'No one will end up dead': 'To feel sore/After our crimes is what/Our crimes cry out for.'

IN THE WILDERNESS AND OTHER POEMS *appeared in 1969 and it seems the least sociable of your books.*
Yes, it's the most metaphysical. The wilderness is where Christ and Lear and anyone on a camping holiday gets away from it all and grows up. It ties in with emigration and pioneering. I think these themes all contribute to a very unified book, as usual welding the exalted to the ordinary. 'I like to camp and read King Lear/We had a lovely fortnight here.' I played Lear once. I sometimes wish I had earned my living as an actor or singer.

The HONEST ULSTERMAN *which you founded in May 1968 was billed as a 'monthly handbook for revolution' via literature; the first editorial quotes Lawrence and Thoreau in support of this case. Do you still see literature as capable of improving society?*
I don't know any more. I know it has changed me, and I think I have seen it change other people. What it doesn't seem capable of is short term political change. But it does contribute. And things certainly do change. Irish anti-clericalism from Joyce to McGahern must have done its fair share to expose the Catholic Church in Ireland. I was denounced from the pulpit once by an Anglican clergyman.

Do the poems in ENERGY TO BURN *(1971) chart tensions between a younger revolutionary self with 'energy to burn' and an older, reflective self?*
No, I don't think so. 'One of the Boys' is an observation of the wild young men I served drink to in The York Hotel in Portrush. I was never one of the boys. And, sure look at me now, sixty six years old and still up to my ears in debt and involved in a high risk idealistic enterprise, 'The Poets' House', married to a forty five year old American poet, very much outside the present establishment when all my contemporaries are securely ensconced except perhaps Derek Mahon, and he's a good deal younger.

In 'Exploration in the Arts' you seem to reject Modernism and in 'Against' you say that in poems you don't 'invent a new/ language... The best — the good best — is a variation on a popular tune...'

Yes. I don't think there's a single poem by Eliot that I relish. His essays are more interesting and endorse my notion (surely every real poet's notion) that you must immerse in the tradition to learn how to write. Pound has his moments, some of the translations from the Chinese; Pound says 'make it new' but I've never read anyone better than Shakespeare and it's often in dialogues that he reveals such incredible knowledge of people. The argument is well enough put in the poems you mention; but I wouldn't want to be dogmatic. All the poets roughly gathered under the Modernist label are so different. You should read my 'No Land is Waste' which is a poem about London roughly based on *The Waste Land.* Is Yeats a Modernist at all? Carlos Williams has some great moments; but his 'experimental' poems are the least readable.

'For the Centenary' chalks 'Yeats lives' on the wall but what about Louis MacNeice and other Irish writers after Yeats?

I like MacNeice's 'Autumn Journal' and a few others — 'Florrie Ford' and 'The Gardener'. He tacks poems together too much. There's late Yeats when he is not too obscure: 'In Memory of Robert Gregory', 'The Municipal Gallery', 'Among School Children', 'Prayer for my Daughter'. I try to use that expansive form in my new collection. Kavanagh has some terrific poems and, of my near contemporaries, Derek Mahon and Paul Durcan seem the best. John Montague has a good solid achievement: all those sad family poems add up; I love it when he talks of the lovers in the morning who 'Lay on both sides of the canal/ Listening on Sony transistors/ To the agony of Pope John/ Yet it didn't seem strange or blasphemous,... *Puritan Ireland's dead and gone,/ A myth of O'Connor and O'Faolain.'* Mahon, like MacNeice, links the unusual in a startling way but he has more sense of the created work of art in poems which never appear thrown ramshackle together; his vision is not swamped by journalism. Of the younger poets Martin Mooney and Paula Meehan seem very good. Of course Janice Fitzpatrick is amongst the best, and people should start accepting her as part of contemporary Irish poetry. Paul Muldoon can be great fun, but very tricksy. There are a lot of good poems in Heaney's *Field Work.* This sort of list can go on and on. I've just read some good poems by Tom French.

The "Troubles" feature in poems in the '70s volumes from 'Bloody Sunday', and 'Claudy' to, more recently, 'Ulster Says Yes'. 'For Jan Bentley' images 'grenades (under mist) ... stored in boxes (which) will wait' — as sinister an image as Paul Muldoon's Volkswagen 'ticking over in the gap'. Is there a polit-

ical position in the poems akin to moderate reform espoused by the SDLP?
It would be silly of me to start to try to sum up all those poems. Personally
I am an unreconstructed liberal and I suppose Hume tries to take some
of the fanaticism out of Nationalist politics. So, yes. Fanatic Gerry Adams,
fanatic Ian Paisley, fanatic Communists: they frighten me. Compromise is
the word. Things improve. Unionist reaction to the first power sharing
was the Ulster Workers Strike of the '70s; there's nothing so bad yet in the
immediate Unionist reactions to the Good Friday Peace Agreement but
democracy is not yet delivered.

*You have not mentioned the poet John Hewitt? His Regionalism, his charting
of identity outwards from Ulster, might be linked to your* HONEST ULSTERMAN
manifesto?
One always forgets somebody... several people. Hewitt wrote some really
central poems and his late autobiographical sonnets are very attractive. Yes,
I'm attracted to the notion of self-government for Ulster. Restore the miss-
ing counties; we are different from Southerners. But I'm not fanatic about
it. Any compromise that will make things better will do me. I am a Derry
man by birth, but I hate sentimentalising about it. I squirm when people tell
you seriously how creative everybody in Derry is! It was beautiful to grow up
in, but there was a limited pool of talent and a lot of complacency. Phil
Coulter country! Everyone harmonising under the lamp posts!

*Irony seems congenial to your soul. One poem claims that the 'rebel' who 'can-
not kiss the head he's cutting off is a bad egg'.*
Perhaps it is the literary manifestation of anti-fanaticism. You want to let
things speak for themselves, give opposite opinion a chance. It's a mar-
vellous compressing agent for defusing or annoying the opposition.
Perhaps it's an Ulster family trait: my father would joke ironically about
his unobtrusive acts of charity rather than preach about them.

You also write musical poems: lullabys, ballads, laments, lyrics and songs.
So do most good poets.

*Yes. Poets like Roy McFadden acknowledge direct inspiration from music and
his 'Sancto's Dog' originates in Paul McCartney's 'Yesterday'. Is there direct
quotation or influence in your poems?*
You know there is. All those sonnets based on Shakespeare sonnets. 'The
Blessed Mary Heggarty' was released by Joni Mitchell's 'I Could Drink a
Case of You and Still Be On My Feet'. 'The Sun' is full of quotations from
Edwin Muir and Edward Thomas. 'Ronadaine Cary' has two stanzas from
Stephen Spender. Music is a key subject — especially in poems I still feel
serious about like 'Didn't He Ramble' but it's often the poignancy or gen-

eral atmosphere that is carried over into poems; you find that too in Derek Mahon's work where he ends a poem thinking that he loves to hear 'that lonesome whistle blow'.

The critical essays in ACROSS A ROARING HILL *explore the thesis that Protestantism directly influences the language of poetry; you use Biblical-sounding language and phrases like 'the further shore'. In 'Cloncha' do you express an insecurity of tenure in the land you love? Does the Protestant background matter?*

I think 'the further shore' is from hymns; but certainly my work is littered with phrases from the Bible. We went to church every Sunday for several years and although the sermons were boring the texts were exciting, and some of the hymns. I don't know if Catholics read the Bible so much. The myth is they don't. I suppose the crucial thing is *how* we use the Bible. It's surely a key text. In 'We Belong Together' the last two stanzas of a family quarrel run:

> I regret even the childish marriage vows
> we giggled in the face of Heaven.
> The ghost of that contract is in our rows
> bargains are struck, bargains are driven.
>
> For this philosophy I burn
> I am sick of love, and my wife leaves
> to consult a solicitor, to turn
> my house into a den of thieves.

I don't think you find that density of reference in Heaney or Muldoon or anywhere. It seems to me rarely passionate and direct and feeding off the Bible.

As for 'insecurity of tenure'. I was made to feel that by history and by the behaviour of many Nationalists — and some poets — during the "Troubles". Growing up in the North, Ulster was my obvious home. Reading history I discovered that my people were among the invaders from Scotland and England... very long ago. Then, in the last thirty years or so, one was often made to feel an outsider; even lapsed Protestants are not always welcome; MacNeice and Elizabeth Bowen and Joyce Cary were made to feel the same way. Kinsella, Montague and Heaney emphasised in their work the Protestant versus Catholic side of the "Troubles" rather than Conservative versus Liberal/Labour betraying, as I thought, the tradition from Joyce to O'Connor to O'Faolain. Is that true? As someone who was brought up in a liberal Presbyterian environment I never could understand how anyone would be frightened by the hellfire sermon in *Portrait of the Artist as a Young Man* just as I was shocked to find that Anglicans read their prayers from a book instead of praying spontaneously.

You seem to share Portrush with other northern poets like Derek Mahon. You entitle a 1974 volume WEST STRAND VISIONS.

Yes. I'm very happy with that. You could make a nice little pamphlet out of poems on that area by Derek and I. I was there much longer but Derek also had a connection with Portballintrae through his wife. Derek is a big figure in my mythology. The *Poète Maudit* — those poets who tried to kill themselves — are important in his work. He went for an exclusive, ill-fated poetic destiny and I tried to stick with the domestic thing. He figures in several of my poems, and our work is very similar. He might have a finer ear; I have more generous scope. Or is he more sophisticated and I more humane, a Donne to his Marvell? This is getting ridiculous... but good fun. Derek says that if he had had better eyesight he would have been a sailor; it turns out his father-in-law was a sailor who wrote poetry. Read his poem 'Father in Law'.

The sea, sailing, is a recurrent metaphor in your poems and many of your homes have been in coastal locations. Is there a connection between the sea voyage and Protestantism, the poem as a Mayflower voyage?

The sea's presence is literal. In an early unpublished poem I am sitting on the rocks at Portrush wanting to escape and thinking that if I sail far enough on this globe I will be home again. The world trap. Joyce Cary's great novel *To Be a Pilgrim*, named after Bunyan's hymn, sees the Protestant protagonist's life as a pilgrimage and, yes, it seems to have been a Protestant impulse to leave persecution for the New World. Were the Catholics more driven out by famine? The early explorers from Spain and Portugal were Catholics so there probably isn't a clear case but there's something in it. Was Odysseus a Protestant? Such a notion is very close to my heart. Maybe you are asking the wrong question. It is very limiting to be always classified as a Protestant, a lapsed Protestant, rather than just a person, a poet.

You were writer-in-residence at Queen's University in the late '80s and you established 'The Poets' House' at Portmuck in Co. Antrim in 1990 which has now moved to Donegal. Did you uncover new young writers?

New writers uncover themselves by writing: at Friends' School I uncovered Sam McBratney who went on to write children's books while Michael Dibdin went on to be a crime writer; the *Honest Ulsterman* helped writers like Michael Foley, Frank Ormsby, Paul Muldoon and Katherine McPhelimy to get their work before the public; at Queen's I ended up with a small group of older writers some of whom are producing good work and Martin Mooney, a talented poet, came as a student and ended up teaching at Portmuck. Many of our students have gone on to publish in England and America like Bridget Meeds, published by Faber and Faber.

In From the Irish *(1985) and in* The Cattle Rustling *(1992) there are links with Irish language poetry and the figure of Cuchulainn. What is your sense of Irish language verse? Why were you attracted to Cuchulainn?*
Teaching the Anglo-Irish literature course at Coleraine I was continually using Irish language poems in translation and reading books like James Stephens's prose versions of the sagas, Kinsella's *Tain*, O'Connor's *The Little Monasteries* or Austin Clarke's translations. I couldn't read the originals, but the translations suggested a use of English and some models I felt I could learn from. Poets like Pearse Hutchinson, Hartnett and McIntyre keep referring to Irish poems and I love Derek Mahon's placing Rafferty in a modern university. (Why does he leave that out of his *Selected Poems?*) I did a similar but more sustained thing with a whole series of Irish originals, like 'The Lament for a Dead Policeman' based on 'The Lament for Art O'Leary'. Irish literature in English has this huge tradition of Irish literature in Irish that most of us are cut off from. I'm just one of those trying to heal the gap without learning Irish. It isn't simple.

As for Cuchulainn, he is a very interesting character, half-gentleman and half-thug. In fact, he isn't even a character. Various authors use him in different stories, as they do with Conor who starts off as an angel and who ends up as a beast. Sagas are not like novels. Obviously anyone who sees Ulster as very separate from the other provinces can see *The Tain* as a separatist myth. Vivian Mercier's *The Irish Comic Tradition* is very good on connecting the sagas' grotesque style with Beckett. My title poem 'From the Irish' is half-quotation from Lady Gregory's translation of the Cuchulainn cycle.

In your recent collection The Company of Children *(1999) there are lines about you as a painter: 'I think about painting as much as work or wife./I've been dabbling all my life'. Is there a difference between painting and writing for you? Which Irish painters do you admire?*
I'm nervous about talking about my Sunday painting. I've been at it all my life without trying to push it much. The scenery is something I love; but it seldom turns up in poems except when I almost force it in, as in 'Cloncha' or in 'Honeysuckle'. I really love Heaney's ability to suggest the feel of the physical world in his poems and wonder why I don't do it more. An artist friend Jimmy Moore in Derry who did talented slapdash landscapes that a lot of people love was my first experience of the artistsic life. He couldn't afford a car but he could make a living by riding his bike out into Donegal and painting landscapes supported by doing adverts for cin-

emas in Derry. A friend of my father, the painter Neil Shawcross, did our posters for The Poets' House. When I taught in Lisburn Colin Middleton was a colleague, and I could see he was the real thing. What I loved about Middleton's landscapes was that they were really abstract but they had a firm sense of place. Apart from that I have to plead ignorance. I have liked what Gerard Dillon I have seen and the younger Jack B. Yeats (the latter seems messy) and a lot of Paul Henry. Internationally Peter Breughel would be my hero and Edward Hopper at a lower level but I do like Van Gogh and Vermeer. You don't want lists. I'm quite a good draughtsman, and some of my charcoal and pastel sketches stand up well in any company; but anything I bring off in colour seems to be good luck. My wife Janice has a really bold sense of colour. There was a painter who taught maths at Campbell College, Cyril W. Bion, who seemed a genius to me at seventeen. I'd love to see his paintings again.

Donegal, your hinterland in youth, is your home now. Do you feel settled? Are you somehow asserting a connection with Donegal as part of Ulster?
Yes. All impossible childhood dreams have come true. The Donegal accent has a gritty Ulster quality but much sweeter than Derry or Belfast, without the tricksyness of Kerry or Dublin. When we moved from Northern Ireland, the Donegal poet Cathal Ó Searcaigh led us here to where people appreciate us and support us and where we can do our good work in an atmosphere of celebration rather than suspicion. That man has a sort of magic about him, he is a wheeler dealer who has kept his integrity intact. I think our new books will show that we are among the best, that we have survived intact and maybe better than ever we were, Janice and the children — Ben and Anna — and me... and of course Charlie, the dog.

SEAMUS HEANEY

You were born in 1939 and grew up on the family farmstead in County Derry. In your Nobel lecture in Stockholm, CREDITING POETRY *(1995), the poet receiving this great honour and the pre-reflective child (who 'lived a kind of den-life' largely 'proofed against the outside world') are linked when you 'credit poetry with making this space-walk possible'. That image seems to indicate a none-too literal or direct ratio between poetry and autobiography (in which imagination is already implicated). There is also, though, the 'umbilical' link with Mossbawn, your parents and friends, a core presence in the life of the poems. Did your parents influence you in different ways in terms of becoming a poet or in terms of the way they 'get into' the poems? As a recent poem, 'Known World' asks: 'How does the real get into the made up?'*

My father figures strongly in the first poems I wrote. I remember being uneasy when *Death of a Naturalist* came out, wondering how he would feel when he read things like 'Follower' and 'Ancestral Photograph'. There was an underground cable between us and whatever messages were exchanged were usually sent through it rather than through any talk we might have had. Whatever influence my father has had on the poetry comes from my tapping into the cable. Or from being one of the terminals. As far as he was concerned, I was in a different world and seemed to be operating in it competently enough, but we had no developed language for linking up on subjects outside the first world we'd shared. The question could equally be, how does the real get out of the unsaid? Sometimes it doesn't, it just stays in there, like a charge. My father's bound to have been aware of that too. There was a touch of the diviner about him, after all. He used to hold a sil-ver pocket watch over the place where there was supposed to be a spring, and the watch would start to oscillate. Or maybe it was he who made it oscillate. Anyway, in those early poems I dug in to get at the source. There was something being broached between us, and I suppose I was anxious that the broaching might lead to a breach. It was serious, but then the seri-ousness made poetry something more than a word game. It was life-chang-ing, life-helping even, and there was emotional risk involved. What I was making up was making a difference in the real. Which had to mean equally that the real was getting into the made up. But how it gets in, that's still a question you can't answer ahead of time.

My mother, for example. It's only relatively recently she enters the poems as the whole mystery a mother is. All my life I'd remembered meeting her in the bus station in Magherafelt at Hallowe'en in 1951, on the day I was coming home from St. Columb's College for the Hallowe'en break. I'd gone off to Derry at the end of August so this was my first time back. There was this special chartered bus that took the south Derry boys from the college, dropping them off in groups at Draperstown and Desertmartin and Magherafelt. And it was a great surprise to me that she was there when I landed, in the old waiting room of the bus station. What I realize now, of course, is that she knew I would be arriving and had arranged to be in Magherafelt, doing the shopping, so that we'd connect for the last part of my journey home, which would be by the regular service bus. I think that was the first moment I saw her and she saw me as other, so to speak. It was a sort of *Sons and Lovers* moment. Anyhow, when the bus station in Magherafelt was blown up in the 1980s, I felt strangely connected to the event and eventually wrote a sestina — of all things — the one called 'Two Lorries' that's in *The Spirit Level*. The plain reality of explosion and obliteration got mixed up with the underlying untold reality of the memory. So the 'umbilical link' you ask about is in that poem, but it's also — as you say 'none too literal'. I suppose the line I once heard from the sculptor Oisin Kelly is one way of putting it: 'These things are not secrets, but mysteries.'

PREOCCUPATIONS *(1980) records Anahorish, primary school in the 1940s, and it recounts encounters with three genres of poetry early on: bawdy, earthy rhymes; patriotic ballads or 'recitations'; school poetry learned by heart, like Keats's 'Odes' where 'midges' were 'gnats'. Do these three forms or tensions between them ghost subsequent poems?*
Undoubtedly. The Anahorish schoolboy was learning big art language and being set on track to become the A-level candidate and the First Arts student. Linguistically upwardly mobile. Except that the sociological metaphor isn't quite right. I've always liked Vincent Buckley's resistance to the idea that a more elaborate and developed language constitutes a displacement: he saw it as an increment of inwardness, an entry to further language. I mean, there was nothing in my actual experience that matched the upper class twit world of Bertie Wooster, and yet as an adolescent I rejoiced in P. G. Wodehouse's prose. I suppose I eventually tuned the further language to the first note. Or better say it tuned itself. I'm conscious, all the same, that some of the recent work I've done in criticism and translation grows out of that old vernacular stuff that's always there, deep down. I got great pleasure a few years ago, for example, going back to Robert Burns, finding the hidden Scotland in me, so to speak. There's a terrific swing and at homeness about the Burns stanza, it collapses the

difference between high and low. You can have your *oxters* and your *Oxford* in the one breath. I did an essay for a book published on the bicentennial of Burns's death and found myself writing a whole page about his use of the word "wee" in his poem to the mouse. 'To a Mouse' as a truly weird, fateful, soothsaying poem, scaresome rather than sentimental. 'Wee' is the first word in the first line, and it goes in like a wedge, like the ploughshare wrecking the mouse's nest, and it opened a channel to all that old stuff back down there in my ear. The result was that last year I found myself doing versions of Robert Henryson. Henryson wrote in Scots, in the fifteenth century, his own versions of fables from Aesop, very down to earth, the kind of thing you could have read out years ago at a local "variety concert". Canny old stories about the town mouse and the country mouse and all that sort of thing. At the same time there's a certain literariness about the writing. The poems are in rhyme royal, in the stanza form Chaucer used for *Troilus and Criseyde*. So I started to do an update of the old Scots just for the pleasure of rhyme and the roll of the stanza and the chance to get the occasional birl of local speech into the venerable text. It's the kind of verse you could imagine Billy Connolly doing for a big audience. Recitation. Back to the variety concert...

Poems in NORTH *and* ELECTRIC LIGHT *recall school at St. Columb's College in Derry (1951-57); your critical essays and Michael Parker's book,* SEAMUS HEANEY: THE MAKING OF THE POET *(1993), record a varied reading syllabus there: Biggles, Robert Louis Stevenson, Maurice Walsh, Lorna Doone, Wordsworth, Hopkins and Hardy. Did some influences from reading, like Hardy and Hopkins, prove more durable havens afterwards than others?*
Well, haven is a great word for it. Hardy is a haven, all right. I don't think of him as an influence. But 'The Oxen', for example, feels like a pre-natal possession. Probably because I learnt it by heart early on. And because from the start the words 'barton' and 'coomb' seemed to take me far away and at the same time to bring me close to something lurking inside me. Then there was the phrase, 'their strawy pen', which had a different familiarity, it brought the byre and the poetry book into alignment. Hopkins was different again, in that he made me want to write. Wordsworth I just gradually grew up to. He has always been a mountain on the horizon. Wordsworth helps you to think about poetry as a way of taking the measure of yourself and the world, and yourself-in-the-world. He has such range. There's a wildness in a poem like 'Loud is the vale' that opens you up to your aloneness and the vastness you inhabit; and then you have a more serene mysteriousness at the end of 'The Ruined Cottage', in that image of tall grass and weeds. Hard to beat. Durable, as you say. The thing you learn, I suppose, is that for poetry to matter, the amount of it you know isn't as important as the meaning any small bit of it can gather up over a lifetime.

The period spent mainly in Belfast as a student at Queen's and as a teacher and lecturer (1962-67), described in PREOCCUPATIONS, *began at a time when contemporary poets were thin of the ground: 'Roy McFadden had drawn the blinds on* RANN. *John Hewitt was in Coventry.' Poets like Patrick Kavanagh, Ted Hughes and Frost seem to have fortified the voice early on. In what way, to what extent, did northern poetry enter the work then and remain as part of its dialogue?*

I can date that precisely. The year after I left Queen's I did a postgraduate course at St. Joseph's Training College, as it was then called, and wrote an extended essay on literary magazines in the North. I read old issues of *Lagan* and *Rann*, I met Jimmy Vitty who was then the librarian of the Linen Hall Library, and began to get a sense of what had been going on on the ground in the '40s and '50s. I was searching around but not quite sure what I was after. I'd got this prize when I did my degree, a book token for £5 that I'd opted for in lieu of a medal — the McMullen Medal — and with it I'd bought several Irish books including MacNeice's *Collected Poems* and the old Everyman editions of Wilde and Synge. In the library in Magherafelt I came on an old *Faber Book of Irish Verse*, edited by Val Iremonger and I think Sean Jennett, that contained Hewitt's 'Townland of Peace'. Michael McLaverty lent me McFadden's books. And so on. I was beginning to take notice during 1962. Then I met the painter Terry Flanagan and his wife Sheelagh, who knew Hewitt, and that too gave me a sense of connection with the living stream.

Michael Parker suggests that you read Corkery's HIDDEN IRELAND *and Irish language poetry early on. Is it fair to suggest language is a key site of struggle between aggravation and assuagement, a move from being represented by or even in language to achieving mastery or 'jurisdiction' over these split syllables (over lyric and aisling) until this becomes an instinctual pleasure or primal delight, 'Anahorish' and 'Sruth'? This would imply a meld of language as etymology and history and language as pleasuring instinct, embrace and escape from the actual site of these struggles — Sweeney's flight and Cuchulainn's stand?*

When I was doing that Burns essay, you know, what came back to me was the memory of a genuine connection I'd felt — when I was sixteen or seventeen — with poets like Cathal Bui MacGiolla Gunna and Art MacCumhthaigh. They were Ulster poets and their work was on the Irish syllabus and the Irish they wrote in was close to the Donegal Irish we were being taught in St. Columb's College two hundred years on. And in the Nationalist and cultural Nationalist conditions we were working in, of course, it was impossible not to link that sense of linguistic closeness to a sense of ethnic closeness. And then when I was doing the Burns piece, I realized that John Hewitt's feel for the Rhyming Weavers was based on a similar sense of kinship. Accent and ancestry as one. 'They were my own people,' Hewitt says somewhere. So that's square one in the Ulster linguistic pysche: you start off with given notions of where your allegiance lies and your studies tend to be directed at a confirmation of those notions. The linguistic politics of the Assembly is a caricature of it all: Irish for Sinn Féin, Ulster Scots for the DUP. But further language is what we need, Sweeney's flight, as you say, to make a change from Cuchlainn's stand. Anyhow, it struck me that a true schooling for Northern Ireland students, a truly literary liberation, would involve a course where they'd have to read both Cathal Bui's poem about the yellow bittern and Burns's poem about the mouse, and they would be shown how the poems are revelations of poetry's power to spring the individual into new awareness of what it is to be alive and at risk in the world. Both of them are poems of tragic intuition, they expose the consciousness to extreme recognitions, they remind you of what happens to Lear on the heath. But I don't propose this ideal syllabus for the sake of community relations, if you know what I mean. My reasons are essentially poetic. In those particular poems, Burns and MacGiolla Gunna fit Nadezhda Mandelstam's definition of the poet as an agent of world harmony and a source of truth... Maybe none of this answers your question about language, but at least it bears on it. The older I get, the more I want to be at home and away in myself, to allow every linguistic link and chink and loophole to bring me through to something uncensored, some gleam of half-extinguished thought flaring up.

DEATH OF A NATURALIST *(1966) was critically acclaimed for its sensuous, muscular, concrete, immediate, exploratory, lyrical processes, its memory made present tense desire. A County Derry woman told me recently that 'Blackberry Picking' has stayed with her as the first poem to put down the real feel of her 'known world' on the page. That synaesthetic bluebottle, though, seems to buzz somewhere between a World War II aerodrome and Seamus Deane's 'Six: After Derry, 30 January 1972': 'This is the honeymoon/ Of the cockroach, the small / Spiderless eternity of the fly.' Is there a militaristic, metaphorically ballistic force moving through those first volumes?*

'The squat pen rests. Snug as a gun.' Well, with hindsight, you can link that and other lines to Ulster in the coming times. But when it was written, it wasn't orientated in any conscious way towards politics or political prospects. This is an area where I am dumb to tell... in this regard I'm as much outside the poems as the next person.

'The Bookcase' in ELECTRIC LIGHT *recalls books as physical objects but there are 'Voices too of Frost and Wallace Stevens/Off a Caedmon double album, off different shelves.' The American influence on northern poetry in the 1960s is explored in Edna Longley's* POETRY AND POSTERITY *(2001). Do you see American poetry impacting on your own work differently than it did in the*

poetry of Derek Mahon and Michael Longley who also played that album cease-lessly at Trinity College?

The album they played is probably the very one I listened to in the Longleys' flat in Malone Avenue. And that's actually the Longleys' book-case I'm describing. Michael was a great Hart Crane man, and Crane is there in all his oceanic majesty in an early Longley poem like 'Circe'. Michael had also heard Richard Wilbur read in London and was a great Wilbur fan. I remember us all meeting Donald Davie at a reception in Queen's in the late '60s and Michael being irritated at Davie's slight put-down of Wilbur for being too graceful. I think we cast ourselves a bit self-consciously as paleface and redskin in those days, me being for Lowell and Hughes, just to keep the edge on things, but also because of a differ-ent phonetic and poetic grounding. Still, John Crowe Ransom, Elizabeth Bishop, Robert Frost — they were all beloved. But I'm not sure how much any one of them entered my writing. Frost is there in the monologues for women in *Door into the Dark* — 'The Wife's Tale', for example. And Lowell is audible in *Field Work*. But that's about it.

Has your Robert Frost and Paul Muldoon's taken different, and complimen-tary, roads?

There is a dazzling Frost and a daunting Frost. The daunting one was the one I connected with, in the writing part of myself, at any rate. The one who wrote 'Home Burial' , 'To Earthward', 'The Subverted Flower', 'Out, Out'... He made me feel that a certain blunt, plonked-down thing within me could have its say. At the same time, the reader in me, the apprecia-tor, took great pleasure in the wizard Frost, the maze maker of 'Two Look at Two' and 'A Hillside Thaw', the dream-surfer of 'After Apple Picking'. And that's the Frost who entered the writing part of Paul.

'The Tollund Man' links poet and burial victim from the Danish bog in nam-ing the 'man-killing parishes' where you become 'lost, /Unhappy and at home.' Richard Kearney suggests this quest echoes Heidegger's view of poetry as a search for the 'estranged', original call of the pure being of language itself, lan-guage as 'homecoming' going back beyond everyday speech which is merely an echo, a 'worn-out, overworked poem'; a search, though, for this primary being which 'accepts the truth that we are no longer at home in the world' (TRANSITIONS: NARRATIVES IN MODERN IRISH POETRY, 1988). *Others have read the 'bog poems' as postmodern events in language which constructs the poet's own subjectivity so that no stable knowledge of a fixed past or history emerges, only its constant reconstruction as a moving film, a fiction. Plato comes into the poems; Barthes and deconstruction are (fleetingly?) in the criti-cism. Are these junctures between philosophy and post-modern theory meaning-ful in terms of the way you yourself read the poems or construct them?*

Richard Kearney's way of talking about the bog poems and linking them to the Heideggerian hypotheses does make sense to me — again in retrospect. I couldn't have put it like that at the time. But yes, I felt carried away by the material, into and out of the material, and probably made a mistake in trying to tame the strangeness of it all. I explicated the poems too trimly in relation to the politics and dangers on the ground at the time. I should probably have just let them abide there in their own exhumed oddity. So 'the events in language' approach makes sense too. But all these sophisticated responses never get far past Frost's homey old declaration that a poem is a 'momentary stay against confusion'.

In critical writing you have emphasized the auditory or 'sounding' faculties, as well as the visual qualities, the 'verbal icon', of the imagination; the primitive oral impulse to imitate owl or widgeon are as vital as the instinct to engage in the 'plastic art' of mud pies. When I read 'Squarings' in THE HAW LANTERN *it was like hearing a new 'clinker-built' music. Have the sounds you are listening for or hearing in making poems altered over the years?*
There was something up and away about the movement in those 'Squarings' pieces that was new for me. Each poem was a twelve-line sprint. I was hurdling along. Trying to do them a poem at a time as opposed to a line at a time. So the line's not force fed or tightly reined, and I think that particular experience of limbering up has increased the stylistic options. Not that options is exactly the word. But the twelve-liners in *Seeing Things* have to be precursors of the loose-weave sequences in *Electric Light.* At the same time, I still love a line like Hewitt's 'heavy, clay-sucked stride'. That's the kind of music I was after in the beginning and I wouldn't ever want to sign away my right to it. Or to the short, tight quatrain.

Many poems evoke paintings and a great number are dedicated to modern or contemporary Irish painters and artists. 'Sunlight' and 'Squarings' seem to evoke, with love, the Dutch interiors of Old Masters ('Stable-straw, Rembrandt-gleam and burnish'); 'An Artist' searches for 'unpainted space/ behind the mountain'. How do you see the relationship between poetry and visual art which the essays also evoke? Does abstraction (the absence of subject matter and narrative, the full presence of the medium) in contemporary art or poetry disturb or invite you?
When we say abstract, you know, it makes the thing in question sound bodiless. The fact is that painting, whether abstract or narrative, is never unbodied. You stand before a Miro, say, or a Klee, and you feel it like a system of checks and balances, you can stretch your arms out and take the strain of it from fingertip to toe-tip. The graph is transposed into your nerves. You join up the dots inside yourself. You stand before a Cezanne and it's more a case of weights and measures than checks and balances.

You stand before David's 'Death of Marat' and you're up against a marble slab. Painting comes into the poems because it's inscribed, if you'll excuse the expression, in my nervous system. I'm not going to say that there's not an intellectual pleasure in knowing something about the historical circumstances and the iconography and the art historical placing and so on. But on the spot, it's the simultaneity of the whole thing that does you good.

To what extent do poems imply a class analysis of left and right? 'Oysters' juxtaposes the 'Glut of privilege' with 'poetry or freedom'; 'Mint' connects the herb with 'prisoners' who 'we failed... by our disregard'; there are the craftsmen, a dying breed economically but alive in the verb of their 'Midas touch'. I guess I'm suggesting the pull of Michael Longley's makars and Joyce's idea of the priesthood.
It's probably more a case of the Sermon on the Mount and the Eight Beatitudes than class analysis. One of the effects of a Catholic childhood as pious as mine was to give special value and even beauty to the concept of passive suffering. The religious vision of Irish Catholicism in the 1940s and 50s was shot through with the idea of sacrifice and self-denial. Anyway, for whatever reason, I was sensitized to the reality of dumb sorrow, helpless endurance. Highly conscious of 'the suffering souls in purgatory'; and developing a kind of answerability for them. I suppose 'Mint' is in some sense about being in thrall to such feelings and then for a moment being absolved from them — by an experience of sudden rapture, some kind of transport — absolved — but for that moment only. That same yearning for absolution and disappointment at its unavailability is in 'Oysters' too: 'I was angry that my trust could not repose/In the clear light, like poetry or freedom/Leaning in from sea.' All a bit priesty, indeed.

Do poems like 'Punishment', 'Casualty', 'The Strand at Lough Beg' (revised in Station Island*) test your key image of water ripple as poetic consciousness widening inclusively, a connective tissue encompassing family, neighbour, 'tribe', province, nation and the international within inner circle and outer ring? Individuals transgress tribal or national values in these poems and pay a 'disproportionately' high price. To what extent do instinctive cultural-political attachments, Unionism and Nationalism, in which the North is 'mired' have to go to attain a liberal humanity here? Surely there is a certain overlap between that figure drinking in the bar in 'Casualty' and the poet in 'Known World' twenty years later quietly ordering a drink on the plane who says: 'Nema problema. Ja. All systems go.' ?*
Well, you're right to link those two occasions, although I would never have thought of doing so myself. They're both a case of absolution once again — self-administered, that is. But the scene at the end of 'Known World' where the poet is flying away from the folk religious world of Macedonia into a kind of Euro-freedom and secularity — that contains

intimations of betrayal too. It's meant to look forward to the no-risk bombing raids by NATO pilots during the Kosovo war. I don't believe in ditching 'attachments' but you're right to bring up that line about being 'mired' in them — being dragged down into soul-destroying solidarity is the problem for people brought up — or is it brought down — in Northern Ireland. I suppose I would still put trust in education, a liberal education, as they say, a humanist education. To quote Frost again: education changes the plane of regard. It helps you to get a new look at yourself.

Does writing love poems present particular problems for the poet? Is there a stance in the love poems that separates them as 'genres' in the work from the other poems?
Maybe in *Death of a Naturalist* the love poems are pitched differently, but in *Field Work* I think they belong in the same register as the rest of the book. And in *Electric Light.* And elsewhere in between — 'The Underground' in *Station Island.* 'The Walk' in *The Spirit Level.* James Wright once said he wanted to write 'the poetry of a grown man'. As stances go, I think that's a pretty good one, and it's one I'd want to adopt for all poems, love poems included.

*In an 'Interview with Seamus Deane' (*CRANE BAG,*1:1, Spring 1977) you talked of the poems in terms of a 'kind of slow, obstinate, papish burn emanating from the ground I was brought up on'. Has religion or a numinous sense changed in the work between the 1980s volumes like* STATION ISLAND *and* THE HAW LANTERN *and 1990s volumes like* SEEING THINGS *and* THE SPIRIT LEVEL*? Does the incredible sense of the liminal or luminous (of the 'beyond', of the 'foreknown' in the event, of the past as a future coming towards us, of 'last things... first things slipping from me', of being 'in step with what escaped me...') suggest a secular, lyric philosophy or a religious teleology, a catechism?*
What I've found myself doing more and more, especially in interviews like this, is emphasising the purely religious, transcendental importance of Catholicism. We have been doomed and demeaned in some of the ways we talk about ourselves in the North. Catholic, even to those who call themselves by the name, tends to be more a sociological term than anything else. 'Papish burn', I'm sorry to say, caves in to that same old clichéd idiom. It doesn't help. It's not further language. Catholic is less conniving than Papish, but if you describe yourself as a Catholic in the North, it can still sound like a defiance or a provocation. In certain circles in the South, it might even be taken to mean that deep down you are unrepentant about child abuse by priests and not altogether against corporal punishment in orphanages. I exaggerate, I know, but only in order to emphasize the way the common mind tends to react when faced with the fact of religion and religious practice and religious value. What I've found myself

doing in a conscious sort of way is countering this with a declaration of the beauty and salvific effect of growing up with the idea of God in his eternal present around and about and above you everywhere, growing up with ideas of continuous creation, of guardian angels, of sanctifying grace, a universe shimmering with light. Of course it all belonged to a medieval world picture, it was Dante for the preliterate, but it formed a luminous private world for individuals in my generation, and as Joseph Brodsky says, 'if art teaches anything, it is the privateness of the human condition.' So the transcendent turn in the poems, if it can be called that, is a matter of following on down that road of truth to self. Not relapse or nostalgia, I hope, more a matter of following those gleams I mentioned earlier, an act of uncensoring.

THE HAW LANTERN *(1987) has the parable poems. What were you after in the form of these poems?*
The first one of those poems to be written was 'From the Republic of Conscience'. I'd been asked by the Sandymount Branch of Amnesty International to write a poem for United Nations Day. They sent me a whole dossier of information about prisoners of conscience in jails all over the world, evidence of the injustice and the torture they were suffering. It was a dreadful catalogue, but it spoke so powerfully for itself, I couldn't see how to match it with a poem. I felt a kind of reticence, some sense that it would be trespass of sorts to cast oneself too promptly as the good guy, and at such a safe distance. Anyway, I could shift nothing and wrote back, ruefully but at least honestly, to say I had to decline the commission. And then, suddenly, once that feeling of obligation was out of the way, a great sense of freedom and playfulness arrived — it was induced by accident when I read Richard Wilbur's poem, 'Shame', which imagines shame as a small cramped country. At any rate, the potential earnestness or righteousness was got through and I began to think up images to suggest the landscape and weather of conscience. I knew there had be a clear and rinsing atmosphere and luckily remembered a moment when I'd stepped out of a British Airways commuter plane on an airfield in Orkney. The propellors phutt-phutted to a stop and there was complete silence. A clunk when the door was opened and the steps were let down. And when I walked down off the plane, across what was more a moor than an aerodrome, I heard a curlew. Solitude, a piercing summons, no hiding place — I had landed in the republic of conscience. It was one of those poems where you don't sound like yourself to yourself, but still know you're on the right track. I suspect Larkin felt the same when he wrote 'Solar'. Then I just followed the track in order to write two or three other poems — 'From the Canton of Expectation', for example. And 'Parable Island'. Of course, the parable mode was familiar from the Eastern European poetry

I'd been reading in translation, and the language of those particular poems is a kind of translatorese. There was an exercise I used to set the students in my poetry workshop at Harvard — to make up a poem that pretended to be translated from an original in a foreign language. The parable poems were that kind of exercise. Basically an attempt to get poetry out of 'the doldrums of what happens'. I'd just finished *Station Island* and was trying to dodge documentary.

Gaston Bachelard's THE POETICS OF SPACE *links poetry not primarily with intellect or reformulations of social or political structures but with a primary, concentrated, instinctive, shock encounter, where the image reverberates until it 'expresses us by making us what it expresses'. He sees the space between the pre-reflective child and adult poet/reader as thin: 'But over and beyond our memories, the house where we were born is physically inscribed in us... The feel of the tiniest latch has remained in our hands.' Is memory an active principle, a key note in your latest volume* ELECTRIC LIGHT*?*
Memory has never ceased to be an active principle. It's where space and language and time come together. It's the material that the Bachelardian house is made of. When I hear the word 'latch' or 'scullery' or 'chimney breast' I don't know whether they're dreaming me or I'm dreaming them. In the second poem of 'Squarings' there's a line that sets the standard and makes it impossible at one and the same time. 'Do not waver into language,' the line says. 'Do not waver in it.' So to conclude with the famous Dublin triad: 'This is it. This is the thing. This is what you're up against.'

MICHAEL LONGLEY

You were born in Belfast in 1939 after your parents had moved there from Clapham Common, London, in the '20s. How would you describe your home or family background?

Lower middle class. Comfortable enough. My father was a commercial traveller for an English furniture manufacturer. He joined up in 1939 and on being demobbed in 1945 found himself without his old job. He scraped a living as a freelance fundraiser until his firm opened up again in the early '50s. He was well-liked locally, so the English background wasn't too much of a handicap for his children. We became socially nimble and fitted in fairly well — which is what all children crave. Despite the fact that there wasn't much money, a young Fermanagh girl, Lena Hardy, was employed for next to nothing to help my mother to look after my twin Peter and me. She became part of the family, a second mother. I treasure my memories of her. Our sister Wendy who is nine years older than us also contributed to an emotionally rich though wobbly childhood. I was a melancholy child. Being a twin was important. I didn't sleep alone until I was fifteen or sixteen. My parents were not particularly well-educated, but they were very bright. Goodness knows what they would have achieved if they'd had my chances. My father looked like a burly T.S. Eliot. He took to painting landscapes in the last years of his life.

In TUPPENNY STUNG (1994) you describe your mother as 'volcanic', your father as 'sedimentary'. Did they influence the geology of your personality and the poems with these dual characteristics? (In your poem 'Self-Portrait' you 'articulate through the nightingale's throat/Sing with the vocal chords of the orang-outang.')

They're bound to have done. Now that my children have grown up, they tell me I'm moody, up-and-down, though as a father I've always tried to avoid being unpredictable. Critics seem to have noticed only the formality. There's wildness in my work as well, a bit of honky-tonk. A lot of *The Ghost Orchid* is meant to be sexually hilarious, subversive. My poems are much more improvised than they seem. I wait for lines and phrases rather than construct them.

Primary School on Belfast's Lisburn Road acquainted you with class divisions: on each side of the road the professional classes' lit lounges and rhododendrons, the cramped conditions and outside lavatories of working class school friends (to paraphrase a passage from TUPPENNY STUNG*). Is class awareness or the politics of class implied in your poems?*

Implied is the *mot juste.* I couldn't sit down to write a political poem on purpose, to versify mere opinion, to tell others what they want to hear or what I want them to hear. I like to think that my concern for the craft of poetry is somehow rooted in the pride I feel in my Grandpa Richard's trade as a carpenter, and his grandfather's trade as a blacksmith. My mother's father taught ballroom dancing and his grandfather was a jeweller and painter of sorts. Poems should be as well-made as chairs. Whatever his visions may be, the poet is a *makar* or he is nothing. I'm more left-wing than I might appear. Old Labour. An Attlee man rather than a Blairite — though Blair and new Labour are a thousand times better than the previous crowd of schmucks. In the South the Labour Party would get my vote. In the Republic or in Britain I would always vote Labour. Here it's more complicated. My hero is Paddy Devlin, but there was no room for what he represented, alas. I often vote strategically in a forlorn attempt to keep out the bigots and pharisees. In the European Election I voted for David Ervine because I admire his intelligence and courage and agree with much that he says.

In CAUSEWAY: THE ARTS IN ULSTER *(1971) you state: 'Ulster must be about the last area in the English speaking world which is still likely to produce poets who write out of a response to religion.' In what way did you assimilate religion as you grew up and how did your poems develop as a 'response' to it?*

Thanks to the easy-going Anglican agnosticism of my parents home was completely free of sectarianism. At primary school I soon tasted its curdling sourness without beginning to understand what it was all about. I still don't really understand. My grammar school, Inst, was quite liberal. We might have squinted at the occasional refugee from Christian Brothers' violence, but that was all. I don't think I caught anything from Ulster religion apart from a suspicion of dog collars. I'm a pantheist, a tree-hugger, a primrose-sniffer. I have a religious sense of life. I hope that gets into my poems — reverence for plants and animals, a sacramental sense of things. When I'm in Italy I love the Romanesque churches and the religious art and the ceremonies so much that I become a sentimental Catholic for a few days. But on the way home, somewhere above the Alps, the mood passes, I'm glad to say. I'm a cultural Christian. I believe Jesus existed, an original, a genius, a poet, a revolutionary. No wonder Church and State reduce him to a cult and blur his message with mumbo-jumbo.

As a pupil at the Royal Belfast Academical Institution in the '50s you chose Yeats's COLLECTED POEMS *when you won the prize for English in third year. Was Yeats your first love? Is Yeats a writer who influenced you?*
My first loves were Keats and Walter de la Mare. I hadn't a clue what Yeats was on about, but liked the sounds. Yeats has been a challenge and an example rather than an influence. He puts the slipshod to shame. His syntactical control and stanzaic artistry refresh me. The more I look at him the greater he appears. As I grow older I love him more and more. Is that influence? OK.

You left Belfast to study classics at Trinity College Dublin in 1958 and, later, shared digs, a typewriter, cigarettes, pints, 'buttery books' and publication in the university magazine ICARUS *with Derek Mahon. In there a distinction between the poems you and Mahon write?*
I hope so. Mahon's early poems are extraordinary. They would scare the shit out of all but the brain-dead. In my first forty years of writing nothing (apart from my marriage) has been more important than that first friendship with Mahon. But you have to disconnect and do your own thing. We have gone our separate ways and taken different risks. We keep in touch, usually at a jocular level. Our friendship is profound and lasting. It seems to have a life of its own. As I've said before, suddenly all the promising young poets are sixty. By the way I've given up the ciggies and Mahon's given up the juice.

Is it fair to see the 1950s as a missing decade in terms of Ulster poetry?
The cultural scene was generally quieter then. But as a sixth-former I went to Mary O'Malley's tiny Lyric Theatre in Derryvolgie Avenue and bought the house magazine *Threshold* (whose poetry editor was John Hewitt). Rodgers and Hewitt were big enough names. We also knew about McFadden and Greacen. But MacNeice was the only poet whose work we would see reviewed in the newspapers. And he only came to Belfast for rugby matches! There was a feeling that poetry happened in 'proper' capital cities like Dublin or London.

You studied Latin and Greek at school and university, and developed 'a long preoccupation with form, with stanzaic pattern and rhyme' — to quote your early pamphlet 'Secret Marriages' (Phoenix, 1968). Latin love poets and elegists appear in the early volumes (Propertius, Tibullus, Sculpicia); Virgil, Horace and Ovid in THE GHOST ORCHID; *and Homer is central in your recent work. Can 'old, unhappy far-off things and battles long ago' be 'kidnapped' — your word — as subject matter now? Is there a gap between ancient and post-modern sensibilities?*
Sub specie aeternitatis Homer wrote only a blink ago. Have we changed all

that much since his time? The moments in Homer that I've tried to render into English feel quite contemporary to me. They release in me strong immediate emotions and allow me to say things about the here-and-now that I wouldn't otherwise be able to manage — personal/political statements. A poem I wrote at the time of the 1994 IRA ceasefire has had more impact than anything else of mine. It was based on a passage in Homer. The *Iliad* is the first great European poem, a vast meditation on war and death. It still illuminates our lives, so it is still relevant. Poetry changed after the *Iliad*. Of course it did. But it didn't get any better. I produced my Tibullus translation 'Peace' in response to the Peace People whom I met by accident in a Belfast pub after they'd won the Nobel Prize. Tibullus sounded in my ear like a gentle, wise Belfast neighbour. He doesn't seem very far away at all. Nor does Ovid whose *Metamorphoses* must be the best collection of yarns in the world. A great hodge-podge of Greek and Latin myths and folk tales. Rather post-modern. Propertius is one of my favourite love poets. I don't think of him as a remote classic.

Among the poets you read at Trinity College you list modern Americans but Eliot and Pound are noticeably absent. Does Modernism leave you cold?
Pound and Eliot are not among my favourite poets. I tried the *Pisan Cantos* yet again last summer, but they read to me like notes for poems. How many people in the world read and really enjoy them? A few dozen? And most of them would be academics with vested interests. Really great English poets like Edward Thomas and Wilfred Owen and Isaac Rosenberg who died in the trenches would have made it more difficult for Pound and Eliot, more complicated. (I tune into Stravinsky and Cubism quite happily by the way.) And is not Yeats a Modernist? Whether he is or is not strikes me as beside the point. In simple terms of wattage Eliot and Pound don't hold a candle to Willie. The war poems of Owen and Rosenberg ring out in my ears like modern versions of Sophocles and Aeschylus. Utterly modern. Huge. Who cares if they're 'Modernist'? And what about Lawrence? His wonderful psalm-like improvisations about animals and the natural world are modern without being alienating. Modernism as I think you mean it seems to have left the lay audience far behind, irritated and suspicious. I find the darker poems of Frost and Hardy more frightening than *The Waste Land*. The twentieth century was a rich century for poetry — partly thanks to Pound and Eliot. But as we get it into perspective they will, I suspect, appear less influential, certainly this side of the Atlantic.

In No Continuing City *(1969) you published poems written over a decade. These poems show enormous stanzaic and metrical variety. Is it fair to see poems like 'A Personal Statement' (a 'zig-zag' dialogue between body, mind and senses)*

and 'Epithalamium' (where four sentences and their many sub-clauses are fer-
ried over thirteen five-line stanzas) as emerging from Metaphysical Poetry?
George Herbert is one of my favourite poets, the ultimate lyric poet. I love
Donne nearly as much, but his poems happen somewhere between the
drama and the lyric, and I find him a bit hairy, a bit too masculine some
of the time, all thrust. I prefer Herbert's ebb and flow. His miraculous son-
net 'Prayer' has influenced me as much as any poem in the language. In
'A Personal Statement' I borrowed the stanzaic pattern of his poem
'Deniall'. In 'The Hebrides' I married the stanzaic restraint of Herbert's
poem 'Peace' to the oceanic surges of Hart Crane and early Robert
Lowell. Heady stuff. Wild and poised like surf-riding. 'Epithalamium' is
the first poem of mine to survive. I wrote it in the summer of 1963 when
I should have been studying for my finals. The stanza shape is Herbert-like
but my own invention. Derek Mahon had sent me a poem written along
similar lines, so I knocked together an even more taxing stanzaic pattern
and rhyme scheme and let my sentences unwind through many stanzas —
a 1500 metres race, only with hurdles. I wrote 'Epithalamium' in an elated
rush, despite the formal difficulties. It's more rhapsodic and impro-
visatory than it appears, quite jazzy. I was jousting with Mahon, and with
George Herbert. I was learning how to jam and show off at the George
Herbert School for sophisticated Swingers. I can't understand why most
young poets nowadays don't educate and exercise themselves in this vig-
orous outward-bound fashion. Writing wee free verse poems in your early
twenties seems to me a bit cissy.

Can the well-wrought medium block as well as deliver message. In the tight for-
mal address to 'Christopher at Birth' — 'Your uncle totem and curator bends...'
— we are surely far from the more 'relaxed' demotic idiom of a later poem like
'Washing' in Gorse Fires: *'All the washing on the line adds up to me alone/*
When the cows go home and the golden plover calls...'
I dislike that pejorative phrase 'the well-made poem'. If it's not well made,
be it in strict stanzas or in Lawrentian free verse, then it isn't a poem. You
might as well talk about a well made flower or a well made snowflake
(both of which are patterned but organic). Symmetry is part of biological
life. I hope there is a natural development from 'Christopher at Birth' to
'Washing', from the early work to the more recent pieces — cellular
growth like the rings of a tree, from the knotty centre to the more
'relaxed' outer circles. A true poet is set free by form. Michael Foley once
described Heaney, Mahon and me as 'the tight-arsed trio' — which is
funny. But early poems by those two, say Mahon's 'In Carrowdore
Churchyard' or Heaney's 'Personal Helicon' seem to me miraculous flow-
erings rather than clever constructions. My own work has grown simpler
over the years — more 'relaxed', though not I trust 'loose-arsed'.

NO CONTINUING CITY *inhabits islands and shorelines — not contemporary Belfast. Why? Is the city of the title real, symbolic, actual, Greek?*
The title comes from St. Paul's 'Letter to the Hebrews': 'For here we have no continuing city, but we seek one to come.' Yes, it's symbolic. The absence of Belfast (or any city) from my poetry is a big gap, I agree. I hope it's not a weakness. But perhaps we're being a bit literal. My writing is bound to be conditioned by my living in Belfast. What is a Belfast poem? There are more than the Derek Mahon and Ciaran Carson templates. As I've said before, you write about what moves you, and I'm moved by trees rather than telegraph poles, by dragonflies rather than helicopters. Life is grass. We'd all starve without flowers and insects. Whether we live in a city or in the countryside, ultimately our lives depend on the plants and animals I write about. I trust I am more than a botaniser among the hedgerows. I would like to think of myself as an ecological poet, and therefore relevant right now when our most pressing problems are ecological — how we share the planet with the insects, the plants and other animals. I want my poetry to be like Noah's ark.

Your second volume, AN EXPLODED VIEW *(1973), takes its title from the poem about the prehistoric site on Orkney, 'Skara Brae'. This poem directs us downwards through an archaelogical window. What is archaelogy for you? Is it a different process from the one in Heaney's* NORTH *or in Montague's excavations of cairns?*
No, I don't think our archaelogical approaches differ all that much. I can't stand in a field in Mayo looking at the wild flowers and the sea birds without being aware of the forgotten lazy bed ridges under the grass and the ghosts of the smallholders who once crowded into what is now a wilderness. The standing stones and cairns and stone circles keep me in my place. Closer to home, the Giant's Ring with its dolmen and big grassy area is just up the road from here. One of my holy places. Edna and I visited Skara Brae on a rainy summer's day in 1966. When I'd written my poem about it, she bought me P.V. Glob's book *The Bog People* as a gentle challenge. But nothing happened inside my head. Heaney read the book as well and produced his remarkable sequence of bog poems. I didn't mind. He's staked his claim with 'Bogland', that lovely poem at the end of his second collection. Anyway, my ancestors lie in English soil. I've traced them on my father's side as far back as William Longley who was born in 1713 and is buried in Cowden churchyard in Kent, south east of Tunbridge Wells. A long line of farmers, farm labourers, shepherds, blacksmiths, carpenters, woodcutters, game keepers, wood reeves. My father's father Richard was a journeyman carpenter. Archaeology includes the less distant past, doesn't it? I've been trying to follow in my father's footsteps through the nightmare of the First World War. I wanted to check some of

his memories that had got into my poems. Documents I discovered in the PRO at Kew confirmed practically everything he told me. So yes, I excavate my own past and the past of my family and the past of the landscapes I love.

Michael Allen points out that AN EXPLODED VIEW *(1973) structurally pairs poems to give two views of one subject in 'Options: The Poetry of Michael Longley'* (EIRE-IRELAND, *Winter, 1975). Is this idea of two thinks at a time intended?*
No, not when I was writing the poems. I'm never too sure what's happening when I'm writing a poem. But when I was putting the book together I must have noticed the twin relationship of, say, 'Options' and 'Alibis', 'The Island' and 'Ghost Town', 'The Fairground' and 'Nightmare'. But there was no long term strategy or programme. I'm superstitiously opposed to that kind of cunning. I'm a twin myself. I wonder if that has anything to do with it...

Contemporary political fissures have led northern poets to engage with Irish history in very different ways: there's Hewitt's 'Once Alien Here' or 'The Colony', Montague's THE ROUGH FIELD, *Heaney's* NORTH. *Do you engage with history or are you 'through with history' like Mahon in 'The Last of the Fire Kings'?*
We've all been asked that kind of question so often now, our answers are in danger of becoming polished and glib. Poetry and the "Troubles". Creativity and Violence. I wish in a way that I could be 'through with history'. But I'm not. Nor is Mahon. Nor can we ever be. The poems we've writtten in response to the thirty year agony should now be allowed to speak for themselves: poems like Heaney's 'Casualty', 'The Tollund Man'; Mahon's 'Afterlives'; Simmons's 'From the Irish'; Muldoon's 'Anseo'; Carson's 'The Bomb Disposal' and many more. I'm proud enough of a few of my own poems — 'Wounds', 'Wreaths', 'Ceasefire' — to suggest their inclusion in the list. I don't know if I will have anything more to say on the subject specifically, though the terrible upheaval and its root causes are part of the fabric of my life and therefore likely to influence what I write in some way or other, between the lines if not as subject matter. I pray that the "Troubles" are over, that the Good Friday Agreement will hold. The best commentary on the "Troubles" remains Frank Ormsby's extraordinary anthology *Rage for Order*.

To what extent do the two World Wars and your reading of the war poets frame your view of the "Troubles"?
They've given me a perspective on the violence. The First World War and the tragic committment of tens of thousands of young Irishmen (from the

North and the South) has engaged my imagination for decades. My father fought in the trenches from 1914 until the armistice, right the way through. It's a miracle he survived. He was wounded at High Wood and won the MC and was a captain at the age of twenty. He's my natural focus. He joined up again in 1939, an oldfashioned patriot. He was too old then for active service. The two World Wars were part of my family history before they became part of my imaginative landscape. Sometimes I listen to Owen and Rosenberg as though they were my dad's drinking and smoking companions, sharing a Woodbine behind the lines during a lull. And sometimes I wonder what he would have to say about the "Troubles". Or I imagine him as a squaddie on patrol in a wet windy field in south Armagh or as one of the soldiers Heaney resents in his poem 'The Toome Road'. He didn't read the war poets. When I was engrossed in Graves's *Goodbye to All That*, he didn't show much interest. But I don't think that the war poets should be penned into a ghetto called 'War Poetry'. Their poems are about everything, about life as well as death. Keith Douglas who died at the age of twenty four on the Normandy beaches in 1944 was another towering genius. These poets provided me with a map and compass when I began to contemplate our own sordid little conflict.

THE ECHO GATE *(1979) is full of death. Does the gate have a symbolic as well as literal function?*
You can find the Echo Gate at Trim in County Meath where my sister-in-law lives. If you stand there and talk loudly enough you get a spooky echo from monastic ruins in the middle distance. Yes, the title's symbolic; but I wouldn't want to over-explain it. The Gates of Horn and Ivory. The underworld. A place where past and present intersect. Somewhere to rendezvous with the dear departed. There's a lot of death in all my books, but that shouldn't make them depressing.

Do you write two types of poem about death: one a funereal mock-serious game ('Detour', 'Three Posthumous Pieces'); the other an attempt to examine atrocity?
More than two types, I hope. Some are personal elegies, others war poems, protest poems, some are funeral games. But I would resist pigeon-holing. Though I want the note of lamentation to ring out loud and clear, there's nothing wrong with laughing at a funeral.

Music — jazz, traditional, classical — appears in the poems and in your auto-biographical book TUPPENY STUNG. *Does the language of jazz or blues or the rhythms from music influence your poems?*
I listen to music every day — mainly classical. I don't know what influence it has apart from being an inspiration. I believe in the singing line in poetry, in verbal melody. So great music is bound to stimulate that

impulse. I believe that the calculating side of writing should be balanced with an openness to improvisatory possibilities. I admire the way that jazz players balance what they call a 'head arrangement' and improvisation. Though I love the blues, especially the classic female blues singers like Bessie Smith and Ma Rainey, the words read pretty poorly on the page without the music.

You have reviewed art exhibitions for the IRISH TIMES *in the past, and you joined the Arts Council initially as a temporary exhibitions officer. Your third collection* MAN LYING ON A WALL *(1976) is named after a painting by L. S. Lowry. Many of your poems and writings are about or dedicated to visual artists: Gerard Dillon, Raymond Piper, Edward Maguire. Visual art as diverse as an Amish Rug or Robert Mapplethorpe's penis-photography seems to interest you. Your poem 'Irish Poetry' sees poetry as a variation on landscape painting with its 'specialisations of light'. How do you see the relationship between poetry and painting? Which painters do you admire?*

You mean as well as Titian, Rembrandt, Chardin, Van Gogh, Bonnard, Vuillard, Matisse, Orpen? In my twenties I was blessed by the friendship of Colin Middleton whom John Hewitt once called Ireland's most accomplished painter. He was a magician, a master draughtsman and technician. Later I got to know George Campbell and Gerard Dillon. I admire all of them — self-taught, self-supporting, courageous, generous. A huge part of my education. Their pictures now fetch astonishing sums. They were invariably short of the price of a pint. Dillon I adored. I'm haunted by him. Blackshaw and Shawcross and Crone are painters of genius. I like to talk with artists about their trade. About once a year I try to write a catalogue note for a kindred spirit. It's like pulling teeth, very difficult, but it's my way of giving something back and it probably does seep into my poetry in mysterious ways. In recent years I've written essays on Felim Egan, David Crone, Brian Ferran, and Jeffrey Morgan who has come to live in Ulster. His big portrait of me now hangs in the Waterfront Hall. I can't tell you how proud I am of that. My dear friend Raymond Piper has taught me a vast amount about the natural world. His orchid paintings are among the wonders of our times. Painters and poets notice things. It's important for them to compare notes.

You have written a lot of love poems. If the "Troubles" brought the political and public world to the door is there a reverse responsibility in making the private public in love poems?

No more than when an artist paints his wife in the nude. If it's a good painting people won't go 'Nudge, nudge, wink, wink, if you go to Fenderesky Gallery you'll see X's misssus without a stitch on!' Rather the painting will plumb their humanity. But being private in public is a problem as you imply. The private material has to be made universal, otherwise it's just embarrassing. I suppose horniness has inspired some of my poems, but generally I approach love poetry as another way of looking at the wide world. The 'you' and 'I' are like two posts holding up a clothes-line. Any image can be hung out there to dry — everything except your dirty washing.

GORSE FIRES *(1991) seems to evoke such incredible space and beauty — starlight and flowers literally and metaphorically on the page. I've read that you can hear a conversation in the Arctic two miles away. Is this the sound and vision that you're after here?*
I like that idea: the ideal reader two miles away or two continents away or two centuries away and still able to hear what the poem is saying.

SEAMUS DEANE

You were born in Derry in 1940. In RUMOURS *(1977) a poem like ' Shelter' depicts real poverty with your mother 'doing the sums/ For food and clothes, the future/In endless hock' while 'The Victim' sees your grandfather and mother on streets known 'with the avarice that poverty can know'. How would you describe your family background in Derry? Is* READING IN THE DARK *a factually accurate autobiographical account of your family background?*

Reading in the Dark is as accurate as can be when we are speaking of fiction, however autobiographical. I grew up in the working-class area now called the Bogside. It was a Catholic, Nationalist, Republican area. The police were hated; and with good reason. The priests were respected, but without good reason; one of the fatalities of the Education Act of 1947-48 was not only the Unionist one-party police state but also the impregnable position of the clerical RC state-within-a-state. For the last thing the church needed was that its priests be exposed on a wide front to the vagaries of teaching; the clumsy or vicious violence or injustice that accompanied it was ultimately harmful to a church whose priests had hithertoo been revered.

The family life was essentially a happy one, but tense in a very profound way; my father and mother were embodiments of the male/female stereotypes of the strong, silent man and the voluble emotional woman; although they were actually very different from those roles in which they were nevertheless cast. But then, everybody in Northern Ireland was more obviously from Central Casting, as men or women, Catholics or Protestants, than is usually the case.

Poems like 'A Distant Beach', located in a 'vistaless' place, 'Between huddled houses' in 'sun-narrowed streets' where 'church bells' or 'shipping growled/Out in the foglands', seem to evoke a Derry geography which also seems deeply imprinted in READING IN THE DARK *(1996)? How would you describe your first and growing awareness of Derry?*

I was aware of Derry as a series of small, interlocked, concentrically widening territories as I grew older. But it was always a ghetto. It had some of the standard features of working class areas too, especially of ports, and Derry was still, during the Second War and up to and including the NATO

North Atlantic fleet visits of the 1950s a port, although in a diminishing sense. There were gangs based on territories. A lot of stone-throwing 'wars'; some, what shall I call it?, hand-to-hand combat as well. From Creggan to the City Walls, that was chiefly my territory; and then beyond, from Creggan to Grianan of Aileach in Donegal; that was the hinterland. I didn't leave the city for more than a brief stay anywhere else until I went to Belfast as an undergraduate at Queen's.

Northern poets from a Nationalist background (John Montague and Padraic Fiacc) speak of their fathers as involved in the "Troubles" or the IRA in the North of the 1920s. READING IN THE DARK *has your uncle and grandfather involved in IRA and police killings in the '20s; does this reflect a factual or typical account of northern Nationalism at that time?*
Yes, it's true but I'm not sure how typical. Certainly not unheard-of. To break the Unionist state, an ambition that was assumed to be widely shared, legitimate and sure to be realised in the long run, there were two weapons available: guns or education. It's hard to persuade those who did not know it, how deep the isolation of the northern Catholics then was. I remember, in the mid '50s, when the RUC as usual baton charged a St. Patrick's Day parade in Shipquay Street in Derry, a then notorious photograph was taken by a *Derry Journal* photographer of a very large policeman with his baton raised above the head of a little girl of five or six; the photo was sent to all the newspapers in Dublin and to many in London. Only the *Manchester Guardian,* as it then was, published it; in Dublin, not even *The Irish Press.* Incidents like that made Catholics realise that they would have to forge their own way against the northern set-up; and that the attraction of world opinion to the violence of the place was a necessity. There were refuges from this. The public library, for instance, which became my auxiliary school, especially with its English and American novels. It was there I read Waugh and Henry Green, Graham Greene and Rosamund Lehmann, translations of Musil, Thomas Mann and then Hemingway, Thomas Wolfe, Scott Fitzgerald, Faulkner. It was a different world in there, in the library; and a different world in the classroom; and another one in the street. It took a while for them to come together in a constellation.

World War II coincided with your early years in Derry; the air-raid shelters feature in the poems while the Army Chaplain in READING IN THE DARK *speaks of Derry as 'a vital port for the great NATO fleets'. To what extent did the Second World War register in your experience as a boy and in your memory as a writer?*
I remember the air-raid sirens, the gas masks, being taken under the stairs for safety when a bombing raid was threatened. And I remember the American soldiers, especially the black men, at whom I stared outra-

geously, fascinated by their amazing black skin; it was only afterwards, when black children were born, that I became mildly aware of what much of the excitement and muttering was about. But all the Americans meant to me were clean uniforms, white teeth, the smell of toasted tobacco.

I remember too the captured submarines brought in at the end of the war; they were towed out and sunk off the coast beyond Eglinton. My father met some of the prisoners; most of them, he told us, were boys of fifteen or sixteen. Sometimes he saw dead bodies in the subs that were brought into the dry dock; they had to clean them out. For me the war was exciting — sirens, sailors, soldiers, air-raid shelters.

You went to secondary school in Derry, to St. Columb's College in the 1950s at virtually the same time as Seamus Heaney and John Hume. Heaney talks of reading Blackcock's Feather *and* Lorna Doone; Reading in the Dark *recalls a boy reading the* Shan Van Voght *and Loyola's* Spiritual Exercises. *Did you encounter writers at secondary school who lasted or who influenced your own poetry, a first love if you like?*
Loyola was enforced punishment reading; not a choice. I do remember *Lorna Doone* and a 1798 novel *The Shan Van Vocht.* And lots of comic-cuts. *Adventure, The Hotspur, The Wizard* and the Dublin-published *Boy's Own.* My liking for French writers dates from the secondary school period; novelists like Mauriac; a few poets, Verlaine, the wonderfully indecipherable Rimbaud, Alfred de Musset and the rather sinister Baudelaire. But I do believe that then and since the French were used by me, not entirely consciously, as a counterbalance to the Irish, English and American climate of reading and of popular culture in which I was formed. But the Irish writers in English — Yeats or Joyce, Kavanagh or any other writer — were unknown to me for a long time. English Romantics — Wordsworth, Keats, Coleridge and Hazlitt in particular — were far more important. And I did have the luck to share with Heaney the same English teacher, Sean B. O'Kelly, a wonderful man.

In 'Counting' in History Lessons *(1983) you describe 'A radio/ Childhood lived in the backwaters of reception…' As a teenager in the '50s North were you aware of divisions primarily in terms of class or nation in popular culture (comics, football, the radio) or in the world of school and the streets?*
Reading was a solitary activity, the great refuge of privacy and a kind of escape. The movies were the communal art form; and the radio, especially the popular music channels — Radio Luxembourg most of all. I mentioned comic cuts; they were influential, little cartoon sheets for British imperial values, published in Dundee, and profoundly racist. I remember being amazed when I first read George Orwell on these: I had thought you could talk about them but that no one would elevate them so far as to write

about them. And then there was sport, especially soccer. If I had not been badly injured, I might have taken it further as a proto-career. But then…

Your SHORT HISTORY OF IRISH LITERATURE (1986) claims that 'few Irish writers have shown any imaginative sympathy for Catholicism as such' and READING IN THE DARK might be read as anti-clerical, a Joycean view of Catholicism (as mathmatically inhuman, blissfully ignorant of sex and abetting the political status quo) while Protestantism is 'really foreign territory', an 'estrangement' of 'bibles and the ache of the railway'. In CRANE BAG (Vol 7, 1, 1983), though, you describe a church interior in the 'monastic town' of Zagorsk in Russia with its 'great iconostasis, the gold of which seemed to smoke both with darkness and with the forms of incense… A rush of priests in Lenten robes'. Do you drop Catholic belief and content and retain an undercurrent of sensibility — what Heaney calls an 'obstinate, papish burn' in your CRANE BAG Interview with him in 1977.

Catholicism is always liable to become a sort of aesthetic, even if it is no more than a bundle of sensations or memories, or the beliefs central to it are abandoned. I like its vertical historical depth. Only the other week I visited Rome's only Gothic Church, built on top of an ancient temple to Minerva. That archaeological sense of the past and a recognition of its weight is one of the potencies of Catholic tradition. But I hated Catholicism's co-operation with the British State in Ireland, since the foundation of Maynooth and the Orange Order in the 1790s, when any Enlightenment possibility for Ireland was sacrificed to a polity of carefully nurtured sectarianism. But the liturgical year, its rhythms and colours, and all the associated practices, is still a pulse that beats, however distantly in the nervous system.

It's not a sensibility that ever found itself at ease in the aggressively Protestant British civilisation; the only great Irish writers in whom we see the merging and the separations involved are Burke and Joyce.

You studied at Queen's University, Belfast (1957-61) and receievd an M.A. from Queen's in 1963. 'Greasy Belfast flats', empty Sunday streets and the Plymouth Brethren 'sunk in heaven' are recalled in 'The Brethren', a poem in RUMOURS (1977). How would you describe Belfast and Queen's at this time? Were there underlying political tensions in Belfast akin to those in Derry?

The English Department at Queen's was an eye-opener for me, largely because of Laurence Lerner, a coloured South African, a poet, a marvellous teacher, and, in general, one of those unexpected influences that silently invades much of your life thereafter. There was also a tutor in the history department, whose name escapes me now, who made me write essays on the Balkans and talked to me endlessly about that part of the world. Between hearing from them about South Africa and the Balkans and hearing them say things about Northern Ireland in a comparative context, I was receiving an important part of my education with only a sleepy half-awareness of the fact. But it was a Unionist university; sectarian then, as it still is, although less so. J.C. Beckett's lectures were straight-fowardly Unionist; 'God Save the Queen' was played every turnabout and violence ensued if you didn't stand for it (in both senses). I discovered at Queen's some mild sense of the literary tradition in Irish through friend-ships with students in the Celtic Department; in poetry in English, my biggest discovery was the Metaphysical poets, particularly Herbert and Donne; and the nineteenth century novelists, particularly Dickens, George Eliot and Hardy. I suspect, but maybe without foundation, that I became aware of Kavanagh via Heaney; he and I shared the same digs off the Ravenhill Road for a year. Yeats was a name and a few phrases. The most exciting contemporary writers for me were the Amercian poets — John Crowe Ranson, Allen Tate, Randall Jarrell, Wallace Stevens and Robert Lowell. I published a long and dreadful poem in an issue of *Gorgon*, the English Department's journal, modelled on Tate's 'Ode to the Confederate Dead'. In the same issue Heaney had a little poem called 'Aran' which was as modest as mine was immodest in its ambition. I also remember John Montague winning a prize for his poem 'Like Dolmens Round My Childhood'; that poem impressed me greatly, but did not lead me to further investigations in contemporary Irish writers. I liked French poetry; René Char... who else? Supervielle and Bonnefoy came later, I believe, although Bonnefoy remained with me for a long time once I got to know him, especially his poems about his native village, like 'De l'im-mobilité de Douve'. And then I read some poems by W.S. Merwin, of whom also I became a longstanding admirer. Later, much later, in California, the American poet James Tate became a close friend, and I think I revised my sense of the American poets through him, although by then there were many more. There are so many American poets who are outstandingly good.

Your poetry pamphlet 'While Jewels Rot' (1966) was published as one of the Belfast Festival series; other northern poets started out at this time. Do you believe that a recognisable group of northern poets emerged in the 1960s? Is there a relationship between your poetry and theirs?
That pamphlet; I destroy any copies I can find. There was a mix-up there; the poems I meant to have published were returned to me, the ones I wanted returned, were published. Not that the difference in quality would have been great. But I have no substantial connection with the northern poets' group or groups. I learned of it via Seamus Heaney when he came to visit me in Cambridge armed with a prize and a bottle of whiskey. I was more surprised by the whiskey, since he had never taken a drink while an

undergraduate. But of the other poets of that era, Derek Mahon's work has remained important to me; no one else's.

Mahon and Heaney are surely very different writers?
Yes. Heaney creates the sense of historical linkage, retrieval, a moral assuredness that is in line with the specificity of the physical world. Mahon's is a bleaker world — more knowledgeable, less rooted, even a cosmopolitan but darkened contrast. Along with the sounds and gestures of MacNeice, Mahon is full of French echoes, and he is a wonderful translator of French poetry. His ambition to make poetry more real than the actual world is of a piece with Heaney's, but Mahon has much more sceptical, subtle-silver ironies in his stance. But the two of them comprise a whole period, are two contrasting aspects of a view of and trust in literature, of its importance, ultimacy. A strange belief, in my view, but there it is.

You taught for two years in Derry (1961-63), went to Cambridge (1963-66), then lectured in Oregon (1966-67) and Berkeley in California (1967-68) before returning to lecture at UCD in Dublin. Did America alter or develop your view of Ireland in a way which registered in your first volume of poems, GRADUAL WARS *(1972)?*
Yes. In Cambridge I wrote some poems but my energies were largely concentrated on my research — this finally centred on the French Enlightenment. After Cambridge, on the west coast of the USA, I came across American poets like Kenneth Rexroth, and James Tate in Berkeley.

In *Gradual Wars* I'm writing about feelings that belong to a lost world, are indeed trapped in it. I want rid of it, but can't leave it. In the poem 'Roots', I find an emblem for that dilemma. If poetry has any enhancing powers for the poet, they surely must include the belief that you must make the effort to break from what formed you, even though this itself is part of an almost predetermined formation. But it does create 'un peu de liberté'. Or the belief in it.

GRADUAL WARS *(1972) is both bleak and elegiac. The 'great times' of the child are a memory overtaken by the 'honeymoon of the cockroach'; the poet is haunted by history and nightmarish, murderous shadows; he carries nitroglycerine in a world of khaki, sirens and 'guerilla laughter' where even the 'water in the bath' is 'Beginning to detonate'. If* GRADUAL WARS *rejects poetry as both 'a planned withdrawal/ In stanzas from every battleground' and as 'realism' ('There is no realism/ For loss...') where does it find a style adequate to political crisis?*
In that book and in *Rumours* there exists the naïve notion that here is a world of public disorder and there is a world of poetry and imagination and order. The outbreak of the "Troubles" exaggerated in me what was already there. It's an unbalancing tension, that remains in *History Lessons*.

It creates too much monotonous pressure which petrifies rather than liberates the poems.

In Rumours *(1977) and* History Lessons *(1983) is there a view of the role and function of poetry? Your* Crane Bag *(Vol 9, 2, 1985) discussion with Jennifer Fitzgerald suggests that the 'relaxed' alliance between the poet of landscape — the Auden of 'In Praise of Limestone' — and a general 'human consciousness' is over for you: ' when you have a political crisis and a very deep division within a society... that kind of belief begins to break down, and then our view of the nature and function of art changes'.*

In Auden, I'm trying to say, there is implicit a tradition that has internally known two hundred years of peace; although that was two hundred years of war for others all over the globe. In Ireland, without that internal continuity, there is a more discordant music, especially when the sense of crisis intensifies. I don't think now and didn't then think that it was poetry's function to naturalise violence or discontinuity but to show the felt disjunctures and breaks they produced.

In your 'Seamus Heaney Interview' in Crane Bag *(Vol 1, 1, 1977) he sees poetry as 'born out of the watermarks and colourings of the self... born into and from literary tradition(s)' -'your own work is your home' — so that political commitment is neither certain nor predetermined but a 'tension'; the 'watermark' in your lecture series,* Strange Country, *is the inescapable, British-Irish, colonial relationship so that writers like Paulin are read as 'politically committed' or in denial, like Muldoon in* Celtic Revivals. *Nation might be seen as an accident of birth and passport; writing as the creation of unofficial passports as writers define themselves in what they do, creating new passports as part of a 'multi-national', a body of writers. For a northern writer like Mahon one senses that political committment to either side was not that attractive, hence his attempt to be 'through with history'; Joyce also talks of escaping the 'net' of nationality in a move out to Europe in images — like John Hewitt's or Heaney's — of rippling through wider concentric circles.*

I agree in many ways. In Ireland there is such an ideological investment in the idea of the artist, the privatisation of writing, the absurd pretensions to a cheap universalisation of feeling and of authority with that, that it is difficult to keep a sense of proportion. Writing that treasures narcissism, writing that is mere propaganda — between these two polarities, there is very little that is worth remembering. And it is difficult to enter into the wider world without denying the inner world. It's not just an escape from nationality, of the British or the Irish variety; it is an escape into the belief that one is 'free', that one is the maker of the world he sings. I think this is a glamorous and vacuous notion. At least in its pseudo-liberal therapeutic form, it is mere garbage, although widely canvassed and admired.

You edited ATLANTIS *in the 1970s and two volumes of the* CRANE BAG *(1979) and as a critic you have written of literary and publishing traditions within Ireland. How did you see your editorship of these in relation to that tradition?*

I remember Derek Mahon and me talking about the need for an 'international' journal and especially for one that would have some respectable standard of commentary on cultural-political matters. So I suppose we believed that we were inaugurating or helping to inaugurate some new phase of re-understanding our situation, internally and in relation to the world beyond.

The OXFORD COMPANION TO IRISH LITERATURE *(1996) described* HISTORY LESSONS *as linking 'contemporary Northern Ireland, personal recollection and the obscure forces that drive historical events' — full of 'the sting and shock of feelings which include the slow burn of anger at wrongs done'. Did you see yourself as a poet working within an Irish tradition? Which literary and historical influences did you assimilate in this volume?*

I did not consciously think of myself as working within any tradition of writing; but inevitably within an historical experience, yes. I find it hard to say what 'influences', so to speak, were active in that volume. At a guess, what was hanging in my mind then then would have been concentrated in various reading areas — in Edmund Burke, in Gibbon, in Carlyle, Arnold, Hegel, Marx; but as far as specifically literary influences, or influences from poets, relatively few, except maybe W.S. Merwin.

Is there a conflict in the poems between pacifism and violence akin to a debate within Nationalism between the pen and the gun? In 'Derry' there is 'The thought of violence a relief,/The act of violence a grief...'; 'A Fable' in RUMOURS *states that the killer of the house painter 'has to be got/that unfinished youth who fires the shot' and there's a poem like 'Send War in our Time O Lord' in* HISTORY LESSONS. *Does unexamined, 'acceptable' liberal pacifism only serve to provide a platform for violence through inaction?*

No, I don't think so. I certainly believe what you call liberal pacifism is not pacifism at all but merely a legitimation of the state that practises violence and claims a monopoly on it — as all states do. But I'm linking a certain kind of writing to the fissures of feeling that the war in Northern Ireland created. Alternating tides of feeling that are hard to govern and yet seek for some ethical dimension that is also political.

To what extent is your poetry a class conscious analysis? 'To all at No. 38' speaks of the breadman's loaves 'That needed a miracle /Of distribution' and in Derry there is 'The unemployment in our bones /Erupting in our hands in stones...' It might be argued — with the Derry commentator Eamonn McCann or the Derry-born poet Robert Greacen — that poetry's primary allegiance is to

SEAMUS DEANE

Socialism as opposed to Nationalism?
Only to a limited extent. I wouldn't say Socialism as opposed to
Nationalism. It's neither one nor the other. Maybe just a diffused anger at
the social and political injustices that are integral to the world I grew up in.

*You have written critically about the great collectors of Irish music in nineteenth
century Ireland and there's your liking for 'The Snowy Breasted Pearl';*
READING IN THE DARK *is prefaced by a quotation from 'She Moved Through
the Fair' and the father in the book obtains a record player in the late 1950s to
play three Italian arias constantly. Is music a direct influence on your poems?*
Music is important to me in many ways, but not as a direct influence. The
music I heard — Italian opera, folksongs, Thomas Moore lyrics, political
ballads, popular American music, jazz — that would have been formative
of my taste in ways I only half-recognise. But it was quite miscellaneous.

*Some poems refer to painters; there's 'A sick man/In Rembrandt darkness' and
'the fauve/Flower lit resilience of the sea' in the second elegy in 'Fourteen
Elegies' in* GRADUAL WARS *while* READING IN THE DARK *frames key sym-
bols like the cathedral in window frames. Is it fair to link your poetry and prose
with painting as opposed to photography?*
I can't say; if I had to chose between the two, I'd say painting.

*You were a founder member and director of Field Day Theatre Company which
was formed in Derry in 1980 and you wrote two pamphlets, 'Civilians and
Barbarians' (1983) and 'Heroic Styles: The Tradition of an Idea' (1984).
How did you envisage Field Day's role in '80s?*
No, I wasn't a founder member. The founders of Field Day were Brian
Friel and Stephen Rea. Everyone else came later. I have written a great
deal about Field Day elsewhere so I'll be brief here. The company's role
was to stimulate discussion, to break from the cul de sac of stereotype and
bigotry, to expose the Unionist state for what it was and would be, to take
some responsibility in the ungoing crisis in the North. I think we suc-
ceeded in that; and further, we succeeded in providing an important cri-
tique of the nature of essentialism in political thinking; less so in literary
terms, although it is perhaps more enduring in the world of letters than
elsewhere. In effect, we tried to redesign the linkage between authority
and power and show that the possession of the latter was no prelude or
condition for the possession of the former.

*Between 1980 and 1993 you were Professor of Modern English and American
literature at University College Dublin. In* CELTIC REVIVALS *(1985) and A
SHORT HISTORY OF IRISH LITERATURE (1986) a key feature of the history
of Irish literature is the loss of the Irish language which leaves the 'native' cul-*

ture 'undelivered' or 'dismembered' and generates a literature that is highly self-conscious of its medium and uncertain of its audience. In READING IN THE DARK *your mother's silence or 'connected remarks disconnected by days' overlie a younger voice which is 'lying in the crypt' while the poet in 'Migration' finds 'his tongue still undelivered, waiting/To be born into the word home'. Is it fair to suggest that your primary emphasis is on a loss (akin to Montague's 'severed head' which 'chokes' to 'speak another tongue' in* THE ROUGH FIELD*) as opposed to Heaney or Muldoon's grafted, bi-lingual, loss and gain (the pun in Heaney's 'government of the tongue' suggesting the loss of Irish through cultural or political imposition might also be seen as gain in literary enrichment and access through English)?*

All my work is about uncovering, especially uncovering of voices that speak without governance, or that speak without being heard. It's the ostensible composure of voice that lives along with the actual dispersion of voice that I admire most in literature. And yes, I think the finest Irish writing is particularly sensitive to this condition, and that inevitably means a sensitivity to loss. But I would say that loss is real in the primary sense that it can't be recovered; but the sense that something cannot be recovered is both a resource for ingenuity, an aggravation and a distorting agency. Irish writing is fertile in its responses to these varied conditions. It must be said too that loss is by no means the only condition; but it is one of those that seems to me inescapable as such.

In CELTIC REVIVALS *and* STRANGE COUNTRY *you document the links between Yeats and Eliot and Pound. Do you see poems like Eliot's* WASTE LAND *or Pound's* CANTOS *as bearing fruit in Ireland in general or in your own work in particular?*

Not in my own work. The writer in whom those two works bear fruit, and magnificently so, is Thomas Kinsella. He is also the writer who has most deeply absorbed Joyce. The combination of those absorptions, to restrict it to those three, is formidable. Kinsella is certainly the most ignored and underrated writer of this and the previous generation. But his work will endure.

Kavanagh in CELTIC REVIVALS *appears to be a poet locked in '50s Monaghan 'nostalgia' for the parish, superceded by the new economics of Lemass in the '60s. Surely, though, Kavanagh represents the kinds of community from which poets like Heaney or Montague emerged — a poet who allowed them to trust their own experience as valid in writing poems?*

I have a great deal of admiration for Kavanagh. There's an 'influence' incarnate! Yes, he rediscovered the local, the regional, the provincial, and made it accessible to Montague and Heaney and others, but particularly those two. I have called him a Free State poet and I think of him and

Flann O'Brien as the two most important writers of that period and in that polity — precisely because they took the usual version of it, as inward-looking, recessed etc. and transformed that into a positive alternative to the cloudy mysticisms and exaggerations of the Revival, the pseudo-cosmopolitanism of Joyce and Yeats and others. It was a necessay reaction; but it does produce a literature that is strangely 'magical' and yet rooted in a disabused realism. I think that an amazing achievement on the part of both.

DEREK MAHON

Knowing your poems and knowing you, I imagine the proper place to hold this conversation might be some sort of terminal: an airport, a train station, a bus depot. You've moved around rather a lot, and the issue of being in place and out of place crops up often in your work. You've also spoken, however, of a 'homeward gravitation in Ulster poetry', and your own poems reverberate, initially, in the six counties of Northern Ireland.

Two of them actually, Antrim and Down: Belfast and the seaside places.

Can you give me a sense of that background?

The poem 'Autobiographies' is an attempt to do a little documentary on that. 'Courtyards in Delft', I think, adds more to it, because it bites off more and manages to chew what it bites off, although it's highly aestheticized. One of the reasons I haven't done much in that explicitly autobiographical line is that it's not for me to do. Others have done it; others who have been content with a documentary mode have done it better than I would ever do it.

What we get in your work, though, are glimpses of the child born during World War II, bombers, the sense of a city that was distinctly different in the island of Ireland, one on which the bombs fell. We have girls, the growth of sexual awareness, the bicycle — that epiphanic bike — and then in 'Courtyards in Delft' that 'strange child with a taste for verse.' Can you put those things together?

They all have Joycean mnemonic contexts: the bike, the girls' names, the war. When I think about the war, I think of a 1940s radio set, wireless set, and other objects with their inherent numina: a Japanese lacquered cigarette case brought back by an uncle in the Merchant Navy — the little things that you saw with a child's eye when you were a child and that will never go away. That's what consciousness is all about. My Aunt Kathleen's white shoes in a rented summer house in 1945. No, I was on the floor, it must have been 1942; I was on the carpet. Those white shoes! I imagine what I call that 'strange child with a taste for verse' emerges from a slow consciousness of the numina inherent in these things. I think that's the beginning.

It's a beginning particularly interesting because of the words 'mute phenomena' that appear much later in your work and become necessary anchorage for so much that you do. Anyway, this kid — this strange kid with a taste for verse — also of course has parents, has a human environment.

I think it was important that I was an only child, an only child whose best friends were the objects I've been talking about. It was a quiet house. Usually my mother was doing this or that, practical things around the house; while my father was usually out at work, away a forty- or forty-eight-hour week perhaps. He worked in the shipyard. A quiet man. He did the same job (with some little promotions) for forty years. Belfast was his life. The shipyard was his life. My mother the same. She was from Belfast. Before she married, she worked in what used to be called the York Street Flax Spinning Company, Ltd., which was the other big Belfast industry: shipbuilding and linen. So they had what you might call blue-to-white-collar jobs in these two industries. The linen industry doesn't exist anymore. My mother stopped working when she got married. That's what they did then. She became a housewife. She had only her husband and an infant to look after, but she became a housewife and very house-proud in the obsessive way that a woman in that position often is. It's almost a question of what else had she to do? She'd keep dusting and keep everything as bright as a new penny. Of course, this was a bit of a strain on the child, an irritant. In fact, with my mother, no harm to her, I think it was pathological. But since little boys are usually rougher than house-proud mothers, there were times I would deliberately do things to be infuriating — knock over a cup or something.

Given that sense of enclosure, do you remember anything that suggested an outside?
Since there wasn't any hurly-burly of siblings, I had time for the eye to dwell on things, for the brain to dream about things. I could spend an afternoon happily staring. In one of those poems, 'The Lost Girls' section in 'Autobiographies', I remember (this is naughty) this little girl who used to dress very prettily: she in her back garden would be visible to me up in my parents' bedroom at the top of our house, and I used to watch her down there. I'd see other things besides, like a coal delivery, the sort of pictorial qualities of coal. That kind of thing — the running of cold water from a kitchen tap, the light. I had time to dwell on these things.

Belfast in the '40s: did you and your parents go to church?
There was a certain amount of churchgoing, although they went for the look of the thing: it was expected that you would show your face in church once in a while. They were serious about being respectable and being seen to do the right thing, but they weren't really serious church people. I mean, they were Protestants! There's no such thing as a devout

Protestant, is there? Protestants aren't devout, they're staunch. So it was all appearances. I tagged along, scrubbed and kempt. But this turned out to be very important because, after a while, my parents were approached by the minister (the Church of Ireland minister, I should say, not Presbyterian) who asked, 'Could young Derek hold a tune, would he be interested in having a go with the choir? We can arrange for Mr. Wood to audition him on Wednesday evening.' So in no time at all I was in the choir, which meant two services on Sunday, one in the evening, as well as choir practice on Wednesday evening. The hymnology invaded the mind: 'Ransomed, healed, restored, forgiven.'

Did you (do you) respond to all this as a believer?
I believe in the words, and in the tunes. I've never seriously asked myself the question, Do you believe in God? I believe in the words and the tunes; that's quite enough for me. As a child, I suppose I brought the same kind of apprehension to these things as to other phenomena: we were singing from sheet music, hymnals, anthologies of hymns, with the music written out and the verses underneath. For example, let's take a verse like this (I won't try to sing, it'd only be embarrassing):

> From Earth's wide bounds, from ocean's farthest coast,
> Through gates of pearl streams in the countless host,
> Singing to Father, Son and Holy Ghost:
> Hallelujah, Hallelujah!

Very imperialistic, 'From Earth's wide bounds, from ocean's furthest coast'. But the way this was printed in the hymnal was important to me: it was under the music, *far-thest*, so somehow I created a whole geography of my own, around ocean's *far-thest*, as it were *far-flung*, coasts. The words themselves became facts, objects; and I believed in those objects, those clumped printed objects.

How did primary school open the world to you?
All I see is sunlight, classrooms full of sunlight, or windows streaked with rain — as everybody does. I don't hear anything. I recently looked at an old school photograph of Skegoneill when I was six or so: all these wee old faces, thirty of them, and we're all, each individual one, absolutely unique and crazy in some way, quite unbelievable.

Was it ever a question of 'there is a child among us taking notes,' a Stephen Dedalus on the edge of the circle?
No, that wasn't me, not at all. I was like any other. I felt at home there. I started feeling not at home when I was at secondary school, at the begin-

ning of adolescence. I started moping, brooding; I didn't go in for sport. Mine was a great rugby school, rugby and cricket. I played some rugby and cricket, but then after a certain point I wasn't interested anymore. I think I can trace this to something in the way I was treated in my family situation. My cousin Conacht and myself, who were the same age, lived just a few streets from each other, and we were quite like brothers a lot of the time. Conacht was a bit taller and he always was considered the more interesting and more manly, more able one. I was a bit of a dead loss in comparison. This was internalized, entirely, and gave me a lot of trouble at the time. And I think that knocked me off the straight (and even narrow) and turned me into an eccentric or, as my mother always said, 'an oddity'. It created a sense of inadequacy, a sense of 'well to hell with that then, I'll opt for the place where I can succeed, for other forms of value.' So I didn't compete. Although I enjoyed rugby and cricket, the competition didn't interest me. There were other boys in the school like this, a little group of us — oddities, weirdos — so I found a coterie, and there I was at home. Age fifteen, sixteen or seventeen, we would go precociously to something that was just coming into existence in a place like Belfast in the late 1950s ... a coffee bar. And talk, and read Aldous Huxley.

Was this where literature put down its conscious roots?
I think there are two kinds of literary life: there was a real, affective literary life, in the sense of my appreciation of early Yeats, getting a thrill out of Dylan Thomas, things like that; and then there was a more pretentious coterie thing. Showy. But this offered me an identity, and an identity that stays with me to this day. It was the beginning, I suppose, of my life as (God spare us!) an "intellectual".

You once mentioned John Boyle, a history and English teacher in secondary school. Was he important to this life?
Well, all this business of sitting in a coffee bar with a Penguin novel by Aldous Huxley, it was somehow disembodied, you know? We thought of everyone else as peasants. But Boyle enabled us somehow to embody the notion of *not* being cut off, not being outsiders in a society that itself was outside something. And the fact that Boyle was from Dublin was important, from some "other" or larger context. He was an articulate representative of the other part of the island. He was active in politics, a member of the old Northern Ireland Labour Party, chairman at one time, though he never sat in any parliament. His field was Irish labour. Boyle was also a teacher of literature, and one of the things he taught was Yeats. He taught Yeats as if Yeats were an historian of the time: Yeats as documentary. When Boyle himself was at Trinity he had gone to a debate where one of the speakers was Maud Gonne. So he was able to make it all real to us.

Was that your first awakening to the sense of Dublin, the sense of the two Irelands, of politics?
Not quite. Because as I went through my teens I saw them with my own eyes. A part of my visual experience was Election Day in Belfast, those lorries full of Unionist supporters, the polling booths. This was part of the whole fabric. I didn't look at these people as terrifying B-Specials and so on — they were my family. I had an uncle who was a sergeant in the B-Specials. My cousin Conacht and I used to play with his unloaded revolver in their house. The man who took the Unionist tally at Skegoneill school polling booth was the father of the little girl I sat beside in school. It was all part of the whole.

At secondary school, however, I first began in that teenage way to develop what you might call a political awareness. That was helped by, possibly prompted by, an uncle who was a rather peculiar character. He had been at sea in the Merchant Navy and he had worked in the Ministry of Transport office in Belfast for many years. He never married. He was a sort of bachelor-student, the kind of man who wanted to read literature, wanted to know about literature. In his room there would be a novel by Sinclair Lewis, *War and Peace*, issues of a French cinema magazine to which he subscribed. He was a self-taught man, a left-wing autodidact. He was the one who bought the Sunday papers that nobody else bought, that kind of thing. He had quite an effect on me at one point, prompting me to become conscious of the political situation.

You took such turnings while you were in secondary school. What were their consequences as you were about to leave Belfast? You had choices to make: some students went to England to go to university. You chose to go to Dublin, to Trinity.
No, it was chosen for me. The way it happened was this: the best boys, those who had done best in the mock exams, were slated for Oxford and Cambridge. The next best were slated for Trinity. Those who had done well, but not exceptionally, were slated for Queen's, Belfast. Tells you a bit about self-esteem in the North doesn't it?

Would you describe Dublin as a watershed time?
I was bewildered by the place at first, bewildered by Trinity. I thought that Dublin was beautiful. I remember going on a bus, in the sunlight, and thinking that it was a gorgeous place. It was a happy alternative to Belfast. In fact, some of us who went down together from the North developed anti-Northern jokes among ourselves.

What about Trinity as a kind of literary awakening?
There was a particular kind of community there, a unique community involving certain very vivid characters: Alec Reid, Con Leventhal, Owen

Sheehy Skeffington. These were both teachers and friends. The professor of English then was Philip Edwards. Philip was English, a nice man, but much more *inspiring* was a reprobate like Alec Reid or a humanly interesting person like Con Leventhal. We grew up in a very pleasant way. Physically the surroundings were extremely attractive. Beautiful college, beautiful trees, beautiful girls: wherever the eye fell there was something to please. At the same time, it was a place apart — golden days, golden moments.

Did you ever start to think of yourself as an academic?
No, I thought of myself as a surly *étranger* in a donkey jacket, with literary pretensions. The way to seem was careless of the academic demands. Some, of course, swotted up furiously at night. I didn't, and that was my mistake. So I drifted away from the academic but, like others, formed my own little university within. It was then that I had the notion that 'this poetry nonsense you've been tinkering at for the past couple of years at school, if you're going to take it seriously, you can do it here and people will pay attention.' It was a very fertile environment, very supportive. Alec Reid was part of it, in a very personal way; he was great fun, and so *human*. A liberal education, was Alec.

To what degree is the sensibility in the poems from your first book, NIGHT-CROSSING, *due to your education at Trinity? Wry, speculative, eloquent, debonair...*
It's hard for me to say, but I suppose it must have a lot to do with it, because those words would describe the environment at Trinity when I was there; probably it's how a contemporary undergraduate there would describe it today. That is the mode, not only the conversational mode, the mode of discourse, but it's also the mode of composition, of imaginative discourse. It's the tone of voice. Of course, there was a struggle going on within myself at the time. It took me a long time to get hold of anything I could begin to think of as being my own voice, with the struggle going on between a surly Belfast working-class thing and something, to use your word, debonair. The *flâneurs* I couldn't help but admire and envy, also on the written page: the way that some of the students had that at their fingertips. So there was a clash in me between one and the other, which Eavan Boland was very conscious of in her poem 'Belfast vs. Dublin'. Those things more or less came together at a later stage, maybe ten years later — those two kinds of rhetoric were able to negotiate with each other and come together in a single voice. In putting together the *Selected Poems* I tried to manufacture belatedly a homogeneous voice, but, in fact, in those early poems there'd be one man on one page and a totally different person on the next page. To my ear anyway.

When you'd finished with Trinity, how would you say the Belfast boy had been altered?
Well, he was grown up now, if he has ever been really. *But I didn't know where I was!* I suppose, looking back on it, that I was in some kind of crisis. Had I been accustomed to a disciplined and purposeful way of life, I would have gone on to whatever I was going to do then — trainee journalism, the BBC, doing a PhD at Oxford, whatever it might have been. I would have proceeded. But I came to a stop because I'd been living indolently, with literary notions, so I had no direction. On leaving Trinity, the only thing I could do was get out of Dublin.

Would you say that the movement from Trinity out into the world was one in which you became more and more identifiable to yourself as a poet? or at least as someone who wasn't anything else?
That's a better way of putting it. It wasn't that of all the things I did poetry was the most interesting. In fact, poetry was the only thing I did. Anyway, I left Trinity in 1965 and came to the States, to Cambridge via Canada. There was this enormous poetic energy in America at that time, and I was very conscious of it around Harvard Square. First of all through Louis Asekoff, whom I'd known at Trinity. The '60s, the protests, the war. A lot of it was very strange to me, of course, and I couldn't get it at all. I suppose my taste was very conservative, perhaps it still is. The other thing I was conscious of was the Harvard dimension: there were people about who had just a year or two previously been taking writing classes with Lowell. So there was a lot going on. The American poetic psyche was very active. But in a way I think I was lost. I was in a transitional phase. At the time it didn't seem transitional, it seemed terminal; but I was in a phase between being a Trinity student and being whatever I was going to be next. The only constant was not being too far away from poetry and from a literary environment.

How did the word home *reverberate under these conditions?*
I felt very far from home in those years. (In fact, for a large part of my life I've been *terrified* of home.) I think that this has a great deal to do with what started happening in Northern Ireland in 1968, 1969 — how it took me by surprise. I'd been away from it for a bit, not too long, but I was still close enough to it to get burned inside. (I'm thinking of the marches, of Burntollet and so on.) I was horrified, and I didn't go up there after a certain point. No, that's not true. I would go up to Belfast from time to time, right up to 1970. In some sense (this may sound very phony) it was almost as if the things that were happening up there were happening literally to me. I felt "beaten-up". I wonder if others felt the same. I felt that I had been guilty of something I wasn't aware of. Although I've never been a motorist, I felt as perhaps a hit-and-run driver must feel when he wakes up

the next morning. It was extremely upsetting, especially when the death toll started mounting. I couldn't deal with it. I could only develop a kind of contempt for what I felt was the barbarism, on both sides. But I *knew* the Protestant side; I knew them inside out. I was one of them, and perhaps I couldn't bear to look at my own face among them. So I adopted a "plague on both your houses" attitude.

Did it provoke, in its anguish, any digging for roots?
Should have. There are various researches that I should have undertaken at that point and that I didn't, that I avoided. Seamus Heaney, for example, did a lot more digging than I did.

In 'Afterlives' you put it like this:

> Perhaps if I'd stayed behind
> And lived it bomb by bomb
> I might have grown up at last
> And learnt what is meant by home.

I think probably there were things that I should have come to terms with, researched, looked into, looked at, but I didn't. At that time, Protestants like James Simmons, Michael Longley, myself could think that this was not our quarrel — our peculiar upbringing as middle-class, grammar-school-educated, liberal, ironical Protestants allowed us to think of ourselves as somehow not implicated. I told myself that I had more important things to do. Which were going to London, getting on with my own literary career as I had now started to conceive of it, marrying Doreen, getting myself together, discovering a sense of purpose. And writing directly about those conditions in the North was not part of that purpose. One of the damnable things about it was that you couldn't take sides. You couldn't take sides. In a kind of way, I still can't. It's possible for me to write about the dead of Treblinka and Pompeii: included in that are the dead of Dungiven and Magherafelt. But I've never been able to write directly about it. In *Crane Bag* they'd call it 'colonial aphasia'. Perhaps, in fact, that's what it is. I was not prepared for what happened. What happened was that myself and all our generation (particularly in the North) were presented with a horror, something that demanded our serious grown-up attention. But, as I say, I was not able to deal with it directly.

I've noticed that whenever you talk about your poems in public you usually talk about form; what you never talk about is the self making the poems. You never let us into the workshop with you. What would be your take on yourself as an actual maker of the poem?

Well, there's no point in beating about the bush. After many years of beating about the bush, the fact is, I am an out-and-out traditionalist. That's the way it is, and that's the way it's going to stay. I find that certain poets want to express certain things, want to be truthful about their emotions, about the nature of the world as they understand it, about the changing nature of society, about their instincts and their opinions. They are full of liberal intentions, they are admirable people; but they are not poets, not to me they're not. They're writing free verse (I suppose you would still call it) — without any specific talent for poetry — to express themselves, to deliver narrative, to state opinions. But they are not doing the thing that poetry does as far as I'm concerned. Formally, that is. I remember talking to Richard Peaver about this, and the three principles that we found ourselves agreeing on were Soul, Song and Formal Necessity — the Coleridgean sense of formal necessity that the poem should 'contain within itself the reason why it is thus and not otherwise'.

The quotation, of course, allows for free verse.
Of course it does. But it's my own experience that writing is a visual experience as well as an aural one. It's important to me what a poem looks like on the page. I'm interested in organization. I'm interested in at least the appearance of control, orchestration, forceful activity; something intense happening, something being intended and achieved — purposefulness instead of randomness.

I find very little worthwhile in the magazines now. I don't read column-fillers — it's been a long time since I've done that. If I pick up a copy of *The New York Review of Books*, the *TLS* or whatever it might be, I don't find much in the poems anymore. They're not interesting, they're little wisps of words. I like to be arrested.

Formally? Materially?
I'd like to think that being formally arrested promises the material arrest. And formal arrest has to do with the appearance of the thing on the page; it has to do with the sound of the thing, some kind of authority. These are dangerous waters, come to think of it — the use of *authority* reminds me of that. There are contemporary theoreticians who will be tapping at the scaffold for my use of *authority*. At the same time, I am as liable as any — and perhaps indeed more than most — to the lures of negative capability and anarchy and all those things. But what I miss in contemporary poetry is the sense of 'here's somebody doing something that he or she knows how to do' — the sense of control. It doesn't have to be a bullying thing; it can be a gentle, gradual, tentative thing, like Elizabeth Bishop in the 'Moose' poem, for example. Or it can be the rather ludicrously authoritative note of something like 'The Quaker Graveyard', which is a parody

of what I'm talking about. But I like to be spoken to in the tone of Lowell's 'Waking Early Sunday Morning':

> Pity the planet, all joy gone
> From this sweet volcanic cone.

Then I'm hearing music loud and clear. I like the tenor of it. Here is a voice that has committed itself to words without hesitation, without irony, without fear. It's a form of giving yourself to life. It's the ability to surrender; to walk into the water without a lifebelt; to do the big thing.

From time to time you've made articulate your suspicion of language, and even of verse itself. Would you say that this is a kind of trouble to you, as well as a kind of pose? The very thing that you admire is something that you oppose some of the time?
I think of it in dramatic terms: if you surround yourself with hesitation and constraint and so on, and yet manage to sing through, then you somehow earn the sound you make. Perhaps something like that is going on. But I suppose that you have to be able to speak without thinking all the time how it sounds — those peculiar moments when you are saying something and even as you are saying it, the objections, the laughter, all these things are going on simultaneously, and yet you are able to say it, without shame or horror or embarrassment. It's all a matter of artistic tact. Let's just say that you must, in order not to go mad, be able to speak.

Many of the neo-formalists see the formalist stance as having implicit moral and political implications. What's your attitude?
Well, I think that there might be something in that. The habitual choice of a certain kind of form does describe a sensibility, so that a formalist poet's politics will also be formalist, in the sense that they will respect abstract notions of ... I'm trying to avoid the words *law and order*. I don't consider myself a right-wing person. Robert Hughes's book *Culture of Complaint*, about the forfeiting of individual responsibility endemic in American culture, says things with which my own thinking about contemporary poetry chimes. He has a chapter, for example, called 'Art and the Therapeutic Fallacy'.

One of the things for which you are valued as a poet is a formal elegance without exhibitionism — form has been digested by content, and content by form. How do these elements relate to one another as you work?
It's almost impossible to describe. It's the sense in which one finds a tone of voice. I want always to bear in mind what I was saying about Soul, Song and Formal Necessity. The best way I can put it is that I like there to be a

certain gravity somewhere in the offing, some residual echo of traditional form. The suggestion should always be there, even in the most talky poem — like 'Ovid in Tomis,' for example — that once upon a time this stuff was sung, not spoken. I'd call it music. And I like there to be an external side to formal organization. I like to see a form on the page, or listen to a poem and be able to measure the page as an organized object, as an authoritative-looking object, as a thing that looks like something interesting — not like one of the thousands of therapeutic poems that you don't want to read because they look so boring on the page. There's nothing putting it together, there's no reason for it.

Your manners as a poet suggest a view of the world that is coherent and continuous, which can be traced from early poems like 'Lives' and 'Afterlives' all the way up through 'The Sea in Winter', the Camus poem and 'The Yaddo Letter'. Camus, in fact says in THE MYTH OF SISYPHUS *that 'the world in itself is not reasonable, that is all that can be said. But what is absurd is the confrontation of this irrational and the wild longing for clarity whose call echoes the human heart.' Your poems seem often to register that wild longing for clarity as a kind of ground note.*
Yes. I like that. I like the wild longing for clarity. I like that phrase. That strikes a chord. It's an interesting use of *wild* isn't it?

We talked one time about the Dionysian and the Apollonian in these terms: the Apollonian as your sense of shape and form; the Dionysian as the manner in which you collide with "stuff", with the "wild". Does this combination make sense to you?
Yes. That's the combination that has the greatest potency, I think. The hissing chemicals inside the well-wrought urn; an urnful of explosives. That's what's so great about Yeats, after all: the Dionysian contained within the Apollonian form, and bursting at the seams — shaking at the bars, but the bars have to be there to be shaken.

So you understand poetry as a cage, with a wild animal inside it?
This is where we quote Robert Frost and Clarke and Henry James. Raymond Chandler, too: 'No art without the resistance of the medium.' But the resistance musn't be gratuitously imported for tactical purposes. It must be organic. I guess that's worked for me in a few poems, sometimes only in a few lines at a stretch. Take 'A Garage in Co. Cork', for example. There's a lot of banging the bars and banging at the windows in that poem — windows being broken, in fact — but it's all very formally contained. I suppose that the same is true of the 'Shed'. Bringing together those two elements makes me hear orchestras and see fireworks. Childish things like that.

You say there have to be bars there to be rattled. So what are *the bars?*
I suppose they are what's usually called 'the human condition.' The constraints, the fact that we can't fly, the fact that we can only be at one place at a time. The constraints that enable us to live, and prevent us from living. In artistic terms, I'd say that when poems feel as if they're working there's nothing quite so... like the gates being thrown open and ... trumpets sounding. A kind of liberation.

Is love *a word you would use in this connection?*
Well, it's all about love, really. This also connects with something that I'm not allowed to do anymore, which is drink. I used to drink a lot. There was a certain kind of consciousness — false consciousness, no doubt, especially the morning-after lucidity, which I thought of as being a kind of revelation. I think there are various points in the *Selected Poems* where that moment is touched upon. I suppose it must be, it must have been, akin to what is considered to be a religious experience — I'm talking about the apparent suspension of time, the transcendence of bother and the quotidian, the sense that life is long and life is full, the sense that if we are here to perceive anything it is this kind of perception that is particularly intended. The surrounding chaos is the stuff that keeps you awake at night in lower Manhattan. For me, the revelation that came the morning after came as a formal thing — the *morning after*, mind you, since the clarity of drunkenness itself, as is well-known, is a complete chimera. A 'systematic derangement of the senses.' I think Rimbaud was well acquainted with what we're talking about, and gave it the kind of weight that I'm giving it here. For me it has great deal to do, it *had* a great deal to do, with a certain bohemian way of being — living at a certain angle to life, spending quite a lot of time having the brain active, having the senses active at certain times of the day and night when other people are asleep or out at work. I think that way of life can help the creative. I don't think that's bohemian sensibility; I think there's truth to it. Before the bohemian clichés, there were bohemians who were originals. There is an original bohemian idea to which I still have an attachment, despite all the nonsense that has been said and done in its name.

What sense do you have that other ways of living — living without drink, for example — can still provide a 'derangement of the senses'? What in the ordinary, the quotidian...
Well, this is my current creative problem. I think one writes a different kind of thing, which is where I am now. I think I've probably entered that middle-age stretch in which, so they say, you have the choice between falling silent or rambling on. Now, I won't ramble on, I know that. I think the pattern that's emerging is a general sort of silence punctuated by sud-

den bursts of noisiness. Aside from translation, I haven't produced a lot of verse in recent years. For some fairly obvious reasons, I think — all kinds of displacements, an inability to concentrate, distractions.

Let's get back to composition itself, which you've described as a shaking of the bars, a link moment between the human condition and the song.
Something like that. There's a certain moment in which that happens, but that's a very rare occurence, of course. Although every poem, I suppose, is an attempt. I suppose it's religious — the notion of art as consolation, the belief that 'everything will be all right.' I suppose I can't finally seriously believe that we're not immortal. So yes, in some sense everything *is* going to be all right. That seems a really crass thing to say. But it would be pernicious to insist that this was the be-all and end-all; it's not. It's only one of the poetic experiences — although it has a kind of privileged status, I think. For example, in 'The Sea in Winter', writing to O'Grady below in Paros, I assign such a moment to him:

> You too have known the curious sense
> of working on the circumference-
> the midnight oil, familiar sea,
> elusive dawn epiphany,
> faith that the trivia doodled here
> will bear their fruit sometime, somewhere.

That reflects on it.

Would you call the poem, then, any poem, a secular act of faith?
I suppose it is. If we're going to start from religion, yes, a 'secular act of faith' would do. A faith in meaningfulness, a defiance of nihilism — to which one is rather prone, of course. I mean, we do all know it's all a lot of nonsense, really, just as Mr. Camus knew, but it doesn't do to say so, even to oneself. Isn't that right?

Although, if you're a poet you have *to say it to yourself, I guess; but you also have to say the other thing — what Yeats would call holding reality and justice in a single thought. You're after that too?*
Yes, of course. 'Derry Morning' has something of what we're talking about: the glimpse of the streets on that morning. As to poems as secular acts of faith... well, everything is an act of faith: getting up in the morning is an act of faith. I like the idea of a defiance of nihilism, that's certainly true in my own case. It's very easy to have said at some point, even to say still, 'It's all a lot of nonsense, it's not to be taken seriously.' But that attitude never produces anything.

When you say 'act of faith', does faith have an object, or is it there for its own sake?
The object is life, I think. The object is to make life possible, and to make life continue. That sounds rather utilitarian. But I think that it is for its own sake in the first instance, to say *yes* rather than *no*. The happy incidental outcome of that is that the side of life is strengthened — one can go on.

In a lot of your poems the final image is of somebody going on 'in spite of'. Do you think that the poem itself is a journey towards going on?
Yes. Heaney quotes a Coventry Patmore phrase, 'the end of art is peace.' *Peace* in the sense of contributing to the world, to life, which is finally all we have, I suppose. That sort of 'going on'. Though perhaps we shouldn't be talking about peace, but only about faith — the poem, as you said, as an act of faith. So let's forget peace; let's stick with the faith.

There's a generosity about your poetry vis-à-vis the ordinary world, as if the poems were some sort of ministration into the world.
Well, that sounds very nice. Ministration. It also sounds a little patronizing. I mean, they are themselves products of a broken world.

But products of a broken world that you want whole. You have a sense of wholeness that you're trying to minister into the world.
Yes, but all that one can do is minister to that sense. I don't think poetry makes anything happen. No, scratch that, because it educates the imagination, so you get more imaginative people, a higher quality of civilization, people behave better toward one another. I'm more inclined to Shelley than Auden on this: 'The great instrument of moral good is the imagination... Poetry contributes to the effect by acting upon the cause.' So no, I don't think Auden is right. It was a very half-hearted declaration of Auden's anyway. It's my observation that not just poetry, but art in any shape or form can tutor the imagination — the imagination can feed and strengthen itself on art, on poetry, in such a way that the sum of goodness and wisdom in the world is infinitesimally increased. I think that is so.

What's the connection between the formal element in your work and the act of faith?
If a thing is worth saying, it's worth going to some trouble to say it in a presentable and memorable fashion. Something like that. But even that's too much of a rationalization. It's more that *that's the way I like to do it*. It's almost as simple as that: *that's what I like to do on the page*. I've often filled a page with free verse, and I've thought, now that's not a bad piece of free verse, and it's hung around for a while. But eventually I throw it out, because it's not interesting to me. A thing has to have shape, profile, it has to clear its throat, make its presence felt, make itself visually interesting and so on. That is simply the way that I understand poetry.

Is that also the way you understand poetry as making something happen?
I don't think that far ahead. In writing, my thinking is on the level of 'this
will interest so-and-so' or 'so-and-so will like this.' Or maybe not even that;
maybe just that 'this is going to be fun when I'm putting the finishing
touches to it, when it's actually taking its final form.'

*Although the self-portrait that comes through your poems is often that of the
solitary, a lot of your poems are dedicated to specific people?*
I invoke a circle of friends, a reading society. I didn't realize that at the
beginning, but I was creating a circle of readers.

Of course, this introduces other issues. If we're going to talk about
solitude and community, we're going to have to talk about non-belonging,
about marriage, about homelessness. All these themes are subject matter
for me just at the moment, which have as their origin the way I shut myself
off from my family, from my family origins. Not entirely: I still see my
mother once a year. But, at the age of eighteen or so, when I left home to
go to Trinity, I wasn't just going on to college; I was actually leaving one
life altogether and stepping into another. Throughout my teens I had a
sense of the immediate community — extended family, the neighbour-
hood and so on — but I felt that there was something terribly amiss and
lacking and skewed about this whole carry-on. It seems a very insufficient
community. The question in the back of my mind all the time was, Is this
all? Is this it? Is this life? These people, this place? In fact, of course, look-
ing back on it now, there's a lot more vividness in actuality about both the
people and the place than, at the time, in my intolerance, I was able to
appreciate. A mistake Heaney has never made. But I was an odd fish.
Heaney was part of his community growing up — part of the extended
family and society — but I found the nature of that society intensely
repressive, neurotic.

You might say that my first model of community was tainted, so I opted
out of community. But, to quote Adrienne Rich, 'the danger in reacting
against coldness is that one becomes oneself cold.' I think that happened
to me. I'm still a pretty cold fish in some ways — it becomes second nature,
first nature, even, to get out of all community, and to turn into an antino-
mian, nasty character. The dangers are solipsism, inhumanity, intolerance.
It's the first step towards, on the one hand, Rimbaud, and on the other
hand, the serial killer. Really it's a psychological risk to deracinate from
your given community. Heaney asks this question somewhere: How dan-
gerous is it to reject the world we're shown? And it *is* dangerous. A more
obvious and easier danger, of course, is to be absorbed by it. So what I did
was to reject the world I was shown, though I later came back to it in vari-
ous ways. But I still went off on this solipsistic trip, on which I in some sense
still am. So all of those dedications amount to the creation of a new family.

You've also been married and have a family of your own. Now you're separated. Do you see that as another community from which you finally isolated yourself?
I suppose the answer is that I'm not very good at community except in a tentative fashion. Just as I don't like parties unless I'm standing near the door talking to people I know well, and able to get away fast. That's my idea of parties — and also of communities. To be essentially solitary (this is all very selfish, I realize that) — not without community, exactly, but a slight distance all around, so that one is dealing with community on one's own terms. And that's the way I live today.

What's the connection between that and the kind of poems you write?
It's practically my subject, my theme: solitude and community; the weirdness and terrors of solitude; the stifling and the consolations of community. Also, the consolations of solitude. But it is important for me to be on the edge looking in. I've been inside, I've spent lots of time inside. Now again, I appear to be outside; perhaps I'll be inside once again. I don't known. On the formal side ... I was talking recently to a very nice young woman who seemed to be coming from the current literary orthodoxy; she used two phrases of her students — one was about 'giving them permission to write' and the other was about 'creating a warm space for them to write.' Now, poetry written with permission in warm spaces, there's far too much of that — and that is the voice of community. What interests me is forbidden poetry written by solitaries in the cold, written by solitaries in the open, which is where the human soul really is. That for me is where poetry really is.

FRANK ORMSBY

You were born in Enniskillen in County Fermanagh in 1947 and grew up in the townland of Makeny near Irvinestown. How would you describe your family background ?

My father left school at the age of eleven to become a farm labourer and later worked on the roads and as a street-sweeper for Fermanagh County Council. My mother, whose maiden name was McMahon, was a farmer's daughter. She too left school at eleven and was no stranger to farm work. My father was a widower in his mid-sixties, she was in her mid-thirties when they married. I am the eldest of their four children.

Your first volume A Store of Candles *(1977) sees education as driving a wedge between you and your family but* The Ghost Train *(1995) surely suggests shared sporting ground. Were you aware of a tension between the values or "speak" of home and the language and writing of school early on?*

There were certainly tensions. My father, for reasons best known to himself, was against my sitting the 11-plus examination, but my mother, supported by the Principal of Irvinestown Boys' Primary School, which I attended at that time, insisted. I was already "bookish" in a way that my parents were not, though with frustratingly little access to actual books and when I started attending St. Michael's Grammar School in Enniskillen my life took a radically different direction. It is true that my father and I shared an interest in sport — Gaelic football, horse racing, boxing — and it pleased the Nationalist in him that one of my subjects at St. Michael's was Irish. He didn't have a word of it himself but clearly there was a political correctness about the fact that I was acquiring it. Nevertheless, my abiding memories are of withdrawing into a world that was largely closed to my parents. There were occasional rows, even with my mother, about the extent to which my 'nose' was 'always stuck in a book'. Maybe my mother recognised earlier and more clearly than I did the gulf that was beginning to open.

You describe Fermanagh in the prose anthology Thirty-two Counties *(1989) as a 'deceptively placid, postcard county' with an underlying 'palpable' border and divisive internal politics. Were you aware of those divisions growing up there?*

Divisions, divided allegiances were in the air. They had a kind of formal embodiment on occasions like the 12 July, 12 August and Remembrance Day. The tricolor was flown and the 'Soldier's Song' sung at Gaelic football matches. Separate schools, separate churches, different flags. There were local tensions that went back to Partition. The population of Fermanagh was predominantly Catholic but the Unionist minority had used the gerrymander system to maintain political control of the county. Furthermore, because Fermanagh was a border county, it was vulnerable to I.R.A. attack from the Free State, as we called the Republic. Between the mid-`50s and early `60s there was a constant campaign of ambushes, explosions, attacks on buses, post office vans, bridges, and on R.U.C. barracks at Lisnaskea, Derrylin and Brookeborough, with fatalities on both sides. When I was ten or eleven there were popular ballads in praise of Fergal O'Hanlon and Sean South, the two I.R.A. men killed in the attack on Brookeborough barracks. As a result of these incidents, many border roads were closed and every barracks in the county became a fortress, protected by ramps, wire-netting and sand-bags. The B-Specials were also active at the time, a kind of Protestant militia who were likely to stop you as you cycled home from the cinema at night and question you. We lived near the boundary of Necarne Castle estate where the Specials had a practice shooting range, so gunfire was part of the sound-track of that time. We did not associate with Protestant children and it was only when I was in my teens and at college in Enniskillen that I made friends with Protestants of my own age.

'Geography' assimilates a Joycean pre-lingual world into Whitehill Primary School; other poems in THE GHOST TRAIN *look at a child's earliest world. Did the world you entered in late 1940s Ulster differ substantially from that entered by children now?*
Yes. In retrospect it seems a very bleak existence — no electricity or running water, no kitchen as such — but we never felt deprived. Growing up in a house where there was no television, no car and, until I was about ten, no radio must have had all sorts of unquantifiable consequences for the imagination. It certainly limited our sense of the outside world, though it also made me a reader and helped turn me to writing at an early age.

You went to St. Michael's College in Enniskillen in 1959. Many northern poets speak of the absence of writers as models bridging the gap between their environment and the world of writing at secondary school. Were you aware of this? Were you interested in poetry or writers at secondary school? When was your first poem published?
When I was nine or ten I moved from Whitehill Primary School, a rural primary, to Irvinestown Boys' Primary and it was shortly after that that I

began to write poems. I think the catalyst was writing a poem as part of a school assignment for Enniskillen Show and winning a prize for it. By the time I got to St. Michael's College, I was already filling notebooks with verse — much of it, I imagine, in imitation of schools' anthology fare at that time — Stevenson, de la Mare, occasionally Irish poets such as Yeats, James Stephens, Padraic Colum, Joseph Campbell. Another big influence was the patriotic verse printed in the poetry centrefold in *Ireland's Own* magazine. I wrote thumping traditional stuff in the style of Thomas Davis, John Boyle O'Reilly, Thomas Keegan Casey, the Young Ireland poets. The first poem I ever had printed was a ballad about Brian Boru and the Battle of Kincora — it appeared in the letters columns of *The Sunday Press* when I was in my early teens with my name and address at the bottom. After that the level of production was feverish, the models ranging from the Augustans (Gray, Cooper, Collins and Goldsmith were on the A level, or Advanced Senior, as it was then called, syllabus), through Hopkins (also a set poet) to the writers in the Penguin Modern Poets series which began to appear in 1962. I did come across Patrick Kavanagh's work — many of the priests who taught me in St. Michael's were from Co. Monaghan so that, for them, Kavanagh had local hero status — but my first sense of contemporary northern poetry came through poems by John Montague and John Hewitt, photocopied by an English teacher and distributed for discussion. Montague's 'Like Dolmens Round My Childhood the Old People', in particular, opened the way into writing about my own background and experience.

Edna Longley, in THE IRISH REVIEW *(No 17/18, Winter 1995) states: 'differences in religious background produce imaginative dialects which are not only thematic, but inform the metaphysics and structure of poetry.' How would you describe your religious background and its subsequent influence on the poems you wrote?*
My parents were staunchly Catholic and I practised fairly devoutly myself until I was about twenty. I served as an altar boy, sang in the chapel choir and so on. Religious instruction was an integral part of our schooling, from the Catechism of primary school to the "Apologetics" taught at St. Michael's. Subsequent influence of this? A big, unanswerable question. I was well on the way to lapsing by the time I published my first poems and I think *A Store of Candles* is a secular book, but complicated by an identification with Catholics' minority status in Northern Ireland. Allegiance and non-allegiance. Was it Michael Foley who used to joke about knowing which side he was on in a showdown?

Poets from the North in the 1930s and 1940s often register a hinterland of both left-wing commitment and social compassion in their work. Your first volume of poems is set in the small farms and village housing estates of Fermanagh and you have written about squatters, prostitutes, tramps, winos and labouring men. Is there a class consciousness at work in your poems?

Yes, in that they reflect my own background and a curiosity about my parents' lives that sometimes seems like obsession and maybe contains an undercurrent of guilt about having seemed to move "beyond" all that. Not that I think the subjects you mention are a salve for the conscience or part of a "compassion" enterprise. There was no question of my deliberately choosing such subjects.

You studied English literature at Queen's University (1966-71). Did you meet writers who encouraged you there? Was there an ethos in terms of the syllabus or a "take" on literature?

Those five years had a huge impact. I married and had two children. I discovered the poems of Heaney, Mahon, Longley and Simmons, first in magazines such as *Phoenix, Threshold* and *Aquarius,* then in their first collections, and met all of them except, I think, Mahon. There were meetings of the Group in the English Department and Heaney's house and regular readings organised by the English Society. I got to know Foley, Muldoon, Carson, Bernard McLaverty, Stewart Parker and others. I had my first "serious" publication, a poem in the *Honest Ulsterman* in February 1969, and became joint-editor of the magazine, with Michael Foley, at the end of that year. I read vast amounts of poetry by both the living and the dead: Herbert, Raleigh, Wordsworth, Hardy, Yeats, Keith Douglas, Alun Lewis, MacNeice, Larkin, Hughes, Roethke, Adcock, Snodgrass — it was intoxicating. If there was a particular "take" on literature in the university I was ignorant of it and more influenced by James Simmons's manifesto for the *Honest Ulsterman* or by conversations with Michael Foley and Tom McLaughlin and Ciaran Carson. I found the whole atmosphere conducive to writing and still think of that period with excitement.

Northern poets often register or re-shape a unique confluence of Irish poetry (in English and Irish) and the English tradition. Yeats and MacNeice are sometimes cited as important exemplars. Do you see Yeats and MacNeice as having influenced what you have written?

Yes, primarily as love poets and as craftsmen. Between *A Store of Candles* and *A Northern Spring* I tried, unsuccessfully, to write a "Belfast Journal" in the style of *Autumn Journal* — attracted by the idea of reflecting the everyday and exploring key concerns in that ranging, inclusive, deceptively relaxed way. Yeats is inescapable — as love poet, war poet, satirical poet, poet of fatherhood, poet of ageing.

Some northern writers relate to Modernism in general or Eliot's Waste Land *in particular. Montague speaks fairly sympathetically of Eliot and, to some extent, reinterprets his 'fragments' as 'scars'; Fiacc translates Eliot's 'fragments' into 'smithereens'. What is your attitude to Eliot and Modernism?*

And of course Jimmy Simmons mugs old Stearns in 'No Land is Waste, Dr. Eliot'. I came across Eliot's *Selected Poems* right at the end of sixth form and studied them in my first year at Queen's and for a while wrote imitations. I still read him with admiration, as I do other Modernist poets such as Wallace Stevens and William Carlos Williams, but I don't think they have had a lasting influence on me. Or traceable influence anyway — since Modernism has become such an integral part of our creative oxygen, how can you tell? On the whole, I'm probably more attracted to the great Modernist prose writers and painters.

From December 1969, either jointly or alone, you edited the HONEST ULSTERMAN. *Simmons initially saw the journal as 'A Handbook for Revolution' in which literature from the North could produce real, radical, political changes akin to those envisaged by Bernadette Devlin. How did you see your editorial role?*

Initially I was an assistant editor to Michael Foley and the polemical thrust of the magazine was in Foley's editorials. As I remember it, neither of us was entirely comfortable with the trumpet sound of the phrase 'handbook for revolution', though both of us agreed broadly with Simmons that literature should be accessible, bold, exploratory and that it could be a force for change. I think we were less evangelical, more sceptical than Simmons. I've always felt that literature is more likely to effect change by infiltration, by getting into the water supply, that good writing works by stealth. As sole editor of the magazine I hardly ever wrote editorials but aimed for a variety of poetry and prose that in itself reflected 'tough reasonableness and lyric grace', as Simmons puts it in his poem 'Didn't He Ramble'.

Since 1971 you have taught English at the Royal Belfast Academical Institution. Are writing poems and teaching poems complementary activities?

In my experience, yes. I went into teaching because it held the promise of a working life discussing poetry and prose and that impulse has not changed significantly. The formal teaching of poetry has taught me a lot about the craft and I hope that, in turn, I have brought a practitioner's edge to the teaching. Nothing like the reading aloud and close exploration of poems to confirm or moderate your excitement about poetry. Whatever inspiration is, the immersion, privately and with others, in great poetry is certainly one of its sources.

You published two pamphlet collections, 'Ripe for Company' (1971) and 'Business As Usual' (1973), before your first volume. There is a colloquial feel to these titles and a later poem, 'Geography', speaks of talk that 'warms the infinite sky/for the space of three minutes'. To what extent do you trust or distrust the colloquial? Is this related to a link between irony and rhetoric in your poems?

The 'important places' I grew up in, the important people there, like my father and mother, had ways of saying that were, in themselves, "poetic". I was educated out of that language, of course, but it has, to some extent, got into the poems — sometimes naturally and unselfconsciously — sort of offering itself as the right way to express something — sometimes very deliberately, as in poems like 'A Fly in the Water' and 'After Mass' and 'News from Home'. There were literary precedents too, as in Hardy and Frost, then Kavanagh, Montague and others. And it seems to me that the rediscovery of the colloquial and the revitalization of cliché are significant features of recent Irish poetry — not to mention poetry from Scotland or Yorkshire or wherever.

Death is a recurrent theme in A STORE OF CANDLES: *the sportsman ('McQuade'); the rich man ('A Death in the Mansion'); the cremated ('Passing the Crematorium'); the 'domestic murders' ('The Police Museum') and the 'Chalk-marks (which) traced the body's line' in 'Aftermath'. Your father's death is remembered in 'In Memoriam' and your mother's death imminent in 'Winter Offerings'. Is there a relationship between your personal elegies and a wider analysis of the North?*

Of the poems you mention, only 'Aftermath' is directly a "Troubles" poem. I don't remember the genesis of 'The Police Museum'. The others are entirely personal, the early rite-of-passage encounters with death that might be expected in a first collection. 'Winter Offerings' reflects a sense of my mother ageing rather than approaching death as such — in fact she lived for another twenty years! The death of my father when I was twelve had a profound effect on me and still surfaces regularly in poems. Of course there are other poems in *A Store of Candles* which address Catholic minority experience in the North —'Sheepman' and 'The Barracks', for example, and others which are about personal, domestic continuities in time of violence — I'm thinking of 'Floods', 'Spot the Ball', 'Moving In', 'Passing the Crematorium', 'Under the Stairs'.

Ronald Marken in the IRISH UNIVERSITY REVIEW *talks of the 'sureness of the form' in* A STORE OF CANDLES, *but there are many "forms" in this collection (from the tight couplets and eight-line stanzas to the three-liners) and in your other volumes. How do you see form or shape? Do you associate particular forms with particular themes or strategies?*

In my experience poems often begin as lines or phrases or images which, as they take hold and develop, suggest the form and shape of the poem. It generally involves an intuitive sense early on that the poem will be formal or relaxed, a villanelle or blank verse. God knows what factors are involved — the mood that induced or is induced by the subject, the poetry you found yourself reading or teaching, perhaps, the week before. In *A Northern Spring*, for example, the title sequence is heavily influenced by the loose dramatic monologues in Edgar Lee Masters' *Spoon River Anthology*. Many of the poems at the end of *The Ghost Train*, about the impending birth of my daughter Helen, suggested themselves as a kind of ceremonial celebration and make use of set stanzas, half-rhymes and so on, while others, like 'The Easter Ceasefire', are built around repetitions. An earlier poem, 'King William Park', is written in stanza form but is also structured around a set of inter-related images — the sea-bird standing on one leg, the public buildings built on underground stilts driven into land reclaimed from the sea, the victims of knee-cappings balanced on crutches. I don't remember which image occurred to me first but it generated the others as the poem was being written. Then again, I've written a large number of haiku recently and while the first few occurred to me in that form those that followed are deliberate workings of the genre — though even in those circumstances you hope for the happy marriage of form and content that will lift the poem above the level of mere exercise.

Do you assimilate influences from Philip Larkin and Thomas Hardy in A Store of Candles *? A poem like 'Mrs. G. Watters' traces a house's former occupant in gas bills and a calendar and there is surely a debate about whether the ordinary or practical might double up as the mystical or luminous? I mention Hardy because in 'Landscape With Figures' there's that rural 'Sadness of dim places, obscure lives', while 'Spot the Ball' might be read as a sardonic update of Hardy.*
Yes, Larkin and Hardy were both influences on *A Store of Candles*. I came to the poetry of both as an undergraduate and related temperamentally to both. I've always been aware of 'Mrs. G. Watters' as Larkinesque but I've never associated 'Spot the Ball' with Hardy. It started out as a lugubrious love poem and then took on a "Troubles" dimension at the end, though that is probably not evident. The concluding image of 'the full hundred crosses filling the sky' was suggested partly by a billboard outside a church in Donegall Square East in Belfast (the building is now the headquarters of the Ulster Bank) on which each death by violence was marked by the addition of a cross.

Northern poets usually make either place or people speak volumes (one emphasis may include the other). Does A Store of Candles *or your poetry, generally, put portraiture first and place, the toponymic, second ?*
I think that people do take precedence over place in the poems, though having said that I know that I tend to think of my poems in terms of loca-

tion — Fermanagh poems, Belfast poems and so on. There are some in which location is particularly important — 'King William Park', 'On Devenish Island', 'At the Jaffe Memorial Fountain, Botanic Gardens', 'Geography', to mention a few, but very few landscapes without figures.

You edited and introduced POETS FROM THE NORTH OF IRELAND *(1979). If an editor wrote a Craig Raine 'Martian' postcard describing the salient features of poetry from the North, what would be on it?*
To me the most striking feature is the sheer multiplicity of voices, so that meaningful generalisations are difficult and potentially reductive. There is, of course, a pervasive sense of wounds, faults, divisions, a poisoned inheritance, and a related uncertainty about what constitutes "home". There is a troubled engagement with the impact of violent public events, past and present, on private lives and an interrogation of the role and value of poetry itself in such circumstances. Conversely, there is a celebration of the stabilities, human values, normalities, if that's the right word, that are under threat. The best poetry from the North has a sophisticated amplitude and assurance that accommodates both the local and an informed global and universal dimension. The quantity and quality of translation is a significant feature that tends to be overlooked. Technically, poetry from the North is characterised by a mastery and, sometimes, a bold handling of traditional forms. Until recently the practitioners have been predominantly male but more and more women have begun to publish in book form.

Is the title POETS FROM THE NORTH OF IRELAND *a recognition that poetry, birth and geography may be embraced as common ground for a canon likely to produce something greater than the sum of all the parts while politics or nationality are elegantly side-stepped because they create factional or problematic boundaries ? Is this a kind of SDLP title as a recipe for consensus ?*
I thought of the contributors as first and foremost poets and, secondly, as poets from a particular place who transcended the specific political boundaries of that place in their poetry. I worded the title of the anthology to reflect this, so I deliberately avoided the designation 'Northern Ireland'. Of course, even the side-step was open to political interpretation. I remember one reviewer describing the title as a coded way of withholding recognition from the Northern Ireland state.

World War II was witnessed by John Montague as a boy in Tyrone and Armagh; Seamus Heaney was aware early of 'war coupons' on the farm; Roy McFadden's family were evacuated when he was a young man and pacifist in Belfast; Michael Longley recalls the war as a dim infant memory (supplemented by family experience and later reading of the war poets). In what way

did World War II come to you?
The war ended before I was born but there had been an American military hospital camp in the woods near our house and as children we played in the air-raid shelters and on the stone floors in the undergrowth. Both the Catholic and Protestant graveyards in Irvinestown contained the graves of Canadian and American airmen, mostly the victims of training accidents. Maybe eight or ten years after the war, you would find rusty beer cans among the bluebells. Some of the Nissen huts were to be seen in local farmyards, serving as outhouses. The GIs had related particularly well to the Catholic community and stories about the 'Yanks' were part of local history and folklore.

Why do you write about World War II? In what ways does the terrain of the World War and the language and structure of A NORTHERN SPRING *parallel or diverge from the landscape of the later Ulster "Troubles"?*
Well, as I've said, the potential imaginative stimulus was already there and long before *A Northern Spring* I had touched on World War II in two poems in *A Store of Candles*, 'The Edge of War' and 'The Air-Raid Shelter'. The 'Northern Spring' sequence was written in the period leading up to the fiftieth anniversary of the Normandy landings partly, as I've mentioned, influenced by the *Spoon River Anthology*. The nature of the military presence in Ulster in spring 1944 and the reasons for that presence differ totally from the situation in the North since 1968. I thought of the sequence as imagining the experiences of individual soldiers — so I suppose the poems could be read as an implicit riposte to the kind of "Troubles" propaganda that presented soldiers as "legitimate targets". In 'Maimed Civilians, Isigny' I had in mind the victims and survivors of La Mon House and the Abercorn. 'From the German' takes its cue partly from MacNeice's lines in *Autumn Journal* about how the Irish 'shoot to kill and never / See the victim's face become their own'. And 'Apples, Normandy, 1944' is, on one level, a reaction against journalistic pressures on Northern poets to write about the "Troubles". One of the things I enjoy most about dramatic monologue is that it offers such ways of being simultaneously oblique and immediate.

You edited John Hewitt's COLLECTED POEMS *(1991) and some northern writers would acknowledge Hewitt or Kavanagh as poets who developed their trust in the parish (not the parochial) as artistically valid material. Does* A NORTHERN SPRING *suggest Hewitt's Regionalist position and the parish boundary has been superceded by the culture of the global village, by 'Europe's aggregate air'? Fermanagh, for American airmen in the 1940s or American tourists now, is often a brief part of a larger, European, itinerary: in 'Seaplanes at Castle Archdale' their uniform 'wings/ are uppermost and seem to catch the sun:/ still butterflies'; 'On Devenish Island' has them pitching a baseball 'through the perfect arch /of a church window's crumbling Romanesque'.*

A Northern Spring is not a conscious, deliberate response to Hewitt and Kavanagh but because their work is part of our cultural oxygen the direction that book took might be said to show their influence indirectly. Somewhere along the line I sensed that it was turning into a book about visitors to and settlers in the North of Ireland, the complicated nature of "home" beyond the usual Northern Irish polarisation. Of course Hewitt's Regionalism had a European dimension and he had hopes that it would help people to transcend sectarian divisions in the North, so there are affinities there... But, as I've said, I think that a lot of Northern Irish and Irish poetry is characterised by a rippling outwards from the local to the global. It's not just a superficial matter of locations ranging from the Falls Road to Estonia, Glengormley to Maine, The Moy to Hopewell, New Jersey, but a matter of restless and inclusive sensibilities and an educated cultural range. I think *A Northern Spring* is affected by that too. I like the expression "this part of the world" as an unpretentious, colloquial summary of the local/global confluence and I smuggled it into the poem 'Darkies'.

In Longley's most direct "Troubles" poems war poets like Owen or Edward Thomas are conscripted for elegies where the key notes are compassion or commemoration for victims; surely A NORTHERN SPRING *deploys more Sassoon-like ironies or a wry anger. In 'Darkies' victims are either selectively remembered or forgotten.*
While *A Northern Spring* was in progress I read a lot about the Normandy landings and about America before, during and after the war. The absurdities could be harmless or poignant or lethal. The wry and ironic elements in the sequence emerged from these stories. In some cases I adapted actual experiences or built on passing references, in other cases I invented.

Do the post-Plantation settlers in Ulster in A NORTHERN SPRING *(American GIs, the Jewish, Chinese and Italian communities, the 'Vietnamese boat-people of Portadown') turn the colonial problem on its head and point to an underlying racism in which both traditional majority and minority are complicit?*
Racism is certainly a theme in the 'Northern Spring' sequence, especially the grim irony that not even a World War against a racist regime could annul such prejudices. However, I thought of the Jewish, Chinese, Italian and Vietnamese settlers not so much as victims of prejudice in the North of Ireland, more as vulnerable but resilient outsiders who have begun to adapt to a new place while retaining something of their ethnicity.

The narrator's vision (through bus or skylight windows or gaps in hedges) looks as if it is being deliberately constricted or else obscured (by mist or darkness) in A STORE OF CANDLES *so that certainties are rendered impossible. Some poems*

in A NORTHERN SPRING *amputate their subjects: 'The War Photographers'
work 'with one eye closed or heads buried'; the 'Mechanics' operate under cars
'united/ with heads and torsos'. Does this reflect a pessimism about poetry's role
or function in violent times — the poet as a partially blind doctor complicit in
accidents and emergencies rather than as a seer or 'midwife to society'?*

Some of the images you single out have a macabre side but I don't regard
'The War Photographers' and 'Mechanics' as pessimistic. The photogra-
phers are working in positive, enhancing ways within their limitations and
the mechanics, though they actually enjoy exuding negative attitudes, 'go
on with the operation'. My own sense of these poems is that they are war-
ily optimistic. Maybe the very writing of poetry is warily optimistic, to a
greater or lesser degree.

*Tom Clyde sees 'Cleo, Oklahoma' as having a 'cinematic sweep reminiscent of
Citizen Kane in the* IRISH REVIEW *(No 1, 1986) and there is a 'chiaroscura
pan' in 'You: The Movie'. Does cinema or film influence your poetry?*

How can you even attempt to define the impact of the cinema — imagi-
natively, morally, emotionally, perceptually? It was in our lives from an
early age, educating the outer and inner eyes in ways that were rich for
poetry. In retrospect, the Adelphi cinema in Irvinestown was as important
a source in its way, of spiritual and imaginative nourishment as the chapel
or school. In my case, the influence is most explicit in 'Sheepman', which
was suggested by a specific Western, *The Sheepman*, with Glenn Ford and
Shirley MacLaine and 'The Aluminium Box' is a kind of homage to the
actors and actresses who loomed large for us in the `50s and `60s.

*Irish myths, standing stones or figures from prehistory like Cuchulainn register
in northern poetry. Apart from 'Home' (with its bi-focal lens on both the Giant's
Ring and on the contemporary) is it fair to suggest that this long sweep of his-
tory is of less interest to you than recent history?*

That's generally true. I don't think I've drawn on Celtic mythology as such
in a poem. However, there are poems in *A Northern Spring*, such as 'On
Devenish Island' and 'Some of Us Stayed Forever' where recent history is
consciously presented as part of a longer perspective, represented by the
monastic ruins on Devenish and the Viking remains at the bottom of
Lough Erne. 'King William Park' begins with images of the coast where
Belfast was built as it might have been in prehistoric times and moves
through a series of historical snapshots to the present.

*Is there a 'generational' difference between poets from the North before/around
1939 and those born after? In Hewitt, Heaney and Longley's poetry nouns are
rooted in the primary industries (farming, fishing, weaving, mining) or
planted before the poet as 'craftsman' or 'priest' or 'botanist' transmits them as*

metaphor. In your poems nouns from manufacturing (Lucky Strikes, Wrigley's Spearmint, candles, 'weedkiller in lemonade bottles') may be dispersed or recycled as uncertain hybrids. Muldoon's 'Mules', Carson's THE STAR FACTORY, *your refugees (in Belfast's Botanic Gardens they are 'random inheritors' improvising a 'style of making do/ from trunks and travelling bags...') surely point to either a changed poetics or a changed world?*

I'd hesitate to pronounce on generational differences in terms of nouns or imagery drawn from the sources you mention. I can think of Muldoon poems in which farming is central, Carson poems that draw on bell-casting, patchwork, poems of my own in which farming and fishing have a place and so on. All generations adapt or build on or engage in dialogues with their predecessors. This is a particularly notable feature in the work of Muldoon, Carson, McGuckian and Paulin. The strands of change and continuity weave through all poetry. The sense of a changing rural world is certainly strong in, say, Montague and Heaney, and of a world 'blown sky-high' in Muldoon and 'gone for a Burton' in the work of Carson. Practically all of the northern poets born since 1939 reflect or address political change or changes in, say, patterns of education or global awareness. All "Troubles" poetry, even when it laments recurring cycles and entrenched attitudes, is in the broadest sense about change. Nevertheless, it is possibly true that poets like Muldoon and Carson reflect, or that their poetry is permeated by, aspects of what is contemporary to them in specific, immediate, ways that are not characteristic of their predecessors. I'm thinking of the hallucinogenic motif, of the way Carson absorbs the names of products or items of military equipment into his poems, of Muldoon writing 'sleeve-notes' for songs by Van Morrison, Bruce Springsteen and others, or attempting, in *The Prince of the Quotidian*, to reclaim the so-called trivia of everyday life for poetry. Of course, as soon as you try to generalise about such matters, the edges blur. MacNeice's *Autumn Journal*, jazz and popular music in the poetry of Simmons and Longley, Derek Mahon's 'Manhattan' poems in *The Hudson Letter* and *The Yellow Book...* arguably all contemporary in the same sense.

You edited NORTHERN WINDOWS: AN ANTHOLOGY OF ULSTER AUTOBIOGRAPHY *(1987). Is poetry in the North of Ireland deeply tracked by the autobiographical?*

Deeply. There is a sense in which every poem is a fragment of spiritual or intellectual autobiography, but in addition to that there are many poems and books by Ulster poets which deal directly with experiences and circumstances in their own lives: MacNeice's *Autumn Journal* again, Hewitt's *Freehold* and *Kites in Spring*, the books in which Montague and Simmons explore their own experience of love, marriage, divorce.

You also edited THE LONG EMBRACE: TWENTIETH CENTURY IRISH LOVE POEMS *(1987) and you've written love poems. Does writing a love poem present difficulties as great as the writing of political poems?*
In my experience, all poems present the same essential difficulty — finding the words, rhythms, weights, balances that come closest to catching, recreating your experience without diminishing it. It's to do with being simultaneously inside the skin of the experience, so that the poem as it accretes, becomes the experience, and also at a retrospective remove in which you are making deliberate aesthetic judgements and choices in relation to diction, line structure and so on. Although I've edited an anthology of love poems and political poems and such terms are useful as thematic descriptors, I've never really thought of love poems, political poems, nature poems, family poems as presenting significantly separate or distinct difficulties.

Your revised edition of POETS FROM THE NORTH OF IRELAND *(1990) takes account of emerging 1980s poets like Medbh McGuckian and Paul Muldoon, their self-reflexive, implosive, poetry of the interior — dense with dream or abstruse reference. Does your editorial selection in the "Troubles" anthology* A RAGE FOR ORDER *(1992) imply that Muldoon is a "Troubles" poet and McGuckian is not?*
The "Troubles" figure as one important subject in northern poetry — but only one — so I don't think of northern poets as ' "Troubles" poets' or 'not "Troubles" poets'. Some address the "Troubles" more explicitly than others, in the same way that some are more direct than others in their exploration of, say, love and marriage. The "Troubles" are more explicitly present in Muldoon's poetry than in McGuckian's. In *A Rage for Order* I tried not to be too prescriptive about what constitutes '"Troubles" poetry'. The Introduction makes the point that the impact of the "Troubles" may be present in oblique and unquantifiable ways in all northern poetry since 1968. Medbh McGuckian is, I think, making the same point by selecting as an epigraph for her 1994 collection *Captain Lavender* Picasso's statement (made in 1944): 'I have not painted the war... but I have no doubt that the war is in ... these paintings I have done'. If the "Troubles" are indeed a current in McGuckian's poetry before 1992, the current runs too deeply for detection, at least by me. Always frustrating this for an editor and one of the drawbacks of the 'thematic' approach — the sense that where you have to draw the line — or, more accurately, where your line wavers in relation to inclusions and exclusions, may represent a blindness on your part or an injustice to poems so elusively oblique in their angles to the 'theme' that you find it difficult to justify their inclusion, so complex indeed as to remind you that the 'theme' based approach breaks down at a certain point and is limited by what it cannot accommodate.

While we're on the subject, I think, in retrospect, that I made a mistake in omitting Derek Mahon's 'A Disused Shed in Co Wexford'...

Surely a volume of 'poetry of the Troubles' is problematic? In POETRY IN THE WARS *(1986) Edna Longley re-iterates Yeats's point — poets search technically and spiritually to find forms which house experienced truth in which both the imagination and the tradition have primacy. She also quotes Edward Thomas to illustrate 'a subject-matter fallacy': 'Anything, however small may make a poem; nothing, however great, is certain to'.*

All anthologies are problematic, for one reason or another. As I've been saying, it's the fate of editors to be plagued by doubts. From among the thousands of "Troubles" poems I read while compiling *A Rage for Order*, I tried to select the ones that seemed to me to work best as poems. You work away as positively as you can within the limitations. The anthologies you mention began and ended in excitement and a sense of riches and some kind of trust in the way poetry can speak memorably and movingly to others. And, reservations aside, there are certain creative satisfactions in organising the material in thematic anthologies so that the final impact is somehow more than the sum of the details, as is the case in a good picture or a good collection of poems.

As editor of the HONEST ULSTERMAN *you used work by contemporary northern painters. In poems like 'The Gatecrasher' and 'A Paris Honeymoon' you refer to Lavery and Monet. Who are your favourite painters? Is it fair to suggest that photography is the visual art closest to your conception of poetry?*

I more or less educated myself in Art, systematically, through, for example, the Phaidon volumes of reproductions and randomly through visits to museums and art galleries. The process is, of course, on-going. From time to time poems have come out of this interest. 'The Bees Nest' in *A Northern Spring*, for example, is based on 'Cupid Complaining to Venus' by Lucas Cranach the Elder and there are painterly elements in 'Landscape with Figures' and 'Apples, Normandy, 1944'. More recently, I based a poem on Colin Middleton's 'Lagan, Annadale' (1941). Favourite painters? Generally the list would include French, American and Irish Impressionists, Picasso, Klee, Edward Hopper ... too many to mention. I know less about photography, though again there are poems which have been influenced by it. 'The War Photographers' draws images from specific Crimean War and American Civil War photographs and 'The Photograph' (in *The Ghost Train*) is based on a particular holiday snap. I suppose there are snapshot images, stills, tableaux and so on in individual poems. There is nothing as systematic or considered as a theory or concept involved here.

Has music — classical, jazz or traditional music — influenced you as a writer?
Very little. I would say, at least directly. Who can tell how much any writer's
sense of rhythm and verbal harmony owes, indirectly, to music? My father
had a repertoire of popular Irish songs, many of them nationalistic. The
wireless was tuned — at least while my father was awake — to Bridie
Gallagher, Eileen Donaghy, Brendan O'Dowda, the Assaroe Ceili Band.
When he dozed off Radio Luxembourg replaced Athlone. As I've said I
sang in the chapel choir but had very little access to music beyond the
wireless — even though areas of my home county were noted for singers,
fiddlers and so on. At school we learned standards like 'Over the Sea to
Skye'. My knowledge of jazz is scrappy and my acquaintance with classical
music hopelessly random.

Is it possible to see your third volume THE GHOST TRAIN *(1995) as charting
a new, fragile optimism after three decades of living in Belfast and the writing
of two volumes where death and World War II are central concerns? 'The
Heart' states that the city your daughter 'will call home/aspires to be the capi-
tal of bereavement', so one might read that future tense as implying that the
unenviable status of the North will change in the next century?*
Well, 'fragile optimism' probably describes the mood of all three collec-
tions, despite the presence of death in the first two. The lines you quote
imply equally that Belfast might *succeed* in its aspiration to become the
capital of bereavement. *The Ghost Train* leads up to a group of personal
and public poems which celebrate expectant fatherhood at a time of ter-
rible atrocities and feuds in the North, but also the first intimations of a
lasting ceasefire. So the book ends with a birth but also, like *A Northern
Spring*, with a sense of how precarious any concept of "home" is in the
North. There is a cautious looking forward, certainly, a sort of hopeful-
ness that also acknowledges the possibility that "peace" may not extend
beyond the family.

You mentioned having written a lot of haiku recently. How did these come about?
I have always been a fan of Bashō and the other Japanese masters. The
recent haiku grew partly out of the experience of editing an anthology
The Hip Flask: Short Poems from Ireland (2000) which brought me back into
contact with the haiku of Irish poets such as Michael Hartnett and Paul
Muldoon and the oriental influence in the work of John Hewitt, Michael
Longley, Aidan Matthews, Tony Curtis, Julie O'Callaghan and others. The
form has a sort of weightless gravity that I like and — back to photogra-
phy — an attractive snapshot quality. We moved house in 1999 and some
of the haiku emerged as part of the settling-in process. Every window you
looked through framed a fresh, compact image of a new place — the trees
in the neighbours' gardens, the hanging baskets on the porch, Cavehill

from an unfamiliar angle — and haiku seemed the ideal form in which to catch this. There is also a narrative line running through the sequence which deals with an imaginary visit by Bashō to contemporary Belfast.

Bashō in Belfast? Did he find more frogs at old or new watering holes in the town? No frogs. But he does visit some watering holes on the Antrim Road and has an encounter with a loyalist blonde and other adventures.

CIARAN CARSON

Born in 1948, you grew up in West Belfast; your father (who knew the streets of the city intimately as a postman) and mother (collecting and re-cycling shirt buttons or jumpers) appear in the poems. The poem 'Bed-Time Story' in BELFAST CONFETTI *(1989) is preceded by Buson's haiku about 'borrowed armour'. Did your parents, your background, make writing likely?*

My parents learned Irish as their second language and spoke it exclusively at home. To the exclusion of English, that is. My father also learned Esperanto, possibly because he thought it might supplant English as a world language. Maybe Irish and Esperanto were his 'borrowed armour'. As for me, Irish must have been a first language, and English something I picked up off the streets. At any rate, that bilingual background has made me deeply suspicious of language in general. Saying things in one language is different from saying them in another. Well, suspicious, but not averse to the pleasure to be had from words. My father was what you might call a yarn-spinner, and I seem to remember him telling us children stories, or episodes of stories, every night for years. The nightly episode would carry you through the next day of school, or whatever else was going on, until the next episode. Outside of the stories, your ordinary life went on, but the extraordinary was also there, in the imagination. There was a sense of stepping from the story into life and from life into the story.

I have a sense of language as morse code in your work.

Or a scepticism about language. How can we know what we say until it's said? Even then the meaning is uncertain. Words are a code. The word code is from codex, the trunk of a tree, a set of tablets, a book.

You went to St. Gall's Public Elementary School in the 1950s run by the De La Salle Christian Brothers. How would you describe the 'margins of the known world', that micro-geography 'hedged' by the Falls Road in relation to the wider world of Belfast? In THE STAR FACTORY *(1997) the 1950s Falls was surely a different place from your 1980s 'Hamlet' version of it as 'A no-go area, a ghetto, a demolition zone.' ?*

I was pleased that *The Star Factory* was read by some people who came from outside my own immediate area as an accurate picture of the experience of growing up at that time. People who were brought up in the Shankill, for example. In the 1950s the Falls and the Shankill were very near to one another; one could slip quite easily from one to the other. And there was a shared industrial landscape. Mills, factories, lots of coal-smoke.

Are you suggesting childhood contains universality?
Well, when you're a child, everything is new to you, and wonderful. I loved the coal-smoke. The brick walls. Everything is beautiful if you see it with the right eyes. I believe that the world exists in such a way that everything relates to something else. Or we make it exist in that way, making links all the time, connecting things up, one thing always leading to another.

In THE STAR FACTORY *this macro geography emerges out of the micro. You learn of the wider geography of Belfast, as a youngster, by being beaten up in Cupar Street, off the home patch and come to see that the Bog Meadows divides Catholic west Belfast from the Protestant Lisburn Road. What was the micro-mosaic of Belfast like in the 1950s?*
Beatings up still happen. I've just said that the '50s Falls and the Shankill were very near to each other; but, of course, they were also remote. I knew exactly where the line was between territories. The Falls Road and its wee streets were the known world; beyond that lay monsters. I think maybe even the language was different: a Shankill language, a Falls language. Then here I was, speaking Irish, something totally foreign, really. An island within an island. The home circle.

That circular image looks familiar: Heaney's water-ripple, Montague's 'circling' as 'failure to return', Joyce or Hewitt's outward bound concentric circles.
I guess so.

As a pupil at St. Mary's Christian Brothers Grammar School in the '60s you learned weights and measures by rote or the strap — a kind of Catholic Imperialism with escapes to smoke on the steps of Belfast Central Library or to a pub on the Limestone Road. Derek Mahon described his (and Michael Longley's) schooling as that of 'Protestant poets from an English education system with an inherited duality of cultural reference.' You have imagined yourself as Biggles/Billy Bunter or an IRA man on the run. How would you describe the cultural/literary orientation of school?
In the '50s and '60s you learned "stuff". The facts of the matter, articulated in a very formal, question-and-answer way. Formal and scholastic. None of this liberal nonsense about finding your way into a subject, or making up your own answers for things. You learned the answers, like you learned a cat-echism. There was no question of exploring how this knowledge (especially history) might relate to one's self. That sort of soul-searching might be all

very well when you got to university; but, in the meantime, you had to get there, and you got there by passing exams. This was your responsibility, as a good, intelligent, Catholic: to pass the exams, and get on in life. Be a civil servant, or a doctor, or a lawyer. Don't rock the boat. Play the game. Ironically, the whole system was based on some Platonic ideal of an English public school, as if the Catholic Church were a kind of British Empire. At any rate, it was a very safe, structured world. Then, in the mid and late '60s, things started to change. There was some revolution in the air, and I watched it evolve with some astonishment, because for the previous one hundred years or so, it seemed, things had remained pretty much the same.

You read Biggles in the Falls Road library and 'extra-curricular' or a-literary genres (comics, science fiction, thrillers, detectives or westerns) appear in the work which seems to draw as much from popular literary culture as it does from 'literary stuff'?
Well, it's all "stuff". The world is everything that is the case. Hierarchies are impositions.

You read poetry as well? Which poets first impressed you?
At school, at fifteen or so, I *was* struck by Gerard Manley Hopkins. I remember the awe and the shock of being exposed to Hopkins in my first day in form four. 'I will pass around two extracts from two elegies', the teacher said. 'You will write an essay evaluating the two pieces.' These, as it turned out, were 'unseen' passages from Tennyson's 'In Memoriam', and from 'The Wreck of the Deutschland'. I was rather gratified when the teacher announced at the end of the class that only one pupil, Carson, had the right answer. Everyone else had supposed the Tennyson to be poetry, and the Hopkins gibberish. Of course *I* didn't *know* what the Hopkins meant; but I knew it was written in a language which was strange and extraordinary; a language that was one's own and yet a language one didn't know. It was foreign, awkward, marvellous. It provoked anxiety and awe. I still think that the experience of a poem should be that: awkward, anxious, strange, new. Who cares if you *know* the thing? If you know things, how can you explore them? How can you ask questions — about yourself, the street where you live, whatever? It's no fun if you already know the answers; it is fun when you are disturbed.

Is this street you live on strange?
Anything, everything you see can be strange. The sign at the top of this street says 'Glandore Avenue'. Glandore is the name of a townland in West Cork. What's it doing up here in Belfast? It means 'Gloomy Glen'. 'Avenue'? That's equally strange. From the French 'to come to', I think. Or from *avenir*, the future?

Going back to other poets you read at secondary school. Robert Frost comes into the poem 'Z' in an overlap with your father, a postman who is carrying a letter that may, or may not, get delivered. Which school poets lasted to become an assimilated influence?

Well, Robert Frost, for instance. Frost sounds very sane and American compared to Hopkins, but the language gets stranger the more you examine it. 'I cannot rub the strangeness from my sight/I got from looking through a pane of glass/ I skimmed this morning from the drinking trough...' 'After Apple-picking' is one of the great poems.

Other poets from the North absorbed the Romantics at school. Keats's 'murmurous haunt of flies on summer eves' accompanies the Black and Decker as murder weapon in one of your poems; Coleridge's 'Milk of Paradise' and 'honey dew' in another poem produces 'eyes as black as creosote'. Are you making the English lyric take ironic reality-injections?

I love Keats. The world of the Odes is made "real" in language. Is it the real world? In 'The Irish for No' I have lines from Keats turning up beside a Black & Decker drill. Is that the real world? Is the language in which we write about the "Troubles" a reflection of their reality? Or their "unreality"?

How does the Second World War register? It's a 'nearly recent' or 'cupboard' memory in THE STAR FACTORY *(where you build models of, or imitate, aircraft): a whole squadron on 'astroglide' appears in* LETTERS FROM THE ALPHABET; *there's 'Dresden' in* THE IRISH FOR NO, *'Apparition' in* Belfast Confetti *and poppies in* THE TWELFTH OF NEVER.

Maybe the Second World War is more real to me in literature. I read lots of Biggles stories at the proper age. Building model aeroplanes was a way of getting close to Biggles. Helped enormously, I should think, by all that glue one inhaled along the way. The boy's own opium poppy.

You were a student at Queen's University (1967-71) when Medbh McGuckian and Paul Muldoon were undergraduates and Seamus Heaney taught there. Muldoon's arm 'sleeved in glass' and Heaney's jam jars appear in the poems; McGuckians' 'velvet stroked the wrong way' and Longley's grandfatherly face as a Vermeer portrait are in FISHING FOR AMBER. *How would you describe the relationship between your poetry and that of other northern poets?*

Well, I don't know if there was such a thing as a school, or a group, even though we attended what they called "The Group". Longley, Ormsby, Muldoon, myself, we all hung around together; but we didn't necessarily talk about poetry. Maybe we did share some notions of what poetry should be — shared concerns about accuracy, precision and craft.

In revamped clichés, puns and riddles, in narrators who split like bubbles of

mercury and in cross-fertilising genres it might be argued that you and Paul Muldoon are engaged on similar poetic adventures although, as Edna Longley has pointed out in THE LIVING STREAM *(1994), you seem more 'extrovert'.*
It has been said. I didn't write very much between 1976 and 1985. Paul Muldoon was doing the thing so well, so why bother? Muldoon wrote — writes — with such enormously impressive, underhanded knowledge about language. When I did come back to writing it was through trying to accommodate bar-talk. Speech and slabber can be entirely odd and strange if you hear it right, or maybe I mean wrong. Sitting in a pub, you can tune into some ostensibly ordinary conversation, and it can become weird and wonderful. I wanted to get that into the poetry.

Pub riddle or wise crack and Zen haiku seem a hairs-breadth apart in your work; haikus are spliced between poems in BELFAST CONFETTI. *The final poem in* LAST NIGHT'S FUN *looks like wise crack in a nutshell. 'Lir' in* THE TWELFTH OF NEVER *has Bashō's transcience: 'Like a scarecrow/Blown by Autumn wind, like dandelion seed.' Is there a tension between the 'circumbendibus' of narrative digressions through 'fields abounding in high cockelorum' and image precision?*
Well, the long line sometimes aspires to be a haiku. About 17 syllables. Each line can be like a haiku-like unit, so that you have all the precision you need in the context of an apparently long rambly poem. Like blackberries on the bramble.

After studying at Queen's University you worked as a civil servant and teacher. You have described 1971-74 as a time when you were 'up to (your) neck' in early Irish literature, writing the poems published in the first volume, THE NEW ESTATE *(1976). How do you see early Irish poetry in relation to your first volume?*
Early Irish poems are written to a very strict and clever agenda. There's a tremendous witty energy at work, playful, ironic, precise, full of crack. Take any poem at random from Gerard Murphy's *Early Irish Lyrics*. They're beautifully done: lovely, assonantal, alliterative structures, so that even when the poem might not be saying much, from a modern perspective, you can at least admire the technique. Maybe it's not fashionable to say that technique can stand outside content, but there you are. I think style *per se* is a thing to aim at. Anyway, I liked the way these apparently ancient poems were right up-to-date in their slickness. I wanted to see the world in the way those people did. I think that's what *The New Estate* aspired to; also, to re-write English through the medium of that older Irish. Much of what is written in Irish nowadays, by the way, is a shambles compared to those early Irish poems. I wish contemporary writers of Irish would pay more heed to that milieu, and to that skill. But I also acknowl-

edge their wish, their need to be contemporary, since it is thought by many non-Irish speakers that Irish has no place in the modern world.

Surely THE NEW ESTATE *also espouses that modern landscape or aesthetic, the high fidelity music and 'lines' of 'washing' like verse in the title poem — the type of deadpan, urban ironies sponsored by Mahon in 'Ecclesiastes': 'Your people await you, their heavy washing flaps in the housing estates.'?*
Certainly. I was very influenced by Mahon then. I loved his clarity and vigour, his sparseness. And it so happens that these are the virtues of early Irish poetry.

The word 'Estate' has connotations with architecture, politics, religion and class; it might be inferred that the volume views these from without the demense walls?
Yes. But I'd hope that whatever views I have are hinted at, and not stated.

THE STAR FACTORY *suggests the 'liturgical exactitude' of Christian Brothers' schooling: the urge to martyrdom, Imperial order, angels as an overarching alternative to the temporal power and the hagiographies and Catholic Encyclopaedias suggest excavation of Catholicism in the work. Your 'Ballad of HMS Belfast' has 'Catestants and Protholics' on the 'prison ship'. In what way does the 'smoking wisp wick' of Catholicism track the imagination, the language of the poems?*
Catholicism deals with the ineffable. Or used to. As a Catholic, you experience certain things which you cannot explain or, perhaps, you are not meant to explain. You know, as a Catholic, that the language of men is ultimately doomed because it can only refer to 'all ye know on earth'; whereas the ultimate reality — for Keats as well — is death, and what lies beyond it. After death is heaven and hell and the uncertain state of a place between, though there's not much talk about purgatory these days. As for limbo, it appears to have been banished from Catholic eschatology. The Catholicism of my childhood seems more ornate, more otherworldly, than today's version. The Latin Mass has gone, and with it a whole concept of language. Latin may have been incomprehensible to the majority of Catholics, but it was universal. 'Introibo ad altare Dei. Ad Deum qui laetificat iuventútem meam.' It purported to express the mystery of liturgy, of eternal truths. Perhaps that's a more interesting idea than vernacular accessibility. As if language can describe things beyond language. Religion should need no prosy explanations.

Catholic prayer in the North becomes electrified at the switch of a candle-button in one poem as does British Army surveillance in another — the helicopters in BELFAST CONFETTI *use '30,000,000 candlepower gimbal-mounted Nitesun'*

searchlights. Gods and muses require more — and faster — flows of information?
The problem with information is that it needs to be processed. The more
information, the more you need interpreters. I'm not on the internet as
yet, but I gather that getting from one place to another on the web can be
pretty slow.

In 1975 you started working as Traditional Arts Officer with the Arts Council,
playing, recording and taping songs and stories throughout Ireland for the next
ten years before your second volume, THE IRISH FOR NO *(1986). What is the*
relationship between music and your poetry? You have talked of the '8 bar basic
unit of the reel' as a parallel for the long lines in this book. In THE TWELFTH
OF NEVER *you put the 'shamrockery' of popular ballads like 'Galway Bay'*
through a mincer.
There are no hierarchies in art. A traditional tune, well-played, should be
perceived with as much joy as a well-made poem. It's about a kind of
grace. It's the wit and humour of the old boy playing in a corner of the
bar, his fingers seeming hardly to move; but you are drawn to listen, and
you discover a beautifully understated elegance. Like a chef using simple
ingredients might give them a new spin and a gourmet meal appears. And
as I've said, maybe style can stand outside the work. Because sometimes
you don't have to be that stylish; the job will get done, the appetite satis-
fied. The style is a bonus, a pleasure, a gift.

In OPERA ET CETTERA *and* THE TWELFTH OF NEVER *style pushes couplets*
and sonnets to breaking point so that it looks as if you are deliberately making
life difficult for yourself. Rhyme chains style and syntax into Houdini contor-
tion-and-escape routines — the first rhyme making life difficult for the second
cuff link to be found to effect an escape.
Yes. Sometimes the strain shows, and maybe that's not good. But at the
same time the reader is meant to laugh, I think.

In THE IRISH FOR NO *(1987) there is surely a sharper engagement than in*
THE NEW ESTATE, *more narrative presence? The first lines of poems have a*
dramatic, anecdotal particularity, a narrative promise. You have acknowl-
edged a debt to C.K. Williams's long line — a poet you read in 1985 and
reviewed in 'Against Oblivion' (IRISH REVIEW, *1986).*
Well, the debt to Williams doesn't seem to me as great now as it did then.
At the same time, I don't think I could have written *The Irish for No* with-
out his voice. It certainly woke me up from some kind of poetic slumber.
I think I also acknowledged a debt to traditional music and storytelling,
which have immense particularity.

Both THE IRISH FOR NO *and* BELFAST CONFETTI *(1989) have three-part*

structures. Does structural similarity hide structural differences? Neil Corcoran's essay 'One Step Forward, Two Steps Back' in THE CHOSEN GROUND *suggests Proustian style memory triggers individual poems so there might be a kind of purl knitting from memory linking across volumes?*
In many ways any structure for a book is arbitrary. But at the same time, I like to structure the thing in some way. It gives you a template, a constraint. The alphabet, for example, is one such device I've played around with a lot. There's no real reason why the alphabet should be in just that sequence. But it is, and we file things accordingly.

What is the relationship between your work and Belfast? In BELFAST CONFETTI *(1989) and* THE STAR FACTORY *(1997) Belfast is 'my metropolis' and a 'universal city', a magic overnight-construct and time-layered, 'dense urban fabric'. Sometimes it's a changing map and 'labyrinth' as well as a 'prison ship' and 'an industrial Armada'. Are there writers who've captured cities — people like Murakami, for instance — who you particularly admire?*
I love the work of Haruki Murakami. *The Hard-boiled Wonderland and the End of the World,* for instance, is a great book. In a way it's very Irish in the way it presents an Otherworld, an alternative reality. The protagonists move in and out of that world through dream portals. I was fortunate to be invited to Tokyo a year or two ago, and I was amazed by that city, the way the antique and the traditional exist side by side with the hyper-new. You walk through a doorway from one into the other. Many of the poems in *The Twelfth of Never* are about that rapid transit system. Then again, I used to read a lot of semiology and urban space stuff. When I was younger I used to have dreams of being an architect. I still have recurrent dreams about Belfast in which the architectural spaces get shifted around and transformed. And of course there's Joyce, Calvino, Borges.

Reviewing Heaney's NORTH *(1975) in the* HONEST ULSTERMAN *(1975) you argued that 'No one really escapes from the massacre... by applying wrong notions of history' although you have acknowledged Heaney as the first northern poet who really worked the vernacular here. In what ways does* BELFAST CONFETTI *attempt to 'face into the massacre'? How do you write about or register the "Troubles" in the poems?*
I can't as a writer, take any kind of moral stance on the "Troubles", beyond registering what happens. And then, as soon as I say that, I realise that 'registering' is a kind of morality. Nor can one, even if one wanted to, escape politics. But my aim was, in that work which deals with the "Troubles", to act as a camera or a tape-recorder, and present things in a kind of edited surreality. An ear overhearing things in bars. Snatches of black Belfast humour. If there's one thing certain about what was or is going on, it's that you don't know the half of it. The official account is

only an account, and there are many others. Poetry offers yet another alternative. It asks questions, I think. It asks about the truth which is never black-and-white.

If 'Snow' in BELFAST CONFETTI *seems more silent and more brutal than MacNeice's 1930s prototype then 'Bagpipe Music' in* FIRST LANGUAGE *sounds more onomatopoeic than MacNeice's version. Perhaps both poems are in 'scorpion's inverted commas' — criticism and compliment. Edna Longley has suggested that MacNeice is a writer you relate to.*
Well, to tell you the truth, I haven't read that much MacNeice. And of the bits I have read, I sometimes suspect his ear.

You share sport as an interest with MacNeice.
Sport is a great model for writing. It can't exist without rules. You need the rules to create wit, skill, humour, irony, play. You play with the rules, and within the rules; sometimes even against the rules. You play your own game.

Your images seem to suggest art as revelation and concealment of itself, illusion: the Russian doll; the Chinese box; the Delft hen with the eggs inside; the zoetrope; synapse; the cup that fits its ring-stain; the typewriter ribbon followed by typex; the star as a narrative hole or link in an interconnecting constellation. It looks like a recurrent idea?
You can fool yourself into believing your own illusions, or your own inspiration. And that's no bad thing, since it makes for good art, or sport. It allows for rehearsed spontaneity. Practising a thing over and over 'til it becomes second nature. Then, when inspiration comes, you ask yourself where it came from, as if it weren't the result of all those hours kicking a ball against a wall.

FIRST LANGUAGE *(1993) looks at the relations between Irish and English. Irish has been imaged as a 'severed head' or a 'tongue' that may be 'lost' — 'governed' or 'in government'. Shakespearean doublets 'mangling Irish' in Belfast appear in* THE STAR FACTORY *but the 'Agincourt of arrows (that) overwhelmed me, shot by Milton, Keats and Shakespeare' in the final poem of* OPERA ET ETCETERA *leave you as 'a redskin, foraging behind the alphabetic frontier'. I'm, suggesting perhaps that you bring humour to the whole high seriousness of this debate?*
Well, too many people who write in Irish, for example, take themselves too seriously.

Dictionaries, encylopaedias, taxonomies, etymologies, books which run A to Z occur in the work. LETTERS FROM THE ALPHABET *(1995) might be read a kind of philosophical reflection on language itself as the exploded font of the*

streets in BELFAST CONFETTI *is re-ordered in alphabetical sequence. 'I' is nar-*
rator and letter; letters start talking to each other; 'Q' nearly always needs 'U'.
Is language a 'boomerang' back into its own deep system as much as a 'cata-
pult' into the world? Is this the sort of book structuralists go wild for?
Letters from the Alphabet lead me into some funny areas. It was a lot of fun,
and it was also strange, because of the constraint of having to make some-
thing up, or discover something, for each of the letters. It started off with
one letter, X, and then I did a few others. Eventually the alphabet led me
along, instead of me thinking to myself that I'd attempt it. So there was a
lot of serendipity about it. Looking for rhymes and scansions, I use the
appropriate dictionaries and thesauruses a lot. These books continually
remind one of one's ignorance of language. There are always words you
never come across till then. And almost always, the word that you have to
hunt for in a dictionary or thesaurus is the right word, the exact word; yet
you'd never used it until then. It makes me think there's some kind of hid-
den law within the language that makes you stumble on the right things.
You don't find the right word, it finds you.

The poem for the letter 'D' attaches you by 'velcro' to the 'Celtic Twilight Zone'
and Yeats's Byzantium. Do you see Yeats's enterprise as very different, more seri-
ously mythic and rhetorical than your own?
'D' is homage. It's also an earnest joke. Sometimes I find it difficult to take
Yeats seriously, but I have to acknowledge the Byzantine splendours of his
work. There are lots of other homages in the book, by the way. To Maigret,
for example, not to mention Holmes, Kant, Keats and others.

You also have those wonderful colour coinages for stamps, inks, pens, model
aircraft paint, fogs, breadvans, trolley buses, phones and lemonade bottles. A
great number of painters and photographers are in the work. Dutch painting
in general and Vermeer in particular are a focus in FISHING FOR AMBER.
How do you see the relationship between poetry and painting?
I liked the challenge of trying to describe painting, and what painting
does. Especially the mimetic kind of painting practised by Vermeer. I like
the idea of the master illusionist, and I wanted to try a few illusions myself,
to convince myself that I could enter a painting through words, and in
doing so, convince someone else as well. To make one thing look like a
thing, or be another thing. Isn't that what art's about?

Is narrative central to painting and writing? Take modern or abstract art
where the discernable shapes of a physical object or person disappears. Are you
saying that the only visual art you really respond to must have a narrative?
Well, it's easier to talk about narrative painting. Often, when people talk
about abstract art, the work itself is merely a jumping-off point for talking

about the artist's life. I'm thinking of Rothko here, where the paintings can be described as portals, and you can hang a great deal of religious symbolism or whatever on to them, and Rothko's despair, or his gloom, or his doom, and so on. Other people might just talk about the paint, and the colours, the rednesses, the blacknesses, that kind of thing. I believe some of the canvases are in a terrible condition, the paint's falling off them, because Rothko used bad paint. You'd never get Vermeer doing that.

FISHING FOR AMBER *also mentions Van Meegren who forged Vermeer. I'm reminded of Derek Mahon's Meegren whose forgery is hidden love, the ultimate compliment.*
Imitation is the sincerest form of flattery. It's true. And we often imitate without knowing we imitate. In fact, when you look at it, everything's imitation.

In OPERA ET CETTERA *you wrote a sequence of poems, a mirror image to* LETTERS FROM THE ALPHABET, *based on the radio operators code. What do you know about that? Is it important for these poems?*
Like most things in those poems, I learned them out of books. That's not to say that I know about them. Some people have used the word "erudite" in connection with my work. But I'm not erudite, I'm only pretending to be erudite. It's a cunning disguise, an illusion. I spend a lot of time in libraries in a magpie kind of way, and anything I learn is superficial, stuff stolen for the sake of a line in a poem or an interesting story. I don't *know* these things. I have no experience of them. If you asked me to speak for thirty minutes on any of the subjects covered in, say, *Fishing for Amber*, I'd be very hard put. Because most of that ostensible knowledge is theft. At the same time I'm amazed at the number of people — this includes many academics — who think they *know* something because they read it in a book.

Language may be a suspect, dodgy epistemology if its truth or knowledge we're after but you have re-worked traditional stories and written sonnet versions of Rimbaud, Mallarmé and Baudelaire in THE ALEXANDRINE PLAN *(1998), so you must surely believe that something from the Babel-babble of language can cross space and time? Walter Benjamin saw non-literal translations as capable of 'pure language', grasping some knowledge or truth or intention that lay behind language. If language itself is so objectively bankrupt why make available the voices of those three French nineteenth century poets now?*
Language may be dodgy but we need it to talk with. Life is dodgy. Matter itself, things, if we are to believe the quantum physicists, is very dodgy indeed. The funny thing is that I think the essences of things can cross space and time, maybe because of that very dodginess. As if the matter of the poems were in the ether, swirling around invisibly for the last century or so. So I loved the enterprise of doing Mallarmé and Rimbaud and

Baudelaire into English, or Hiberno-English. On the way, it struck me that their negotiations with the idea of a republic, with freedom, whether it be of language or of morals, with drugs, were directly related to ourselves, now. So I thought of these very French poets as being very Irish, and tried to make myself into something very French. I hope it was a fair exchange.

The "Troubles" brought junctures, the exchange between politics and poetry into focus. One of the Latin-tag poems in OPERA ET CETERA *(1996), 'Jacta Est Alea', finds you in 'The Half-Way House' split by the border and then wading 'Siamese-like... into the Rubicon'. 'X Ray' looks ambivalently at Irish history's repeated battles as seen from the stars. Is there a juncture between poetry and politics for you?*
I feel I'm in the Rubicon. Maybe we all are. It's a big river, and sometimes the other bank seems very far away. Politically, I'm like a lot of people who would like to live in a liberal, allowable state which so far hasn't happened here. A state which allows you to be yourself.

Do you see that liberal state in evidence in FISHING FOR AMBER *(1999) in the Dutch Republic of the seventeenth century? Is there something there that both sides in Ireland might take on board, a new orange republic?*
The Dutch Republic in the seventeenth century seems to be a model of what is possible. A state overseen by the House of Orange. It seems that in the Dutch Republic of that time you could say what you wanted, within reason, as long as you did your job. If people here want to be Orangemen, then look to that as your model. Civic pride and responsibility. A willingness to explore the universe through commerce, art, science. An examination of the physical world, which brought into focus the beauty of the particulars of that world. A humility in front of things. A freedom to be many things, because of that humility and reverence for the bounty of nature, and its humanly created counterparts. If Northern Ireland — if Ireland — could aspire to a tenth of that! Culture? The word is much abused here. Was it Goebbels who said, 'When I hear the word "culture", I reach for my gun'? And as for guns, like a lot of people, I say, 'Well, if I was in the IRA, I'd make a token gesture of decommissioning, give them eight guns, whatever.' Then someone turns to me and says, 'That's the reason you're not in the IRA. They wouldn't let you in.'

TOM PAULIN

You were born in Leeds in 1949 and moved to Belfast when you were four. In VIEWPOINTS: POETS IN CONVERSATION *by John Haffenden (1981) you describe your mother as 'an Ulster-Scot' from a 'very strenuous and Victorian' family and your father, a teacher from Tyneside, as 'a great liberal'. The poem 'Seaside House' recalls books and 'parental strangeness'. How would you describe your family background?*

My mother's parents moved from Glasgow to Belfast in 1912 and my grandfather, whom I never knew — he died in the 1930s, managed the Iceworks which is now a car park off Great Victoria Street. My grandparents sent their son and daughters to Queen's University and so my mother studied medicine there and then went to work in London during the Blitz. She met my father in Belfast — he was in the army, stationed at Ballykinlar — when she came back to the North of Ireland and they married in 1944. My father was a teacher. He had been in the war and he liked Ireland. If you wanted a headship in those days there were opportunities in the North of Ireland and, like many of his contemporaries — the Head of Methodist College and Belfast Inst., who had been British Army officers in the war he got a job and came to Belfast in 1953. I grew up in a household with books and without television. My parents read; they were members of the Linen Hall Library; they subscribed to the *New Statesman* and they talked about politics and ideas.

There is Philip Larkin's childhood formation in an essentially 'English culture' of 'bows and arrows...cricket bats and oak trees' in MINOTAUR *(1992) but a poem like 'Kinship Ties' in* WALKING A LINE *(with its Latin-English and Celtic typography) suggests a more complex, hybrid cultural formation. In* THE WIND DOG *which 'carbon dates' your childhood one hears your mother's voice talking about a 'modrun nuvel'. How would you describe the cultural apparatus of your own childhood in Belfast?*

I've often a curse of a memory for what happened yesterday but I do remember some things from long ago. December 1953. I'm four years of age. We're on the Heysham boat coming down Belfast Lough and it's pitch dark. I can see the yellow street lights of this strange city they call Belfast and I'm thinking about the name of the place and seeing it as one of those great buoys bobbing on the water. I think, too, there was a picture of a ship that had been cut in half by another ship in a newspaper down in the panelled cabin. And then there's the strange smell of hay and horse dung on the docks. In Belfast you grew up on comics. *The Topper* serialised Robert Louis Stevenson on the back pages and there were boys' adventure stories by Rider Haggard or books — tales by W. A. Henty — that sort of thing. Hopalong Cassidy and the Lone Ranger were hip in the '50s. My parents got a TV in order to watch *That Was the Week That Was*. My mother talking in an Ulster Scots accent of the 'modrun nuvel' in *The Wind Dog*? It's simply that there's never one seamless way of talking and that there are microclimates of pronounciation in any locality; I remember, for instance, a girl at primary school saying 'tar' as 'tarr' and, coming to Belfast from Leeds, I was conscious that my Yorkshire accent was different from the way the kids I played with spoke around North Parade. I do remember being stopped in the streets by one of the kids and asked whether I was a Protestant or Catholic and so, early on, you were aware of questions about identity which I don't really give a shite about now.

Introducing THE FABER BOOK OF VERNACULAR VERSE *(1990) you recall the impact of reading* HUCKLEBERRY FINN *at primary school in the '50s and there's your '60s secondary schooling and the south Belfast geography in many poems. Did school include or exclude the history, language or 'speak' that lay around you in Belfast?*
I went to Rosetta Primary School off the Ormeau Road in the '50s and then on to Annadale Grammar School in the '60s. Annadale has now merged with Carolan to become Wellington College; then it was one of the new state Grammar Schools which came into existence as a result of the Butler Education Act which the Unionist government, as we all know, held back for three years in the North of Ireland. The school was built from scrap aluminium and hardboard left over from the war, from Harland and Wolff, and its four houses were named after the four Ulster Field Marshals: Dill, Allenbrooke, Alexander and Montgomery. At the time you weren't really aware that this existed in parallel with another heritage where Catholics went to other schools and you were friendly with them and you played together in the streets outside of school. When I was fourteen we moved across to the Malone Road. Those were happy times. As an adolescent you really don't know much about where or what you are so I can't say I was aware of much difference in the spoken register between school and way you spoke in the streets then.

Other northern poets — John Hewitt, MacNeice, Roy McFadden and Robert Greacen — encountered Socialism and the left in Ulster in the '30s or '40s at school or university. Did you come across this? Does Socialism matter to you as a writer?

When I was fifteen I was a member of the Socialist Labour League. There was a group of us in a Trotskyite cell — a philosophy student from Queen's, a worker from Harland and Wolff, someone from Shorts and myself. We met on Fridays and Saturdays in a room off Donegal Pass and we went off up the Falls and Turf Lodge and the Shankill to sell the newspaper called the *Newsletter*. I read Deutscher's big three volume biography of Trotsky when I was sixteen. I read Marx and Engels and I remember going to a young Socialist conference in Morecambe at that time. We sold the socialist *Newsletter* in pubs on the New Lodge Road which were like impoverished sheebeens from the wild west with ancient stoves in the corners and bare floorboards. Sometimes you'd get attacked or people would get angry. Our activity came out of an analysis that there was something wrong with the society we lived in but, like many people on the left and many in the Civil Rights campaign for whom it was not an issue, we didn't take on board Nationalism because we thought that the state was reformable from within. I'd been thrown into a politics and I was trying to make sense of the experience and so, as I've continued to do for most of my adult life, I looked to literature. I read Conrad's *Under Western Eyes*, which is his great novel; I read Greek tragedy later on; earlier, Dostoevsky's *Crime and Punishment* which — when you're an adolescent — is a big experience. I was trying to get a purchase on my experience. I'm conscious of the danger that, through sheer historical accident you have access to a kind of privileged knowledge but I'm also conscious, reading many English or British contemporaries around the same age as myself, that they simply don't have a clue about politics. In Michael Frayn's play *Copenhagen*, for instance, he simply does not understand politics. When you get a politics outside democracy then it's a tragic politics and you have to chose one position or the other. I'd rather not know that and I'm nervous of talking about it.

You're saying though that the choice between left and right was superceded by an unavoidable choice between Unionism and Republicanism and you chose the latter?
Yes. I chose Republicanism. I don't and never did support violence but it did come down to having to chose. Now traditional Irish Nationalism is having to take on board a British identity and history — to which I've all kinds of fealties — that is represented by Unionism while Unionism is obviously having to re-invent itself.

In '50s Ulster two poet's analysis of the rot were available — John Hewitt's image of complacent, middle class 'coasting' in the suburbs and Montague's image of 'poisoned lands'. There was also pop art, pop music, sex and Lawrentian court cases about 'the weight of a man's balls' in the London '60s although Mahon's point about the North is that if two 'coat hangers' knocked together in a wardrobe then that was a ' great event'? Were you aware of these images then?

Although I spent a lot of my spare time on Donegal holidays in the '60s — and I've visited there on and off for more than forty years — my experience then was largely of urban Belfast. At the 'O' level stage you took part in the school debating society and came up against powerful speakers like Frances Tomelty, who came over from the Convent School in Finaghy and Michael Farrell spoke powerfully at the debating society at Queen's. I read writers like Graham Greene and Orwell and I studied Synge for 'A' Levels but, most of all, it was Joyce who was fundamental to both me and my mates. I was also reading Rimbaud and Verlaine and Baudelaire; I listened to the Stones or the Beatles who visited Belfast in 1964. My adolescence had nothing to do with anything rural. I remember Eamonn McCann, the Derry Socialist, getting kicked out of Queen's University and taking a libel case against Philip Hobsbaum over the publication of his poem in *The New Statesman*. One knew about Hobsbaum's Group at Queen's. My teacher at school, Carroll Spence, had been to Trinity with Michael Longley and Derek Mahon and I remember him giving us an early cyclostyled Mahon poem, 'Spring', with its line about 'the insubstantial co-inhabitants of my bed'. 'Sir', said one class mate, 'He's talking about dreams'. The point is you had access to the poets who published poems in the '60s and there was that glorious, historic moment when Heaney published *Death of a Naturalist* (1966). I link that volume with the Divis Street Riots. I remember feeling sympathy for the rioters; it was the summer, after 'A' level exams, that I went with school mates to work in Guernsey and on the camp site we met three guys from the Falls Road and Seamus, from Turf Lodge, showed me his lumpy elbow — he'd a big silver bolt put through his elbow. He'd flung a grating in the riots and the police had pinned his arm behind his back and broken it at the elbow. At night these guys would play guitar and sing traditional songs — ' I wish , I wish I were a maid again...' — and after listening to the songs one night in the tent I asked my school mates if they'd seen Seamus's arm. I remember being greeted with absolute silence. You realised they were all Unionists and that even though you identified with the Northern Ireland Labour Party — you had Unionist sympathies too — you came to see that you could only cross the sectarian divide away from the place — smoking dope and chasin' wimmen.

In 1967 you left Belfast to study English at Hull University and these new English co-ordinates seem to register in some poems. Did Philip Larkin and the Douglas Dunn of TERRY STREET *influence your first volume* A STATE OF JUSTICE *(1977)? In the poem 'A New Society', set amidst bulldozed terraces, you too wish someone 'grass'.*

When I arrived in England I was amazed at the sheer confidence people seemed to have. Douglas Dunn is an old friend; I owe everything to him; he was a year ahead of me at Hull. We met when I started to scribble at poetry and he was encouraging; *Terry Street* came out in my second year as an undergraduate at Hull and it's a classic. Look at the last line in 'A Removal from Terry Street': 'That man. I wish him well. I wish him grass.' It's a lovely line, beautifully spoken iambic pentameter, and I'm interested in that kind of Puritan plain style which comes right down from Defoe where you hear the spoken immediacy. In Larkin you have also got that but there's also a Yeatsian lift-off in the language, a waiting for the big moment. In Larkin you have the psychopathology of traditional English males of that generation — men who are now in their seventies or eighties — a kind of bunkered mentality induced by historical circumstances like the war and imperial decline. You read Larkin and find there's also a lot of Emily Dickinson and Christina Rossetti and a great deal of anguish in the poems.

In your THOMAS HARDY: THE POETRY OF PERCEPTION *(1975) he emerges from struggles with agnoticism, provincialism and the historically determined to write powerful, spontaneous poetry — full of oral textures and eidetic images. Hardy surely proved particularly attractive in that these concerns were still very much alive in Ulster? Surely his sensibility, that sense of lyric absence, tracks a poem like your 'Fin de Siècle' with its 'dead... webbing through the afternoon' and the pond mirroring 'a culture(which) sends/ A hopeless man to love a drifting girl'?*

I'd read some of Hardy's poems in Hull and then came to Oxford to do research on Hardy because I felt that most critics had written about the novels but neglected the poems and so I read his *Collected Poems* in my first term there. I'd also come to Hardy via Robert Frost who I had read on sentence sound as a teenager and my English teacher, Eric Brown, in Annadale had a record of Frost reading 'After Apple Picking' which he'd played to us. Frost and Edward Thomas were really important for me and I have a student who is working on Frost's influence on northern poets. Frost's absolutely crucial and there's something about his speaking voice that links in with Hardy. Recently I was re-reading Hardy's 'The Shadow on the Stone' with secondary school kids; he uses 'discover' in the second stanza and, because of the rhyme pattern in the other stanzas, you expect a rhyme on this line until you realise that it's not there but it might have been 'lover' because the poem is about the ghost of his dead wife. There are hard rhymes on 'track' and soft rhymes on 'grief' and 'leaf': Hardy had a very delicate ear; he knew a great number of traditional songs and, maybe because his father was a fiddler, I sometimes think I can hear fiddles playing reels behind the poems. I was twenty one when I started work on Hardy as a research student — it took two years and when I got a job lecturing in Nottingham I re-wrote the thesis as a book in my first couple of years there.

Some critics have seen poetry from the North of Ireland as essentially lyrical, a re-write of the Georgian or Hardyesque lyric of place. Does this idea wash with you?
I really have to go back to Frost and Edward Thomas — poets I read early and whose work I love deeply. I read a little bit of Yeats at secondary school but I couldn't make head nor tail of his 'Long Legged Fly' so I came back later to Yeats as an undergraduate. Critics now have very mixed views of Georgian poetry and there are all those poets with rural names — Brooke and Marsh and Masefield — but Frost, who is sometimes linked with the Georgians, is really much bigger. There's the irony of a poem like 'A Written Answer' but that's really a guilt poem. At that time English journalists would ask you about the North of Ireland and they'd talk about war poets; you would try to answer but you were also aware of your safe position tucked away in England.

Concrete, clocks and 'permafrost'; the poet travelling through a world of coded radio signals or becoming a dead voice ('Firelight'). Your first volume sparks a chain of associations with the 'hyberborean north' (Finland, Russia, Belfast, Iceland) which starkly contrasts with India and the warmer south. Is there a north-south border to be crossed in your work?
It's certainly one of the big themes in many writers' work. There a fascinating essay by Robert Lowell on Elizabeth Bishop's view of it and it's in her work. Ruskin too wrote on the nature of the Gothic — he has a big panoramic view of it, moving through Europe — north to south; Auden does it in his later work where there's the moral north of Byron, a beer and potato culture, and a warmer south of wine and opera. I suppose Yeats started all those binary opposites as an antithethical way of thinking about cultures this century and there's Bishop's poem about the lighthouse which begins with all those wonderful Catholic baroque images and then becomes Prod naif. Gaskell's *North and South*? So many have written so seriously on the matter that I'm not sure if there's much more to add.

In THE STRANGE MUSEUM *(1980) there are many genres ('maritime pastoral... light verse... limericks') but there's little history — the North is 'without' or 'before' history — and the cultural void in the 'deadlands of the mullahs' is being exposed in a 'dull' hard light. To what extent did the crisis in the Ulster in the 1970s and the intense media saturation documenting violence and breakdown produce a crisis in poetry? Heaney, and Muldoon seem conscious of walking a line between poetry as public utterance (imaged as poetic exploitation or political responsibility) or as private craft (imaged as 'ostrich in the sand' ignorance or an 'eddy of semantic scruple'/ a concern for shape and form). In what way did you as a poet deal with this crisis in the poems?*
I'm not sure how my poetry works as a concept in relation to this. People write as they feel impelled — I know that's a truism. At a certain point I

stopped using punctuation. I was looking at a review in Desmond Greaves's Socialist newspaper of *The Liberty Tree* and the reviewer was talking about how my poems resembled traditional stanzas but had lower case initial letters and I thought — to hell with it — I'll get rid of the whole apparatus of the poem.

In poems the Bible seems to act as both a launching pad for the spirit and as a source of 'sour' or 'parched' 'Desertmartin' certainties. In Minotaur *there's detailed Biblical know how and your essay on Conor Cruise O'Brien suggests there is a Catholic and Protestant style? In what way did Protestantism shape your own imagination and style?*
I guess that there are two different sensibilities. Writers like Joyce and Hopkins share a fascination with language and pattern which is central to the Catholic imagination. Protestant writers like Bunyan often face the problem of being brought up in a religion which suspects the imagination and so they construct an aesthethic that's an anti-aesthetic to get over the problem. Certain Protestant writers seem to carry the guilt that they should be doing something doctrinal or useful which makes writing problematic, although writers like Heaney have also talked about having to overcome this in a Catholic background. I'm fascinated by Conor Cruise O'Brien's first book *Maria Cross* and its application of Catholicism to writing. Perhaps I've overrated this book, but in his later work he became febrile and emotional. In Joseph Conrad's imagination, shaped by Polish Catholicism, there's a concept of community and solidarity — you are not simply an autonomous individual. The curse of the Protestant sensibility, which Larkin writes interestingly about, is that bunkered, blocked sense of being an autonomous individual. Recently I had to visit the Millennium Dome and I remembered Blake's view of St. Pauls as representing Adam Smith's eighteenth century economics and the age of reason, inside of which you are simply a random social atom, and you have Blake's deep identification with English Gothic. Perhaps the dome, which is a big circus tent, also represents this. When I spent a year in the United States I thought of it as a deeply Calvinist culture. When you were awake you could almost hear the constant hum coming off the hammer on the anvil — you know that image in the Preface to the Authorized King James Bible — the image of the anvil presbyters. And it's going on the whole time, even when you are asleep, that work ethic pushed to the limits. I do think it is a kind of curse in the consciousness.

Perhaps your first two volumes operate mainly in ironic and satiric modes around that consciousness? In 'In the Meat Safe' (with its cheap 'utility furniture' and 'Exchange and Mart' objects) and in 'Still Century' (where 'hard captains' of 'linen mills and black tabernacles' make us 'the stuff/That visions, cutlery and Belleek/ China are laid on') Belfast surely merits the satiric mode of Ben Jonson rather than textured narrative whirly-ma-gig of Ciaran Carson? Perhaps. Certainly I'm interested in dead ends, cul de sacs and painting yourself into a corner — you know Barthes' essay 'Writing Degree Zero'. There's not always a conscious volition in writing, though, and you usually just follow your nose.

You were a founder-member and director of Field Day in the early 1980s and you published a pamphlet on the language question advocating a new diction-ary as a "home" for Hiberno-English and Ulster Scots. Field Day Theatre Company first performed THE RIOT ACT *in 1984. There is Edna Longley's critique though in* POETRY IN THE WARS: *Irish writing post-Yeats can 'coarsen' into propaganda if it too readily accepts inherited political ideologies or sees language as politically determined rather than imaginatively shaped? Political ideology can block creativity.*

I suppose that this can happen. The pamphlet I did on the language ques-tion, though, was simply an attempt to rectify the absence of a home for Irish-English. It struck me as extraordinary at that time that there were dictionaries for Newfoundland English, Trinidadian English, Canadian English and Australian English but there was nothing in existence for Irish-English. That seemed odd. I got the idea from reading a book by Ian Adamson — there was a chapter on the language of Ulster so I was really following a civic argument for the institutionalization of a language that you hear in Ireland where you are constantly hearing unexpected words that are outside the standard. There are now dictionaries of Ulster Scots and Irish-English and I was delighted to contribute a Preface to one of these in 1999 because dictionaries are important things.

Surely there is also the danger of relegating the language to something "couthy" and enforcing a "proud of our wee Ulster" mentality?

Yes, but what strikes me is the great 'whap' of the language. You read nine-teenth century American fiction and American poetry; you read Whitman and Dickinson, you read Melville and Twain and you think — my God what must that language have been like to use for the first time in print. I've been re-reading *Huckleberry Finn* recently and you find words like 'galoot' and Irish-English words lying about in the novel. You are really thinking about how this vernacular energy can be released — that's all; it can be provincial but it's also oceanic.

LIBERTY TREE *and Paul Muldoon's* QUOOF *were both published in 1983. Surely these volumes move in totally different directions: Muldoon's is implo-sive, following the crypto-currents of language whereas* LIBERTY TREE *is pub-lic, projecting outwards into the world of politics?*

Quoof is fascinating and the title poem plays wonderfully with the language of the family, the community, the province and then the monstrous public language which lies beyond these — to put the family word into print, outside the family and in the public domain, there had to be terrible things happening in the public domain.

In LIBERTY TREE *(1983) the United Irishmen and radical Ulster Presbyterianism are retrieved as evidence of a more expansive, radical Republican vision of Irish unity lost by twentieth-century Ulster Unionism and 'buried' in Belfast's Linen Hall Library. Can there be a "national" political solution in Ulster (un-doing Imperialism) though before a regional solution without a repetition of double-colonisation on either side? In rejecting the worst features of Nationalism and Imperialism in England and proposing a multi-cultural democracy with regional and vernacular energy, in* IRELAND AND THE ENGLISH CRISIS, *you have surely got to attack Irish Nationalism's centralising tendencies — its violence and amnesia. If Unionist schools forgot the United Irishmen so too did the Republicans who fire-bombed the Linen Hall Library in Belfast in the mid-80s?*

Of course Irish Nationalism needs to be deconstructed as well as Unionism, but you start with what you know about first, you criticise cultures from within themselves. I'd a wonderful teacher at secondary school, Victor Kelly, who taught us about the United Irishmen and so I took my own thing apart first. If you looked at England in the nineteen eighties that was also what was happening with the rise of critical theory; there was a specific English identity crisis within the intellegentsia in which the canon of English literature — which is almost all I've got — went through a nervous breakdown of deconstruction. It was a bloody awful experience in which I had many rows with academics because I did not see the canon as a terrible, fixed hegemony of texts oppressing the population — a series of Stormonts to be overcome — and for years I'd been trying to look at relatively neglected writers like Clare or Christina Rossetti or Hardy the poet with the aim of calling more attention to them. Certainly Nationalism does have to be deconstructed; I tried to do that in a particularly heavy-metal essay on Yeats and Nationalism using a Walter Benjamin' production-history of the text approach to look at Yeats's 'Easter 1916' but I had students walk out of that lecture accusing me of political bias or of being boring, I don't know which.

I have difficulty though with Yeats and Joyce as cultural Nationalists. Surely they too largely deconstructed Nationalism?

Yeats, of course, can have it both ways but at the end of 'Easter 1916' — 'was it needless love after all?' — it's like a mother talking about a child and what comes through is a deep vatic Nationalism, atavism; of course there is also the 'stone in the midst of all' and he wants to have it every way. Joyce took Nationalism apart and yet there is also the sense that he was the great international Republican.

In the Haffenden conversation there's your shared sense of 'community' with Frank Ormsby's POETS FROM THE NORTH OF IRELAND *and there's a melt-down of many Ulster poets in* THE WIND DOG. *Louis MacNeice is directly invoked in 'Thinking of Iceland' (A* STATE OF JUSTICE*) although 'Song for February' in the same volume suggests a colder more contracted world than MacNeice's 'Snow' with the poet behind double-glazing watching 'dead headed roses waste over the pocked snow'. MacNeice too left Belfast for Oxford and he's also a documentary poet full of brand names and products like your 'snowcem' and 'velux windows'.*

I do identify with MacNeice. I remember vividly MacNeice's death being announced on the radio when I was at school and I read the *Collected Poems* in the early '70s. I have a great admiration for the poems and there is an attractive displacement in them which I can relate to. Although MacNeice came out of the North there's also his Anglo-Irish background — his father was a bishop who came up from the South — and I see him as a free spirit, critical of both Unionism and Nationalism. The Ulster '60s poets were also crucial when I was growing up there and I got their books as soon as they came out. I remember reading Derek Mahon's 'Disused Shed' when it came out and Seamus Heaney's 'Casualty' was being quoted in Vancouver at a conference shortly after it came out. *The Wind Dog* is a patchwork or cento. MacNeice published a novel under the pseudonym of Louis Malone and that haunted me; my grandmother lived off the Malone Road in Belfast — in Deramore Park — which I altered to Drive in the poem to alliterate — and so you have that world of sagging tennis nets and Victorian red-brick houses where one of the kids I played with had a governess like MacNeice. I believe that the Bishop's house on Malone Road became Aquinas Hall. Just as many of Betjeman's *Collected Poems* are tributes to Hardy, full of gentle irony and tenderness and a con-servationist's heritage — so you develop your own wee religion, your own cargo cult of what is important for your imagination and that often keeps you in touch with dead writers like MacNeice. I guess that for me he was a prophet figure.

LIBERTY TREE *(1983) rejects Heaney and Hewitt's Antrim weavers as ances-tors — 'I can't come from that' — and — 'mid-Mahon with a tang/of Manhatten' in* FIVEMILETOWN *has an ambivalent feel?*
No, that's a Unionist civil servant talking.

As well as claiming kin with other poets writers often seem drawn to specific objects or landscapes; there are all those temporary makeshift buildings and metallic materials you seem drawn to in WALKING A LINE. *'Cheap tin trays/that's the music speaks me' you say in one poem.*

I've a long-standing fascination with Nissen huts and I remember as a kid being drawn to one in the Botanic Gardens in Belfast, near the Ormeau Bridge, which is long gone and it took me ages to write the poem about that. I'm fascinated by warehouses and I've read Heidegger on buildings and perhaps that takes you into an ontological sense of dwelling in the world. I'm interested too in modern materials — the oil stains in Emily Dickinson and Frost talks about the minerals that are in his car. I am interested in architecture — although I've this awful notion that architects have authoritarian personalities — but I've only scraps of knowledge about it so maybe there is a classic book somewhere on the idea of architecture. At the moment I'm fascinated by bad taste and I've tried to give a lecture recently on bad taste. I wish critics like Susan Sontag would cover it — it is a missing critical term. I was in Moscow recently with Frank Ormsby, Nuala Ní Dhomhnaill, Paul Muldoon and Thomas MacCarthy and we went to Lenin's tomb: that's the epitome of bad taste, the absolute peak of it.

Your poems too — like one Heaney essay in PREOCCUPATIONS — *dissect popular iconographic symbolism in Ulster visually and seem to register Protestantism's flags, bunting, gable-end murals, banners and male, masonic images and there's a sense of Catholic kitsch in the temple on top of Croagh Patrick. Is there a profound difference between Catholic and Protestant images and kitsch in Ulster?*

I'm not sure that I've thought about this as deeply as you suggest although it is an interesting subject with its own aridity. I think I became particularly interested in the masons when I was in the United States for a year where you often come across masonic temples and people like Jefferson and Washington were masons and there are all those masonic symbols on gravestones there. I started to read quite a bit about freemasonry — books like Margaret Jacob's *The Radical Enlightenment* — and I've spotted its symbols at times in art — in Poussin's painting — or come across masonic symbols like the open book or Blake's compass image in 'Urizen'.

A STATE OF JUSTICE *journeys to England — 'Exile in the sticks' — while* FIVEMILETOWN *makes a return journey to Fermanagh where you are ' a gaberdine stranger... so near and far from home'. 'An Ulster-Unionist in Kentish Town' is 'half-foreign' in one poem and in another the only Catholic Ulsterman to win the V.C. in the war is unrewarded in Belfast and called a 'Paddy' in England. Is there such a theme as exile in contemporary Irish poetry? Does a shift in location — poems with binocular visions of Ireland written from England — produce different kinds of poems?*

It comes down to personal experience and in my own experience 'exile' is probably too grandiose a term. In the '60s, after 'A' levels, we hitched around Europe and then, like some schoolfriends, I chose to go to university in England although Hull — my first choice — was everyone else's sixth choice. In 1972, after finishing at Oxford, I applied for jobs in Belfast (at Queen's University) and at the Education Department in Coleraine which I didn't get and so — my God! — I ended up stuck as a lecturer in Nottingham for twenty two years. *Fivemiletown* came out of that perspective; I was stuck in the Midlands before I came back to Oxford. Luckily enough these days young lecturers have mentors who tell you to get out after a couple of years, to move on. I think Ireland, generally, still has a view that you come from one place. I was reading a piece by John Montague in *The New Yorker* about a terrible murder case in Co. Cork and it ends with a local getting angry with him, telling him 'You're only a blow-in'. In England people also now tend to come from more than one place or country so you end up with people speaking many languages within a mono-lingual culture. My wife is Indian and she grew up in Ireland and as part of an extended family we have Indian relatives with Irish accents and relatives in India so you move between two — three — countries.

In THE RIOT ACT *(1985) and* SEIZE THE FIRE *(1990) you re-work two Greek dramatists, Sophocles and Aeschylus. Do these two Greek dramatists offer very different perspectives on contemporary events and power structures in the '80s and '90s.*
I first came across a modern Greek film version of *Antigone* in the News and Cartoon cinema in the centre of Belfast way back in the '60s when I was at school. When I studied Hardy I became fascinated by Donald Davie's reference to *Antigone* in *Thomas Hardy and British Poetry* where he mentions the play in relation to Conor Cruise O'Brien's *States of Ireland* which I had not read at the time. And so I read *Antigone* and A.C. Bradley's great essay on Hegel and Greek tragedy and then in the '80s we decided at Field Day that I should do a version of the play which I wrote in three months when I was teaching at the University of Virginia. *The Riot Act* is definitely connected with the North of Ireland as is *Seize the Fire*, which was commissioned later for an Open University course. I suppose, at some level, I'm kicking around the notion of a looney Prod individualism, although a friend of mine groaned at a quote from Luther in it.

MINOTAUR *(1992), Seamus Heaney's* GOVERNMENT OF THE TONGUE *(1988), and Seamus Deane's* STRANGE COUNTRY *(1997) — three critical volumes by Irish poets from the North look at the poet's allegiance to inherited individual conscience, to fellow poets and to nation state(s). Do you each place different emphasis on these three factors? One might suggest that for Heaney both Yeats and Joyce were primarily conduits to Kavanagh (the regional in dia-*

logue with the international via an entente cordial between Irish and English literary traditions) whereas for Seamus Deane and yourself the regional is a cul de sac, subject to sharper political divisions between Ireland and England?
I have a great love, a great reverence for Kavanagh and 'Kerr's Ass' is a wonderful poem and Raglan Road is a great song. These are different critical books but I would say that Heaney and Deane's way of writing about national cultures would have influenced me.

Cuchulainn is associated with Ian Paisley and his Third Force (in 'The Red Handshake') and you link him with both Yeats and Ted Hughes in Minotaur. *Will Cuchulainn and the sense of myth be killed of in the 21st century?*
I have no interest in Cuchulainn; my myths don't go back that far. The Reformation is really where I begin.

Your view of T.S. Eliot in the 1980s (as an inclusive Anglican seeking the moment of epiphany 'in a draughty church') contrasts with the pulpit-bashing evangelicalism of Paisleyism but it also seems to have undergone revision to take account of his disfiguring anti-semitism. Bad faith though can surely also make great art — it could be argued that Eliot made possible important ways of writing which were assimilated by Irish poets like yourself, John Montague and Seamus Deane?
I encountered Eliot when I was at school; I've been reading him for most of my life and I've a great admiration for his work. The 'Four Quartets' I used to admire as the last great religious poem written in England but I'm losing that and I now suspect this really ends with Hopkins's 'The Wreck of the Deutschland'. Donald Davie's essay on 'The Dry Salvages' is very severe but there's some point in what he's saying. I'm aware that the big influence on Eliot is Keynes's *The Economic Consequences of the Peace* and that's a different Eliot. Keynes is a great humane genius who prophesied the Second World War just after the First and that's in *The Waste Land.* Eliot has a Doestoevskian sensibility; there's his risk taking but there's also the immersing of yourself in the gutter and a huge self-disgust and self-hatred and his rejection of Unitarianism which he projected on to the Jews and there's his absurd wish to be taken as English. I vividly remember reading Anthony Julius's book on Eliot's anti-semitism and being totally absorbed with the realization that you had been in collusion with the notion of Eliot as a great poet who is central in the canon. People avoided reviewing the book but I wanted to review it and when no one really noticed I wrote another piece to stir things up. There's a problem specifically in England with over-reverence for writers as part of a great heritage. Jane Austen and the slave trade? Mention that and people get angry and attack Edward Said. Larkin and racism? If you mention that you can't appreciate his poetry. And there's Eliot and anti-semitism? Certain

embedded forms of cultural esteem for images of writers like Betjeman in bed with his teddy bear mean that talking, for instance, about Shakespeare as a Catholic does not fit with the kinds of ratification of Shakespeare expected by the culture. There's the alternative Puritan disdain for or deconstruction of high art as a kind of antique. In Ireland there's probably a more healthy argumentativeness; people can admire Yeats but they're not frightened to fling a punch at him — it's not an either/or thing to admire and criticize writers.

Eliot read Hazlitt's *Lectures on English Poets* around 1910 — his essay on Dryden and Pope — and he takes one quote and dismisses him but, before this essay there's another essay on Milton and Shakespeare; Hazlitt says Milton is a writer of centos but second only to Homer in originality. Hazlitt puts the epic form and the cento together and maybe it's not entirely fanciful to see that as the seed of *The Waste Land*. Eliot too, like Hazlitt's father, comes out of Unitarian culture. The collage, the cento, the Schwitters-like techniques are central in Eliot but you can go back and find these techniques in Hazlitt's critical essays where he uses patchworks of quotations.

Painting is a recurrent parallel for poetry in MINOTAUR *(Frost/Cezanne; D.H. Lawrence/Gaugin; the Polish poet Rosewicz/ Richard Hamilton and Pop Art; Elizabeth Bishop/ primitive painting; Zbigniew Herbert/ anonymous Old Masters). Do you feel that the relationship between poetry and painting has changed? One might suggest that in Ireland poetry leaned increasing on painting rather than vice-versa in the twentieth century? Are there Irish painters you admire?*
I get worried about writing poems about paintings and maybe it's a phase but it's writing about something I cannot reach, or do, so perhaps its a kind of myth of Sisyphus. And maybe that myth is a variation on the kind of thing that attracted Hazlitt to Titian when he notices that Titian's signature — *Titianus faciebat* — on the paintings implies that they are incomplete or imperfect. Certainly Hazlitt was both a painter and the first great art critic writing in English.

I'm tediously obsessed with painters like Jackson Pollock where painting is a very physical act, a process of work; he was from a Scots-Irish background and he's a real head-banging, Calvinist painter. In Ireland I've admired work by Jack B. Yeats and James Dixon, the primitive painter from Tory Island, and I admire Felim Egan's work. Annadale Grammar School produced a whole series of good painters — Ken Jamieson who taught there before I arrived went on to become head of the Arts Council in the North — and there were two very gifted painters who were teachers in the art department when I was there, David Crone and Richard Croft. I was no good at painting at school but we'd meet at lunch times in a store between classrooms in the art department to smoke and talk about art. I guess I had visual art around me and friends who were visual artists. There's that wee throw-away poem in *Walking a Line* recalling those days before we left for London for the first time in the summer of 1966: *'Painting's the most primitive of all the arts/* Was it Moore Kenny said that/or Davey Jamieson?'. My mother paints water-colours and my granny too painted.

Tom Moore's IRISH MELODIES *come off a poor second to the vernacular vigour and smack of the streets in David Hammond's Belfast songs in your critical writing and you set up an invigoratingly fricative racket in* WALKING A LINE. *Does the sound of your poetry come from within a written or oral tradition as opposed to a musical tradition?*
I'm not musical and I'm fairly ignorant about music apart from listening to the odd piece of classical music on the radio when I'm washing the dishes. I liked listening to blues music and Bob Dylan and Woody Guthrie when I was young and I've read a biography of Shostakovitch and I do like his music. I don't think though there is a carry-over from a musical tradition in the poems.

As we move into the 21st century to what extent has your view of the North of Ireland altered from the 1970s or '80s essays? How do you see your own work and Ireland (North and South) evolving?
There has to be an evolution. When I wrote that essay on Paisley, way back, I was trying to explain the context or the evolution of a relentlessly negative figure. Defoe's *Robinson Crusoe* as the great dissenting prose epic interests me. I'm particularly interested though in figuring a particularly British kind of identity — its culmination around the time of World War II; perhaps I can write about it before it totally disappears which it may well do if Scotland gains independence. The Irish thing? Just before Christmas 1999, the *Irish Times* was talking about the release of the Cabinet papers which are kept secret for thirty years and I was thinking about Richard Crossman writing in the *New Statesman* around 1970-71 about Ireland being united and everyone being horrified at that. As Tony Benn pointed out, if someone had said to the cabinet, that sending the army in would mean that for thirty years there would be the loss of over one hundred lives every year and billions of pounds — would they have chosen that? If someone had said that to the population of both islands? History unfortunately does not work like that — it does not send a Tiresias figure and so the whole thing went banging on for most of our lives. Everyone from the North can find the names of the dead in that book *Lost Lives* — we've all been scarred by the last thirty years or touched by them in some way. The North is evolving but who knows whether all the weapons — even the rusty rifles from 1912 — will be handed in or whether what will happen will be enough to secure peace?

MEDBH McGUCKIAN

You were born in Belfast in 1950. Your mother Margaret's family were from near Randalstown (the poem 'My Mother' in THE FLOWER MASTER *envisages her among 'her boxes, lace and tins' with the inscrutability of 'a clock') and your father Hugh McCaughan's family were from near Ballycastle (a poem in* CAPTAIN LAVENDER *recalls your father and 'the passionate polygamy /of four hands (ours) at one piano.') How would you describe your family background, its influence on you?*

The four hands playing the piano are my mother's and mine; my father didn't play the piano although he was musical so, I suppose, the image is of both of them. The image of the clock does relate to my mother because she is obsessed with time. My father, as a man from Ballycastle described him recently, was a person who had no enemies although that's a negative way of putting his positive qualities. My parents' generation of rural Catholics suffered a lot; they had to work hard. My father, who was a primary school teacher for many years, became a vice principal at the Holy Family School; it was one of the roughest schools in Belfast, especially after the "Troubles", and he was never out of the hospital with kids falling out of trees or hurting themselves. I think he was a father to all the children at that school and I know, from talking to people since, that he did have a real effect on many of the children's lives. My mother worked in the post-office until she had her children in the '50s — myself, my two brothers and my three sisters. My mother is very much a city woman, even though she is not particularly sociable or out-going, and she feels very secure in Belfast. She is more deeply religious than my father; as a Catholic who had grown up in the Markets, where she had many Protestant neighbours, she went through the hardships of the Second World War and she was more moderately Unionist than my father — in the sense that she was happy with the status quo in the North. When the bombs started going off my mother would condemn the violence; my father, who was a liberal who never supported violence, would more readily try to understand why rather than criticize.

In 'Slips' in THE FLOWER MASTER *your 'childhood is preserved as a nation's history'. The rich, pictorial, imagination of children appears in some poems and there's their theatrical sense of play in* MARCONI'S COTTAGE. *How would you describe your own childhood in Belfast? In a prose anthology* THIRTY TWO COUNTIES *(1989) you describe World War II and the airfield at Bishopscourt with a sense of 'presentiment of the long occupation still to come'.*

My primary years were very safe, very romantic. We grew up before the "Troubles". Although you never went to certain areas you still knew you were safe because the boundaries were clearly demarcated in north Belfast. You would go to the park which was a "mixed" area; you couldn't go down to the Grove although you didn't quite know why. You had a sense that you knew where you were all the time in childhood and the church, my daddy's school and the street where we lived were all within a tightly knit, circumscribed, world. I never remember being unhappy even though it was a rough area and you sometimes saw children cry in the streets. In the '50s we went on holidays to my granny's house, my mother's mother's, in Ballyhornan near Downpatrick. I loved visiting her and going on walks down those lanes with the honeysuckle in the hedges or on the beach; that landscape around Downpatrick is flat and beautiful. I think that the dark view of the airfield and barricades from the war is possibly retrospective but I do remember, in the '50s, walking down a lane full of poppies and seeing two soldiers being killed when their jeep overturned in the lane and that did seem, in some way, to prefigure what lay ahead.

Your 'Aunts', in an early poem, also 'jived their way /Through the '50s to my teens'; 'Eavesdropper' seems to chart a space between being a girl in the '50s and an adolescent/woman in the '60s, 'shackling, unshackling the breasts'.

I was talking to my mother the other day; she was telling me that all the married men in Dublin have gone gay and all that young girls talk or think about these days is sex and getting pregnant but — 'sure she never told me anything about this when I was growing up and look how I turned out'. I tried to explain that sex was not all that easy to figure out as a girl. I never realised, even when I was eleven, that my mother was two weeks "overdue" and pregnant with my sister Maria. I did not know what was happening. No one talked to you about sex. I was innocent.

You went to secondary school at the Dominican Convent (1961-68). You've mentioned Hopkins as influential at school and you read Keats and Wordsworth for 'A' level according to an Interview in GOWN LITERARY SUPPLEMENT *(1986). You seem to share Hopkins's love of birds; in* VENUS AND THE RAIN *there are those moon-lit rooms with deep windows, shutters and 'brass-studded doors' — 'valerian drops' and the 'lips (which) disturb the vespered world/ Of grapes'; Coleridge, Shelley, Keats and Byron appear in the next two volumes. Were Hopkins and the English Romantics important in forming you as a poet?*

Hopkins is a very sensual poet. He was probably seen as a very safe poet to teach us in the convent but he managed to keep his life running on a moral line and kept his sins for his poetry and so he erected a space in which it was safe to play. Poetry became a playground where nothing was wrong because it was imaginary; Hopkins allowed you that sense that in poetry you could sleep with the Virgin Mary if you chose and not get into bother. My early life was almost entirely surrounded with females — I remember someone asking the nuns how long a French kiss should last — so poets on the syllabus like Hopkins and Wilfred Owen, who I didn't know was gay, were a way of finding out about men through poetry. Hopkins's love of birds is in his poems but there are also so many birds in Emily Dickinson and they are all male as they are in my work. People sometimes think, from my books, that I'm the kind of poet who is sup-posed to be a complete expert who knows everything about birds and flowers but I'm not. Michael Longley is the real botanist and when I was in a car with Michael, driving in Scotland, he had to stop to look at a rare flower by the roadside whereas I was more interested in the name of the thing and what that meant. Between sixteen and eighteen I was totally, totally, in love with Keats — his 'Ode to St. Agnes'. I wandered around thinking about him and reading him constantly. He became mixed up in my head with a cousin of mine, who was slightly smaller and darker, who I also fell in love with so there was that tension between the living and the dead which I seem to need to write poems. At that time I read everything I could about Keats; I could have told you then what he had for breakfast.

You studied English literature for a B.A. and Anglo-Irish literature for an M.A. at Queen's (1968-1974) when Paul Muldoon was a student there. 'Horsepower, Pass By!' (1999) is a pamphlet study of Seamus Heaney and the car; there's a poem dedicated to Derek Mahon (in which you share a sense of home and look at his 'general thirsting after death' and there's his voice like 'thawing ice or dry straw') and one for Seamus Deane; Michael Longley's female tenderness is acknowledged in a previous interview. How do you see your poems in relation to the Belfast '60s poets?

It was a scarey time going to Queen's and leaving the streets I grew up in. Until then I had read English poets, the Romantics and Milton, but Seamus (Heaney) was my teacher there and I met Paul (Muldoon), who was a few years younger, and this brought an Irish dimension in the form of living writers. I did not really know Seamus Deane well then. I feel that this '60s generation of writers were very supportive, in no way competitive, when I started out. I was learning, especially from Paul who was younger. These writers were father figures and still are. Every book Paul does is unbelievable but his first, early, poems are very special to me; they evoke the dances and music and the mood and experiences that all of us who were there in those early years at Queen's can recall but which we never quite understood — and he found words for these things. Later Paul's work became more wordy and clever and the emotion is more tongue-in-cheek but I like those early poems because he is so utterly sincere.

'I drive words abreast/Into the interior of words...': is your poetry triggered by language itself so that it is, in part, philology or etymology in which language is a living creature more than a referent to, or a fixing of, meaning on the outer world? One might suggest that your poems are layered, associative — tacking, ducking and diving in language that's deep as opposed to transparent so that 'a word has only/an aroma of meaning' as you say in 'Pulsus Paradoxus' — and this way of using language means you are technically close to Paul Muldoon?
I think of this inwardness more as a female thing, an inward physical and mental reserve that I learned to channel outwards as I became more adventurous. At the beginning I felt poems had to be logical and artistic but, after marriage and the children in the '80s and the "Troubles" and the Hunger Strikes, I felt that I had to go further. Emily Dickinson gave me scope in that direction; she managed to say things that it was thought could not be said in language. Seamus (Heaney) recently said to me that you would need a critic like a nuclear physicist to understand Dickinson's poems but she allowed me to create what I liked. At Queen's I resented, very much, not having a Gaelic side or being able to incorporate Irish in a genuine way. I was listening to Gregory Peck, in the film *The Yearling*, give an old-fashioned funeral oration recently where he says that 'it pleasures us, O Lord, to think...' and that archaic language reminded one of Irish. I was trying to make the language do something for myself and others, to simply make it less ordinary.

I've been reading Paul (Muldoon) recently and I am not that close to him in the sense that his poetry rhymes and fits together in way that is unlike mine: it has different satisfactions; it is more finished and complete. He takes a delight in word patterns that I am unable to; it's like Joseph Conrad who chose to write in English rather than Polish because of the freedom of syntax it allowed him. I find, in me, a longing for wordlessness almost or for something poetry can achieve through words but leaving them behind; maybe writing in Irish would not have made that any easier although there is a natural rather than civilised sound that's genuine — like water or leaves — but a bit like Tennyson's 'murmuring of innumerable elms', a kind of mimesis. English has words that have many other meanings and words which contain other words like "love" or "held in a glove". Paul does not scruple to play with personal names or any kind of word so he can rhyme "Merlin" with "Marilyn" and obtain subtle effects. I would not say my poetry is 'triggered' by language but certain explosives go off when "t" and "d" happen to come together and words can ignite each other. I like putting words together that have never, or could never, have been conceived of by others as being possible friends. When I say "drive" or "aroma", in connecting with them, I'm thinking of them as animals or soldiers or a country or a growing plant or nourishing food — all of these things.

After marrying the teacher and writer John McGuckian (1977) you wrote two Ulsterman pamphlets with thirty two poems: 'Portrait of Joanna' (1980), and 'Single Ladies' (1980) in which Paul Muldoon's Introduction mentions your 'unique voice' with 'shades of Emily Dickinson' and 'Sylvia Plath looking over (your) shoulder' although 'neither (are) breathing down (your) neck'. Was Plath an assimilated influence?

Plath's poetry and her life frighten me. Her ending in the gas oven terrifies me. She was much more of a socialite then Emily Dickinson but I find some of her poems more gross, more vulgar and, in terms of an inner world, I'm closer to Dickinson.

You contributed poems to TRIO 2 *(Blackstaff Press, 1981) and* INTRODUCTIONS 5 *(Faber, 1982) in which there are grandmother's samplers, your mother's sewing machine, lipstick and henna, Waterford crystal, spoons in drawers, the noise of the electric fridge and the bag apron in the house in the folk museum. Heaney noticed that Katherine Mansfield hoped to tell 'how the laundry basket squeaked'. Is there a sense in which you link household objects and female identity?*

I went through marriage and all that orthodoxy associated with the stage of nest-building and so there are the cushions and carpets of those household objects in the poems and I guess that these are linked with a woman's confinement in a home. Some people have linked the tulips in *The Flower Master* with Plath's tulips but they were simply an image from early married life, from the back garden of the house in Downpatrick where we settled for three years after we were married. They are an image of being fertilised — a tangible, real, image that I saw and found in the garden when I moved from the street I had lived in to that kind of suburban street, to that world so well described by Eavan Boland in her poems.

THE FLOWER MASTER *(1982) has poems written around the time of the conception and bearing of your first baby and there are images of seeds and flowers and harvest; you mention 'regression' in* VENUS AND THE RAIN *(1984) due to post-natal depression, a 'mental breakdown after the first child' in* GOWN LITERARY SUPPLEMENT *(1986);* ON BALLYCASTLE BEACH *(1988) is dedicated to your son Hugh Oisin; there's your daughter Emer's poem in* MARCONI'S COTTAGE *(1991). Does the birth of your four children register in each of your first four volumes as a theme of motherhood?*

Absolutely. In one poem I say that 'a man needs a woman for every book'; I might have said that a woman needs a child for every book. I didn't plan things this way but that is the way it happened; with each of the children

I felt totally fulfilled and soaring during pregnancy and then there was the plunge afterwards and that learning experience is in the poems. My third son is fifteen this year; maybe my children would be horrified at the idea of "book-making" from the experience of their birth but that is the way it was. Childbirth can also be horrific and involve suffering — both physical and mental — and there was also the fact that my father started getting ill as I was having my babies which increasingly affected those four volumes.

Michael Allen sees the central theme of THE FLOWER MASTER *as a shift between the 'emotional energy' of 'young maturity' and 'the ascetic strategy required by age' in* CONTEMPORARY IRISH POETRY: A COLLECTION OF CRITICAL ESSAYS *edited by Elmer Andrews (1992).*
If Michael means cutting out or turning your back on the flesh then I don't think that is in that volume because I was trying to deal with the body and flesh very much as well as the spirit. I would say *Marconi's Cottage* is more full of the ascetic with its deaths and its angels and heaven and coffins but then, in the early '90s, everyone had an angel or archangel hanging out of them, including Muldoon — it was a big fashion then.

A poem like 'The Invalid's Echo' talks of 'our grandmothers,/Who spoke God's name continually' and there are Saints' Days, church feasts and the atmosphere of Catholicism in the poems. In what way does Catholicism register in the language and subject matter of your poems? Does Protestantism and Catholicism — Mahon as the individual atom/ Heaney as familial and integrated — transmit differently into poetry?
Catholicism is simply part of the way my mind thinks. I was talking to Seamus after he had been on holiday to St. Lucia; we were soon talking about Saint Lucia, St. Lucy's Day, John Donne — all those Catholic associations which do hold a kind of glamour. For me saints are real people who have given names to real people; one of my names is Philomena so I was very upset when the Church made up its mind that she was not a real saint and I lost someone I had been praying to for years. Some might see this way of thinking as like the way you would think about the fairies or Irish mythology but I think it's simply enjoyable. I can't think of a word like Christmas, for instance, without splitting it into Christ-Mass, its separate associations. There is a spiritual dimension with Catholicism which sometimes influences the way you see things like nature. I can't spent too long inside William Blake's head when he cuts down Wordsworth for seeing nature as the devil which blinds him to God. Now where would you be with that kind of thinking? Maybe I'm driving at something about Protestantism and Catholicism in *Shelmalier* in returning to the sense that your 'childhood contains a nation's history' because it was a fantastic revelation to find out that there were a whole range of Protestant martyrs

during the 1798 Rebellion; it made sense of the fact that two religions produced martyrs and that we might all be going to the same place by two different roads. I don't have the same sense of the Bible in my work as Jimmy Simmons — he has carnal knowledge of it — and he can use hymns in poems but hymns don't turn me on like the litany. You could say that Michael Longley goes for the Greek jugular whereas myself and Seamus gravitate towards the Latin, the Italian, Dante and the French.

Your first volume is earthed in seeds, flowers and harvest; Clair Wills notes that Venus, in your second volume, is the planet of 'ideal love and womanhood', obscured from the earth, 'an inhuman place unreached by man' in IMPROPRIETIES, POLITICS AND SEXUALITY IN NORTHERN IRISH POETRY *(1993). Yeats is often seen as the beginning of the contemporary in Irish poetry with his experience embedded in a 'stylistic arrangement' of shifting symbols — like the moon and stars. Does Yeats's poetry, his symbolic, anti-rational, way of thinking, relate to you?*

I was trying to be pagan in *Venus and the Rain* — a kind of pre-Christian Medbh — and the title conveys a sense of the mound or Mount Venus and the rain is the nuclear rain of that time. That book also came out of a horrendous mental breakdown and periods of hallucination which drove me back into the arms of the church. There are deliberately ugly rhymes in that volume which are unlike my lyrical or romantic side — 'bottle' rhyming with 'farm' — and for a whole year I couldn't read or think so there is no sense of development. Yeats has always been a fixed star despite his arrogance and contempt for women. I admire fervently his utter dedication and the sense of Ireland and its people, even if it was wrong-headed.

Between 1982-85 you taught English at St. Patrick's College; you were the first women writer-in-residence at Queen's University (1985-88) and you taught creative writing at the University of Ulster in Coleraine (1996-98). Are teaching and writing linked?

My father was a teacher and I've a great deal of sympathy for teachers. Seamus (Heaney) was a great teacher at Queen's and I have the sense that whatever he does I am going to do — not literally, I'm not going to write *Beowolf* — so there is a kind of assurance that he and others like Ciaran (Carson), who has recently written a new prose book are still going on. Everyone you read in a sense is a teacher. I'm reading Theodore Adorno at the minute and, like Eliza Doolittle, I'm slow and so with a writer as dense as this you have to read every sentence four times. Once I get it, though, I really do get it.

You changed your name with marriage and Maeve became Medbh; there's your 'shared pormanteau name' in one poem although 'The Invalid's Echo' speaks of your name as 'ownerless' while in 'Lighthouse with Dead Leaves' you state, 'I am three girls or the same girl... a ruptured seed'. Poems often appear not to have a single narrator, 'I', but an 'I' who is a riddle, a multiple metaphor, a Russian doll identity while a poem in ON BALLYCASTLE BEACH *'dreams of being written without the pronoun I'. To what extent are your poems experiments in different voices, the single lyric voice enacting a dramatic dialogue?*

Perhaps I use the 'I' too carelessly but as you grow older and you travel — I was talking to Edna O'Brien about this — pain scrapes away the hard edges of the self. You also come to make poems that are like jumping off into the sea with faith that you will be caught in a net of language. Sometimes I feel that I should be like Stravinsky, down on my knees worshiping the lord or a single creator in my creative work, but there is nearly always that sense of talking to a least one person who can become two people — a bit like Keats and my cousin — and I've never believed that a single creator would want us to stop talking to each other as human beings. There are many 'I' s. There is the writer being interviewed and another 'I' that wonders whether I have enough pampers for the children or what they will have for tea.

Are their different ways in which the form of your poems take shape? What is form to you?

Poems seem to rise organically in some kind of yeast. I have a certain amount I want to say, or feel my way into saying, and I have a certain number of gathered words (liked and chosen and interesting to me and maybe never used before) that I try to mould into a coherent, readable argument that might parallel what is going on deep in my subconscious or somewhere unreached by words, like a fear of pregnancy or an unspeakable guilt. I don't think of all the elements separately when I'm writing. I have a moment of energy I want to cage. I have, maybe, a book, a journey, an ecstasy, a loss, a fantasy, a street, an evening to record, or a person to address. The form seems to just evolve as I concentrate on being honest and real, inside the safety net of non-communicating, which is like acupuncture. I am more concerned with drawing together incompatibles, to somehow harness all the cancelling-out hatred and love, going towards and retreating from everything all the time, as one does, the sentence holding within the laws it has to but going up and down the way that no sentence (like this one) is allowed to.

Many northern writers relate to either Kavanagh (with his sense of the soil-rooted, the pagan or timeless place like Monaghan) or MacNeice (with his sense of constant shift and change in a colder more rootless modern world, the cityscapes like Derek Mahon's). Do you relate to the world either of these writers created in poetry?

I'm not that close to MacNeice. I cannot read his 'Prayer Before Birth' without being deeply frightened and you get the sense that there was something troubled in his relationship with his mother; there is a sense of great warmth in Kavanagh's relationship with his mother. Their poems are as different as potatoes and chips.

THE FLOWER MASTER *had Georgia O'Keefe on the cover; 'The Seed-Picture' is a sampler painting from pulses and lentils; 'The Sitting' has painted hair like a 'net of lemons'. There's 'a small Matisse in the inglenook' in* ON BALLYCASTLE BEACH. MARCONI'S COTTAGE *has Gwen John's numeric scheme for colours.* CAPTAIN LAVENDER *opens with a quotation from Picasso and there are book covers by Jack B. Yeats, the Belfast painter Barbara Freeman and a poem for the Irish painter Barrie Cooke. What is the relationship between painting and poetry in your work?*

Painting and music are in some way related to class. When I visited the Metropolitan Museum of Modern Art in New York I was aware of painting as sheer luxury. We had music at home when I was growing up but we did not have paintings other than reproductions of religious paintings, holy pictures, and I know my father would have given a lot to have seen those paintings in the Metropolitan Museum, let alone have owned a reproduction of one of them. I don't have an original painting by anyone so I associate paintings with the rich. Perhaps I write about painting so much because I can't paint although I think of painting and music as more primary or direct whereas words seem much further down the line and more complicated. I'm aware that my parents' had a hard life — much harder than mine — although in the area of north Belfast where I grew up I found out that others, like John Luke or James Galway who lived nearby, could make their lives with painting or music. Poetry is my bread and butter: I earn my living from that but I'm conscious that it's not physical work, in the same way that my parents' generation worked from nine to five; so, although I've been fated to work like my father as a teacher for long periods, I see poetry as a luxury that sometimes offers escape from those regular hours. I like French painting of the nineteenth century and Dutch seventeenth century painting and Ireland does not seem to have painting like that.

No one talks about class in relation to your work: in 'Waterford' there are 'rich families' with cut crystal; 'The Albert Chain' in CAPTAIN LAVENDER *speaks of how 'every inch of soil has been paid for/ by the life of a man, the funerals of the poor.'*

I suppose I should prefer O'Casey's plays to Synge's emotionally, even though they are less poetic. I realise that very deprived or even handicapped people would get nothing from my work — they are so beyond it. Because my father taught me so thoroughly that 'the poor are always with ye', some part of me is always on the St. Vincent de Paul level and full of conscience about how the world is 'ill-divid'.

You have lived mainly in Belfast and in the THIRTY TWO COUNTIES *prose piece you wonder if Belfast is 'my propellor, my engine, fuel and wind?' 'Porcelain Bells' mentions a city in which 'nothing is forgiven'.*

If Belfast is my propellor did I ever leave it in Bilbao? The quotation in 'Porcelain Bells' is from Marina Tzvetaeva. In Belfast people place you and you try to place the place. I was on the bus today from home and I was looking at these two men who had their politics tattooed on their fore-arms for everyone to see and I also had the sense that they would know me and my background. This street we are on (Fitzwilliam Street) is named for, and this room (in the school of Irish Studies) evokes, some-one who is deeply associated with the United Irishmen in 1798. I have the sense, too, that I feel very safe in my own area in north Belfast but if I'm in east Belfast or even in the Ardoyne or Falls Road in west Belfast then I'm less secure unless I'm in the car and perhaps that is why I wrote that piece on Heaney and the car (*Horsepower Pass By!*). The city is changing with more trees being planted in the streets and a pleasure boat now goes up and down the Lagan and bridges, like in Dublin, have lights which also reveal the grime in the architecture; even though the place is coming down around us there is also the sense that the more they knock down the more they reveal of an older place, stuck in time, like Manchester in the 1820s. Belfast lags way behind Dublin and other cities. When you arrive in Belfast on the train you still feel that there is still *there* and there is noth-ing else. When I wrote *Shelmalier* I became aware that a good night out in Belfast was looking for Henry Joy McCracken's grave in Clifton Street Cemetery — which is not there — or his sister's, Mary Anne's, which is.

In Ciaran Carson's BELFAST CONFETTI *Belfast is a literal maze; for Fiacc it's 'hellfast' and in* THE ROUGH FIELD *it's bleak, rainy and sectarian. Your street directory (Minus 18 Street, Gendarme and Bird Street) seems more metaphorical?*
In the '50s you were aware of the divisions in north Belfast as people moved and the city became a place where the last house in one street ended with people of one religion and the next street began with another. Those ways I developed for talking about it tried to see it as French, or Chinese or Russian, part of some kind of European evolution however backward it was. The street names in Belfast were not of the local people's choosing. They were imperially and politically stamped so that even when people said where they lived they were remembering a tyrant like Cromwell on their tongues; so I never used those names but I did use any-thing else, a number or a word they would not use, like 'Prison Street' which would be the reality. I use 'Bird Street' because of all the symbolism weighted there. Maybe I just wanted to have my own city to upset all the Ordinance Surveys; it seems important to have a sense of where you really are, of where the helicopters cannot photograph.

On Ballycastle Beach *(1988) was divided into two parts. Why? Clair Wills suggests that sea and sky give way to ships and aeroplanes, the book enacting a return journey to reclaim the land. A return flight of the Earls? Is this a fair analysis?*
The latest edition is no longer divided. At the time I felt a break and a journey had been accomplished, since we began to spend a lot of time near Ballycastle and I began to understand more of my father's complex relationship to the sea and land. Simultaneously I was starting to travel internationally and learn from that. So I was aware of two processes, inward and outward, back and forward.

Eileen Cahill suggests your poetry commits 'sins against the laws of logic, syntax, congruity, grammar, causality, linear structure and unity' in 'Because I Never Garden' in the Irish University Review *(Vol 24. No 2, 1994).*
I feel, if I sin, these laws are man-made, not woman-made. Words are tools that men mostly created to suit themselves and although I buy into them, necessarily, they do not rule me or, at least, I rebel and fight against their empire. It's an attitude that also has to do with the language I have to use being an imposed and foreign one, at a psychic point.

'A Dream in Three Colours' (language as 'pearls that have lost their clasp') and 'The Dream-Language of Fergus' (language as a sleeping tongue and 'seed fund') which refracts Mandelstam appear to be about the loss of Irish and 'Elegy for an Irish Speaker' has its 'scarecrow language' and 'simile lost'. John Montague images a 'severed head' and 'lost tongue' (execution and suture) while Seamus Heaney suggests both silence and power (the tongue governed/governing), loss and reclamation. The loss of Irish/the use of English in Irish poetry is a theme in your work?
It has become more directly so. I have a poem mourning my inability to regain the Irish language addressed to Cathal Ó Searcaigh. I don't see much point on dwelling on it poetically; in fact it can be rhythmically recalled and evoked through English, in a redemptive and healing way. Bob Welch has said to me that when he reads 'The Aisling Hat' it sounds to him like a restoration of seventeenth century Gaelic which is very encouraging.

There is the poem that 'makes diamonds' as you put in Venus and the Rain *and the poem of continuously opening doors: indeterminate, inconclusive, growing. Do your metaphors signal constant shifts — an awareness of the comparison as not only an exact or stable likeness but as being more or less or half-alike — so that the image also becomes an interregnum (between realities) — carrying doubts like an 'or'. I'm suggesting your imagery is a battle between fixing and un-fixing?*
Nothing is ever certain, but I would say, at this stage, my own tentativeness

was an expression of unease in a very turbulent war situation here where we had to be very guarded and one *was* very guarded so one always kept one's back covered, linguistically and literally, so that you could not be pinned down accusingly perhaps, by any group or side. How does the imagery work in the poems? 'On Her Second Birthday', the last poem from *Marconi's Cottage*, has the image of a mother talking to an infant daughter which is really used to give voice to the broken nature of Ireland addressing a future new Ireland. The poem operates on these levels simultaneously and I want it to. My contours are at once my own physical boundaries and the political shape of the "Six Counties". Like I say earlier, in 'The War Ending', the unborn child's movements are a wave, a rainbow or a painting; this is an expression of fear for her safety or security in a violent outer world. The external hand is the hand of force or repression that I feel has caused my fear. 'The Rosary Dress' was an attempt to describe 'giving birth' in the medical, backless, white garment they put you in to do that so all the imagery is about a woman's mental state in labour, in those helpless hours, and what your consciousness does; the lily ceiling is all she sees, really, though she's a heatwave beneath it, as it were.

French literature has often attracted Northern poets (Mahon, Carson and Montague) and you have French phrases or titles for poems. Michael Allen suggests Mallarmé echoes in 'Next Day Hill' and there's the 'French born sea' in BALLYCASTLE BEACH. *Do you admire French poetry or writing?*
There is a conference next week where I am looking forward to meeting French poets. I do not know enough about contemporary French literature but, certainly, their culture — Napoleon, their novelists — I admire tremendously. I see France as a dream world because I have so seldom been there.

In 'Death of a Ceiling' 'The sounds that shapes make in the air, /The shapes that sounds make, matter' and in 'The Time Before You' images work like an 'accordion'. 'Through the Round Window' has a 'child playing Brahms'; a poem sees Mozart as music's 'drudge' or 'stepchild'. Does music, contemporary or classical, influence your poetry?
The first music I really encountered was the Beatles and Leonard Cohen at Queen's. When the Beatles sang 'I wanna hold your hand' or 'she loves you' they seemed to be talking about sex, not love; I would not say that the Beatles produced the best music in the world but they opened up areas which the previous generation had been embarrassed about and they had words — unlike a lot of popular music now. If I think of painting as French, I often think of music as German — or as coming out of middle-Europe — something martial. In many ways I'm critical of both music and painting because I'm aware that both were often enjoyed while people were dying so you have to think about what art costs. I write poetry

and that too has a cost because if I'm doing that I'm not looking after the children. I have to believe that a poem can have an effect, that it might just save someone's life. If I could have submitted more to the disciplines of dance or music as a child I might not have found poetry such a release but it has, for me, that sort of soothing, entertainment, quality at its finest.

Piano notes, the sudden scent of a room's cut flowers, 'Fragments of once-achieved meaning, ready to leave /The flesh' in 'Breaking the Blue'. I'm reminded that T. S. Eliot worked through inklings where music declares a mood or an epiphany or a moment of synaesthesia. Is Modernism, Eliot or Pound, important for you?
Eliot does not speak to me in his earlier work. Although I like some of his later poems I feel much closer to Yeats and I have the sense that Eliot became very British. Pound's *Cantos?* No. I feel very cold when I read these two. The American poet I prefer is Frost.

Letters, envelopes, postage stamps, postcards, coloured pens and paper — poems as 'vital transfusions through the post'. Are poems like letters?
Well, they should be! Ideally they are, for me, addressed to a single/double person, perhaps even as love letters. They certainly intend the total one-to-one communication that is possible between people and so they are illicit, and, of course, unanswerable.

Poems are also full of colour: 'Marie-Louise blue', 'grass green', salmon pinks, 'quaker brown' and all those shades or gradations of white (and black) that gather around the self. 'Scenes from a Brothel' laments that there are 'So few words for so many colours' and 'Woman with a Blue-Ringed Bowl' wishes for 'a pen that wrote in four colours'; there is even 'A colour (that) walks around with people hidden in it.'
I started playing around with colour, daubing and dabbing and mixing paint and sometimes I'm aware of its religious connotations — those blue and whites that recall vestments in the church — and sometimes it is political, as in 'Dream of Three Colours' which was written after my son was born and where I offer him a choice and wonder whether one set of colours is as bad as the other.

I liked the self-indulgence of all that then but I feel now that it is probably a vein I have outgrown or exhausted although — maybe not.

MARCONI'S COTTAGE *(1991) feels like a book 'on a war footing': there are black swans and roses, a torn dress and curtains ('Dear Rain'); 'the sign of the cross in window frames... coffins being brought into the hall'; 'Shefari' refers to the 'most closely watched place/in the Empire'; there is 'Gendarme and Prison Street'; the wind 'knocks cameras out of newspapermen's /Haphazard hands' and clouds*

wear 'Army uniforms'. In what way did the "Troubles" register in your poetry?
I think that the "Troubles" did not really register in my early work — perhaps not until the mid '80s although I had written a poem after Bobby Sands died which I did not publish simply because it was not a good poem. I never thought of myself as a "Troubles" poet; it was not part of my oeuvre and I couldn't do it simply as an exercise, so I didn't take it on. I was conscious though of the number of victims and I went into the prison in 1993 and became aware that here there were people writing poems and that changed the way I wrote. It brought me up against the reality of people's lives and sacrifices in a way that did filter into my own writing — maybe not in a salutary fashion.

In CAPTAIN LAVENDER *there is the link between politics and the North. Nationality is often a vexed question for northern poets. You could argue that Joyce saw it as an entrapping net. Does nationality matter in your poems?*
I don't like the word 'nationality' and Adorno says that 'the nation that thinks it is special is doomed'. Maybe Americans have got it right; they have such a big empire that you can be both an American and from a state, although there are differences from state to state and it makes someone from Idaho mad if you mistake them as being from Illinois. I know I'm Irish though — I can't help it — and maybe I'm proud to be Irish although I don't want to be patted on the back for it, considering it is so sexy to be Irish now when it certainly was not in my mother's day. While it would be lovely to be James Joyce, and feel that you had escaped the whole thing, I also think that Joyce did come back to it. I'm not sure whether you would know if I was Irish from reading the work; it is something I've only gradually allowed myself to be.

Pomoma, Venus, Aphrodite. Your myths seem more classical than Irish?
Yes, because of the Roman and Latin influence. Other poets like Nuala Ní Dhomhnaill have a more authentic right to explore the more Irish myths; I have never felt any great desire to but these creatures I refer to are pretty incidental.

In CAPTAIN LAVENDER *(1994) what are you exploring in the title poem?*
It was quite a dense discussion with myself, in the stages of bereavement, of the metaphysics of my father's immortality; I invoked him as a time-traveller across the Atlantic of space I would have to follow. I made him very much a part of this world and, at the same time, a figure from film or literature. The poem is also the twin sides of the military coin.

Radio voices sometimes drift into some poems by Michael Longley and Seamus Heaney. Does television or cinema inspire or enter poems you have written?

Television never really does — except some news reports of bombs or killings as in 'The Dead are More Alive' where I talked about not seeing the lynchings in Casement Park but of watching my children watching them. Cinema has recently become a more important inspiration and I have written, for instance, a poem for Neil Jordan after seeing *The Butcher Boy* and I've also written about *The Guns of Navarone* (which is a war film very much from the British perspective). Like Paul Muldoon I have a poem about Lord Haw Haw and his peculiar position. Mostly though it seems like a very second, or third-hand, sort of experience to be directly reacting to. I have been 'commissioned' — that grand word — to try to respond to paintings or photographs and I always do that in an oblique way. I was asked to write about the painter John Lavery for a book so I used a bit of Hegel who was the subject of his painting.

'The Third Chessplayer' in SHELMALIER *is dedicated to Barrie Cooke. Can you tell me about this poem? It might be argued that literature (the classics, history, the Bible) used to inspire painters but that now more and more poems come from paintings and painters?*
Well, that poem is more of a personal encounter with a painter I've always admired than just about being inspired by his work. I visited Barrie at his studio in Sligo and had one of those epiphany moments when you are out of time. Barrie is English and yet he loves Ireland and he celebrates it. I felt a transcendence above the narrow politics of place. Barrie's work is very earthy and there are dull colours but as I was leaving he threw a rose into the car, which dissolved in my lap as I drove home, so that was part of the imagery. He had shown me twelve small drawings that were very sacred to him and I was trying to create some of the power and effect he created there in my approach. I felt his work was very honest and intimate and I had not experienced anything quite so scarey, really, as a male artist allowing a female one into the mystery of his art — that sanction. I felt compelled to a response, a game where his eye was with me but not party to the connections he established: it set up a lot of questions in my head because Barrie cares a lot about rivers and pollution and the environment and the world's survival; he's just a major figure I wanted to thank and celebrate.

There is also a poem like 'The Feminine Christs' in SHELMALIER. *What is it about?*
Yes. I was visiting my father's grave on Christmas Day and it's in a Catholic part of a mainly Protestant cemetery, in an area that used to be mainly Protestant but is now mainly Catholic. I walked around the very beautiful, older, part of the cemetery which had ancient Protestant graves of people who were not being visited by relatives. I was just addressing them as my opposites and yet my selves in many ways. I was thinking of the time over two hundred years ago — some of them were from around the time of the

Rebellion —when they would have been caught up in those events, so the poem comes from that human emotion of standing at the grave of a person who lived where you lived but who was very different from you. Somehow I had that feeling of connection not only to the Nationalist Presbyterians but a fellow-feeling with the Church of Ireland dead obviously in that 'Death Be Not Proud' kind of setting. It was probably a way of detaching from the ongoing obsession with my own father's mortality.

SHELMALIER *(1998) recalls the United Irishmen, two hundred years after the rising, though this period of history in Ireland seems as much to do with the future as the past. Tom Paulin's* LIBERTY TREE *recalls forgotten examples for Unionism; Seamus Heaney has linked the 1798 with a continuum that is recurrent and leads to 1916; there's Stewart Parker's great play* NORTHERN STAR. *How did you see the rebellion?*

The United Irishmen are such fluid muses, romantic figures; it was a time when Protestants produced martyrs and Thomas Russell was hanged in Downpatrick and priests were carrying arms. Keats would have been barely a babe in his mother's arms when they were planning the rising. When I talked of Belfast going back to the 1820s you might also see it as city deeply influenced by the 1798 and marked by that time. The nineteenth century produced further complications; recently I went to teach a class in a Catholic school near Emily Brontë's territory here and found that many of the schoolchildren were in some way related to the Brontës. When I started to read and research the United Irish period — a time when the North was not divided — the peace process was coming together and it became very vivid and shocking for me to realize what a blood-bath for everyone concerned it was and so it helped very much explain the roots of what is happening now.

Post the Good-Friday Agreement and into in a new century — how do you see your poetry and the North develop?

I have a book on the ceasefire and the millennium with Gallery Press. I'm not sure if I want the North to develop into a tourist haven with all those usual high street shops which is likely to happen if the peace holds. My poetry and the North are hardly synonymous. My teenage son is absailing or climbing up the side of the Europa — the most bombed hotel in twentieth century Europe — and when he gets to the top he will be in Kenya because it's a sponsored event. Is that what is coming next?

PAUL MULDOON

Were you brought up in a rural environment in Ulster?
Yes, I was, but not on a farm as such. I came to live in a place called
Collegelands in north Armagh when I was about four, because my mother,
who was a schoolteacher, got a job there. My father was essentially a
labourer, and for some time a market gardener. He first grew cauliflowers
and peas, and then moved to mushroom farming: that particular area of
Armagh is an important mushroom-growing area, and there are also many
orchards. But having said that, I should add that it's not essentially rural.

There's a nearby village called the Moy which figures quite strongly in
my poems, though I've fictionalized it to a great extent. It's an area very
rich in history and folklore, just as every square mile of Ireland is coming
down with history and is burdened by it. The Moy itself was built by a man
called James Caulfeild, who was at one stage Lord Lieutenant of Ireland,
Earl of Charlemont, which is a little sister hamlet to the Moy. This story
may be totally apocryphal, but Caulfeild is supposed to have designed it on
the principle of an Italian town, Marengo. I've fictionalized the place to
this extent — as I see it, one of my main duties as a writer is to write about
what is immediately in front of me, or immediately over my shoulder.
Clearly any landscape or locale is going to be re-mapped by a writer —
Hardy's Wessex, Faulkner's Yoknapatawpha, Joyce's Dublin, Yeats Country
— I'm not setting myself against any of them, but these are places which
are recognizable in their fixtures yet are changed by the creative process.
I'm very interested in the way in which a small place, a parish, can come to
stand for the world. As I began to read I became aware that several writers
— particularly those from the North like Seamus Heaney, Derek Mahon
and Michael Longley — were writing about places I knew, and that what
they had to say about them was accepted beyond those places.

You were brought up with a religion?
Yes, I was brought up as a Catholic. Both my parents were Catholic. My
poem called 'The Mixed Marriage' is not about a marriage mixed by reli-
gion. I merely try to some extent to describe them and their relationship.
They would have been something like the Morels — though that's an over-
stated comparison — in *Sons and Lovers*. My father is anything but a coarse,

185

lumbering man — he's a very refined man — but not educated. My mother was the youngest of a large family, and she was the only one they could afford to educate, so she went to a teacher's training college in Belfast.

The poem seems to present the sort of geometry which might have led to a division in yourself.
Yes, and being geometrical its edges are rather sharp. The Latin Quarter, Proust, and Castor and Pollux is perhaps over-simply set against the hole in the hedge, the life lived close to the earth.

Do you feel that you've shown more loyalty to your mother's career in following a life in letters, while at the same time harking back to the rurality of your father?
To begin with, I don't see myself as a man of letters. But I suppose that in the second book, *Mules*, I was trying to explore these lives that couldn't quite reproduce themselves, and that were sterile in themselves. It's too programmatic to describe it in these terms... but lives caught between heaven and earth. The poem 'Mules' itself: the mule is the offspring of a jack-ass and a mare, and the mare came to stand for me as some sort of basic earth force — a pagan force, if we can use that word — an animal that was worshipped by the Celts. On the other hand, the donkey is significant in Christian mythology.

Through living in Ireland and having the kind of education I had, I was very much aware of the Irish language and history, and of the energy of the Celtic civilization. When I went to grammar school, St. Patrick's College in Armagh, I came under quite exceptional influences. One man, Sean O'Boyle, who was a scholar of the Irish language and music, taught me Irish and gave me, and everyone round me, a sense of this marvellous heritage of literature and song in Gaelic. I was also blessed — it may sound corny, but I really do feel blessed — by a man called Gerry Hicks, a singer, who taught English. They were people whose knowledge exuded from them. A man called John McCarter really started me writing, I suppose. He'd been involved, peripherally I think, in the Dublin literary scene, and he gave me the sense that there were writers alive in Dublin. He also introduced me to the *Faber Book of Modern Verse*, which I more or less learned off by heart. He introduced me to T. S. Eliot, whom I thought was God, though I no longer think that. When he set English essays for the weekend, I wrote a poem, which seemed a much shorter and simpler thing to do. I'm a great believer in that definition of poetry as the stuff that doesn't quite reach the margins. I got away with it again and again, with the upshot that I didn't do very well in English Language exams. That's how I got started.

Was your experience at Queen's University, Belfast, equally fulfilling?

I met Seamus Heaney and Michael Longley just before I left grammar school in 1968, and I asked Seamus if he'd look at my poems if I sent them to him. He subsequently published a couple of them in a magazine he was then editing. Strangely enough the very first poems I had published were in Irish, but I soon gave that up because, though I'd studied Irish, I didn't have a real control of the language. Heaney was my tutor at Queen's, and there was a lot happening at Belfast — the aftermath of the famous London group that Philip Hobsbaum had run when he taught at Belfast. Hobsbaum had left, but the group was still in operation — Heaney, Longley, various other writers, and a very good critic called Michael Allen who teaches at Queen's. There were weekly meetings, for a time in Seamus Heaney's house, and later in a pub, where new poems were discussed. It was very important for me, since a writer must be a good critic of his work. There was no sloppiness in the group, everyone was quite outspoken. It was a very healthy kind of society, and I use the word 'society' to describe the group. It's scarcely a group at all, even though it's become a critical convenience to see them as presenting a united front to the world: you have only to read them to be aware of the variety. They're not united by any kind of manifesto.

Do you feel you're answerable as much to the principles of that goup as to your own imaginative direction?
I think one can only be faithful to the language and the way in which it presents itself to you, and to the world in the way it presents itself to you... faithful in the sense of the meeting between language and experience. I believe in inspiration, it's a valid way of describing the process of being open. My poems begin with a couple of ideas which try to work themselves out into some kind of shape.

A number of your poems seem to work a single image...
I'm very interested in the Metaphysicals and in the conceit. I look on each poem as being a little world in itself. I'm very interested in the narrative, the story, and in wanting almost to write novels in the poem. I like to think that a whole society is informing the lines of a poem, that every detail is accurate. And I'm interested in the dramatic persona. I like using different characters, to present different views of the world.

I think the writer who excited me most at university was Robert Frost: an apparently simple, almost naïve, tone of voice and use of language, underneath which all kinds of complex things are happening. I believe very firmly that the most complex notions in the world can be presented in a simple, immediate way, and can have a primary, direct effect on the reader. If you take a poem like Frost's 'The Road Not Taken', the complexity is astounding, and yet it just flies off the page.

What you're saying immediately makes me think of your poem 'The Country Club'...
Yes, the first eight lines of that poem are taken directly from Frost's 'The
Mountain'. It's a strange poem. I was trying, I suppose, to write about
being implicated in a society, and more specifically in a violent event in a
society — implicated simply by being on the sidelines. In my first book, a
poem called 'Party Piece' concerns characters who wished for 'the explo-
sion's heart' — where in fact you're least likely to get damaged, I'm told
— 'not / Pain's edge where we take shelter'. In 'The Field Hospital', the
characters, for all their rather blasé view of blood and gore, are on the
edge but implicated. That poem partly emerged from a viewing of the
film *M.A.S.H.*, and a viewing of *The Good, The Bad and The Ugly*, the
spaghetti western in which, I would guess, the Civil War scenes must be a
most faithful reconstruction of what it would have been like; also the fact
that when I was sitting in the house in Arboe one night a big yellow moth
came in the window and landed on my sleeve.

Do you regard Frost as a model in your work, or do you have many models?
I don't think there are any models as such. I don't care very much for the
notion of a single canon of a poet's work to which one must be faithful. I
like a great number of poems by a great number of people from Michael
Drayton to Craig Raine. Frost was important to me early on because his
line, his tone of voice, was so much a bare canvas. He's a good man to
learn from in that he has no particular nervous tics, no characteristics but
the strong, classic, lyric line. But the most important thing for me in Frost
was his mischievous, sly, multi-layered quality under the surface. One
thing that does come across for me in my own poems is a wryness, a mis-
chievousness in the voice, and I'm never quite sure whether I want to
believe that voice, this person who's presenting a piece of the world to me.

*The wryness you speak of is not something which you first intended but some-
thing you now recognize in your voice after three books?*
Indeed, I think it's unfortunate and dangerous that I can recognize it.
One is running very grave risks of self-parody in becoming overly self-con-
scious, self-aware. I think by and large I've escaped that, since I'm inter-
ested in ventriloquism, in speaking through other people, other voices. I
suppose some kind of tone creeps through but I don't want to locate it:
I'm not pleading for ignorance but against circumspection. The writer's
duty is to be open, and not to have too many preconceptions about how
it is and how it should be set down.

*Do you acknowledge my feeling that in a number of poems you're trying to cat-
echize certain received attitudes of the Irish, mythical and legendary... St.
Brendan and his boat, for example? Are you conscious of refusing to take his-
tory and tradition on trust?*

Yes, and this goes back to what we were saying about the voice: we must-n't take anything at face value, not even the man who is presenting things at face value. For all our simplifications of the world — and a work of art is a simplification in terms of its process of selection, a continual reduc-tion of the variables in what a thing might mean — that process of sim-plification must not become simplistic. We all know that if we try to nail a thing down it can pull the nail out and walk away, and perhaps that has something to do with my slyness and wryness. The poem can engage for thirty seconds in a little fiction: it has moved me, it will hopefully move you, disturb you, excite you; and having said and done that, we go our sep-arate ways back into the welter.

Would you say that you detect a strong moral drive in your work?
It's apparent to me as a reader of the poems in *New Weather* in particu-lar,many of which I don't like because of exactly that tone. I don't happen to like the moralizing tone in myself. Of course, you may not like how you are, but you have to accept that that's how it is, or was. So many of the last lines in *New Weather* come thumping off the soap-box, like 'None could describe / Electrocution, falling, the age of innocence' — how more pon-derous can you get? ... or 'Yet by my broken bones / I tell new weather' — which is silly and imperious.

It's a kind of knowing tone you indulged as a younger man, but not all the poems are of that kind.
No, 'The Cure for Warts' seems all right, though it uses a slightly tricksy typographical switch from 'nippling' to 'nibbling'. Well, it's apparently tricksy, but to describe those warts as 'nippling' and 'nibbling' is reason-ably accurate: I can tell you that because they're my own warts which I transposed to someone else. I'm very much against revision, however, since those poems were written at a particular time. I view the business of writing as a way of dealing with how we are. We keep changing, but we can't deny how we were at that given moment.

Do you have a sense of coordination between one poem and another in WHY BROWNLEE LEFT *or in* MULES, *of certain consistent imaginative notes being struck, and of an order to each book?*
I think both those books do run the risk of *appearing* slightly program-matic in that, in each case, only two or three concerns recur. They just happen to be ideas which obsessed me for two or three years, and still do. In *Why Brownlee Left* I'm interested in random behaviour, in swervings, deviations: and set against that a sense of purpose and idealism, be it in terms of romantic views of women or ideal societies or revolutionary pol-itics. The sort of thing Buñuel explored in *That Obscure Object of Desire.*

So you have a sense of unity about that book as perhaps never before? It builds through each poem.

Yes, I think it does. I think a poem should be intact in itself, but I think interesting things happen when a number of poems come out of a single, if dislocated, personality. They're bound to have some kind of unity. I've become very interested in structures that can be fixed like mirrors at angles to each other — it relates to narrative form — so that new images can emerge from the setting up of the poems in relation to each other: further ironies are possible, further mischief is possible. I hope the mischief I make is of a rewarding kind, not that of a practical joker, and will outline the complexities of being here.

The resonances of a poem like 'Anseo' seem immense in that respect ... since it treats the possibilities of behaviouristic conditioning in a rather chilling way.

If it works, it works because everything in it is absolutely dead-on, the details in it are really accurate. It's fiction, of course.

I suppose one must make a distinction between the poet using his words as a register of experience and using them as an interpretation of that experience, perhaps making quite a purposeful comment on a situation, though not necessarily in a ratiocinative or diagnostic way?

Yes, a poem does make a comment; if you live in a society, you're bound to reflect what happens in that society. That becomes complicated in the case of living in the North of Ireland. The poems I've written about the political situation there tend to be oblique, and I think properly so: they tend to look slightly farther back at the society from which the situation erupted, at *why* we are how we are now. What can you say about *how* we are? What I have to say about the politics of Northern Ireland is no more significant, probably much less informed, than what A, B or C has to say; it's pure opinion. Of course there is a place in poetry for opinion, but there's no place for the opinionated. If I believed there were a revolution, for example, and you can take it that I *don't* — I don't believe that Catholics are good guys and Protestants are bad guys, or vice-versa — if we were living in a banana republic and were being truly, monstrously oppressed, one can imagine pamphleteering, but not in Northern Ireland. The society is much too complex. 'Anseo' is about a very complex society indeed.

Do you think that at the least the attitude should be valid within the terms of the form and language of the poem?

Clearly one's allegiances, or bigotries, are going to be hinted at or guessed at, though I have no proper allegiances except to tell it like it is.

If you're saying that we have to make imaginative discriminations, I think you're quite right, but would you say that as a poet living in Ulster you have to strive for an immunity from political and historical pressures, or has it become necessary for you to assimilate them and try to synthesize them? Does the oppressive quality of life put an undue pressure on your writing? I mean, obliquity can pretend to be a poetic in its own right.

Sure, and I might appear to be evasive. But I don't have committed beliefs — it's as simple as that. Perhaps one makes a virtue of the necessity of how one is. I consider it important that I shouldn't have preconceptions, or that if I have them they shouldn't get in the way of the language, which I suppose is what I'm really interested in. I'm in awe of the language. But I'm not just in love with words, they've got to take on shapes that mean something. I think my response is quite responsible. In 'Early Warning', the figure of 'Our Protestant neighbour, Billy Wetherall' is not aware of his mess. I myself grew up, through geography lessons, to think of Northern Ireland as a linen-weaving, ship-building Utopia, and there's just no denying that when the Protestants had power they misused it. The poem is saying all that, but in no way as directly as I'm saying it now. Which would you prefer? All the things that are happening in the poem are true of a Catholic response, if you want to read it most overtly in that way: it's using all the clichés about Catholics and Protestants — Catholics have loads of children, they are notoriously given to factions, and they depend on more than they can see in terms of their religion and in terms of their Nationalist aspirations...

... and all that is conveyed by the images, not by exposition.

Right. What I object to is that to précis what's happening in the poem the way I'm doing now is to overstate it, to make it crude, and not to allow for the complexity of the poem. The poems are true and they make statements, but they're not standing on a box at Speaker's Corner. 'Anseo' is a very strong statement, if you want to read the poem that way: it's saying the society from which the child emerges is an oppressive, cruel one, and it's a Catholic society. I'm saying it now, but it's more powerfully embodied in the poem.

And another factor is that the figure of Joseph Mary Plunkett Ward makes a virtue of being oppressed.

Yes. I know these people, and some of them love the notion of being oppressed. The society that Joe Ward posits for the future, the society that the IRA posits for the future, is not a society I want to know. I'm making these crude statements now only to underline how much more *effectively* I do it in verse. 'Lunch with Pancho Villa' (*Mules*) is a poem in which the old pamphleteer is upbraiding the protagonist in the kind of way that I might be upbraided —

> 'Look, son. Just look around you.
> People are getting themselves killed
> Left, right and centre
> While you do what? Write rondeaux?
> There's more to living in this country
> Than stars and horses, pigs and trees,
> Not that you'd guess it from your poems.
> Do you never listen to the news?
> You want to get down to something true,
> Something a little nearer home.'

— and my point is that an understanding of the people who keep those pigs and shelter under those trees is true, and *is* at home.

I'd like to ask you here about your long poem 'Immram' in WHY BROWNLEE LEFT...
Yes ... 'Immram' means 'voyage tale'. Under the influence of the *Navigatio Sancti Brendani* the earlier forms of voyage tales were given a Christian veneer. One of the best known of them is 'Immram Mael Duin' (another is the 'Voyage of Bran', which partly explains a small joke in an earlier poem), in which the hero sets out to avenge his father's death, goes through many fabulous adventures, and at the end discovers an old hermit sitting on a rock — who turns out to be a Howard Hughes figure in my version — who tells him that he should turn the other cheek. Swift was very likely aware of the genre, and Tennyson has a dreadful version of it. I've tried to write a version which gives it a contemporary setting, because one of the few genres in which the heroic mode is possible is the thriller. Apart from that, I like Chandler a great deal; I think he's a very good writer, a good stylist. Byron is knocking around there too.

Are you faithful to the individual episodes of 'Immram Mael Duin'?
My poem takes the episodes and motifs of the original and twists them around, sometimes out of all recognition. At one stage, for instance, a confrontation with a white cat becomes a confrontation with a black cat...

... which is slang for a black.
Yes.
    'Immram' runs a real risk of appearing a piece of sheer ventriloquism, but it does pull together a lot of the things that the book concerns itself with: the central notion, for example, of the Howard Hughes figure who lives at the top of an hotel with a deserted floor just underneath him ... that whole sense of the layers of perception is something I try to explore in other poems. One of the things that set me off was this vision of an old

hermit who's visited every day by an otter bringing him a loaf of bread and a jug of ale, which I treat in terms of Hughes's penchant for Baskin-Robbins banana-nut ice-cream. The quest is the powerful and important centre of the poem. Both the protagonist and his father are led through a maze. The protagonist is a cipher, the world envelops him, everything happens to him; he directs very little, and I'm very sceptical about how much we direct anything that happens to us. And the end of it is this whimsical — I would tend to use the word 'whimful', which doesn't exist — this whimsical dismissal by the bane of both their lives. 'I forgive you ... and I forget'.

How does the earlier, shorter poem 'Immrama' relate to 'Immram'?
I wrote it some time ago, when I had no notion of writing the longer poem, though certainly with a sense of 'Immram Mael Duin' at the back of my head. In a way, 'Immrama' is a poem about never having been born ... the father leads a totally different life (which he might easily have done) in which I would not have figured. 'Immrama' means 'voyages'; it's the plural of 'Immram'.

As you say, it's consistent with certain motifs in the book as a whole: the possibility of alternative lives, capricious disappearances, the possibility that certain figures might have been the victims of sectarian killings or might just have opted out.
Yes ... as to why Brownlee left, for example. That poem began, I think, when I saw a photograph of two horses standing in a field, or perhaps I *did* see two horses — such a powerful image — and I started to think about what might have happened. The name itself, Brownlee, suggests a brown meadow, a ploughed field, and so — in a strange sort of way — his end is in his name; he's fulfilled his purpose even before he begins. I use names perhaps far too often in a Jonsonian, emblematic way.

Why do you think the notion of alternative lives is peculiarly fetching, philosophically attractive, to your imagination?
I think it's central to us. One of the ways in which we are most ourselves is that we imagine ourselves to be going somewhere else. It's important to most societies to have the notion of something out there to which we belong, that our home is somewhere else ... there's another dimension, something around us and beyond us, which is our inheritance. There are undesirable elements to that wish to be elsewhere, in the form, for instance, of escapism.

Would you say that you're looking for an imagined order, though the phrase has religious overtones?
It's pretty well established in my mind that the world has an order. There

is an order among things which has got to do with more than our order-ing of them, our perception of them.

Several of the poems in WHY BROWNLEE LEFT *have more comedy than you've managed in earlier books.*
A lot of them should be read as rather funny. The tone of voice, the slightly tongue-in-cheek quality, allows for humour and irony.

Can you say why you've been drawn, on the whole, to work in forms of estab-lished prosody, stanzaic patterns, and rhyme?
Sometimes, I'm sure, there's an element of laziness about it. The only use I can see for formal structures is to help the writer himself decide the shape and size of the canvas. What has to be said determines its own form, or should do. It then helps the reader to have some kind of fixity. I don't scan, however, but use a purely intuitive process within each line. My only concern is that the lines are speakable. I have rather loose notions of what a rhyme is, since many of mine are assonantal. I've been described as someone who would rhyme 'cat' with 'dog'. But I've also managed 'moon' and 'June'.

D. E. S. Maxwell, in an essay which took brief stock of your early work, said that your world is threatening, and at times disheartening. Is that an aspect of your work that you recognize or that has gone further?
Disheartening? I find it difficult to talk about, since it goes back to a 'view of the world'. I would say it's not disheartening. But it's not always a bar-rel of laughs, is it?

Anything that swims into your world picture is *in* your world picture. That's why I'm very much against expressing a categorical view of the world. I hope I can continue to discover something, and not to underline or bolster up what I already think I know.

GERALD DAWE

*Born in 1952 you grew up in Belfast. 'What our family "means" and how we gather all such "things" into our "selves"?' is a question you ask of the poet Thomas Kinsella (*AGAINST PIETY, *1995). How would you answer this question about yourself?*

I think it was an important part of my background that I grew up in a house full of women. My mother and father separated when I was quite young; I moved with my mother and sister from Downview to my grandmother's house in Skegoneill so I grew up there in north Belfast. My grandmother, who had separated from her husband in Canada and returned to Belfast to work in a well-know Jewish retail shop, Goorwiches in Royal Avenue, gave piano and elocution lessons from the house. She had a public life as a light opera singer so I was often referred to as Ethel Chartres's grandson. My mother, a more intensely private woman than my grandmother, stayed at home to run the house only going to work in retail shops in town and, later on, in the civil service when I was in my early teens. It was a fairly typical lower middle class family with a fair share of tenacity and vulnerability and, I see now, an intriguing mask of being only these things. I was often unwell with asthma as a young boy but I was very well looked after by these women. Off school periodically I'd read alone at the top of this quiet house with just the clock ticking — all the women of the house out and my sister at school. I recall reading dictionaries or magazines on films which my mother, as a great cinema-goer, would collect. I grew up very much on my own but the house alternated between tranquillity and calm and a very dynamic family life: my grandmother, as an out-going woman, had friends around for parties or piano recitals; London relatives visited periodically; when my uncle was demobbed from the RAF he would bring his mates and girlfriends around so there was also this whole new dynamic of animated discussions and good-natured arguments.

We lived in a row of seven terrace houses — a self-contained little canton of Protestants and Catholics with a surrounding immigrant Jewish community, a lower middle class world of small shopkeepers, senior clerks and widowers. Originally my great grandfather's people had come from Hugenot France; my great grandmother's people came, we suspect, from central Europe and both had married in Belfast early on in the twentieth century. My grandmother was very friendly with the Jewish community and my best friend as a youngster was a Jewish boy. As a boy you knew the territory between home and primary school like the back of your hand. There was a seasonal rhythm with 'marbles', conkers and the yearly holiday in Bangor or Portrush (which seemed more risque) that has probably gone. During the July fortnight we took a house in Bangor and my grandmother's friends, like the stunningly handsome Annie Orr, would visit. Annie would recount stories of the B-Specials shooting up a family on the Cliftonville Road; early on she rooted me into a Catholic Nationalist experience of Belfast. Later you bussed across town to secondary school in east Belfast and a whole new geography with its own rhythms opened up.

How would you describe your early childhood awareness of that first environment though — the language or speech of home and the Belfast streets?
Language and speech have always fascinated me; there was the way people spoke "proper" English through Belfast accents, a kind of Empire English that was slightly embarrassing and intriguing. On Wednesday afternoons when my grandmother gave elocution lessons, which were popular, you would hear the girls and boys reciting poems in that kind of accent. I was intrigued by the feeling that the way we spoke was somehow inadequate and that there was a "proper" way to speak. I remember visiting my extended family, in the late '50s and early '60s, who had moved to London between the wars, and being asked by a great aunt to stand up and say certain words like "mirror" in my Belfast accent. The request came from affection — not from an urge to humiliate or embarrass — from a sense that the way we spoke was somehow authentic. If you were mindful of the English spoken on the street and the extraordinary language the girls would use on the bus travelling across town, (an incantatory, half-mocking language which ended with them shouting each other's names like *'Jean-ne-o'*), there was also the language that you were supposed to aspire to (a type of tortured Cherryvalley English); between these two there was the language of the place itself with its own phrases, words and terms — a Pandora's box, a treasure trove — and you discover that it is not totally understood everywhere (when you travel) and you become conscious of it (when you write poetry) later on. Every family has its own codes, its language, but there was a symmetry or fluency between the language of the house, the street and the Belfast buses and that is a tremendous resource for any writer to have. I've always been bothered, though, when a writer's sense of the vernacular or the idiomatic or demotic becomes too self-conscious so that it becomes exotic, an interest in itself, a turning of language into a zoo.

Poems like 'Innocence' and 'Safe Houses' in SUNDAY SCHOOL *(1991) have dif-*

ferent perspectives on the Second World War; 'Child of the Empire' in HEART OF
HEARTS *(1995) dreams up Churchill; there is your primary school headmaster
with a spitfire in* THE REST IS HISTORY *(1998). World War II was important?*
The Second World War influenced everything from the clothes men wore
to the style of their moustaches through to the attitude to cooking
(where, if things was not quite hoarded, you still did not throw food out)
and it influenced the physical environment in memorials and pre-fabs,
which I can still recall, on the Shore Road where people had been moved
to after the Belfast Blitz in 1941. This was only fifteen years later after all;
there were still ration books and black-out blinds in the house. Then
there was the whole military sense of the Empire in annual parades —
Remembrance Day and V-Day — and the flags in the churches repre-
sented the various battalions. In the history taught at school the Second
War was an all pervasive background and, indirectly, it suffused the
metaphorical backdrop of the films my generation watched where the
Attenboroughs or John Mills appeared. The political background was
largely not taught but I remember Churchill's televised *History of the World*
with Richard Burton's voice-over coming in. The Second War was our
world and, in some senses, it had never really ended. You would see war
veterans on the buses (with their navy blazers and regimental insignia
badges); there were those damaged war-veterans who could not adjust to
civilian life; some of the neighbours in north Belfast were Jewish or
refugees; our next door neighbour had fought in the war and met his wife
in Vienna and my grandmother had worked in an ammunitions factory.
The war crossed divisions; it affected the whole tapestry of civic life in
Belfast. The people who were honoured, or who we thought we should
honour or who we were told to honour, were all connected with the war.
From Camp coffee in the cupboards to our awareness of battles in
Holland or north Africa there was the sense of Imperial connectedness,
the sense that in some way we were all part of the one story.

The war penetrated consciousness that deeply? What about popular literature?
Yes. On Fridays you had that whole series of magazines or comics like *The
Tiger* where the Germans snapped out instructions and there was always a
good Tommy, a Scottish soldier or a Gurka. Christmas bumper editions,
annuals, covered the story of particular tanks or battalions. We lived not
too far away from the Capitol cinema on the Antrim Road; I remember
my mother telling me, in my teens, about seeing the Pathe News images
of the concentration camps so the full story did leak through. A friend,
Ken, whose father had been attacked by Messerschmitts described the
attack and that lit up another world. There were war posters and, at one
level, the entire imaginative life was lived around the Imperial armies,
navys and airforces; there were the military tattoos, "Army Days" when

you'd visit camps and jump into tanks and television was full of it as well. There was also the sense — built in behind all this but never really explicated — that the war was linked with the defence of democracy and "our" whole way of life. There was a fad in constructing little Airfix aircraft that you built and arranged in the bay window on perspex stands. So there was this construction of your own little bit of the Empire in symbolic miniature in the front room.

You went to Orangefield Boys' School in the 1960s; Van Morrison had been there in the 1950s only to find 'There was no school for people like me.' You note Mahon's description of himself and Longley as 'Protestant poets of an English educational system with an inherited duality of cultural reference' in AGAINST PIETY. *Did the poetry or culture you encountered at school relate to the needs of your imagination or to the place you were from? Are these contradictory needs?*
These senses of place and needs of the imagination are not necessarily the same; we were taught English literature, very English work, and I now feel that this was a good thing; only to have had confirmation of where and what you are, as a fourteen year old from north Belfast, would not necessarily have been that healthy. I was lucky to have good teachers, Dai Francis and Sam McCready. Part of the deal was that you read, learnt and stood up in class to recite, chunks of English literature. I absorbed Chaucer, Keats, Milton, the Victorians and Shakespeare. Literature was this grounding in, and probing of, the great English writers which gave me some sense of the language and its structure, its material fabric. Later you heard sympathetic notes and echoes outside the main English tradition (like Yeats's early poems or ballads or a classic poem like *The Lake Isle of Innisfree*) so you had a sense of contrariness — that this was different from the great English writers like Keats or Chaucer or Milton. The real echo though, which blew my mind, was reading the American poets in *The Faber Book of Modern Verse* edited by Michael Roberts; their language seemed very different — entirely fresh; a contemporary kind of language — and that electrified me, as did Stewart Parker's school talk on Sylvia Plath's work. Alongside these writers you read novels like D.H. Lawrence's *Sons and Lovers* so you had the sense that you could write out of the ordinary, domestic suburban life that was mundane or the family orientated — this *could* be the subject for writing. I suppose I read a lot of fiction — particularly in translation in those Penguin Classics: Gide, Dostoevsky...

Your reading of American poets like Lowell and Wallace Stevens instilled a sense of language as transparent, democratic? English literature by the back door?
For a writer it is all down to how you hear language and energize it in poems. You can hear the language of the street or the bus or the looser, less formalized English of American poetry but you have to know how to

convert this and transform it into formal structures. I'm sure Keats heard the language of the street and knew how to convert it into more operatic structures while Milton created muscular, very literary lines in his poems; it is surely not one thing against another, or vice-versa, but a merger of these things so that one energizes the other. Sometimes you can fall between the gaps when the street language lacks formal structures or the literary language of a poem lacks its own life or energy. To write just idiomatically and think it's a poem is pure fantasy just as it is to purely try to situate yourself within a literary tradition and to do no more than that. You can have all the language in the world but it will not add up unless you have actually something to say.

Robert Lowell added up?
I read Robert Lowell in a hardback Faber edition in Bangor in 1968; the poems which struck me were in *For the Union Dead* and some in *Life Studies*. There was a sense of Lowell's anger and bitterness so that it felt as if these poems had come out of my immediate environment. Here was a voice full of clarity, an unrepentantly modern voice, a voice with erudition without showing off. I picked up on the tone of voice even though a lot of the references went clean over my head. Lowell's poems were full of edginess and irony and that sounded not too far removed from the language of Belfast in fact.

You also read the French existentialists — Camus and Sartre — in Belfast and somehow that seems appropriate?
Camus was the easier writer to read and listen to; Sartre was much more demanding. In *Nausea* and *Roads to Freedom* you have this story of a man cutting his way through a heavily politicised, problematical landscape so those were novels that a sixteen or eighteen year old from Belfast could draw on. Camus was much more intimate and in many ways he meant more; there was Sartre's haughtiness which was partly class-based. And yet Sartre give an extraordinary weight to the intellectual life — life had this extraordinary other world within it which should not be decried; coming from a political climate such as "official" Belfast then was, where the intellect was frowned on and where everything was signed, sealed and delivered — so what was there to talk or *think* about? — that was refreshing. Camus told a story which was more intimate, closer to himself, and he converted these into austere and structured narratives in the essays; there's the powerful, theatrical essay, *The Myth of Sisyphus*; in *The Rebel* (which I read at about sixteen) you had this opening into a huge miracle world, invisible to us until then; there's the violence in *L'Etranger* but there is also a life lived in the sheer brightness of the sun, which is appealing when you are looking out of a Belfast window at the rain. Camus lived in

French Algeria so there was the whole subtextual level about which nation you identify with but I would not have picked up on that much at the time. Strangely, since I wrote about reading these writers in *The Rest is History*, a number of people from my generation have related similar experiences so maybe there was a season for these things in Belfast. The city had a youth culture, an intense club life going on at that time (and much in Camus also came from the similar circumstances in that house on the hill in Algeria, although the entirely different climate offers no parallels) so, maybe, we identified with that energy in the writing; it has that helter-skelter, breezy, out-and-about energy which also existed in Belfast then. This energy and "freedom", particularly in the underground life of Belfast from the early '50s and mid-'60s, has not really been logged, so the dour, dark, drab image of the city predominates or else the fairly artificially constructed, lopsided one of more recent times. Certainly, in many ways, Camus was my hero.

You sought Michael Longley's advice about writing in the mid-1960s and met Padraic Fiacc (1973) whose selected poems, RUINED PAGES *(1994), you would later co-edit. You see Fiacc as having 'bridged the link between poetry and violence' in* THE REST IS HISTORY *to produce 'central, indeed definitive, poetic statements on the northern conflict' in* HOW'S THE POETRY GOING?. *Surely these writers are poles apart in terms of poems and dealing with the North? There's Longley's construction and Fiacc's fragmentation.*
A friend of mine, Gary Williamson, had a sister who was taught by Michael Longley, so I sent him some poems through her and he wrote back a marvellous letter, a real schooling before workshops were invented, with a list of books to read; that was important. When I met Fiacc I found a guy who had a sense of the Modernist aesthetic; he had read and absorbed people like Beckett so there was this edginess and fragmentation and disruption, the breaking down of formal English and its shapes. Longley, and Derek Mahon, both have composure and produce what was once, foolishly, called the 'well-made poem'. Surely all poems, to exist as poems, have to be 'well-made'? Fiacc made poems out of the landscape in which I was literally walking and that authorizing of the landscape was extremely important for me at that time in the early 1970s. Reading his early poems, like 'By the Black Stream', which is about a Belfast man being caught in the half-light of the moon, floored me. There is also an extraordinary irony and self-mockery in Fiacc whereby he deconstructs the whole notion of "the poet" and the pretentiousness that goes with that title. The integrity of his work, at that level, is unimpeachable; it is driven by a need to get the right form for the experience that lies behind the work. Michael Longley's work draws down the classical world and marries it with the suburban world I had grown up in. So here were two writers virtually dia-

metrically opposed in every way — although the Modernist aesthetic in Fiacc is almost counterposed by the security, stability and artistic mass you find in Longley. To some extent, I have tried to marry those two things. At least, that merger was the project, quite a job.

AGAINST PIETY *sums up the period between leaving school and university (1968-71) as ' London, hanging out in Belfast…(applying for a job) as a cub reporter at my great-grandfather's editorial home,* THE BELFAST TELEGRAPH'. HOW'S THE POETRY GOING? *(1991) describes it as a time when 'our lives took on a new weird meaning — we began to live more recklessly with a perverse bravado'. I have a sense that "home" and "homelessness" imbedded itself in northern poetry then; did you write poems in this period?*
I did write poems although they were absolutely impenetrable, a form of Theosophy you could make neither head nor tail of. I wrote one poem called 'I'm Through', the title taken from Sylvia Plath's 'Daddy' poem, and it was eventually published in *Sheltering Places* in 1978. I did not write many poems which will survive in that period but I read an extraordinary amount.

I do have a sense now of 1969 as the year in which the curtain fell. The recklessness and bravado existed amongst a group of us who went to dances or parties virtually every night. Up to 1969 we were spoiled for choice; there was the extraordinary riches of John Mayall's Bluesbreakers, and Cream and Fleetwood Mac visited Belfast. There was also a vibrant club and R & B scene. You could leave a girl home after a dance and walk for twenty minutes across town into any area up to 1968-69 but we kept on doing that into 1970, pretending that nothing was happening, and that was crazy. It was pure luck that no one was badly damaged; by 1972-73 all that stopped as Belfast became sectionalised. After I was threatened with being shot — (I was simply a Protestant in the wrong place) — the penny dropped; the bravado had to go. As Belfast became segmented, a desert town, it's possible to see 1969-70 as the last gasp of that decade's openness; after that it went toke. I'm still angry about that. Something was taken away from us all, stolen by the violence.

Looking back at the early '70s I think we experienced a state of shock, akin to the trauma after a car crash, as we realised that the world we had grown up in had concealed this poison. Like some writers I felt then that you had to respond by writing politically. You might have tried to rationalise the situation and work out the anger and frustration (to create a space that was personal and self-sustaining as a rampart against all of this). I also tried then to conscript poetry to politically motivated writing. I realise now you cannot do that without allowing time or space for the experience to settle. Increasingly I've felt there were no "lessons" to be drawn from history; History (with a capital 'H') was, if anything, an encumbrance — and certainly not some kind of rudder. Some writers looked to Eastern

Europe (to Poland, Russia or Czechoslovakia) for historical parallels and poets like Mandelstam were read but there's a certain artificiality in the historical parallels; what happened in the North, in Belfast, was more intimate and on a smaller scale. If parallels existed at all then surely Spain, with its civil war and religious struggle, was closer? This was a time when I was looking in the wrong direction for political solutions; I feel now, without fatalism, that what happened was inevitable because the opportunity for change had already been lost and squandered in the '60s. The way things were run in the North had not been challenged early enough and so, for two and a half decades, we had the "Troubles" out of which people began living as the paramilitaries moved in and the civic space in Belfast was lost. Only now is that whole problem getting slowly sorted out. People made choices to plant bombs or take lives but the main responsibility for political failure rests with the old Unionist Party and the sectarian nature of the society while the pursuance of a military solution by the IRA was the other major factor in keeping the situation going; we have had to pay for both. How could any one poet weave a way through those two massive, self excluding forces? I just don't think it was possible. Maybe there was a withdrawal by writers into their own spaces. You have Michael Longley reimagining the whole thing through great classical texts like the *Iliad*; you have Mahon meditating on the whole notion of history; you have Fiacc, who I think is unique in this regard, actually challenging it in the structure of his verse. The whole scene was simply uncontrollable; writers should not feel responsible for that. There was the demand on writers to have an easy "take" on the situation but most poets were not giving that so the responses naturally varied; for poets it is primarily important to write poems that work and to that end it does not matter where the inspiration or subject matter comes from. I have always felt a little outside the whole "northern poetry" thing. Probably because I went to college in Coleraine and then left the North in 1974 I wasn't part of the scene although I knew some of the poets individually. I suppose I've always been a bit cagey about being part of anything. I don't know why that should be. It hasn't helped really over the years.

You studied literature at the New University of Ulster at Coleraine between 1971-74 where you wrote two plays, THE SKULL *and* THE PAWNBROKER. *What were these plays about? Are dramatic forms essential different from those required in poetry?*
I had published some poems in *The Irish Press* and read on BBC radio so I was asked by the Irish Language Society in Coleraine to write two plays which they would translate into Irish. The first, *The Skull*, was about a speaking skull sitting on a rock becoming excited by the presence of women and so on. The idea was lifted from Robin Flower's *The Irish*

Tradition; it travelled down to An Damer, the Irish-speaking theatre in Stephen's Green, for a season of one act plays and then it was sent to The Gate but I never got the script back so the play's details are vague. *The Pawnbroker* was a verse drama, a mix and match of priest and Orangeman but these were two undergraduate plays; I now teach theatre so I know the kinds of things needed to write well for the theatre and it's a different discipline than poetry. But you never know when an idea might come along. The theatre is such an interior world: it has its very own codes and conduct; I don't think you can just 'write a play'. You really need to know what you're doing and why.

In Coleraine you joined the Labour Club, helped to set up the James Larkin Defence Committee and played in a band, 'Fir Uladh', at anti-internment gigs; a poem like 'Speedboats, 1972' indicates little sympathy for the North's middle classes. Does class consciousness register in your poetry? A loosely left-wing position might be inferred from reading many northern poets; there's MacNeice's generalised sympathy for the left and Longley's sympathy for artisans.

At that stage I was very much on the left. I read Trotsky and Marx in the hope of getting away from the cramped politics of the complacent Unionist position on the one side and the very heavily authoritarian position of Catholic Nationalism on the other. The hope was that Socialism might create an effective wedge to drive change though. Coleraine drew a mix of students and lecturers from Scotland, the Republic of Ireland and England; Walter Allen taught there and he had been part of that 1930s generation of writers which had included Louis MacNeice. Allen was *very* influential at Coleraine when I was there. He opened up American and Russian literature for us. He was a great teacher. If the teaching staff were generally on the left, the student bodies, with Scottish influence in the Labour Clubs, were totally permeated by left-wing radicalism. As students we would go to Derry to sell newspapers or we mounted protests against internment, that quick fix which energized opposition in the 1970s in the same way that Thatcher's treatment of the Hunger Strikes did in the 1980s. In the modern literary traditions of Scotland and the North of Ireland there has been a very strong left-wing influence; it seems to have congregated in bars and meeting rooms and parlours without really having an impact on northern power-structures or government. You would have thought that Queen's University might have been a cultural centre for the left but that was hardly the case; a writer like MacNeice would have been encountered at Queen's by pure fluke before Edna and Michael Longley repatriated him to the North. There was John Hewitt's egalitarianism, his respect for the political ideals of the left, his Republicanism — he would probably have baulked at that description but the prose and poems are for an active contract between citizens and the state which is a classic Republican position. I imagine Hanna Bell, Roy McFadden, John Boyd — would all be identified as left-wingers. Although it's not entirely visible in the cultural climate, the ether among writers was left-wing; the tragedy was that this had never really been generally imbedded in the educational system so as to produce a generation in the 1970s who could effectively counter the sectarian environment. I suppose, having grown up in a household of women, I have very little interest in delineations of men at work in the poems. I've difficulty with the notion that only work defines you but I have a great deal of respect for Hewitt's and Longley's artisans. I can see that virtues accrue from certain kinds of work. What really imaginatively interests me though is the way art is made or the ways in which you define a landscape through a mood or a shade or an angle of perception. 'Speedboats 1972' points up the complacency and acquiescence of the middle class in the North — in the same way that Hewitt did in his marvellous poem 'The Coasters' — but I hope I'm not just taking an easy swipe because there are also virtues in that class; they helped to create stability but, being deeply uneasy with culture, they created a parody of it which amounted to wearing cravats at the Arts Club and, in some senses, this art world became a kind of refuge for political failure. Here was a "gross industrial city like Belfast but we'll still read our Forrest Reid and hang on to that specialist knowledge which marks one out above others". You come across the same attitude occasionally in the South of Ireland although it is less pronounced. I can't stand it.

The north-west 'triangle' — Portrush, Portstewart, Coleraine — has inspired northern poems by Simmons, McFadden and Mahon. Does it surface in your work?
I've always been drawn to coasts. I grew up within sight, sound and smell of Belfast Lough. I don't think I consciously wrote out of the geographical scene of the Triangle although one or two poems set there appear in *Sheltering Places*, and this landscape often merges with poems written later or set in and around Galway. I think of Portstewart or Portrush now as signifying the staunchness and steadfastness of Ulster Protestantism; it's a landscape on the edge of things, both bracing and abrasive.

AGAINST PIETY *and* HOW'S THE POETRY GOING? *record the 'importance' of Derek Mahon's work. 'Is there a poet of the 1990s for whom one will wait as one did in the 1970s for Derek Mahon's* LIVES *or* THE SNOW PARTY?' *you ask. What is it in Mahon's work you relate to?*
Mahon, for me, brought together different elements into the one imaginative frame: a modern contemporary idiom; the self-dramatising, self-ironising voice; the link with European writing and writers like Beckett (which I found attractive) and the anonymous, austere, remote, controlled shape of the poem. He creates these poems of extraordinary light-

ness and depth — there is a certain chilliness and the more recent work is analytical. There is an imaginative weight in his work, a tremendous amount of understanding and learning so that his poetry surpasses that of all the other poets I greatly admire from Ireland and elsewhere.

Moving to Galway in 1974 to research William Carleton you lectured there until 1992 while commuting 'through those complicated and sometimes deadly chambers that divide one part of this island from another' as you put it in FALSE FACES *(1994). The west has often magnetised poets: Yeats, W.R. Rodgers, MacNeice, Longley, Norman Dugdale. How does it register in your work?*
I had been to the west in 1973, but I moved down in 1974 after working for a brief spell as a librarian in the Central Library in Belfast. I really grew up in Galway as the pressures in the North of the early 70s, that I carried inside me, began to unwind. Galway provided a contrast I needed to discover; I'd been stung to the quick by what had happened in Belfast. Living in the west of Ireland I began to find that there were Irelands — not just physically but culturally and psychologically. *Sheltering Places* comes from the initial awe I felt as a young fellow of twenty two moving into an awesome, even denatured, landscape and, as I started to live in a place where I would work for twenty two years, I began to see through the landscape to the people and to the more domestic customs of the place. I wrote all of *Lundys Letter* from the west; there are quite a few poems about the west in *Sunday School* and *Heart of Hearts*. Between *Sheltering Places* in 1978 and *The Lundys Letter* in 1985 I started to re-imagine the Belfast Protestant background I had grow up in and wonder about my own family's diverse provincial and "refugee" roots. As I was trying to understand my life in Galway I was — ironically and simultaneously — discovering my own background in Belfast and what these terms mean — "background", "Belfast", "my own".

SHELTERING PLACES *has that key image of a storm which threatens shelter in the title poem which makes it look, very much, like a Belfast poem. Are there also tensions between literary/historical traditions and the subjective 'now' — 'the passion that cries out of the ordinary' in this your first volume?*
I wrote the title poem, 'Sheltering Places', in 1970-71 when I lived for a brief period in Ballybeen in east Belfast; it's not a west of Ireland poem. The hills in that poem are the Craigantlet Hills behind the estate and the storm clouds are literal as much as they refer to the "Troubles" which threaten to eclipse the ordinary lives of people. On the whole though that book is emotionally stunned; a big influence and probably too strong a presence was Padraic Fiacc. I was trying to find a language that was non-poetic so Fiacc's voice was important and the poems are responses of which I was not entirely in control. I now think that the lack of control shows but I was trying to create a voice and to understand the literary tra-

dition; I think there's a more realised voice in *The Lundys Letter* which came after I had read more poetry — Yeats and Longley — and absorbed it into my own voice.

If SHELTERING PLACES *alternates between a bleak western, almost existential, landscape (rocky, stony, rainy and empty) and Belfast's 'poisoned... sloblands' where a river is 'a haemorrhaged vein', there is also the traveller in 'Seanchai' with 'baseball boots' and 'an inarticulate/mythology that/has no place/to cele-brate.' Your essay on John Hewitt and your poems set in Europe (with the moth as travelling 'muse' in a suitcase) might be taken as indicating that outward horizons, not inward roots, are more important in your poetry? It also raises that old juncture between home and exile in Irish poetry.*

I think you are like a metronome early on. You move between the need to place yourself, to put down roots and stabilise artistic foundations, and yet you cannot just remain on that ground; that tension lies behind many of the poems. At some level I have always felt rootless and maybe it's a genetic throwback! I need horizons and the sense of space to oxygenize or aerate roots, to avoid the work collapsing inside itself, getting consti-pated. It's not that travel to other places particularly interests me but being in them does; I like observing the "otherness" of other places. Of course I've carried Belfast with me — Belfast is partly a state of mind — but I have chosen where and when I've moved so I can't help but feel that there's often sentimentality in much of the talk around the notion of exile. Of course, a man from Achill who had to leave for work in New York or Boston or London in the 1940s or '50s, would find that exile had an entirely different resonance. These days though, with many Irish kids jet-ting back and forward on Virgin Atlantic Airlines between Ireland and the States, the whole notion of Irish exile can sound like phoney rhetoric, more to do with American perceptions of Ireland rooted in the past than with contemporary realities. If you are from Kosovo or Bosnia Hercegovina exile has a very real and current meaning too.

You edited THE YOUNGER IRISH POETS *(1982) which includes northern poets who 'grew up in the poetically charged literary environment of the 1980s' with their 'unpretentious confidence... self-deprecating wit' and 'keen tactics of evasion'. Is there such a thing as 'northern poetry'? Were the tactics of 1980s northern poets different from those of the 1960s?*

Take it chronologically. There was a big breakthrough with the '60s gen-eration — Heaney, Longley, Mahon and Simmons — who all wrote poems of the first rank. Earlier poets like John Montague and Fiacc, a little before him, had fed into '60s writing but these poets wrote poems here through which they achieved an extraordinary degree of world recogni-tion which was unthinkable up to that point. The second generation —

Medbh McGuckian, Paul Muldoon, Ciaran Carson and Frank Ormsby — could call down that achievement and play with it. Certainly Paul Muldoon has many self-ironising strategies and he can turn the tradition to lightly make fun of it but he's also sustained by it and, partly, its amanuensis. More recent writers, like John Hughes, have moved through that Muldoon playfulness and avoided the more magisterial sense of poetry. Critics, though, prefer groups to individuals; in that first big movement of northern writers, so floodlit by history, you have writers who are so very different that, with hindsight, it's possible to see the differences as more defining than what they have in common as poets from "the North". The differences between Muldoon and Mahon are enormous; very little links Mahon and Heaney. Mahon might be linked with Beckett but where does that leave "the North"? To simply force these writers into categories under the auspices of '*northern* poetry' is fundamentally limiting; their differences have as much to do with specific cultural or religious experiences as they have to do with anything called "The North" with a capital 'T' and 'N'.

Across a ROARING HILL *(1985), which you edited with Edna Longley, looks at the religious factor; it is not a 'sectarian sociology of art' but a reflection on the 'distinction between Protestant and Catholic...'; 'only one, albeit major, part of Irish experience... has determined so much of what I am' in* HOW'S THE POETRY GOING? *(1991). How do different religious backgrounds register differently in the style, language or subject matter of poetry in Ireland and in your work in particular?*
I'll talk within a strictly literary axis. I think that people from a Protestant background have a different imaginative make-up from those of a Catholic background although there are cross-overs and differences within Protestantism — the Church of Ireland and Methodism, for instance — because there has been a different schooling and cultural formation and this can produce different echoes in the writing. The Mass and its whole iconography, the whole sacred notion of the altar and "serving" it, is fundamentally different from the more chaste emblematic furniture and the austerity of language which defines the after-world in Protestant churches. I'm not just talking about spirituality or mystery; the ways in which Protestants are called upon to honour the after-world is entirely different. There is no incense and colour is so shocking because it's use is so limited; this means that every phrase or nuance carries a rigorous kind of significance. I went to the Church of Ireland on the Antrim Road as a boy and it inhabited a middle distance, a limbo land, between Catholicism and Presbyterianism. Early on I was struck by the purity of language in the hymns, the iconography of the Empire in the flags; those Old Testament stories and New Testament parables have stayed with me. There was also a sense of individual, even civic, responsibilities or moral-

ity that you could not just dump outside and leave at the church door. Some Bible stories, like the one about Jericho, surface in the poems as little cartoons. I'm not particularly interested, though, in either hitting the church or exploring its ministry or environment; I've not been scarred by this formation within cultural Protestantism to either want to do that or to fake a Catholic "Irish" sense of what I'm doing as a writer. There is the fascinating encounter between the renegade Joyce and Beckett in Paris; one tries to pull the entire world into the book and the other to flush it all away. Yet you still hear the whispered echo of the Church of Ireland hymnal or vespers — 'Now the day is over, night is drawing nigh' — in Beckett's *Krapp*. In Beckett that takes on a shocking poetic charge; sung in church it can sound just like another cliché. I think that chasteness, that austerity of language is one inheritance of Protestantism for which I am thankful.

Your first three poetry volumes between 1986 and 1991 share, with Tom Paulin, the Belfast-Protestant background and landscape: clocks, mission huts, Orange Halls, terraced streets, the poet questioning recent Unionist history (Edward Carson and Covenants), 'bibles and ledgers', living rooms crowded with knick-knacks. The language, narrative strategies and ways in which history is refracted through poetry seem radically different though?

How conscious this focus is in the writing of the poems I'm not sure but when I wrote 'Secrets' in *Lundys Letter* I felt I had got inside a world I had not read about, the type of domestic interior I had encountered in friends' houses which opened out into the wider civic landscape of Belfast. Initially I felt that this world had not been registered in literature although, re-reading Mahon, I came to realise that he often echoed this world and, in many cases, had been there before me. It took me ages to get a poem like 'Little Palaces' right, to try to capture that sense of decorum and of everything in its place. No doubt there's a kind of psycho-babble that could easily caricature the rituals and routines of this whole Protestant way of life — painted kerb stones, wound clocks, mission huts and Boy Scouts — as defence mechanisms in a consciousness that is either unfulfilled or which has not engaged sufficiently with *any* other-world or other side; I dare say the same analysis might be made in reverse of Catholicism. Primarily these poems register a world, a civilisation, which was changing — which has now gone. I thought it was important to register the integrity of the life in these streets rather than to stand outside and mock it and that's a tricky line to walk. Some people have read these poems as authorizing a narrow world view but there is a critical stance. I see the poet's role as primarily bearing witness — although that sounds a bit grand — and the excitement in the writing came from the attempt to get the visual imagery and metaphors right. I was trying, in those poems, to record what I saw and recreate what I imagined in much the same way as a painter might; if there's commentary it comes out of that.

Do poems ever "come out" of the radio or televison? The sound of the radio sometimes penetrates the work of Ulster poets born in the 1940s; regional tele-vision came in the '50s as you have pointed out.
Radio and television often stand in for codes of passivity by which the world comes into the poems so there is the sound of the radio or the flick-ering televison screen in some of the poems in *Sunday School.* I'm not really that interested in furniture or easy statements of modernity — the 'pylon thing' — and some critics have wanted more of the contemporary world in my poems. Television, radio, these kind of things are not that rel-evant unless as a backdrop.

You acknowledge Seamus Deane's critical writing in the '70s as an important influence on your own work; his STRANGE COUNTRY, *though, looks at litera-ture through the lens of history and politics (which are inescapable); your 1990s criticism surely tries to establish the imagination as having 'priority' in seeking its own 'freedom'?*
I started off with the belief in the 1970s that literature should be deeply engaged with politics; I have now arrived at the view that politics can ham-per or constrain the imagination. The books of essays in the 1990s attempt to see the value of poems — even where poems attempt tran-scendence or take politics on the wing — as poems, irrespective of what they are about. I'm interested in the poem that stands on its own ground so that its validity is not taken from the bigger picture. I'm interested in the poem which defies politics and history, the poem which creates another voice which is earned. There are some great political imagina-tions, particularly amongst novelists, but I'm primarily interested in the achievement of the poet when he or she moves into an imaginative world which is both recorded and recreated, substantial and standing alone.

You commend, though, the 'passionate understanding of the political life of the imagination' of Brigid O'Toole and Derek Mahon's contention that ' A good poem is a paradigm of good politics — of people talking to each other with hon-est subtlety, at a profound level.' Given that you 'grew to despise the rhetoric of nationalism and unionism which no longer fitted into the realities of life in the Republic of Ireland or the Britain of the 1980s' is it possible to see the peace process post the Good Friday Agreement as a space where poetry and politics might meet?
I think that poetry and politics should never meet under orders; I think they are in constitutional antipathy to each other. I'd paraphrase MacNeice in seeing the poet as a critical presence, challenging rather

than conforming to political orthodoxies or communal beliefs. As a citizen in Ireland I have written critically about politics or cultural matters and will continue to do so; I think, though, that there is no real middle ground between poetry and politics in the sense that poetry should be superintending the political world rather than the other way around.

The "Troubles" though brought questions of national allegiance and writers' responsibilties; it's possible you might be read in the North as 'the union's son turned republican' while in the South your critique of Field Day or Nationalist culture as lacking 'forms of inclusiveness'(Stewart Parker's phrase) was hardly sympathetic to an unexamined alliance between literature and Nationalism. 'What -ish my nation?' Has Joyce's Shakespearean question been superceded?
The whole notion of nationhood and those grand cultural categories have become less relevant because there is the whole notion of fluidity and of opening up now. I was walking down the street in Dun Laoghaire a few hours ago and there are now many Romanians and Nigerians and other emigrants and asylum seekers there. That's the world I now live in. The old rigidities of nation lead us into a thirty year war in the North. It's much more interesting to find out the Englishness or Britishness of Ireland and the Irishness of Britain or the role of Scotland in the north-east without in any way losing the independence of these places as distinctive, self-governments. You only have a problem when people feel that by somehow engaging with these issues you are somehow diminishing what you were or are. Talk about 'nation' is very cramped in Ireland and far too many critics and writers from other places like to treat 'Ireland' as a special endearing case of and for Nationalism. They're out of touch, most of them.

Why did you call your second volume of poems THE LUNDYS LETTER *(1985)?*
It was originally going to be called 'The Clock on a Wall of Farringdon Gardens, August 1971' after a poem in that volume. The publisher, Peter Fallon at Gallery Press, was absolutely right when he suggested that anyone asking for that in a bookshop would hardly remember the full title. I came up with *The Lundys Letter* as an alternative. Even though Lundy is abominated within the Unionist tradition as someone who turned traitor, I liked that notion of the transgressor and the historical backdrop. Surely the artist might be someone outside the camp who sends messages back?

'The Likelihood of Snow/The Danger of Fire' from SUNDAY SCHOOL *(1991) reads like an Australian/Irish poem; you visited Australia in 1987 and you have written about the poet Les Murray. Are there links?*
The connection with Les is at a different level; in his poem 'Driving through Sawmills Towns' he gives imaginative life to a community most people would consider unsympathetically as being anti-art or against the

imaginative life. He also wrote an essay on the way that the community he was from was viewed with disdain; I'd also witnessed that in terms of negative or simplistic caricatures of the Belfast Protestant side of my background. Les was exploring a world heretofore seen as distasteful. He was an empowering presence. I kept reading the work after I came back from Australia. 'The Likelihood of Snow/The Danger of Fire', one of the more ample poems, is a letter back to the North to my mother who was in Belfast from the sunlit suburban suburb of Canberra where my wife and family were staying. The fire is the force of history which then seemed in danger of razing us all to the ground. It was the first poem where I actually started to talk about language and the way people use it to create identities for themselves as a community. Les also uses the vernacular in that way; he was important in that sense.

Your next volume, HEART OF HEARTS *(1995), was described as 'the most lyrical' of your volumes. How accurate is this word as applied to your work?*
I would not consider myself to be a lyrical or musical writer although when I write I do read the work out so the sound of the line is important; it is the visual dimension of poetry which fascinates me. It is not just the look of the poem on the page that is important — it's also the way you try to draw your reader in with the hope that they can actually physically *see* something. Some would consider poetry to be all sound so this idea would be anathema but it really does interest me. Perhaps the poems are lyrical in the sense that they are not big epic poems; they're generally small in their physical dimensions — if you blink they are gone — and I do put the demands of speech rhythm in poems so that the reader can hear a voice directing them to what is seen.

Three line verse, between tightly buttoned couplet and quatrain, is a form you often use. Do you have ways of thinking about form which recur in writing poems?
I tend to try to edit poems down even though I often have wanted to write big chunky poems but I generally know what a poem has to look like after living with it for a while. The Greek writer Yannis Ritsos who wrote chunky poems which are almost sonnets did fascinate me but, when I was starting out, I read Yeats's 'Cuchulainn Comforted' and became really fascinated with the three line poem, terza rima, which he took from Dante's *Divine Comedy*. Passolini's 'Gramsci's Ashes' also takes that form. I tried my hand at it in 'A Fire in My Head' with these in mind. Sometimes I've tried to draw something from Yeats for more solid poems such as 'Straws in the Wind', or earlier in something like 'The Proven Deed' or 'The Lundys Letter'. As I've developed I've come to see form as secondary to the tone of voice; that often tells you if you're casting the poem in the right shape. 'Sin' in *Heart of Hearts* was initially written as a big block but, as the tone

seemed to reject the form, I opened the poem out into quatrains to sus-
tain the voice. In that sense the voice or tone is primary for me in that it
directs the form to its shape. There's no way I can be acerbic or self-mock-
ing in quatrains (for me they have too much composure without irony)
but I'd use eight line stanzas to build up a head of steam while couplets
suggest you are going to spring. Some forms seem commodious, some
witholding; trying to work out which will work best is part of the trick.

*You have written about the jazz, rhythm and blues and traditional music scene
in Belfast in the 1950s and '60s, the club scene from which Van Morrison
emerged. In* HEART OF HEARTS *(1995) 'Questions, Questions' with its
repeated 'you' and wisps of rhyme remind me of a Leonard Cohen lyric; poems
in* THE MORNING TRAIN *sound musical. Do your poems assimilate the lan-
guage or rhythms of particular music?*
The connection between some of these poems and music is through the
singer — not so much through the sound; there's a voice in these poems
singing. The voice matters to me very much. The pick up from jazz, R. &
B. or from people like Morrison is subtle, not conscious, but it's there like
a refrain in a song. There's a connection between music and the poems
although I have never directly re-worked the lyrics of a song.

*You re-located from Galway to Dublin to lecture at Trinity College in 1987. Is there
a Dublin perspective in the late 1980s and 1990s which registers in the poems?*
I moved to Dublin in 1987 and lived in college for a year before moving
out to south County Dublin to a friend's house. Moving to Dun Laoghaire
a few years later I had the extraordinary sense of returning home. South
County Dublin has the feeling of an architectural and civic landscape akin
to the north Belfast where I grew up in 1950s. I think this registers in some
poems in *Sunday School* like 'The Messages' which is set in Glenageary. At
the time I wrote that volume, in the late 1980s, I was also reading the great
American novelist and short story writer John Cheever whose suburban
landscapes — and his daughter's memoirs *Out After Dark* — seemed to
chime with being here. I also discovered that it was very likely that my
great grandfather's family — he was a Chartres — had lived in Dun
Laoghaire and some of the family are buried in Monkstown — so there is
that charge although I'm not a great roots-tracker and I am aware of
genealogies as fictions at the best of times. After we moved from Galway
in 1992 — my daughter went to school and my son to college here — I
started to get more poems out of that relaxed feeling of living here.
Dublin Bay is just below us and the mix of working class, middle and lower
middle class houses and upper-class villas registers in the poems in the
same way, I hope, that a visual artist would draw these out of his or her
ordinary surroundings like the painters Utrillo or Dufy.

Visual art surely registers in your work. Marcel Duchamp rages in 'A Fire in My Head'; a woman's face in a bomb blast overlaps with Munch's 'The Scream' while Picasso, Magritte and Chagall enter your latest volume of poems. You point out that Michael Longley looked to the Ulster painter Gerard Dillon and L. S. Lowry for inspiration while Van Gogh, Uccello and Dutch painting have inspired Mahon. In what way does visual art influence your poetry?

When I was at school I had a great teacher, David Craig, who taught History of Art and, at one stage, I even planned to go to Sussex University to study art history but I changed direction after school and stayed in the North. I'm no good at painting or sketching but I've always been fascinated by painting in particular. There's often that sense around painters or visual artists that what they do is physical work which becomes art. I envy that. So much gets in the way of working as a poet; so much ego — fluff about "being a poet". I'm interested in images — as opposed to metaphor which can seem to be clever or artificial — and to get an image right seems honest, integral to a poem; it's also integral to a painter like Chagall who assembles the various diverse elements of ordinary life, in a little village for instance, and then suddenly turns the world around or upside down. Even in Miro's abstractions you sense the physical playing with the canvas and an awareness of the perceiver. There is an intense relationship between the arrangement of the whole physical object and the structure of looking. I've always been interested in the way in which we see what we see and that has developed as a serious interest in the latest volume, *The Morning Train.* I went once to Magritte's house in Brussels; here was this very exciting, perception-changing artist who led a fairly standard bourgeois life and you have a real sense, looking through the windows of that little house, that he's still there. I'm intrigued by painters because I am fascinated by how we see what we see and many painters seem to have an honest unencumbered way of looking so devoid of the ego.

Do Irish poets now assimilate narratives from art whereas art used to assimilate or even illustrate literature in the past? Literature, perhaps, has lost a primary function or its number one position?

We live in a world drowned in visual imagery and bombarded with television advertising and electronic images: the MTV world. I sometimes wonder if the rigour and demand, or the integrity and patience to read or hear a poem, is becoming a lost art in a world with quick fixes. Even the visual imaging of a popular song has become more important than the song. The superficial speed of a contemporary film or advertising seem to be more highly rated than the quiet reading of a poem that lays a depth charge. Perhaps things have changed so that the visual dimension of the poem, which was once rated, is on its way out because it lacks the expected speed of the images of the MTV world. I've a poem about all this half-drafted.

Few Irish critics warm to Modernism or suggest that it has influenced Irish poetry. You note MacNeice's sympathy with Eliot's merger of street talk and the classics in HOW'S THE POETRY GOING?; *when you founded* KRINO *in 1985 as a literary journal you named it after Ezra Pound's lexical gloss on the Greek word meaning 'to pick out for oneself, to choose'. Are these poets an under-explored influence in northern poets' work in general or your own work in particular?*

It's embarrassing to talk about my own work in relation to an absolute master like Eliot. I've always been intrigued, though, by the way Eliot could move images around in a poem like 'The Waste Land' or 'The Four Quartets'. There's an extraordinary stunning clarity and ambition in Pound. I'd never try to imitate this — I simply can't write that way — but I think that that kind of ambition lies behind Kinsella or Brian Coffey's 'The Death of Hektor' without ever being adequately assimilated into the Irish poetic tradition. Eliot can locate a poem in a vast arena and then move in and out of different sounds and tones; similarly Coffey, in *The Death of Hektor*, breaks down the complacent solidities to give you a different read on the world as does Beckett. It scares the shite out of you; it's much more comfortable to live inside the mainstream world. Perhaps I've tried to draw this world into some poems like 'A Fire in my Head' (while there's a kind of marriage of Eliot and a jazz beat in 'At Ron's Place') without going the whole hog. It's the tension between street talk, the classics and beat that matters: creating a medium out of the differences; a living balance.

You edited YEATS: THE POEMS, A NEW SELECTION *(1991); your first poetry pamphlet had the Yeatsian title* BLOOD AND MOON *(1976). Surely Yeats's use of myth and heightened poetic rhetoric is a long way from the voice of your own work where even Joyce might encounter a U2 badge? Are you distrustful of myth or rhetoric?*

I have a healthy disrespect for myth; I do not understand much of the information contained within it but I have a sense of its importance in Ireland and Europe. Having gone on holidays to Crete in the 1980s I became fascinated by the labyrinth at Knossos; I started to read this back into Ovid's *Metamorphosis* and see the maze as a template. *Heart of Hearts* emerges out of that "birthing"; the shape of that collection is very much determined by the shape of the maze. I also became interested in Minos the bull, the grotesque imagined creature in the labyrinth, and that became part of the opening poem in *The Morning Train*, 'The Minos Hotel'. I'm interested in the gap or disjunction between the mythical past and the contemporary world, the way shards of a mythological membrane turn up in the present through the conduit of the imagination. The exact mechanism by which this happens I don't know; and I don't want to know.

In THE MORNING TRAIN *(1999) the North seems largely to have disappeared as you travel into a landscape that is 'neither here nor there' but still recognisably modern. The book seems full of questions. Are you optimistic or bleak about where this new century is going?*

The Morning Train is a journey out of Ireland into Europe carrying the freight of my own narrative and my own sense of discovery of what Europe is — the dark history as well as the light. I worked hard on the book's shape trying, constantly, to cross two things over in it: the sense of calmness, tranquillity and repose as well as the sense of the shadows from the past. I hope it's neither a bleak or optimistic book; I hope it's an artistic one. In the final poem, *Human Wishes*, I'm trying to reconcile the entire volume and to understand through writing how things live and die and are made lasting by the imagination.

JEAN BLEAKNEY

You were born in the border town of Newry in 1956 and it's a location sometimes glimpsed in your poems. How would you describe the place, growing up there?
Actually, my parents were both Fermanagh people, but my father's work (Customs and Excise) brought them to Newry in the mid '50s. So the word "home" had several connotations for me from early on. For most of my seventeen years there, we (my parents and two sisters) lived on the very steep Doran's Hill with a spectacular view of the town. We were very happy — 'The Folks Who Lived On The Hill' as Peggy Lee used to sing about on *Two-Way Family Favourites*! Schools were across town so I did a lot of walking, but it was/is such a busy and attractive town with all that granite and plenty of shop windows and the canal and the river (which sometimes ran red... a local carpet factory?) and the Thursday Market. The bad times were when my father was ill, and, of course, later on. During the '60s, there was a large housing estate built across the road and when the rioting started in Newry, well, we were on the wrong side of town. Policemen and their families, who had been our friends and neighbours for many years, were either burned out or bombed out. We sold up in 1972, and bought a house across town from one of Dad's colleagues who was returning home with his young family to Scotland to live and work. Nightmarishly, the man was killed in the Customs House explosion a few weeks before his move. It was hard to settle, and in '73, we moved, with heavy hearts, to Lisburn; my father swapping the Border for VAT.

One poem, 'Knitting', reflects on primary school years (1960-67) as needlework as opposed to poetry: 'the very mention of No 8's and 4-ply wool/hauls me back to P5 Needlework/and long, long afternoons in Newry Model School.' Language and poetry did not figure in your early life?
I dreaded needlework and knitting in particular, but I also remember being very uncomfortable with some aspects of reading and writing. My spelling and vocabulary were fine, but I sometimes found it very hard to finish a class library book; and I especially hated having to fill a page. In P7 the teacher handed out long scrolls of paper which were stored from week to week in a toilet roll inner. Each Friday, we were supposed to write another chapter in our adventure stories. As all around me were merrily

scribbling and drawing, I'd sit, my stomach churning, in a blind panic. My preferred reading would have been fact books and annuals; especially 'Rupert' with all that weirdness and magic painting, and, yes of course, the rhyming couplets!

In a 'Literary Tour' of Newry for the radio programme 'Artzone' on Lyric FM (November 1999) you return to your childhood house and recall your father, Eddie Kerr, working as a customs' man. Did your family background make poetry or writing likely?
My parents were both educated at small country schools, where learning by rote was the usual approach. Apparently, at some stage, my father was able to recite 'The Rime of the Ancient Mariner'! But he would rarely have sat down with a book. My mother has always loved reading, and has a literary or biblical quote for most occasions. She got great satisfaction, I think, from going to Lisburn Tech. in her forties to get 'O' and 'A' Level English. Also, my older sister (by three years) studied English at Queen's. I absorbed her enthusiasm for Gerard Manley Hopkins, and was grateful to her (and him!) when he featured prominently in my 'O' Level English Lit. paper. But I was set on doing science which, as far as I was concerned, had little or nothing to do with English. Back then, you either went the arts road or the science road.

At Newry High School (1967-73) and Wallace High School, Lisburn (1973-74), you studied science. You spent four years on Biochemistry as a student at Queen's University (1974-78) and nine years working in the City Hospital and the Royal Victoria in Belfast in Medical Research. Do science and poetry overlap for you?
I think I was seduced by one of those turquoise Pelican books. I loved that series. There was one called *The Chemistry of Life* by Steven Rose. I thought I'd find out how the body, and especially the brain, worked. Biochemistry was a bit of a let down in that respect. I enjoyed the research; well, the library more than the lab. in retrospect. My second child arrived at a time when I was becoming cynical about the work; in particular, my own commitment and abilities. So I opted for full-time motherhood. I certainly didn't see a connection between poetry and science; but I loved discovering and using the huge pool of vocabulary.

Like the German language, science seems to have many composites, compound words with bolt-on parts.
Yes. I was working in the rapidly expanding area of regulatory peptides, which were being discovered and isolated before their neurotransmitter/hormonal functions had been fully understood. For example, GIP, variously known as Gastric Inhibitory Polypeptide, or, Glucose-dependent

Insulinotrophic Peptide. There's a nice story about two scientists, Ross and Chance, who accidentally discovered a new peptide in the pancreas. They thought to call it 'Serendipitin', but Ross objected on the grounds that it could be described as a 'chance' discovery! So they settled for PP (Pancreatic Polypeptide).

Yes, science and poetry overlap in many ways. Both interrogate, and the processes are not dissimilar. Elizabeth Bishop talked about 'a self-forgetful, perfectly useless concentration' that can produce poems. The German scientist, Kekule, solved the mystery of the structure of benzene after waking up from a dream about a snake chasing its own tail. He suddenly realised it was a ring structure. Bishop also said of writing a poem, 'It's a mystery, then a surprise, then a lot of hard work.' Well, ditto science!

Let's talk about the poets who interested you first? When did you start writing poetry?
Apart from Hopkins, I suppose it was the War Poets and John Betjeman. Then, about 1990, when I'd exhausted the gardening section in the local library, I discovered Wendy Cope's *Making Cocoa for Kingsley Amis.* I remember standing there thinking…this is really good…I'd like to do this. Also, being at home with my two young children was a trigger. Their language development made me think about words in a new way and I had 'time to stop and stare' (and lie and stare, on sleepless nights!). So I 'Coped' badly for a while! Then, in early '93, I started going to the Wednesday afternoon Queen's Creative Writing Workshop. Carol Rumens was writer-in-residence at the time. Her advice and encouragement were hugely important.

In one poem 'The Sanderlings' you reflect on birds that can 'read the tide like a book, like a biblical epic' and yet, in general, your poetry — compared with that of other poets from Northern Ireland — seems remarkably free from religious or Biblical reference. Is that a fair point? In a recent poem by the Portadown-born poet Sam Gardiner, 'Sanity Tablets' he talks of these as eradicating 'visions or Virgins… you can forget angels on the steeple.'
I was baptised and confirmed in The Church of Ireland, but I don't ever remember having any sense of conviction as regards religious beliefs (Sorry Mum et al!). I suppose I miss the hymn-singing and the lovely language, which has largely been rewritten of course. Anyway, it's not unreasonable to feel scunnered with religion in this country. I don't think I'd feel comfortable about being as directly critical as Sam, though. I've too many connections!

Do poems evolve in certain ways? Does a poem have to have a certain formal shape — or visual shape as in 'Depending on the Angle' — which relates to content?

For me, it starts with a phrase or a line... not infrequently, the last line! That's the seed and there are a lot of requirements for germination. I'm inclined towards rhyme — it's a great supplier of momentum. I like form, and the subversion of form. Carol introduced me to the notion of a serious limerick. My response to the Omagh bombing ('Postcard') was a truncated villanelle. I always think my poems, like my house, look untidy. 'Depending on the Angle' was shaped for mood and pace and it's a beach poem. Maybe I wanted it to look like a bay!

Metaphors from gardening — plants and flowers — abound in the poetry: in Michael Longley's poetry the botanical often leads me out into nature, to the actual wild flowers or birds and bees that an accurate botanical drawing or a florilegium can evoke; in Medbh McGuckian I'm more often drawn from symbolic flowers towards their 'master' — the human mood or relationship or sexuality. What way does gardening work in your poetry?
Although gardening had a headstart, I became passionate about it and poetry around the same time, in my mid-thirties. I just began noticing plants and words. I started working part-time in a garden centre in 1991. I'm still there! As you say, the garden is a bottomless pit of metaphors; for the best and worst of life. I'm fascinated by gardens; their vulnerability to nature, and how all is rarely as it seems. Like those old Dutch flower paintings — only on close inspection do you see the wilted flower, eaten leaf and slug. I suppose I use the garden as part-lens, to give a hopefully fresh view on some aspect of living and part-camouflage, to allow me to say the otherwise unsayable!

The words 'native', 'indigenous', 'blow-in', 'hybrid' or 'transplant' come to mind reading your poetry and they appear in debates about poetic influence or political lineage. Does your gardening language invoke these other spheres — the poetic and political undercurrents?
I'm well aware that, as Carlo Gebler says, 'every word carries its own freight'. But, like most poets, I probably invoke rather more than I intend to.

Why did you call your first volume of poems THE RIPPLE TANK EXPERIMENT?
I used the term in the poem 'The Physics of a Marriage'. It's a reference to a very dodgy and damp experiment from Form 4 Physics where wave patterns were supposed to be generated in a shallow perspex water-bath. It seemed like a good metaphor for marriage and allowed playfulness with words that have assorted meanings, some scientific like 'amplitude' (abundance, extent of vibratory movement etc.). I thought *The Ripple Tank Experiment* was a nice-sounding title and, well, I thought it was a bit witty in relation to a first collection.

Writing about THE RIPPLE TANK EXPERIMENT *Carol Rumens suggests 'the MacNeicean tradition' is important for you and that you have 'absorbed the lessons of "Snow"'. You participated in a marathon reading of* AUTUMN JOURNAL *in the Belfast Festival in 1998. Are there things about MacNeice you admire? Is he an assimilated influence?*

That felt like a huge pat on the back from Carol. 'The drunkenness of things being various' and 'There is more than glass between the snow and the huge roses' would be two of my favourite and most quotable lines from any poet. There is so much colour and energy and music in his work. His voice seems so intelligent and questioning. I love the recurrence of that word 'between'; from an early poem 'Spring Sunshine' (1929) which opens, 'In a between world, a bottom world of amber' to one of his last 'Coda' (1962), 'There are moments caught between heartbeats/When maybe we know each other better'. I've learnt a lot about poetry, and life, from MacNeice.

Maybe that 'between' is deeply embedded, inherent, in much of the 'northern situation'?

Yes I suppose it is, a suitably neither-one-thing-nor-the-other word. Aside from the two implied poles, it's a word that can be used in a searching or tentative or downright noncommittal sense. Yeats referred to 'the fascination of what's difficult'. For me, it's the fascination of what's between.

Does that reference to Yeats suggest he is a less of an influence than MacNeice?

Probably. Apart from my favourites, which would be the popular poems especially 'He wishes for the Cloths of Heaven' and 'An Irish Airman…', I find him a bit overwrought and otherwordly (in a kooky way). Maybe I haven't tried hard enough! Meantime, I'm content to be influenced by later poets who've been (allegedly) influenced by him.

A slightly bemused take on the quotidian, an un-illusioned vision balancing acceptance and questioning via irony, an 'all's mostly well or as well as can be' beside a dying fall of 'ah, well' — these are notes I detect in Larkin and in some of your poems like 'Fidelity, Fidelity' with its railway/marriage analogy: 'The view can pale. The sun might never shine/Hearts are mostly safest when they hold/a season ticket for the local line.'

I like that tone in Larkin. Maybe he caught it over here. It's endemic in parts of the North, especially Fermanagh where you'd hear lots of 'aye…', 'that's the way…' and, as my Aunt Ivy would say, 'anyhow and everyhow'. All delivered with a knowing fatalism!

Yeats and Auden quickened a whole debate about what poetry does, or does not, make happen. In 'Breaking the Surface' you skim stones 'to rearrange the shore-

line — in a minimalist sort of way'. Is this a reflection on poetry? Heaney has reinforced the idea that 'the end of art is peace' and one poem seeks a place where 'hope and history rhyme'. Mahon mentions 'faith' or a 'rage for order' amidst disorder. Paul Muldoon, in the context of Frost, speaks of 'upset', shifts in consciousness: 'Something falls out of place in one sense but falls into place in another. One will never look at a birch tree, after the Robert Frost poem, in exactly the same way. If it upsets our notion of things in one way, it also sets them in another.' How do you hope your poetry functions?

At a very basic level, I'd hope to affect the autonomic nervous system of the reader; to provoke some (minor!) gut, vascular, respiratory or goosebump-type response; to niggle the brain enough that it feels the need to rally the troops. It's easier for music to do this than words, but it's what I look for in poetry; what I find in Michael Longley's 'Ghost Orchid'. That last line 'Just touching the petals bruises them into darkness' connects with the solar plexus every time! I think that a poem sets out to simulate a train of thought (in the reader), outflanking the senses in a way that, yes, 'upsets' consciousness in a pleasurable or disquieting way. A modest rewiring!

Yes, 'Breaking the Surface' is a reflection on my poetry and its aims. Also, skimming stones is not unlike poetry; it's obsessive and attention-seeking!

In 'Holiday Poetry' you read a volume of American verse and talk of the experience as 'Bishop-ish'. You mention Elizabeth Bishop in your 'Literary Tour' of Newry for the radio. Is Bishop — American poetry — important to you?

Yes, very. I'd come across and liked Frost and Dickinson. Then, at one of the workshops, Carol read out 'The Moose', a long dreamy poem about a bus journey in Nova Scotia. That made a big impact. The poems are well-worked gems and I love that wit and moral tone which seem very familiar to me, in relation to my parents' generation. She once said, 'In general, I deplore the confessional.' I can't help speculating (with no grounds) about her roots. Her mother was a Boomer from Nova Scotia. Boomer is a common enough name in these parts.

I read lots of American poetry. The internet makes it much more accessible. Discovering Moore, Williams, Merrill, Collins and many more has been a great joy.

There are 'glitzy, newly honed nouns' from political journalism and the 'vernacular' in 'Out to Tender'; there's the 'attenuated Latin' from botany and gardening and 'a whole new rubric' of 'vasodilatory words' in 'Whenever'. Does your poetry attempt to 'yoke the heterogonous' to misquote what was said of the Metaphysical poets?

Absolutely! I like to mix'n'match the botanical, the scientific and the vernacular. It's a fascination with words and their origins. Some scientific words lie outside common usage for too long. The nice-sounding 'vasodilatory' is in my new Chambers Dictionary, but wasn't in the last. Brand names can work well, but they're a bit risky. Also I love the reckless extravagance, especially with adjectives, that I overhear from my west Fermanagh roots where rain might be described as 'wild' or 'fierce' or even 'ojus' (odious?).

Poetry and the "Troubles" — or the still tentative peace sprung out of the '90s. One poem talks of 'the preferred touch of drama in the border' in relation to plants and there are poems which might be read in the light of the victims ('Postcard' or 'In Memoriam'), of Orangeism ('Mock Orange') or the emerging political "speak" of Good Friday consensus ('Out to Tender'). Is there a juncture between your poetry and politics?

'Out to Tender' was written in response to the 1994 ceasefire. At the time, there was, understandably, much jubilation. But I was well aware of, and in sympathy with, Unionist anxieties. 'In Memoriam' was written, more from the heart, around the same time. I didn't write directly about the "Troubles" again until 1998, that awful summer (weather-wise and everywise). The night after the Quinn boys died, I stood outside in the garden. I was suddenly aware of a white patch on the lawn, like a shadow in negative. It took a few seconds to register that it was the petals of Philadelphus (Mock Orange). The rain had ripped them off. That image, and an associated image of soured milk, provided the poem 'Mock Orange'. There are some other poems in the book such as 'Equinoctial Imperatives' and 'Black and White', which address the "Troubles" in a less obvious way.

Otherwise, I've felt uncomfortable, exposed, writing directly about politics and the "Troubles". My parents came from big families — I've thirty-two cousins — so even by the law of averages, a lot of my relatives served/serve in the security forces. 'Whatever you say, say nothing' and 'Careless talk costs lives' were, and remain, deeply ingrained.

Should poetry be politically committed to one side or the other, to the somewhat monolithic cultures of Unionism or Nationalism?

I think poetry should be questioning, unsettling, rather than propagandist. The middle ground can be a damning position in itself, of course; although MacNeice and Hewitt were able to rail successfully against both sides. It comes back to that word 'between' or, maybe even, Hopkins's 'betweenpie' ('as skies betweenpie mountains — lights a lovely mile'). To betweenpie the monoliths would be a good result, I think.

Your 'Letters from Cyprus' mention Boticelli in relation to Venus or Aphrodite and you have recently contributed to a book of poets on paintings in the Ulster Museum. Madeline Dewhurst's review of THE RIPPLE TANK EXPERIMENT *in*

WOMEN'S NEWS *(November 1999) sees 'The Sanderlings' as akin to 'the microscopic observation of Seurat's The Bathers'. Does visual art interest you? Is it related to poetry?*
I don't feel I've a great appreciation of visual art. I'm more attracted to images from the microscope or telescope — small things magnified and distant things brought close. Like Sunday Supplement photos of cells and galaxies. I very much like the work of Fleur Olby, who photographs flowers and leaves in clinical close-up. I reckon the relationship between art and poetry is a bit one-sided. Poets seem to get an awful lot of mileage from paintings!

Jim Reeves and Frank Sinatra appear in the poems. Why? I remember these singers in my own childhood. Are poetry and music linked?
I particularly remember *Two-Way Family Favourites*, all those crooners and BFPO numbers, and *100 Best Tunes*. There's great nostalgia value for me in my parents' music. Like a lot of my generation, I suppose, I'm acquiring it on CD, rediscovering it. Music is important to me, to my emotional well-being. I enjoy most popular types — more songs/singers than rock — and I'm grateful to my teenagers for exposure to the new and exciting. Honest! Top of the pile these days are Dolly Parton, Bap Kennedy, Ella Fitzgerald and Film Music. It's that 'drunkenness of things being various' again! I generally need unchallenging background music when I'm writing.

In Sinatra's songs the stars are now part of the movies of the American city skyline at night but your 'Starlight on Narin Strand' is quieter — it reminds me of Heaney's 'Exposure' — the Perseids or comets bring both the possibility of meteoric vision and an 'afterglow of spent wishes'. Is it fair to suggest your poems shun the epic, the dramatic, the meteoric arrival — for more tentative, oblique arrivals and departures?
Yes, it's fair. I'm more inclined to offer glimpses, be tangential. There is something compulsive about star-gazing, and meteor-watching in particular. That primitive urge to look for a sign, I suppose. But there's irony in the fact that a small light source, such as a star, seems to dim when viewed directly by the human eye. Looking to one side of a star makes it appear brighter. That poem touches on the need to look at 'the between-blackness of starlight'. For me, it affirms the tentative and the oblique and it informs my approach to poetry.

In the 1990's you were a 'regular' at Queen's writing workshops: you helped edit the poetry magazine BRANGLE *with the writer-in-residence, Carol Rumens. Her 'Variant Readings' (*THINKING OF SKINS, *1993) reflects on Belfast where she 'expected bleachworks and burnt-out cars, not fuschias' recalling 'home' in England (which 'was like this long ago'); it is this 'Most English of Ireland's,* *our difference seemingly less/Than that between neighbourly hedges, depths of green.' You've worked in Belfast for twenty three years but, with the exception of some glimpses of the city, it doesn't appear to feature hugely in your work. Have you 'variant readings' of the city?*

Belfast, even my bit of it, the Lisburn Road and environs, has never really felt like home; except when I'm away. But it's been good to me. And certainly not a 'muse city' in the way it has been, so successfully, for Carol. Like most cities, I suppose, it can disappoint. Carol has a terrific image of a Belfast rainbow in 'Best China Sky': 'You'd think it was the rim/ Of some resplendent turquoise plate,/ Offering hills and cranes and streets and us/ Fancies designed to melt/ As our fingers touched them'. I've no desire to live anywhere else, though. I'd miss the mountain.

Love poems? Are there different "takes" on love in THE RIPPLE TANK EXPERIMENT. *I'm thinking of 'Summer Love' and 'Dangerous Driving' in relation to 'The Physics of a Marriage' and 'Every Little Helps' ?*

Yes, there are the "happily-married" poems and others which address the themes of desire and obsession and loss which afflict us all from time to time; which we recover from, eventually, like sinusitis. I reckon there's still a market for comfort poetry in those respects.

You have favourite love poems by other poets?

Again, it comes back to poems with an ache. I'm very fond of Hardy, Mew and Housman in that mode. From contemporary poetry, I'd pick Carol Rumens's 'Unplayed Music' and 'Last Day of March'; Bernard O'Donoghue's 'The Definition of Love' and Carol Ann Duffy's 'Warming Her Pearls'.

You have written poems about car journeys; Medbh McGuckian reminds me of the link between feeling safe and the car (especially in the northern context) and she has written about cars in Seamus Heaney's work.

As a child, I used to get sick in the car. I'm still not a great traveller. But I loved the long snug journey home, especially on starry nights; and being a captive audience to my current fantasies; and all that excitement if there was snow or fog or floods. Nostalgia again! Heaney's 'Postscript' captures that dichotomy when, in a wind-buffeted car, the head feels safe, but the heart is caught 'off guard', 'blown... open'. The power of the poem is that the reader experiences the buffeting. Didn't Heaney get inspiration for 'Digging' when he was changing down to round a corner? I reckon driving, like peeling spuds, is the sort of automatic activity which can unleash that 'self-forgetful, perfectly useless concentration'…

In poems like 'Afterwards', 'A Woman of Our Times' and 'Stargazing for Feminists' is there a specifically female perspective and to what extent can one differentiate this perspective from a feminist one?

'Stargazing for Feminists' came from looking up and seeing Orion flanked by the moon and Venus. I couldn't resist a playfully feminist viewpoint. 'Afterwards' and 'A Woman of Our Times' came from what I perceive to be the unbearable pointlessness of housework. It's not a gender issue. I'm railing against myself and convention.

I like 'Afterwards', it's re-work of Hardy into a double-negative: he hopes to be remembered for noticing nature; you hope they won't remember that you did not notice housework.

That poem, which ends 'Will the neighbours say/ "She was a woman who never noticed such things?"' is a sort of silent scream. I notice my dust and clutter so much, I actually write poems about them! Irony... it beats ironing every time!

From the 1970s a number of female poets emerged in the Irish Republic although Eavan Boland states in OBJECT LESSONS *that in '60s Dublin she 'began writing in a country where the word woman and the word poet were almost magnetically opposed. One word was used to invoke collective nurture, the other to sketch out reflective individualism.' She envisaged her task as finding a voice to bridge those worlds, those words. Does Boland's view reflect on the/ your relation to other women or writing in the North in the '90s and 2000's?*

It's hard to relate to my experience. There seems to have been an exponential rise in the number of women poets. But John Wakeman has highlighted a problem, in his editorial for *The Shop* (#4): poetry magazines receive far fewer submissions from women than from men. He speculates as to the reasons: 'are they less eager for publication? Are they more protective of their progeny, reluctant to expose them to the cold wind of rejection?' I think this issue, women's commitment to poetry, is an interesting one.

W.R. Rodgers observed in THRESHOLD *(2:4, Winter 1958) that 'The Irish have never been bitten by the T.S.E. fly: they are not given to explore the waste land of the spirit or the private condition of man.' Has the 'T.S.E. fly' ever infected your garden?*

Not that I'm aware of, but then you never know what bugs are out there. And they come and go a lot. A few years ago, New Zealand Flatworm was the big worry. A horrible looking thing that hid under stones and pots and ate earthworms. Apparently there was no natural predator. Well, I haven't seen one in ages.

Having encountered Wendy Cope's 'Wasteland Limericks' first, I find it hard to be serious about T.S.E., I'm afraid!

THE RIPPLE TANK EXPERIMENT *ends with 'A Windless Night in June, There Being No Stars'. Why does the volume close with a poem about star watching and listening for the 1930's pebbledash 'to fall'?*

The poem is about listening in to the sounds of a garden, in lieu of stargazing, on a cloudy night. I thought that listening for falling pebbledash would be a good counterpoint to the opening poem's skimmed stones. Maybe I'm lowering my aim, reflecting on ageing. There is certainly a sadness or coming to terms. The closing words 'part vindicated, part in mourning' refer to how I feel as I go back into the house after meteor-watching; which is not unlike how I felt when I'd put together this first collection of poems.

MOYRA DONALDSON

You were born in 1956. In the poem 'Exiles' you recall your grandfather's 'flinty faith/in mission tents, visions of eternal life/on soft Ulster evenings'; another poem recalls 'the white linen your (mother's) grandmother sewed by candlelight'. In Don Delillo's novel WHITE NOISE *the character Murray concludes: 'The family is the cradle of the world's misinformation... (it) generates factual error... works toward sealing off the world. Small errors grow heads, fictions proliferate... Magic and superstition become entrenched as the powerful orthodoxy of the clan...' Are you also rejecting the ancestral lineage of grandparents, of the clan?*

I suppose that family does teach you how to lie. You are told that inside the family is safe and outside it is dangerous but things happen within the family which are equally dangerous or harmful. When I think of my family or grandparents I think of the pain that's handed on from generation to generation which Larkin writes about: 'they fuck you up, your mum and dad, / they may not mean to but they do.' It doesn't have to be like that though. When you become self-aware you try to break certain cycles — the lack of love or understanding — and put the psychological damage right. I think there's a lot of pain inflicted within the family unintentionally through assumptions like — 'that's the way we think' or 'that's the way we vote'. I've wanted to try to work these things out for myself.

The poem 'Exiles' attempts to question or work out family assumptions about religion?

Much of my whole family life came down to religion and its incredible narrowness, its inability to allow anyone else to think alternatively or outside its inherited confines. I think religion can be an incredible curse; it can impose on these other alternative ways of thinking a sense of sin. My grandparents were Presbyterians who were also involved with the Brethren so it was a very religious family. We were sent to church at least twice every Sunday and to Sunday School as well and there was that whole sense that enjoying yourself was sinful. I felt the damage of this as a child though, later on, when I got to know my mother as an adult I came to see the damage it had also inflicted on her life.

Poems commemorate you mother with great tenderness and an extended version of 'Babe in the Woods' recalls your father working in the ticket office in Bangor railway station. How would you describe the influence of your immediate family background?

My father worked in the railway station all his life. My mother was a teacher. She was an incredibly strong, intelligent, woman who was very frustrated by life but very ambitious for me. My childhood and teenage relationship with my mother, a love-hate relationship, coloured my whole life but most people seem to have picked up on the tenderness in that poem, where she has senile dementia, where she was in an extremely vulnerable position. It was then she told me all the stories from her childhood and I began to understand the guilt and get beyond apportioning blame.

Where did you grow up? Were you aware of social class early on?

I grew up in a small bungalow with a big garden on the outskirts of Bangor. We later moved to a small farm between Bangor and Newtownards. We led quite a sheltered life there so I wasn't all that aware of class as a child growing up. As a teenager I was more aware and began to see the stereotypes my family subscribed to.

In 'My Turn to be the Horse' imaginative play ends with the school bell and you are 'coralled': 'Horse and rider tamed by long division,/ comprehension, back to little girls.' At Glenlola Primary School (Bangor) in the 1960s were you aware of language and literature, the imaginative world of books?

I remember a cupboard in the hallway at home lined with shelves of books that seemed to go on forever. It was a magical place, a gateway. I was read to as a child and I lived a lot in the imagination. The mix of books in the house was quite eclectic: religious books, old novels, encyclopaedias and 'knowledge-magazines'. I suppose I read anything that came my way. I was one of that generation who learnt to love reading courtesy of Enid Blyton.

As a teenager at Glenlola Collegiate School (1968-75) did poetry or poets matter?

I loved poetry early on; it has always seemed important to me — perhaps because, early on, I was sent to elocution classes where I'd recite poems — and you grew to love the sound or the sensuous rhythms in poems you learnt by heart. At secondary school in Bangor we read the ALBATROSS BOOK OF VERSE. I fell in love with poets like Keats. You came across John Donne or Edith Sitwell and, later on, Sylvia Plath and the Liverpool poets, like Roger McGough, where you heard a more contemporary language talking. I remember writing poems at secondary school and writing out poems by other people. I'd learn the poems by heart and carry them around with me and say them to myself.

The language of poems (concentrated, formally ordered, charged, sometimes archaic) was surely different from the language or speech around you, more difficult to integrate within your life?

No. I felt, reading poems, that many of them said some things you'd really have liked to have said or written yourself. With my religious upbringing I'd already encountered the formal, archaic, language of the King James Bible so I didn't mind this "strange" language in poems which added something or set them apart. You found, too, in poets like Keats, echoes of your own teenage angst.

Ginsberg, Jane Austen, Leonard Cohen and Germaine Greer also feature in 'Emma, Leonard and Germaine' which dates their pull to the early 1970s; by '1971' you're 'existentialist', within a gravitational pull that has attracted other northern poets. What did you find in existentialism?

There was something in writers like Camus which spoke of how I was feeling or spoke out of the space I was living in. As a teenager, though, you read anything and everything — novels by Iris Murdoch, Aldous Huxley — and I distinctly remember the effect of reading Germaine Greer's *The Female Eunuch* as a teenager. I felt that book, in particular, shone light into certain areas or levels of my own experience. You became aware that some patterns did not have to be the way they were in suburban Northern Ireland. Around 1974 I was reading poetry non-stop: Donne, Keats, Blake, Eliot. I was in love with Jean-Paul Sartre. I wanted to be Simone de Beauvoir.

You studied English Language and Literature at Queen's University (1975-79). Did you encounter literature or writing groups there which mattered?

I was turned off writing and literature at Queen's. That felt strange. Up to that point in my life all I'd wanted to do was to become a writer. Something quite strange happened. I'd written short stories or poems at school but I didn't feel a sense of belonging at Queen's and I'd no awareness of an atmosphere of creativity or of writing groups going on there. I wouldn't want to blame Queen's for all of that because, maybe, there were things happening that I simply wasn't aware of — there was also a lot going on in my own life — but I can only remember showing one person a poem there and going off writing when I was told it was 'slight'. At 'A' Level I'd loved *Hamlet* with a teenager's passion for tragedy but at Queen's I felt creatively sterile. I stopped writing and I'd little pleasure in reading; I'm not sure whether that was down to the place or to me — it was probably a little of both. I discovered the influence of absences at Queen's. The image systems within poetry, referential and historic, seemed to have no place for me as a young Protestant woman. I felt lost, mute. I'd no sense of identity, national or personal, and I lost confidence in my own ability to create. After I left I went on to do a postgraduate course in social work in Coleraine and I spent two years up there.

One poem, 'A Temporary Lease', is set on that north-west coast in the Umbra, a stone's throw from the 'watch-towers' of Magilligan Prison (recorded in Heaney's 'Sandstone Keepsake') and the 'glow of... its arc-lights' (which suffuse Mahon's prose piece about 'The Coleraine Triangle'). I'm contrasting your private serendipity with their evocations of a landscape marked by politics and the "Troubles".
Well, I'd an overwhelming sense that the landscape and the people there were different from Belfast. I enjoyed the landscape, the sea and coast, and I listened to a lot of live music and made a lot of friends. I simply enjoyed being there in a very personal sense.

You wrote three one-act stage plays and your screenplay L was filmed in 1996. How would you describe the genesis of these in 1980s before you returned to the north-east?
In the time before I started writing again I worked really hard at my job in the '80s. I expected a promotion (which I didn't get); that threw me back on the question of what really mattered to me and I was drawn back to writing again. I was attracted to drama because I was simply interested in telling stories. The first play came after I was approached by a theatre company in Ballybeen, in east Belfast, who wanted someone to help tell the stories from that area. I did workshops based in people's houses there and the play was based on the actual experiences of people there which often involved domestic violence.

How did you marry these stories with the demands of drama as a literary form with its emphasis on situation, encounter and character.
I didn't particularly worry about these things when I took the play on. I'm one of those people who takes something on and worries about how they're going to do it later — so, it was a learning process. I'd seen plays work on stage before so I knew about the intensity and contraction involved in staging one act plays. *L*, the screenplay, emerged from a short story I'd written which won a competition, but the screenplay ended up so far from the original story that I found the whole process a bit disappointing. The story, set in the '60s and '90s, involved a girl who falls in love with a teenage Catholic boy; they come up against sectarianism — he's beaten up as a result of that and the experience repeats itself when he has a son — so the story involves flash-back.

Do these dramatic concerns or elements carry over into the poems?
Some of my poems are like little mini-dramas. I find it intriguing that a huge story can be told in a few lines just by focusing on one element that captures everything else. It's almost as if the wider story is in the silence around the poem.

Is there a tension though between the dramatic and the lyric as two urges within one form?
Yes. I think there is. I was attracted to poetry by language and its lyrical qualities and it can be tempting to allow the lyrical to direct the content or the way a poem heads and to go with the flow. I have to resist that urge although I'm not saying that to write a good lyric is easy. I guess the dramatic mainly comes in through my thinking of the poem as a scene or set of scenes and wanting it to tell stories.

When did you write the poems which appeared in your first volume Snakeskin Stilettos *(1998)?*
I came back to writing poems around 1990-91 and started the poems which went to make up that volume then.

The shoes in the title poem, uncovered by the eight year old girl, seem to prefigure adult sexuality as 'forbidden... live... dangerous...'; there's that tender sexuality in Longley and Medbh McGuckian's work is often bristlingly tactile like 'velvet stroked the wrong way' and there's the homoerotic in Ó Searcaigh. Is sexuality, sexiness, an important element in your poetry?
Yes. Sexuality was never mentioned within the family context but it's part of the self, the make-up, and so — when I found the shoes — I was coming up against something important which was being hidden away. I came across these shoes, the snakeskin stilettos, wrapped up in paper in the back of the cupboard at home. Sexuality is important but in family life here it's often hidden away.

In the work of the Belfast painter, Rita Duffy, one image depicts a girl with a bow and arrow, a self which will go underground as the girl acquires adult sexuality or the decorum of womanhood. Is this a different process for girls?
Is it different for a girl becoming a woman than a boy becoming a man? Yes, I think so. It felt to me that certain feelings were supposed to be put away. My own upbringing was so repressive — sexuality was never talked about at home except as something negative — and I've struggled with this, with finding someone to talk to about it, with reclaiming it.

Is there a relationship between formal shape and subject matter in your poems? Louis MacNeice, in The Poetry of W. B. Yeats *(1941) stated that 'matter must find itself in form and form must find itself in matter.' There's Robert Frost's idea of a poem as a piece of ice on a hot stove, 'riding' on its own melting. How do your poems evolve? Do you have a working method?*
I find that I come across a word or phrase around which other words or images or energies gather. Poems often gestate over long periods. I find, increasingly, that the ideas have to come of their own accord as opposed

to being generated by a workshop exercise where the poem is written around, or to, a certain idea. I like the image of the sculptor uncovering a shape hidden in the stone, the shape being found or emerging organically although sometimes that feels like an impossible task, like 'jewels to be dug from concrete with a blunt knife' as a recent poem has it. Sometimes you take an idea a certain distance and it just refuses to have a form put on it. I love sonnets. I think of that form as a faceted jewel so I enjoy trying to shape something like that.

In a review of Snakeskin Stilettos *in* Fortnight *(March 1999) Medbh McGuckian suggests that Hewitt is one of the 'powerful influences' assimilated and the idea of ancestral ghosts seems important in the book. Is Hewitt's attitude to ancestry and place — his poetry — important to you?*
I remember reading, on the back cover of Hewitt's *Selected Poems*, the claim that he was 'probably the last self-consciously Ulster poet' — as if no one ever again would want to define themselves as an 'Ulster poet'. The comment felt like another gag being put on. I'm aware of all of the bad connotations of calling myself an Ulster anything — but I've lived here all my life. I found myself wondering if it was possible to be sub-consciously — or even unconsciously — an Ulster poet. How did I do that?

Well, there's place of birth or location or address — passport information — but is there such a thing as 'Ulster poetry' as characterised by language or idiom. Poets like W.R. Rodgers have contended that this is the case?
I think that the language here is different. There's a hardness or granite in the language — maybe even in the blood, in the cells. The north in many countries is usually different from the south — geographically and culturally. You find that in European countries. I think some of those distinctions apply here.

In the 1960s poets from the North of Ireland came to the fore and they feature with other, earlier, poets in Frank Ormsby's Poets from the North of Ireland. *Are there writers you relate to or admire from the North?*
I felt at Queen's that there was no tradition for me that I could relate to or find my way into. Of course, I came across the bigger names from here but it was mainly the tradition of English literature that was taught and I didn't come across any other woman's voice when I was there. Maybe the gender issue impacts on that kind of question. I'm not making absolute distinctions between female writers who I relate to and male writers I admire but, at the time when I started to write and most needed a poet or a tradition of women poets I felt it was not there. I think that situation has changed a little in the last ten years and it continues to change.

Which other influences — Irish poetry (in English), English poetry, poetry from Europe or the United States — matter in your work? Does any one influence predominate?

The main influences came from the English tradition and the American tradition, through writers like Ginsberg and Kerouac. The Irish tradition was probably less influential, possibly because it was less visible at school and university. In rejecting my family's values I've always felt a little 'traditionless', with no fixed point from which to move from, and I think the same is true of the influences in my work. They are a hotch-potch of things picked up from different sources: no north, south, east or west.

Noah's ark, transubstantiation and remedies as a 'litany' in your poems remind me that in Ireland, as Peter Fallon puts it in 'The Herd', 'every lamb's a lamb of God'. In what way does religion or its language feature in your work?

I was soaked in the language of religion, soaked in the blood of the lamb, and that language is part of the whole landscape here. I still love some of the phrases from the Bible and hymns like 'Immortal, invisible, God only wise' were all part of a childhood where I was forced to learn huge chunks of the Bible by heart. All that is still there, in my memory and as part of my language, which is paradoxical because I have very little time for religion or its beliefs.

In 'Raven' it's this bird that is released from the womb of the ark — not the dove from Noah's hand. The male, Biblical, image is being converted to a female variant?

You often question the images you inherit. Christian imagery of the female splits her into the virgin or whore but there are older images, particularly from myths, which are less restrictive. I'm trying to reclaim some sense of spirituality as opposed to religion.

Myths like Leda or Lir's children and prehistoric sites, like Newgrange, appear in the poems but it might be suggested that myth is sublimated or substitute religion in poetry proposed, if not quite patented, by poets like Yeats. Some critics see poetry's function as demythologising, facing the 'now' of a more concrete reality. Why include myth in poetry?

I think it is important to reclaim or restore or reinterpret images — it's almost like going back to an earlier text. Take an image like the rose or a story from fairy tales. You can always go back to these familiar things and still find, in their re-telling, something new or relevant or alive, archetypal. You can, of course, make anything you want from these stories. Myths can be politicised, as Cuchulainn has been in the North, but just because a different spin can be put on a story that doesn't mean the story should be silenced. Maybe my use of myth is linked to my rejection of religion and my acceptance that life still has a spiritual dimension, that it's not just physical. I think that this way of talking about sides of yourself will always have a place because if you don't have this dimension you end up with a very reductionist view. I struggle with the notion of the purely concrete in poetry, with the idea of poetry as absolutely devoid of either myth or metaphor, as much as I do with the idea of gender. It's a generalisation but I think there's something that's not concrete about the feminine.

Sometimes — even in Yeats — myth can be motored by over-active rhetoric? Medbh McGuckian's 'Fortnight Review' praises SNAKESKIN STILETTOS *but she is critical of the rhetorical note.*
Maybe I would agree with her point; sometimes, in reclaiming things, you can overstate your case. Perhaps, even sometimes, I'm trying to convince myself.

I'm not sure if I understand your 'Poem for Four Children' in SNAKESKIN STILETTOS. *Can you tell me what it's about?*
The poem is about four children: two born, one un-born and one un-conceived and, perhaps, it's about aspects of myself.

Carol Rumens refers to Medbh McGuckian's poems as 'dramas of adult sexuality and childbirth' in POETRY IRELAND *(No 56, Spring 1998); there seems to be a link between childbirth and her successive volumes. Is there a link between these things for you?*
There is something that links being a woman creating life with being creative in life although, from a totally physical point of view, I didn't find that being pregnant was conducive to any other type of creativity. When I was pregnant I just couldn't write. My hormones detached me from my brain. I was sterile as a writer. Having children, though, and seeing them grow was — is — often conducive to creativity.

In the love poems you have written are there ground rules for this space where privacy and the reader meet?
I really don't know the answer to that question but I try to stick to the emotional truth of situations in the writing. Whether or not the facts or events actually happened is largely irrelevant. I worry sometimes about the extent to which I use people, their stories and emotions. I wouldn't want to hurt people in writing poems.

Betrayal and fidelity feel like key concerns and 'Infidelties' is such a poignantly succinct poem: 'Small change for a call/he couldn't make from the house'. I'm reminded of Longley's 'The Adulterer' where 'I have laid my adulteries/Beneath the floorboards, then resettled/ The linoleum so that/The pattern aligns

exactly...' Are infidelities and guilt, more difficult to write about than fidelity and love?
No. I think that, in some respects, these are easier poems to write possibly because these things actually fascinate me. Everyone has stories about what happened when it went wrong; these are often more fascinating tales than the happy stories where everything is alright.

Your 'Muse' as 'bird/tiger/hoarder/storyteller/wisewoman/fool' implies that the muse can change shape or molecular structure and make things happen? Do you have an image for the way that poetry, the muse, functions?
There are "muse poems" which arise out of the sub-conscious and its changing shapes and there are poems akin to therapy where, in shaping things, you gain a certain control. This shape-changing is in the poems. I think there's a strangely, almost inexplicable, prophetic element in poetry; you sometimes write things which you yourself do not even understand at the time but which, perhaps at a subconscious level, you've grasped or intuited, and you then go on to meet these things in the future, to understand more. I'm not sure whether I'm saying that poetry makes the future happen or that it apprehends, at a sub-conscious level, what will take shape — what you will meet and understand later, when you allow this to happen. As for poetry's public function, I think that change always and only ever happens at an individual level. I don't see any evidence of a great public role for poetry although it possibly does change individuals which, in turn, might amount to changing other things, elsewhere, over a period of time.

Poetry enacts 'slight' but vital shifts in the consciousness; I'm reminded of Conor O'Callaghan's poem 'Silver Birch' where the 'shadows of a story will survive like this', like the two-tone leaves of these trees near Birkenau.
Yes. I think it can out in that way.

Your idea of poetry, shaped by intuition but half-understood at the time of writing, takes me back to T.S. Eliot's, 'poetry can communicate before it is understood'. Do you relate to Eliot?
'The Love Song of Alfred J. Prufrock' was one of the poems I learnt off by heart as a teenager. It definitely communicated something that I didn't understand at an intellectual level. I think that's why I love poetry — because it can communicate on more than one level and, at its best, it's a perfect communion of heart and head.

There are a few Belfast locations in the poems (India Street, the City Hall, The Club Bar) and locations in the North of Ireland. Does location matter in the poems in the same way as it might in drama, where its often 'location, location,

location' — a fixed here and nowhere else, a territorial imperative like an estate agent's sign — or is it more incidental than that? Do you feel at home in the North of Ireland?

Where you are located, being somewhere, is purely accidental — a given unless you deliberately, consciously choose to be elsewhere. There's a sense in which the actual locations in poems don't matter that much although, in another sense, the location inescapably impacts on you. I don't have a sense of this place being "home" and yet, in another sense, it's entirely home. I've lived all of my life in Northern Ireland — I've not moved elsewhere — so there are very relatively small changes in geography in the poems but these are quite significant to me because they mark various stages in my own life. Maybe I'm saying that it's not so much the place in itself that matters as what it means to me. Perhaps location is within.

There are many different birds in flight in this volume and many 'skins' which contain the many selves. Is there a tension between flight out of the self, out of the territory, and this urge to explore the interior, the constantly shifting problematic "I" who appears in the poems.

There is a kind of interior examination of the self within the poems. Sometimes I've no real strong sense of who I am but I do have a strong sense of being able to use poetry to explore the different selves. I suppose there's a tension between the desire to know who you are under your skin and the other urge, to forget the self altogether.

Do Irish/northern politics, the politics of Unionism and Nationalism, and the "Troubles" matter or figure in your poetry?

It's not that I'm not interested in these things — it's impossible to say that I've not been influenced as a person by the "Troubles" — but I don't want to write about them. I have been touched by some of the things that have happened here, and maybe that emerges at some level in the poems, but I'm not drawn to write about politics. The "Troubles" impact on your psyche. Even if you haven't been directly or physically affected by that dark cloud that weighed us down here you did become aware of it when you escaped to go somewhere else for a while — but I've not really written about Northern Ireland politics in the poems. Possibly I've tried to escape these things.

In some poems, though, there is an urge to re-create history or the map. 'Driving Back Alone from Mayo' mentions 're-inventing our history' through stories, so that the 'fiction of what might have been/is a map unfolding, a way home.' 'Hibernating' seeks to 'sleep out the past' because the 'Muse' has 'made the past no place'.

My overwhelming feeling about the past is that those things which have damaged you there will damage others in the future unless you consciously lay them down and stop carrying them with you. It's not easy and you don't always succeed but you have to try. I've mentioned this in relation to my own background. You have to look back and decide what you take forward and where you draw the line. If you dwell on all that was bad or wrong, all the injustice or hurt, you run the inevitable danger of carrying this on your back into the future. I think you can say 'it was like that' but you can also say: 'it can be like this'.

Is part of the juncture between being a woman and being a poet reflected in the number of women coffined (Snow White) or imprisoned (Rapunzel) or poisoned or hospitalised or tempted or confined in the poems. Does gender matter in your poetry or in terms of the way you see contemporary Irish or Northern Irish poetry?
Part of me would like to say that gender doesn't matter but I think it does; there are so many things which you have constantly to examine, to fight against, to reclaim and I think that many of these things go with being a woman. I write out of being a woman. I've mentioned the impact of reading Germaine Greer at around sixteen. What happened to feminism in the North? Many people will tell you about the gains that woman have made in public since then but I don't quite see it. You hear stories about how even the few women MP's here are treated at the Assembly. Are we fully conscious of the ways in which many men still treat woman? The relationships between men and women are important on every level and yet so often unresolved; these things are bound to impact on the writing. I still have the feeling about writing, and certain other walks of life, that that you will be "allowed in" if you are a woman, that you are not really there as of right.

In OBJECT LESSONS *Eavan Boland refers to the nearly unbridgeable gulf between the words or roles of 'woman' and 'poet' in 1960s Dublin as she struggled to write her way between the two; you're suggesting that gap still has not narrowed?*
Absolutely. There is still the feeling among many woman that I know here in the North that even now you are still up against it as a woman so that would suggest that this gap is not just historic. There was more of a trellis of support and encouragement for women writers when I started writing again in 1990 than there had been in 1979 when I was finishing my degree. It's only now, though, that the North's deep conservatism and its disregard for woman is, at last, beginning to crack under the pressure of more radical forces. Recently I read in my home town with a young woman of eighteen, Erin Halliday — young poet of the year — who went to the same school as I did. Her voice is strong so I'm hopeful.

There is that sense of 'between', connoting perhaps ambiguity or transition rather than the absolute or concrete fact, in the poems: the 'gap between seconds...

the spaces/ between things... What's wrong between them...' Carol Rumens has connected Medbh McGuckian's poetry to 'Keat's ability to be in uncertainties, mysteries, doubts, without any irritable reaching after fact or reason'.

The core of all those gaps express something about being human: the gap between aspirations and reality, between hope and fact, between the self and other selves, between male and female, between two people. Sometimes even time seems to be split up into gaps which can open up between seconds. I think that sex is one of the things we use to try to close the gaps even if it's just for a few seconds that you lose all sense of separateness.

That sounds like Leonard Cohen, who you've referred to, his conflation of sex and the sacred in that moment when 'I knelt and my heart was ease'. Is there an influence carried over from music, from popular music, into the poems.

Certainly Leonard Cohen is one of the first names that comes to mind in that respect and some popular musicians, singers and songwriters, do deliver on a poetic level. I fell in love with Leonard when I was about sixteen and that's lasted. I enjoy good songs and there are many songwriters who have written musical poetry — like Van Morrison — songs that enter your consciousness in the way that a good poem does. My daughter is seventeen — we listen to each other's music — and I've found there are still many good bands around.

In Morrison's 'Rave On John Donne' there's that Romantic vision which descends from Blake and, perhaps, Protestantism: innocence and experience; Walt Whitman 'nose down in the wet grass' (of the Castlereagh Hills?) and the 'industrial and mechanical age' (of the Belfast shipyards?). You too invoke Blake in the poems.

I'm a big fan of Blake. He turns things on their head to make something else. The idea of original sin, which I was brought up with as a child, that unless you were redeemed you were some kind of evil person carrying a virus called original sin, occurs in Blake. I've come to feel that the only redemption to be had is through the self, by identifying and dealing with this idea as a virus in itself. Blake suggests that you recognise the demons and deal with the things that can reek incredible havoc — I suppose that goes even further back to the Greek's recognition of Dionysus — so there's the refusal to deny the part of yourself which creates havoc and the necessity of dealing with these things.

Blake was both a visual artist and a writer and in 'Visits' you have a 'raggle of crows/blown sideways... across a flat canvas' although there appear to be more references to photography than to painting in the poems. 'But o, photography!' says Larkin in 'Lines on a Young Lady's Photograph Album', 'As no

art is, /Faithful and disappointing! That records/ Dull days as dull, and hold-
it smiles as frauds...'

My memory works photographically. I often can't remember the whole pic-
ture but I've an instinct for the clarity of a few frames which tell you what
has happened and that's probably why I'm attracted to photography. I'm
more keen on taking photographs than on having my own photograph
taken so I often carry a camera everywhere with me and bore my family to
death with the photographs afterwards. I like the idea that you can freeze
a panel of the past, that you can recall the emotion of that time exactly, and
sometimes see past the "fraud" of the smile. This takes me back to your
question about the 'selves'. I don't know too many people who feel secure
with one, single, image of the self from the past. So you look at all those
many recorded images because you can accommodate the contradictions
of who you are or were and where you've been. I'm conscious too that pho-
tography has probably changed our perceptions in the twentieth century.
The press photograph became one of the main ways to record the past.
We've acquired a record that other centuries don't have but we're proba-
bly much more conscious of wars and other horrors as a result.

Photography, moving images, are powerful mediums and their cultural pri-
macy as a way of reading the world might be seen as threatening or supplant-
ing literature's functions. Pictures or paintings often used to illustrate stories as
subsidiary mediums whereas now the reverse is often the case. The text is
squeezed into space. Maybe we're back with medieval formats like stained glass,
pictures with text as subtitles.

I think there's a limit, though, to what photographs convey even through
the most immediate or striking image. I recently looked at quite a famous
press photograph of a starving child with a vulture sitting waiting in the
background. It's an image which has become famous in terms of cover-
age; it is a striking image and it hits you. The story with the photograph
was about the way it fitted into the photographer's life, about how he had
walked away from that scene, how that had plagued him for the rest of his
life, how he had eventually killed himself. The image, while it's powerful
or strong, is simply not enough to capture all of that on its own.

You're linking language with story, with morality?
I guess that, from a child, morality and working out your own morality has
been a theme that runs through my life and poetry because I didn't
accept the morality I inherited. I was once told as a child that I had no
morals. I've had to try to work out my own morality. Language, having
words to use, feels to me almost a magical thing — a force for good or evil,
a tool — but, ultimately, what you do and how you behave is more impor-
tant than what you have to say.

You currently work as a senior social worker and live in Newtownards with your family. The poem 'Dreaming Houses' concludes SNAKESKIN STILETTOS. *Do you see this as a concluding poem for this volume which you might carry over into recent work?*
Yes. I'm very much interested in architecture and houses. Concluding that first volume felt like a cut-off point; you wanted to kick out into something else but there was also a sense of post-natal blues mixed up with the feeling of having achieved something. I stopped writing for a while. Perhaps I feel that thinking too much about where I'm heading doesn't necessarily help me. I'm not an intellectual and I prefer to let things happen of their own accord although there is a new collection now taking shape.

Thinking into new territory though... surely Dionysus needs Apollo?
I wouldn't deny the importance of that, of the rational and the intellectual, but to think too much about future poems runs the danger of closing them down.

CATHAL Ó SEARCAIGH

Born in Cloughaneely (1956) you grew up in north-west Donegal, within sight of Errigal and Tory Island. How would you describe the influence of your parents on your formation as a child or as a writer?

I can best answer that question by telling you two stories about my parents. The first one is about my mother. She was a simple, guileless, illiterate woman, very earthy in her demeanour and very bawdy in her humour. Having no education, no particular skills, she worked in Scotland in low, mean, servile jobs be it as a tatie-hoker on the farms or as a skivvy in a big house in Glasgow or as a herring girl gutting fish in the Shetlands. While my father laboured in Scotland as a seasonal farmhand, my mother worked our small hill-farm here. She took pleasure, I think, in tough toil; the heave and slog of carrying a creel of turf, of mucking out a byre, of digging potatoes. She was better at heavy outdoor duties than she was at domestic niceties like cooking and cleaning.

Every fortnight my father wrote home, enclosing money with the letter, and my mother would take these letters to Mary Gallagher, our gracious next-door neighbour, to have them read for her. I remember once, when Mary was not available to read the letter, my mother approached another woman, an abrupt, heedless woman. It was on the day the grocery van came to our townland. The locals gathered around the van, waiting their turn to buy the week's supply of groceries. My mother, clutching the letter in her hand, asked this woman if she would oblige her by reading the letter, whenever the grocery van had gone. This woman rudely snatched the letter out of my mother's hand and said, 'I don't have time to read it later. I'll do it now.' She proceeded to read our letter out aloud to the assembled neighbours. My mother was always diffident in the presence of people who could read and write and she was overwhelmed by the insolence of this woman. She stood there sheepishly and let this woman humiliate her, ridicule her. I was six or seven at the time and mortified at this affront to my mother, angry at the outrage of it, the discourtesy of it. I vowed to myself that I would learn to read and write immediately, so that my poor, timid, mother would not have to suffer this sort of public disgrace. And I did. I picked up the basics of reading and writing so that I could correspond with my father. I remember my first letter to him in a childlike squiggle. It looked as if a bird had clawed its way across the page, mysterious and illegible. Anyway, my father kept that letter in his purse for the rest of his life. When he died in 1995 the letter had crumbled into a fine papery dust. I still remember the enormous thrill I got from that letter. To take words out of the air — those winged birds that made the air around me whirr with excitement — and coop them up in a scrawly cage of blue on the page. It was an empowering exercise. Still is.

The second story concerns my father. It was Christmas Day and I must have been nine or ten. The previous night I had hung my biggest knee-length stocking on the soot-black crane above the fire. Santa would stuff it with gifts. I glowed with childish expectancy. You could count upon Santa. I noticed before I went to bed that my father looked glum and down-hearted. How could he be unhappy at Christmas? I wondered what ailed him? Next morning I got up at break of day without disturbing my parents. I slept with them. We only had the one bed in the house. No wonder they didn't have any more children. I approached the chimney crane with a thumping heart. And there was my stocking hanging with a streak of soot down the side, empty and limp. Had Santa passed me over? I wasn't a particularly bad boy. Why had he overlooked me, ignored me? I searched around the kitchen frantically hoping he had hid his gifts. But no, there was nothing — nothing! I went up to the room and told my parents, tearfully, that Santa had forgotten me. I was crushed. They were equally distraught. I could sense that. My father, rather unsteadily, his voice faltering, started to tell me startling things. He said that there was no Santa Claus, that it was parents who filled their children's stockings, that he was so poor, so much in debt that Christmas, that he couldn't afford to buy me anything. We had barely enough, he said, to buy extra food. But things would improve when he went to Scotland. He would buy me something lovely with his first pay cheque. We would survive and some day, he said, things would be brighter and better for all of us. I could see the tears welling up in my father's eyes but he resolutely held back the flow by shutting them tight. I was stunned by these revelations. I knew that it cut him to the quick to have to tell me all of this. I heard him say to my mother, 'Is bocht an saol é go gcaithfidh mé an fhirinne a ínse do chomh luath seo ina shaol.' (It's a poor life that I had to tell the truth to one so early in this life.) I was stunned by this, as I said, but also touched by my father's forthrightness. This knowledge, rather than crushing me, strengthened me. If Santa was a fraud, was God also a hoax? It dawned on me that adults were as gullible as I was, equally in need of make-believe. From now on I would have to examine everything I was taught at school. Adults would not dupe me anymore. There was no Santa. I was curious to find out what else was false or pretence or suspect. That Christmas morning I knew I had crossed the threshold into an adult world. I now possessed something rare, something unknown to my peers. There was no Santa! I felt strengthened by this shocking revelation. From now on I would have to find my own truths, shape my own construct of the world.

You've recalled, at four or five, hearing your father recite Robbie Burns like the Latin Mass in an 'Interview with Niall McGrath' in the HONEST ULSTERMAN *(108, Winter 1999-2000). Does this imply that sound is as important as sense in poetry, the voice as important as the printed word?*
As I've already said in that interview I was spellbound by the chant, by the soaring exultation in my father's voice as he uttered those strange sounds. I didn't have any English at the time. Of course, that soundscape is crucial. The pronounciation-charm of words aligned in such a way that they chime off each other. That effect is mantric. The sound of poetry is a mantric experience, an 'om-like' incantation that opens the clogged pores of the senses. Listening to poetry we became more ear, more inner ear, anyway; more in tune with the potency of sound and more aware of the potentiality of silence. Perhaps we have to experience silence before we can appreciate sound. A poem is also a breathing body of words. The voice of the reader becomes the stethoscope, the amplifying apparatus, through which we hear the gasp and gulp of it. I always urge students to read the poem out loud to hear it 'breathing'. If you put your ear to it, so to say, you will hear its heartbeat, its pulse. In Irish language poetry the vowel sounds are vitally important. How we align and arrange our vowels channels the life-force of the poem, creates its sound; the vowel in Gaelic is the animating principle of the word. It's the soul within the body of the consonants. A good poem in Gaelic, you could say, is a successful vowel movement.

Seamus Heaney's PREOCCUPATIONS: SELECTED PROSE *(1980) recalls that 'verse, however humble had a place in the life of the home as one of the ordinary rituals of life'. According to Michael Parker's* SEAMUS HEANEY: THE MAKING OF THE POET *(1993) he encountered Corkery and Irish language poetry early on. Paul Muldoon's first poems were in Irish. Irish language and verse — were these part of home and community life?*
The Irish language was and still is the local community language. After all, I live in one of the heartlands of Gaelic near Gort a' Choirce where a significant number of the population conduct their lives socially, commercially and romantically in Irish. It was Gaelic that rocked my cradle. My mother sang her 'suntraí', her sleep-inducing songs, to hush and soothe me when I cried. The hum and purr of her voice as she intoned 'Seothín Seothó' usually lulled me into a deep swoon of contentment. The mantric experience again, I suppose. I started learning English at the primary school but it was only in the summertime that I got a chance to put it into practice when many locals, who had emigrated to Glasgow, would return with their brood of kids to stay with their relatives. We called them "the

Scotties". Mothers and children spent entire summers here and working fathers came for a short vacation from mid-July to early August. During these summers playing with "the Scotties" I became fluent in English and spoke it with a slight Glasgow accent in an attempt to imitate or to integrate with them. We Gaelic kids thought they were so "with it", so worldly-wise, with their talk about television, rock and roll and teddy boys and they looked so trendy with their stylishly sleek haircuts. Our hair was chopped off, sheared off unfashionable, by some local farmer. We wore shoddy odds-and-ends while they looked so smart and snazzy in their well-matched outfits, their colour-combinations, their sturdy shoes. We wanted to be them. The capital of our childish world was Glasgow, the city of our imagination, where our dreams would be realised. But they also envied us with our wild mountain playground: our cows and sheep and hens; our scampering nimbleness up hills, over ditches, across bogs. Gaelic wasn't alien to them. They often heard their parents speak Gaelic to each other in Glasgow. Anyway, there was an exchange of ideas going on between us kids, a cultural dialogue unbeknownst to us. They spoke of an urban world of superstores, gang rivalry, high-rise living, Celtic soccer matches. We showed them farming life: a cow being bulled; how to harness a donkey; bottle-feed a lamb; footing turf; handling frogspawn. We opened windows of wonder on to the world for each other.

It was liberating becoming aware of two languages, two different cyphers to denote the same thing. How could 'cnoc' be 'hill'? I favoured 'cnoc' because it sounded more rounded. It seemed to fit those bulbously plump swells that surrounded me. Hill seemed to me then to be too slender, too blunt. It sounded more like an upthrust, a stone pillar. On the other hand I learned that fridge was called 'cuisneoir' in Gaelic. We didn't have a fridge at home but I knew what it was from a shop in Gort a' Choirce. It was where they kept ice-cream. 'Fridge' was an ice-cold box that shut tight with a rubbery, sluddgy, snap. 'Cuisneoir' I'd never heard as a spoken word, a living word in the mouth of any local. When I asked somebody about it they said, 'Ó sin gaeilge mhaide na leabhair'. It was a school word and, because of my distaste for school, a dead word. Now I'm very fond of 'cuisneoir'. It's an apt evocation of the fridge in Gaelic. It comes from the word 'cuisne' meaning frosty or cold-haze. It's the kind of linguistic adaptability I admire. Using a root word in Gaelic and extending and enlarging its meaning, its 'brí'. 'Brí', in Irish, signifies 'meaning' but it also means strength and vigour. In short, having two languages enabled me to see the world through two different lenses. You came, later, to realise that each lens was tilted differently; it became apparent that Gaelic allowed me to see the world in emotional close-up while English provided, for me, a conceptual wide-shot of the world.

Was verse part of your upbringing in the locality?
As a child I often heard the locals speaking verse, particularly in the wake houses. Those sitting up to wake the corpse passed the night by telling yarns and by reciting 'ramáis'. 'Abair Ramás', they would say, meaning some quirky doggerel verse. 'Bó bhán! Bó Bhán! / Ag doras thigh Mhanais / D'itheadh sí an saol/Is cha chacfadh sí a dhath.' Riddle me that, Mr Brown! In instant English it goes something like this: 'White cow! White cow! / At Manus's door / It would devour the world/and never shit a turd.' Now, what's that? It's a graveyard. Another one? Now let me think. O yes, a sort of haiku-like riddle for something which can be quite sloppy if you are into 'hot Oriental fare'. 'Saolaíodh gan anam é / baisteadh gan corp é / agus fuair sé bás ag gabháil cheoil.' Baffling, isn't it? 'Born without a soul/ baptised without a body / and died while it sang!' Isn't that gas? And that's exactly what it is: a fart. Of course, anyone growing up in the sort of Gaelic community that nourished me was bound to hear songs and stories. People would listen to a song, follow its narrative —which was recreated anew each time it was sung — and you'd admire the melodic twists and turns, the embellishments that the singer gave to the song. It was a shared, communal, vibe. The listener was as much part of the experience as was the singer. The song happened in that warm emotive clearing where the singer and listener met and fused. You get a similar vibe at a modern-day 'poultry reading' where the poet squawks and the audience cackles. I've often been introduced in the States as Cackle Ó Squawky.

You went to your first school nearby and then to Gort a' Choirce Technical School at the age of twelve; you started out writing poems in English there which continued when you went to London in the 1970s. Was there a teacher who first nourished your interest in poetry? Which poets first attracted you?
I attended national school in Caiseal na gCorr. It was mostly a grim experience. We had one lovely teacher in second and third class, a Mrs Cannon, who mothered us. She told us stories from the Old Testament. As a result I'm still very fond of that book, a very fine travelogue for inner-space trippers. It's a book of sublime Jewish 'seanchas'. Otherwise school was cruel and brutal and we were whacked and flogged in a callous and heartless system. We have to forgive and forget those ruthless teachers, who were probably damaged themselves by the abusiveness of their own schooling, if we're to avoid becoming victims of our own past. At that time none of our parents had the voice or the authority or the gumption to oppose that cruel system. So, we suffered in silence. My classmates at Caiseal na gCorr abhorred their schooldays there — everyone still shudders at the thought of it — even though it was regarded as one of the best primary schools in the parish because so many students successfully passed their scholarship exams. The school had windows but, looking

back on it now, it seems to me that no light got in to brighten that grim dispiriting room where we sat in fear. Still, I read voluminously at that time, everything and anything that came my way, be it the missionary magazines like *Africa* and *The Far East* or the pictorially naughty *Kama Sutra* — that emissionary 'mag' my father brought home to me from Glasgow, by mischance in a bag of books. Or was my daddy really trying to prepare me for bizarre sex in Oriental bazaars with some insight into my oriental bent? Studying those pictures in the *Kama Sutra* with their full-frontal acrobatics made the facts of life for an eleven year old kid rather circus-like.

I hated school so much I'd no desire to continue my education, but when some friends decided to enrol at the Technical School in Gort a' Choirce I decided to follow them. Technical education was considered then to be inferior — for 'low-grade dimwits' or rejects 'lucky to pick up a trade' — compared to the more exalted academic pursuits of secondary schools, but that first day at the Tech. changed my life forever. A tall, youngish, energetic teacher read from an English book. His delivery was dramatic, captivating; he held our attention effortlessly. When he finished reading he asked us mischievously, 'What do you think about that prose passage you have just heard?' Jesus, I nearly jumped out of my skin with surprise. I'd never been asked that kind of question at primary school where there was no discussion, where we were empty vessels waiting to be filled to the brim with facts. This was exhilaratingly new. I ventured an opinion, tentatively, of course. It was received with graciousness, weighed and pondered, by our smiling teacher. Someone else spoke. Soon everyone was eager to contribute to the discussion. That day I embarked on a glorious five year voyage of discovery under the guidance of Tom Walsh. His English classes were encounter groups, therapy sessions, where we discussed the world of ourselves and the text. He impressed upon us that our questions were as important as our answers. I thrived under this sort of tuition. School was no longer a dreaded chore but a welcoming challenge. We put on plays and toured them throughout the area: we participated in debating competitions, locally and nationally; we were taught public speaking. For its time it was an enlightened environment. As I've said, I was reading a lot at the time, voyaging by diving into the floodwaters of a book and coming up worlds away. Having an outlet like that I was never bored or confined.

You've talked in the 'Interview with Niall McGrath' of being 'awestruck' as a child with Catholicism's sensuous rituals before a teenage revolt against its 'downright totalitarianism' meant you 'copped out'. Poems like 'Words of a Brother' or 'Carnal Knowledge' seem to play ironies against religion from inside its ideolect; others, like 'A Chorus of Characters', feel devotional, prayerful, supplicatory. How does Catholicism register in the language or imagination of the poems?

The poem 'Ceremony', for example, is a Mass-like celebration of love-making: 'On the altar of the bed / I celebrate your body tonight...' That enraptured, frenzied, relationship between God and man was often expressed in ecstatic sexual terms. The poetry of St. John of the Cross is a blissful sexual communion with the body of Christ. 'The Song of Songs' is one of the horniest poems ever written. The Catholicism that I got at primary school was dour and dark; sex was serpent-energy, where the devil inserted his horn into my little dick and made it sinfully rigid; if I touched it I was fondling the devil. One day my little schoolmate told me that he had a strange experience the night before. He'd rubbed his dick too roughly and the devil had spat at him. He enjoyed it, he said, but was terribly frightened because he must have hurt and angered the devil with his rough handling. As yet I'd had no experience like that, I told him, but I reassured him that anything that hurt the devil was good, positively good. He then suggested that we would 'hurt' the devil together. And we did. Over the next few weeks we walloped the devil every chance we got, so much so that he could barely spit in the end. And thus began my love for my fellow men. Catholicism tried to instil a terrible sense of guilt in us because, that way, they knew that they could control us. We were all collectively guilty of the first fuck in the Garden of Eden and we would pay the penalty. Religions are extremely deft at making a ceremony of death out of the miracle of life. I try to travel through life in the safety of my Karma. Those barking, biting, dogmas may chase my Karma but they won't get me, I hope.

As a teenager in the early 1970s you encountered the American Beats. Ginsberg, Ferlinghetti, Corso and Snyder are 'nightingales' who bring 'vodoo verses' to you in London in the '70s poems; Kerouac's ON THE ROAD has you 'hooked', around 1970-73, offering a way of 'Californicating Cill Ulta, Friscying Falcarragh'. Did Gaeltacht writers have an equivalent impact or are these influences an implicit criticism of Irish language poetry as largely conservative apart from Ó'Riordáin's experimentalism which was often slammed?
That's right. When Seán Ó Riordáin's first collection *Eireaball Spideóige* was published in 1952 it received very harsh criticism. Eminent critics said that he was a poor craftsman who had sundered the link with tradition; most scornful of all the judgements made against him was the accusation that he had misused the Irish language. The usual parade of fascist clichés marched forth and tramped over the body of Ó Riordáin's verse. It hurt him greatly and it was twelve years before he issued his next volume, a slim tour de force; *Brosna* is my favourite Ó Riordáin collection. The early encounters with Ó Riordáin's poetry were, for me, both breath-taking and distressing. In an extreme effort to isolate the true self, 'an mise ceart', there's a sort of self-mutilation going on in his poetry. He cuts himself up

with his razor-sharp intelligence. His poetry is full of loathing and self-doubt. He introduces into Gaelic the whole idea of the self as drama. The self is the stage where a drama of the absurd takes place. He managed, very successfully, to dramatise that kind of reflective material. It's interesting that it was during the years of his greatest literary achievements (in the late '40s, '50s and early '60s) that dramatists like Beckett, Eugène Ionesco and Anton Artaud produced their most coherent, most profound, realisations of the absurd in drama. For Sean Ó Riordáin the drama, the conflict, takes place in the interior arena of the spirit. The themes of the drama are the search for the unseeable self and the saying of the unsayable in an absurdist world. In a poem called 'Fan' he says: 'Create if you have to /an unutterable clutter', a 'treanglam dolabhartha' as he terms it in Irish. That's why his Irish sounded so strange to those early critics of his work. He was an activator of language, a pusher of it; he made it get-up-and-go. Rather than letting language speak through him, he forcibly spoke through language. The given language was often inadequate for his needs and he began to coin new words, especially compound words. It was stimulating to read him from that point of view; to encounter that exciting, individualistic, expressiveness which was so utterly new to the Gaelic of our times.

My early encounter with the poetry of Maíre Mhac an tSaoi was, for me, also a thrilling event. She was, of course, a fierce critic of the early Ó Riordáin. It has to be said that she was young and brash at that time and in our youthful impulsiveness we often say rash and hasty things that we regret later. Anyway, I adore her, the person and the poet. The publication of her first book, *Margadh na Saoire*, in 1956 was a momentous occasion in Irish language poetry: that book is a pivotal book in our poetry; a book where passion and precision have become one. I loved it from the moment I picked it up in 1970. I was charmed by its vowel harmonies and verbal music. I was struck by the stunning songlike intensity of the poems, the 'lyric cry' of them. She used classically restrained forms but, oh boy, did she infuse them with a wild throbbing sensuality. Evidently she has influenced me, hugely. By 1970 the *Innti* poets (Michael Davitt, Gabriel Rosenstock, Nuala Ní Dhomhnaill and Liam Ó Muirthile) were beginning their literary swagger. By way of Irish language magazines I had an ear to their dashing, swinging sounds. Michael Davitt, at that time, was the tuned-in, amped-up, street-wise cosmopolitan who set the stances, with *Innti* as his flamboyantly youthful magazine. For a lot of us who took to poetry in the '70s he was the rather raffish, maverick, lyric tenor of our bohemian rhapsody. We loved the sounds he made, the jazzy urgency of his style that made Gaelic go bebop in the night with a swinging, snazzy, self-confidence. It was compelling stuff. Funky, defiant and free.

I met Gabriel Rosenstock in the early '70s at 'Slogadh' the annual

Gael-Linn youth extravaganza that, in those early years, was always held in St. Patrick's College in Drumcondra, Dublin. I had read his poems in the magazines and I was excited by their affirmations, their openness to the world, their dialogue with other cultures. I admired the Chekovian eye for detail. Around that time I was also reading Chekov's short stories and plays. Gabriel, like Chekov, was and is a visionary of the real. Many of his poems are moments of illumination. Haiku-like, they glow with the energy of their perceptions. Gabriel is such a vast subject matter, an expanding universe of words that daily keeps growing and growing. I'd need a book-length interview to discuss him. Suffice to say, that he is a great friend to me and to all involved in the art and craft of verse in Gaelic. He is the Johnny Appleseed of Gaelic Literature. Poet, dramatist, novelist, children's writer, editor, actor, encourager. By the generosity of his imagination he has scattered many seeds that all of us have benefited from. He has given many bulbs of encouragement, many roots of council, many saplings of guidance, many seeds of suggestion. I love the huge and humane enterprise of his writing. The poets associated with *Innti* were the Gaelic response to the Beat Poets. So I did have role models, contemporary ones within the Gaelic tradition, when I set out to write.

Is there ever a tension in your work between Beat freedom or free verse and the 'Gaelic classical forms' that Máire an tSaoi and Sean Lysaght associate with your poetry? How do you see form or shape in relation to content?
The poem decides to a large extent on the face its going to present to the world. In its period of gestation it decides how it's going to manifest itself. I have to do the best I can to help it achieve its own original impulse. Between the thought and the word there are many miscarriages of intent, many aborted impulses. Form, as Charles Olsen rightly pointed out, should be an extension of content. The poem knows the kind of body that is best suited to its needs, to its weight, to its carriage. The poet, by being earfully perceptive to its prompts and its pushes, allows the poem to find its intended form.

In Michael Donaghy's 'A Conversation with Paul Muldoon' in the CHICAGO REVIEW *(35, 1, Autumn 1985) Muldoon suggests comparisons with Seamus Heaney were inevitable because they emerged from the same, small, northern territory where shared Catholic backgrounds, early career paths and subject matter were, to some extent, inevitable; the age-gap was less often noticed — 'a significant fifteen years'. As a poet born in the 1950's do you see different eras or generational factors as being as important as any shared geography in informing or shaping your poems?*
We are all formed and informed by the times we live in. That "state of mind" known as the '60s has certainly conditioned me, shaped my imagination. Although that psychedelic explosion was not happening in Mín 'a

Leá I got an earful of its vibrations from radio. My father, when he came home from Scotland, talked about Beatlemania in Glasgow. He told me about a bald man who went into a barber shop in Sauchiehall Street and requested a 'Beatles haircut'. He also brought home a poster of those four Liverpool moptops. I also loved the colourful tribalism of the Hippies. At the Technical School Tom Walsh asked us to write an essay about Flower Power. By the early '70s I was into long hair, ethnic clothes, beads and patchouli oil. I was getting high on expansiveness be it in pop or in poetry or in politics. I was into the bliss business of Eastern beliefs. Swami Vive Kananada, the Maharishi, Sri Yukteswar and Krishnamurti were my guardian angels, my spirit guides. That '60s tilt towards the Orient has certainly affected my poems but a wise man never "blows his knows".

In the early 1970s, aged 15, you set out for London and the city's whole '70s geography — even daisies in the pavement cracks — registers in poems. Part 4 of OUT IN THE OPEN *(1997) opens with Lawrence Ferlinghetti's 'London Crossfigured': 'It / could have been any place / but it wasn't / it was/London.' Why London as opposed to, say, New York or Dublin?*
I went to London because it was the closest I could get to San Francisco. I wanted to hang out in Haight Ashbury but, for the present, High Street Kensington would be the stop-gap, the substitute. I knew of "swinging London" but by the time I arrived there in the early '70s the swing had gone out of Carnaby Street. The poems were attempts to make some sense of my West-End metaphysics, my hippy-darma. They were also snap-shots of the Picadilly life of my prick.

You've mentioned the 'profound effect' of encountering Derek Mahon's poem 'Afterlives' and his volume THE SNOW PARTY *in 1975 when you were working in a London bar in an 'Interview with Liz Curtis' in* FORTNIGHT *(April 1996, No 349). It was a poem which, quite literally, brought you home. You also studied French, Russian and Irish at the National Institute of Higher Education at Limerick and Celtic Studies at Maynooth. Yevtushenko, for instance, is acknowledged in* HOMECOMING *as providing the idea for the poem, 'Lament for Friendship'. Are there other French and Russian poets you are 'friendly' with?*
I was a student of European studies in the early days of the NIHE. The two years I spent in Limerick were passed in the library rather than the lecture hall. I read my way through the library pursuing my own course of studies — Asiatic rather than European — and then moved on to London, to a bigger library. At Maynooth I enrolled to do Celtic Studies but once I entered the library it became 'Galactic Studies'. I was off again on my own wayward course. Recently I was conferred with an honourary doctorate in Celtic Studies at Maynooth and, as an academic drop-out, it was both strange and funny to be honoured like this. Initially some of my neigh-

bours thought that I was a fully-fledged medical doctor but I'm more of a specialist than a general practitioner. If you have a blockage in one of your passage graves or a priapic problem with one of your standing stones, I'm your doctor. In the bookshops in London, particularly around Charing Cross Road, I began to familiarise myself with European, Russian and South American poets. The Penguin Modern European Poets series was an incalculable asset to all of us interested in what was happening in poetry throughout Europe. The verse translations from unfamiliar languages — Hungarian, Czech, Polish, Serbo-Croat, Russian — stirred my imagination. They were not airy flights of fancy, written as a mental exercise. These poems had to be written; they were wounds that spoke. Nina Cassian, a Romanian poet under Ceausescu's dictatorship could write with conviction and without self-pity in her 'Self-Portrait': 'I am nothing / but a drop of blood / that speaks'. Likewise Paul Celan, who suffered the horrors of the concentration camp, could write in *Fadensonnen*: 'You were my death: / you I could hold / when all else fell away from me.' So through books, those wonderful bureaus of friendship, I became acquainted with Yevtushenko, Neruda, Vasko Popa, Umberto Saba, Yehuda Amichai, Tomas Tranströmer, Fernando Pesoa, Miroslav Holub, Eugenio Montale, Nicanor Parra, to name just a fraction of the company I kept in my imagination.

Your debut collection of poems SÚILE SHUIBHNE *(1983) was published when you were in your late twenties. Are you comfortable or ambivalent with this collection?*
Actually my first collection was published in 1975 when Seán Ó Cuirreáin, a very enterprising school friend of mine, published it privately. I mean privately in the sense that he set up his own small imprint, Cló Uí Chuirreáin, to facilitate publication. The book was called *Miontragóid Chathrach / A Trivial City Tragedy*. The only tragedy in it was that it was ever published. But I had a chance to redress all of that recently when my selected poems, *Ag Tnúth Leis An tSolas (Poems 1975-2000)*, were published which allowed me the opportunity to doctor those first, fine, careless, ruptures. My next venture was a book in which I shared equal billing with Gabriel Rosenstock, *Tuirlingt / Descending*, which was published in 1978. I'm not sure what we were descending from — perhaps the last bus to Gleann na nGealt. Anyway, my poems looked and sounded as if they had jumped off a vehicle in full flight. They were in shreds, concussed and incoherent. So, by the time I published *Súile Shuibhne / The Eyes Of Sweeney* in 1983 I had trained my eye to look at a thing intently. I was more focused, more capable of seeing. In Gaelic the word for poet is 'file' meaning to see, to be a "See-R". Sweeney was the great See-R.

In quotations you acknowledge poets like Gary Snyder and Guillevic, both inspirations for John Montague who is also quoted in HOMECOMING. *Do you relate to elements in John Montague's poetry?*

Of course, I admire the scope and resonance of his work. You have to admire the staying power of poets like Heaney, Mahon, Longley, Kinsella, Montague and their ability to recreate themselves. Montague's artistic odyssey, embarked upon fifty years ago, goes on and on, charting the troubled and turbulent waters of our times with consistent clarity. He has made a meaningful contribution to the canon of literature in our times with his extraordinary sensitivity to people and to places. I like his connectedness to his *Garbh Achaidh*, his *Rough Field*, that registers what is past or passing, always acknowledging the local. In that sense he is one of the Gaelic poets come back, an Art Mac Cumhaidh with a grafted tongue and (like those Ulster Gaelic poets of the seventeenth and eighteenth century) Montague's poems are full of the candle glow of the story, the bright glimmers of memory, the will o' the wisp gleams of myth. 'Like Dolmens Round My Childhood' is a poem of that ilk; the past flows into the present with an earthy, commonsense, mysticism. 'Last Journey' is a particular favourite of mine. In its slow cadences I hear the train chugging its way through —

> the rushy meadows,
> small hills and hidden villages –
> Beragh, Carrickmore,
>
> Pomeroy, Fintona –
> place names that sigh
> like a pressed melodeon
> across this forgotten
> Northern landscape.

The rich immediacy of those lines goes beyond their local geography, and of course, I love his enumeration of place names, a very Gaelic concern. Life is lived forward as Nietzsche said but understood backwards. John Montague's monumental *Collected Poems* testifies to that statement.

Is there such a thing as peripheral worry for a poet? In 'Here and There' Douglas Dunn, in Tayport, is addressed by a correspondent who warns via Heaney: '...You'll twist your art on the parochial lie... An inner émigré, you'll versify/Not write. You'll turn your back on history.' Donegal, a source in many poems, is a border county: in the North, geographically; in the Republic of Ireland, politically. Has it been enriched or denuded by a 'peripheral' or ambivalent position between two powerful histories?
Donegal is often seen as a detached limb of the South, a distant appendage that doesn't receive its fair share of the blood-flow of economic well-being. On the other hand, as a ruggedly beautiful and extremely friendly hinterland to the North it has benefited from a steady flow of Northern tourists. Personally I like its sort of indeterminate, borderland position. These sort

of places tend to be enigmatic and ambiguous — places where different ideas, different identities, different histories, meet and challenge each other. These places are frontiers. From here we can develop new approaches, explore unknown territories. I myself live in an area where the interaction between Gaelic and English is most challenging. It's a linguistic borderland. As Gaelic speakers we are adapting and absorbing, aligning our language to the needs and nuances of our times. We listen to sean-nós singing on ghetto-blasters made in Japan. We tell our stories around German radiators. A friend of mine has a libidinous tomcat called 'Pangur Bán'. Another friend has a little mini car called 'An Bonnán Buí' — 'The Yellow Bittern'. Lovely outrageous ways of repossessing the tradition and breathing new life into it. I think Donegal artistes like Brian Friel, Frank McGuinness, Matthew Sweeney, Altán, Clannad and Enya have all drawn inspiration from Donegal's frontier-like location. It has conditioned how they have reshaped and renewed the tradition.

Haiku, distillations smaller than 'hip-flasks' to borrow Frank Ormsby's image, seem to attract you.
It only takes a spit second to read a haiku but, as Susan Sontag said about a photograph, it also takes a lifetime of preparation... a lifetime of walking around with one's eyes open. Those small, luminous, moments of insight don't come easy. I like the haiku because, at its core, there's the belief that all things are interconnected. Therefore, within that framework, no thing is alone and nothing is unimportant. That sort of sympathy is, for me anyway, reassuring. The haiku, it seems to me, knows no bounds, no borders, no barricades. Like light it's boundless in its capacity to cross over, to connect. A haiku by Buson speaks volumes about love, marriage, loneliness, death, separation. 'The piercing chill I feel: / my dead wife's comb, in our bedroom, / under my heel...' It wrenches the heart out of me everytime I read that. The heart-aching poignancy of it. I also like iconoclastic clarity: ' Pissing through the doorway / I make a clean hole / in the snow.' I don't know who wrote that but it goes to prove that the penis is mightier than the pen at clearing the snow.

In THE WAY OF ZEN Alan Watt's sees Zen as a drunk man on a bicycle; he's lost the fear of falling, connected up, Flann O'Brien wise. How do you see Zen Buddhism?
Zen Buddhism is the ability to take a long walk around the table in your dining room and enjoy the journey. It's about attentiveness, being attentive to the immediate. Travels around the table can be breathtaking if you are open to the experience. You become a mystic of the domestic. For me Zen is about cultivating a sense of awareness in your life, a sense of readiness, an openness to experience not blinkered by preconceptions or

dulled by dogma. Robert Creeley tells of the American artist Franz Kline's approach to painting: 'If I paint what I know it bores me; if I paint what you know it bores you, so I paint what I don't know.' Zen is not about ideology or theology; it's not about conceptions. It's about perceptions. 'Logic and sermons never convince', to paraphrase Walt Whitman, but 'the damp of the night drives deeper into the soul'. Zen celebrates the experience of being alive, the awe-inspiring daily occurrence of our everyday lives. Trying to define Zen is as useless as searching for the claw-mark of a bird in the sky. You breathe Zen. You embody it. Then you are Zen.

How do you see the relationship between Irish and English language poetry and national identity in Ireland? Douglas Dunn's 'Audenesques for 1960' ambiguously suggests: 'Nationality doesn't identify 'our side'. /Muses are international, and mine is a lady/Who speaks all sorts of languages (in translation)....' Derek Walcott's 'The Schooner's Flight' implicates language in history far less benignly — 'that's all them bastards have left us: words'. Do 'Lament' and 'Native Speaker' suggest that you approach this question from different angles?

A number of years ago, Nuala Ní Dhomhnaill described the Gaelic writer as a sort of 'exotica' on the margins of English language writing in Ireland. We were not represented in the anthologies. We were not part of the discourse of Irish literature. We were the 'Hidden Ireland', rustic buffoons still writing in a dead language. Translations have made us more accessible, more Anglo-friendly. Now it would be unwise to publish an anthology of Irish writing without including some contemporary Gaelic literature. The reality is, of course, that you have to receive the approval or the blessing of English before you are ratified and recognised as a writer. Until I was decoded into English I wasn't in demand as a poet. 'Native Speaker' is a humourous look at the criss-crossings, the cross-dressings, that can take place between Irish and English. I find these linguistic encounters between the two languages a great source of poetry. Those tangos between Irish and English are quite dashing and provocative. They are attention-grabbing flings. I think we have yet to explore the full possibilities of these "meetings". New marriages of ideas will emerge, new unions of sound and, of course, very saucy rhythmic pairings.

Gearóid MacLochlainn's recent poem 'Translations' opens: 'Tonight, my friends, there will be no translations,/Nothing trans-lated, altered, diluted/with hub-bubbly English/that turns my poetry to lemonade.' Translation as 'skeleton keys' (Sean Lysaght) or 'cunning linguism' (Frank Sewell) or ag obair as lámha a chéile/ working out of one another's hands (Declan Kiberd and Gabriel Fitzmaurice) or 'writing with English bones, covered with Gaelic skin' (a rough paraphrase from ROGHA AN CHÉID / SELECTION OF THE CENTURY *edited by Gearóid Denvir)? How do you see translation?*

I look upon Frankie Sewell as someone who ferries my poems across the abyss to the safe harbour of English. I have to say that translation into English has given me a new lease of life, an opportunity to survive as a poet in the Irish language. I don't do translations of my own work; it's a safeguard against compromising the originals. If I did translations I would be conscious of English all the time, conceding to its register, forfeiting anything that I felt was alien to its usage. I want to write out of the linguistic experience of Gaelic. I don't want another language whispering in my ear, bidding me to be its agent. As to the translation of poetry? To me poetry is *language* articulating itself at its most acute. Each word in a language has its own precise shape, its own particular soundscape, its own psychic substratum. You just can't take a word from one language and have it reproduced exactly in another linguistic system. It's not possible to have a perfect likeness. You may find a counterpart, of course, but it's never the exact same. 'Fuinneag', for all practical purposes, is comparable to 'window' but they're not the same. That's obvious. There is a huge difference in how they look, how they behave in the sound structure of a sentence. Each language has its own lens through which it filters reality. Our perceptions, our poetries, are conditioned by that fact. The common greeting in Irish 'Dia dhuit' is theologically loaded compared to 'Hello', its more laid-back, secular, counterpart in English. I often hear people say that literal translations of poems are preferable but even there you also have to reconstitute the words in the target language. As far as I'm concerned I prefer those translations (those versions, those substitutions, whatever you want to call them) that are true to the spirit of the text. That means that you retain a sense of the words as far as possible; you amplify them rather than alter them. Some poets are easier to translate than others. Pablo Neruda, let's say, with his verbal fireworks, his lavish displays of imagery, his spectacle of symbols, is easier to translate than Máire Mhac an tSaoi. Her poems exist in the Irish language as pure sound, as diction purified, cadenced, charged. It's nearly impossible to reproduce that sort of verbal magic.

You've written numerous, highly-charged, love poems — Michael Longley has referred to your 'erotic candour' in POETRY IRELAND *(No 39, 1993); it might be suggested that human relationships or redemptive ecology (in poems like 'Odd Man Out' or 'Sanctuary') are more central concerns than Irish politics? You suggest, though, that poetry does have a 'profound' political function and effect in the preface to the poems you selected for the anthology* WATCHING THE RIVER FLOW *(1999)?*

Yes, I believe that. We all inhabit history, some more than others of course. The collective anguish of the past is with us all. 'Words may not defeat evil' Kafka said, 'but they help us cope better with it.' Poems can be alert to politics, to the shadows cast by history, without being head-on confrontations.

I feel that my poem 'Examination of Conscience Before Going to Bed' about the slaughter of a corncrake is a political poem. It is a poem that carries, I hope, a quality of moral weight; an attempt to make some sense of the concealed furies that lie savagely within our psyche waiting to unsettle us, to seize us. Those that kill a corncrake today can, under certain conditions, massacre people tomorrow. We can't remain silent in those situations. We have to bear witness. Like anyone with a spark of humanity I do feel for people trapped helplessly by social or historical forces, the public powers that impinge upon their private lives with disastrous results. You can't have self-respect if you abuse and mistreat others. You can't have love and tenderness for your fellow-creatures unless you embody a modicum of these virtues in yourself. In order to attain this empathy, this rapport, you have to rely on the imagination — the imagination of what it is like to be these other forms of life that want to live with you on the same plane of existence. And isn't that what compassion is about? An imaginative recognition of, and a humane understanding towards, all these life forms. I do believe that good poetry affirms human values. It opposes conflicts and oppression. It cares. That's my 'Gúrú na gCnoc' sermon, John; it's easy to talk like that, of course, when you are not in 'an bhearna bhaoil', the breach of battle. Roger McGough sums up this sort of armchair homily in a little poem, 'Survivor', where he says that he does think about everyday things like large-scale starvation, ethnic strife, bloodshed, ruthless tyrannies, oppressed multitudes, the end of the world — and — then he deflates the whole thing by saying, 'It helps/ keep my mind off things.'

In METRE *(7/8, 2000), though, the American poet Robert Pinsky contends that Walt Whitman's vision of poetry as social cement is no longer possible as television, sport, popular music or global media occupy that role. Could the bardic role or Dinnseanchas (linking history, place and people) and the tight-knit society of John Montague's 'The Road's End' or your 'Corner Boys' disappear in the 21st century?*

That's tantamount to saying that poetry has no future. I don't believe that. Adam-like, the poet has always been preoccupied with naming things; things temporal and things eternal. To name a thing is to perfect its being, its existence, its consciousness. Juan Ramon Jimenez, a Spanish poet, puts it even more precisely in 'Intelligence' which I'll paraphrase: 'Let those who do not know them / go through me to things / Let those who forget them /go through me to things / Let them, themselves, who love them / Go through me to things. / Intelligence, give me / the name, exact and yours /and its, and mine, of things.' Science can, of course, name things but it does it conceptually. Poetry does it emotionally. The poet as archivist of the tribe, recording and registering what is past or passing, will always be an element in humanity's need to name things.

Robert McLiam Wilson's EUREKA STREET *(1996) critiques contemporary Irish poetry as being lost among hedgerows, implicitly failing, perhaps, to live with the multi-storied urban society and violence of his novels? A fair critique?* Violence is not specific to urban living. The hedgerows themselves are places where barbarities are often committed. Infanticide, for instance, and rape. Poetry at its best is experience made vivid in 'shocks of recognition'. It makes us aware by intensifying our perceptions. A poem that makes us aware, also, broadens our compassion, deepens our care. A good poem about a hedgerow would, it seems to me, embody a sympathy for all that lives. Therefore a poem like that reinforces our fellow feeling and strengthens our pity for victims of urban violence. The subject matter itself is not what is important but the poet's handling of it is; his search for meaning, for truth within it. Anyway, poets often allude to the times they live in obliquely, rather than directly. As to the hedgerows — Kavanagh fortified all Irish poets of the bucolic variety against this sort of cantankerous critique in 'Epic'. 'I inclined / To lose my faith in Ballyrush and Gortin/ Till Homer's ghost came whispering to my mind./ He said: I made the Illiad from such / A local row. Gods make their own importance.' Amen! As a gay man I should say, 'A-man'.

You use the first person narrative in many poems. How far can we take this 'I' at face value?
Aye! I like how we use that "aye" — and the 'I' too — rather than yes as an affirmative statement. The 'I' that I use in the poems may not necessarily be my present self. The human psyche is a deep, dark, labyrinth inhabited by many selves past and present. If you believe, as I do, in reincarnation, then the number of 'selves' or even fragments of them leave the labyrinth pretty overcrowded. Out of that sprawling habitation of the spirit some of those personas voice themselves in my poems. How I give tongue to the silence that choked them in other times, other lives. You are not talking to Cathal, you're talking to a crowd. Aye!

What of Randall Jarrell's idea that, for some critics, asking a poet about the work is akin to asking the pig to judge the bacon competition? This might mean we can trust neither teller nor tale or that the 'I' is dispersed and belongs to language itself — to Dineen or structuralism or the critic — to the language speaking us?
Randall Jarrell was a very astute critic. I think he abhored the proliferation of creative writing courses at American Universities. He believed he'd lost God and been given students or words to that end. Asking a poet to explain his work is like asking God to lie down on the analyst's couch and talk about the trauma of creation.

Your selection of 1980s poems in WATCHING THE RIVER FLOW *includes Heaney's 'Terminus' and Carson's 'Dresden' (one of his 'daringly digressive, thickly textured innovations' in that decade); your plays were performed in West Belfast and you were writer-in-residence at the University of Ulster in the 1990s. Has northern poetry a 'distinctive' voice or way of saying things?*

All great poets have their own inimitable, memorable, voice. It's what endears them to us. MacNeice, Heaney, Mahon, Longley, McGuckian, Simmons, Paulin, Muldoon: all have "northernised" the English lyric. Their uniquely individual styles of strumming that lyric is what makes me so attentive to their music.

Cuchulainn as a wonderful gay lover? How do you see the juncture between myth and poetry?

I'll tell you about that when I get a ride in Cuchulainn's chariot. Steered by that bulging manhood. I'm not sure whether I would have a stroke or a strophe. All poetry is, I think, myth. It's telling the tales of our psyche, the stories of the soul.

Some poems evoke visual art as erotic life drawings made tactile, rich as honey; there are London tube poems which have the terrifyingly anonymous feeling of a Henry Moore sketch. 'Colours', personified in one poem, 'make friends'. Are there visual artists whose work you empathise with? Is art an influence or inspiration?

I love the visual arts. I often open exhibitions for my painter friends. And from time to time I buy art. When I get that urge to buy something in oils for the house the question always is whether it's going to be a painting or a tin of sardines. Too often the tin of sardines gets priority. As a writer I envy the painter. As I speak, as I write, I'm giving birth to words: words that are smeared with an afterbirth of ambiguity; words that need to be nourished and nurtured in the school of meaning; words that eat, sleep and excrete in the house of sense; words that scream and smile, laugh and cry, in the lap of language. A painter's little tube of colour speaks with silence. Those colours 'repose in the stability of truth' as Samuel Johnson put it. I envy the painter who can speak to us wordlessly, who speaks to us with silence. We writers have to confront our audience with words that carry the nightmare of histories, the trauma of etymologies on their backs; words that have been used, misused, abused. I love the human frailties of words without wanting to mollycuddle them with meaning, my meaning.

You've written poem-songs like 'Bealtaine Blues' or 'Let's Hit the Road Jack' and blues or fragments of quotations from modern pop music turn up in poems. Gearóid MacLochlainn, the Belfast Irish language poet/musician, tells me that he sees your work as fusing sean-nos and blues. Are there singers you love? How

does music from outside the literary tradition work within it for you?
Musically, I was weaned on Radio Luxembourg. In the evenings I would nuzzle up to our little transistor and let that fantastic ferment of '60s sounds flow through me. I was nurtured by Dusty Springfield, the Troggs, the Beatles, the Rolling Stones, Bob Dylan, the Monkees, the Zombies, Manfred Mann, Procul Harum, the Moody Blues, Small Faces, the Kinks, Roy Orbison, the Beach Boys, Elvis Presley, the Bee Gees, Andy Williams, Tom Jones. This music provided the soundtrack to my sexual awakening. Songs like Amen Corner's 'Bend me, Shape me'; Herman's Hermits' 'I'm Into Something Good'; Steppenwolf's 'Born To Be Wild'; Manfred Man's 'Doo Wah Diddy Diddy'; The Equals' 'Baby Come Back' and the Monkees' 'I'm a Believer' were, for me, libido liberation songs. Reading Kerouac made me aware of jazz, especially Charlie Parker, and that led me to Charlie Mingus and Miles Davis and John Coltrane. In London I became familiar with the Blues; Muddy Waters, Howlin' Wolf, Memphis Slim, Big Bill Broonzy, Sonny Boy Williamson, Robert Johnson, John Lee Hooker. In the very early '80s Rachel Brown (or Rachel Giese as she was known back then) introduced me to classical music. She was living in Mìn A Léa at the time while she was working on her superb documentation here, *The Donegal Pictures*. That book is a classic of photography. Music, as much as literature, has been for me a mind-altering substance. It has changed, shaped and transformed me. The Sex Pistols and Sean-nós; Ravi Shankar and Rostrovopich; Billie Holiday and Bridie Gallagher; all have left their mark on me. Somehow they fondled my 'feith na filíochta' and caused it to stir excitedly.

You are currently working on a piece of travel writing and considering trans-lating poetry from Nepal which you now visit regularly. Do you think it's pos-sible to read Nepal from an Irish perspective and to read contemporary Ireland through Nepal? Could the shortest way to Tara be via Kathmandu?
The shortest way to Kathmandu is by astral projection. I'm working on that at the moment. 'Astral travelling in ten easy lessons', a stellar-seller, I hope, followed up by 'Increase your libido with Origami'. Anything to make more money so I can spend more time in Nepal! I feel at home in Nepal. The tight knit communities in the mountains with their rustic domesticity, their seasonal routines, their ritualistic lifetstyles are similar to the way of life I experienced as a child. Nepalese people are laid back, affable, good-humoured. Like my own people they are prone to put off things. They love to dillydally and delay. What they can do today they can do twice as good tomorrow or, better still, next week. I have been raised with a similar work ethic. 'What is this life if full of care/We have no time to stand and stare' encapsulates their outlook on life. A proper attitude for a poet I think.

CHERRY SMYTH

Born in 1960, you grew up in Portstewart in Co Derry. Your poem 'Coming Home' states: 'Family engulfs me. I search their eyes for myself,/ see only the nice wee girl they want, not the proud woman I am.' Your presentation, 'Area of Detail' (2001), at Cork University refers to poetry as 'creating family. On my own terms.' How did family influence your formation as a poet and how does family register in the poems?

Family and tradition are important to me and yet I've broken with both irrevocably. I am the first woman in my extended family, as far back as memory goes, not to have married. I am the second to have had no kids — the first was a born-again Christian, who was pitied for her barrenness and perceived as seeking consolation through her relationship with her Saviour. Disenfranchisement was not something that being a middle-class Prod prepared me for. I resented it. I fought it. I developed a reputation. 'Family Tree', for instance, addresses this sense of exclusion:

> Everyone has been given branches,
> but my lover. The tree stops with her.
> I want to give her a baby now. I want to have hers now.
> I will be on that tree. I hate that tree
> and want to sabotage it because I know its branches
> will never extend to us. I hate that tree.

Julia Kristeva's *Nations Without Nationalism* describes the 'cult of origins' as a 'hate reaction' which creates 'a sullen, warm private world, unnameable and biological, the impregnable "aloofness"of a weird primal paradise — family, ethnicity, nation, race.' It's the loss of this 'weird primal paradise' that fires my work and the sharp relief of 'exile' gives it both context and constancy. The expression of loss is unifying. It creates an intimation of homeland wherever I am. It's warm. I'm sullen. It becomes cold. I recover that private world by making it nameable. It may try to shut me out, but I come back to expose its secrets, mess up its symmetry and their fantasy images of what constitutes family, Irishness and Ireland. I insist on belonging where I have not always been wanted. 'It's all very well,' my mother once said, 'doing those things in England, so long as you don't do them here. The ill feeling runs too deep.' My father is a storyteller, with no need to write things down or rescue them, so I fasten memories and give them back to him on paper. As with any artist, the texture and tension of my work is to harness two feelings at once — the particular, everyday and the mythic, universal. The best homage to me as an artist has been my father reading poems I've written aloud to company, as though they penned his own thoughts and are an inextricable part of him. He taught me language and I'm delivering it back in another form. It's a tacit, tactful exchange of worth and flattery. He inspires me and I make him a character in a shared fiction. As you say, it's my way of 'creating family — on my own terms.' It helps me bridge the rift of shame. I give him myself and my perception of the world through my relationship with words. Between us, we make a truth — a father-daughter, straight man-gay girl truth. Is it poetry as reparation? Les Murray says in 'Poetry and Religion': 'Nothing's said till it's dreamed out in words // And nothing's true that figures in words only.' Maybe through poetry I'm creating a proxy of myself. I'm giving myself back. Establishing complicity. As Michael Cunningham put it in 'The Hours': 'You want to give him the book of his own life, the book that will locate him, parent him, arm him for the changes.' This is what I look for in poetry — location, parenting and armour.

Your childhood location — the northern, seaside, town of Portstewart — between Magilligan Prison and the amusement arcades of Portrush. It's a different place seen with adult eyes?

My love for the beauty of the coastal landscape remains unchanged, as is my sense of claustrophobia. No matter how over-developed Portstewart becomes, there's no taming the Atlantic and the wild reaches of the strand itself on a rough winter's day. Living so near the beach made solitude acceptable. I'm grateful for that. Finding places to walk alone for hours in London is not easy. But some of the tranquillity I feel there, I also sense on beaches in Donegal as long as there's a jutting headland and wide sweep of dunes. For years I'd seek it in vain on English coastlines. There's something about living with the rhythm of the sea that makes the place "yours". On any other beach, you're merely a visitor and that knowledge of transience is painfully acute.

Yes. That painfully acute, cold, North Atlantic drift among headlands where Derek Mahon heard 'A lost tribe... singing 'Abide with Me'. How would you describe your first encounters with language and poetry at grammar school up there between 1971-78?

Well, it goes further back. I'm three or four. I shout, 'Lukin' out the winda at the washin'.' Mum corrects me: 'Looking out the window at the washing' with a huge emphasis on vowel sounds and "i.n.g." I repeat it regularly to get a rise out of her. 'Talk properly.' My father is fascinated by language. He delights in using a polysyllabic word where several shorter ones would suffice. He enjoys the look of mystery and relishes a lengthy explanation. I used to love listening to my mother reading and reciting poems by Robert Louis Stevenson at bedtime. Its sleepy spell worked on me. Poetry was revered, if distant. There was also the influence of Auntie Vi, the Methodist Holy Roller, who introduced me to the poetry of the Bible and Christina Rossetti. The incantatory rhythms of the Protestant hymn and sermon are threaded through my work. For many years Dad drove me to school and he would correct my pronunciation, coercing me out of my local vernacular and into something approaching BBC English. Words that were arrowed for correction in particular were 'schul/school, pul/pool, flutt/flute.' He'd ask questions, laying ambushes for the tricky, sticky words and then pounce and make us repeat the word till it shone, alien, posh and ludicrously distinct. It wasn't until thirty years later, after a couple of glasses of Cabernet, that he told me that during the Second World War, his regular teachers went to fight and stand-ins were engaged. Their cruelty was legion. One teacher brought young Jimmy Dallas from Garvagh up to the front of the class and asked him to repeat the word 'flute'. Jimmy answered 'flutt' and was whacked about the head with such force that he fell over. He got to his feet and the master asked him again. 'Flutt' was all Jimmy could manage. He was hit to the floor for the rest of the lesson and was unable to leave the classroom on his own two feet. My father's eyes were wide as he told this story. He'd learnt the lesson well. For the rest of that evening, Dallas's 'flutt' played in my head, as it had in my father's for sixty years. Till then, I'd never known where the 'flute' lesson had come from.

You mention Stevenson; he's a real bedtime lamplighter. You've also referred to your education as British in an Irish context. Were there other poets who deeply influenced the work early on — and — in what way?
In school I remember loving Louis MacNeice, Seamus Heaney, R.S. Thomas, Patrick Kavanagh and Wilfred Owen. MacNeice and Heaney are the ones I still read. I remember in particular MacNeice's *Autumn Journal* and 'Snow', Kavanagh's 'The Hunger' and of course, 'Digging', 'Death of a Naturalist', 'At a Potato Digging' and 'The Otter' by Heaney.

I loved T.S. Eliot's *The Four Quartets*. But I was just as influenced by the prose of Mary Lavin, Elizabeth Bowen, James Joyce and Carson McCullers. I hate the influence question. It is 'incorrigibly plural'. My writing was stymied more than encouraged by education. Understanding feminism, anti-semitism, racism and imperialism, seriously dented my unquestioning enjoyment of many early poets. I was powerfully influenced by African-American women writers when I travelled in America in 1981: Maya Angelou, Alice Walker and Toni Morrison. None of whom I read now. Their directness, simplicity and sexual openness gave me permission. Later I loved the work of Olga Broumas, Adrienne Rich, Eavan Boland, Marilyn Hacker, Carol Ann Duffy, Sharon Olds, Essex Hemphill and Jackie Kay. I would also count novelist and screenwriter Marguerite Duras, film director John Cassavetes and playwrights, Harold Pinter and Samuel Beckett, as powerful influences.

The poet's ethics or politics can impair the text? Surely the poem is more (or less) than a carrier or nexus of ideas/ideologies (Marxism) or of philosophically explicable concepts or morality — its language has a different specific gravity, a kind of immanent concreteness? Eliot's FOUR QUARTETS *are more that the sum of the man's morality in the life in letters?*
Yes, I like that expression 'immanent concreteness' and to some extent you're right but my certain unease with Eliot became more defined as I developed politically. It was as much a turning away from certain literary traditions in order to embrace and value neglected ones. That for me had to be conscious and dedicated. The canon is very binding and demands both loyalty and emulation. It takes 'courage' as Adrienne Rich says, 'to do without authorities'.

You left school and the North to study at Trinity College Dublin (1978-82). Did you associate Dublin with writing in choosing to go there? Did you find writing there?
Anger and repudiation fuelled my departure from the North. I found it stifling, regressive, confusing, patriarchal, provincial and deeply conservative. To become who I wanted to be could only evolve beyond the narrow confines of Ulster, with its tight-knit community and culture of conformity. If I say nothing, I will belong. If it hadn't been for my love of Irish writers and literature I might not have identified with Ireland so strongly and I might have followed my more radical peers to universities in England, but I chose TCD, thinking I was following in the footsteps of James Joyce. It was only some time after arrival that I learnt that the sectarian divide had thrived until recently at the hallowed college. I was shocked and chastened. By choosing Trinity, I'd merely reinforced generations of Protestant ascendancy. I wanted an Irishness I could claim and so I perceived going to England as a betrayal. At TCD I encountered the work of Yevtushenko, Anna Akhmatova, Paul Celan, Thom Gunn, Marianne Moore, William Carlos Williams and Wallace Stevens. Perhaps there was a more willing embrace of American poets than I would have experienced in an English university.

In 1983 you undertook postgraduate research in Film and Television Studies at Middlesex University, London: you've written about film, scripted a documentary on post-colonial Ireland (Besom Productions, 1994) and a short film,

SALVAGE *(1999). Television programmes flicker in the first poetry volume where the title poem evokes the cinema. Are there links between television or film writing and poetry for you?*
Certainly, yes. I admire the sparse, dialogic quality of good screenwriting. I appreciate *Hiroshima Mon Amour* by Duras like a poem. I love the emotional rawness of Albee's *Who's Afraid of Virginia Woolf?* and Cassavetes's work, especially *Woman Under the Influence.* I like the possibility of a form that leans in and out of poetry but screenwriting never gives me back to myself in the intimate and revelatory way that writing poetry can. I also found the process of seeing my carefully crafted script being adapted, adopted and edited by actors, director and editor both humbling and troubling. I love that poetry doesn't require a huge budget or an unwieldy team of technicians and equipment.

There's also your non-fiction book QUEER NOTIONS *(1992). What are its themes?*
Queer Notions investigates how a post-shame, radically queer political movement in Britain took on homophobic establishments, art and culture in direct action, in non-apologetic ways. It is an introduction to the academic theory as well as the "in your face" movement birthed by reclaiming the word "queer".

In Íde O'Carroll and Eoin Collins's LESBIAN AND GAY VISIONS OF IRELAND *(1995) your essay, 'Keeping It Close: Experiencing Emigration in England', mentions 'internal emigration' and literal exile, a 'perpetual sense of disappearance'. You left Ireland in 1982, aged 22. Paul Muldoon writes in one poem: 'I'm not "in exile",/ Though I can't deny/ That I've been in Fintona twice.' In 'Coming Home' you say: 'Coming home is like dying/and coming back from the dead all at once.' Is there a tension between home and belonging as compliment and antithesis in the poetry?*
Seamus Heaney defines place as 'known and cherished' in his essay 'A Sense of Place' in *Preoccupations.* He argues that 'one is lived, illiterate and conscious.' For me, there is the literal, geographic setting of the North, which is mundane, quotidian, changing and isolated, while the North of my memory and imagination is eternal, fixed, and peopled with acute emotional and physical detail. If I were to live there permanently, to renounce my nomadism, would I lose this need to fix and fasten the imaginary in art? Would it alter my focus of lack and turn my longing towards the cosmopolitan, the vast, the anonymous, the urban? As Slavoj Zizek wrote in *Looking Awry:* 'Anxiety occurs not when the object-cause of desire is lacking; it is not the lack of the object that gives rise to anxiety but, on the contrary, the danger of our getting too close to the object and thus losing the lack itself.' To create a character and place him or her in the small radius of the North gives them a dimension, a sense of being, that I

find hard to construe in an English city. But I am concerned that this redemptive act of returning risks sentimentality and infantalisation or what Eavan Boland has called 'elegy, invention and idealisation'. Hopefully, the edge of lesbian sexuality counters or even cancels the tendency towards nostalgia for a belonging that will always be riven with ambivalences. These ambivalences are worked through to some sort of resolution through the inner topography of my work. I'm reminded of how the British artist Michael Andrews described his painting as 'the most marvellous, elaborate way of making up my mind.'

Poetry then is — essentially — longing for, or distance from, or 'lack' of, the real: a road taken imaginatively which keeps its literal or biographical loss alive as recurrent possibility or is poetry a way of claiming autonomy, a way of changing what is historically given or inherited?
If the question of life is answered, it's the end. To be fulfilled without writing. To not feel the need to use words to shore up in the face of death. If family and traditional culture silenced my voice, poetry is my opposite. Yes autonomy, if you like. An answering back.

'Keeping It Close' states: 'Somewhere in those crossings I became a lesbian feminist, a queer dyke, a femme top.' Is the juncture between sexual or gender identity and language important in your poetry?
Less so than when I started. I wrote at first to be seen. Be heard. I was very conscious of giving the state of being an Irish lesbian a presence. It was a way of writing myself into language, into love, into being. I began to write before Mary Dorcey or Emma Donoghue were published. I am still amazed that 'cunt' remains the one word that cannot be said on TV or radio.

You mention 'writing myself into language... into being'. Kristeva, who you mention, writes of a 'not-I' in literature in 'The Malady of Grief'. Theodore Adorno says 'the better the work (of art) the smaller the subjective component in it.' From certain critical perspectives, as author, you've been written out of (or into) the anonymity of language; we can't reconstruct your subjectivity or rebuild you like a bionic woman from words. The poetry is print-full and thumb-printless?
I do wrestle with the question of subjectivity. I am less interested in creating a coherent self across time than in showing a shifting, contextual, contingent self. I like the idea of drawing the reader into a critical intimacy between our respective subject-selves. I interrogate the self through the work. As Hélène Cixious put it in *The Passion According to G.H.*: 'the most difficult thing to do is to arrive at the most extreme proximity while guarding against the trap of projection, of identification. The other must remain absolutely strange within the greatest possible proximity.'

How do you feel about the nature or accuracy of female personifications of Ireland in Irish poetry?

I hope you asked the male poets the same question! Eavan Boland has answered this very well in her essay 'Mise Éire'. Gendered personifications of countries/planets are ideologically motivated. Try Father Earth, Grandpa Ireland. It doesn't often make for good poetry.

I've connected gender and Ireland via your essay on emigration which links the urge to speak freely and 'come out' as a lesbian with the British government's media-silencing of Sinn Féin in the '80s. Were there other key events in the North which, for you, defined underlying poetic or political realities? I'm thinking of poems like 'Maybe It Was 1970' and 'The Roadside'.

I never set out to write about a political reality in 'Maybe It Was 1970' — rather — I was trying to work out the skelf of pain that I carried after my father's business was destroyed in the '70s. Several of my poems investigate the unease within apparent ease, which mirrors the experience of growing up in a lush, scenic landscape, while less than forty miles away, people were being bombed to bits. There was the view from the window and the view from the telly. In 'Maybe it was 1970', adolescent sexuality and fear of being maimed or killed were fused and time itself became hard to track. I'm fascinated by the complex cluster of simultaneous realities:

> I'm missing "Crossroads"
> leave the room loudly
> and slip behind the kitchen curtain
> to search for Derry burning.
> The news is too far away.

Meanwhile, elsewhere commerce and agriculture continue as though nothing is wrong. It was deeply chilling that paramilitary murders were carried out on victims that the murderer could have gone to school with. The same farmer who lovingly tends his sheep later blows a man's brain apart: ' It is midsummer and the farmer longs for dark. / The etiquette of execution sharply honed / keeps silence chain-smoked in the carpark.'

Although 'The Roadside' was sparked by the newspaper story of a woman who was killed because she knew too much about her informer-boyfriend, I was much more drawn to attempting to understand the minds of the men themselves — ordinary, local, rural men — "culchies" even. Like the men I'd grown up among. There were so many strategies we learnt as teenagers to normalise what was in fact highly abnormal around us that we became gifted in repression, in coping, in taking risks, in being thankful for being on the next street, the next bus, for being alive. There are ways in which "the war" affected me that poetry cannot yet reach. Each of those — my two most explicit poems about the "Troubles" — are troubled, inadequate, contested in themselves. We can't even agree on a language to name it.

What then is language in poems? A fraction of the ice-berg of experience we're able to name in concentrated language because everyday speech or silence fall short in the face of death or suffering? Or is poetry itself complicit with death — its language annihilating particular things or people or the individual consciousness for the sake of the life of the poem?
I think it was Adrienne Rich who said, that 'poems are like dreams, in them you put what you don't know you know'. I tried to write a poem about knee-capping last summer. I realised that I had heard that word and used it for many years and yet never really considered the reality of the suffering behind it. There was a name and yet I hadn't 'felt' the impact of the need to name it. Through the excavating layers of poetry, I wanted to deliver up its meaning. And my shame.

Have poems you have written over the past twenty years altered in terms of the way you perceive the North? Does your first volume, WHEN THE LIGHTS GO UP *(2001) chart changes in the North over the last thirty years?*
I was very naive. In part because of the emotional blocking we all strived to perfect and also because my social environment did not allow for sympathy towards Nationalism. By viewing the North from London, and by experiencing anti-Irish racism first-hand, I was able to draw a different map. Both 'From Uqbar' and 'The End of July' are poems written on the crest of the millennial hopes for peace. I haven't lived in the North though since 1982 and that also shows. 'From Uqbar' says:

> 'The river reaches its full winter height,
> choked by a century of effort,
> and glittering with acquiescent light.
> Gun shadows yield in the red reeds.'

'The transgressive sexual subject' was an essay you published in QUEER ROMANCE *(Routledge, 1995). Does transgression have stylistic or formal implications for poetry as well as implications for a social/political stance or subject matter?*
I aspire to a more experimental style and often read the poet Caroline Bergval to remind me that I can be more free formally. Yet, I seem to be moving more towards classical form and maybe that acts as a cover for the explicitness of my content, which is often regarded as transgressive.

In your book on international, lesbian, visual art of the 1990s, DAMN FINE ART BY NEW LESBIAN ARTISTS *(1996) you state: 'Emerging lesbian artists have adopted a very different set of priorities and strategies from those of their predecessors... engaging with popular culture, medical texts, pornography, comix and art history, analysing their identity within and in relation to their cultural and historical contexts.' Surely these strategies (not exclusively lesbian) make a case for the art (its formal, genre procedures) as overriding the gender identity or sexual orientation of the artist? If not then one could also host an exhibition privileging white, male, heterosexual art?*

As long as the art world is run by and for white straight men, there will be a need to champion those excluded from their white walls. In *Damn Fine Art* I was keen to contextualise lesbian artists in the broader world of art and culture, rather than simply in terms of sexuality and politics. For most of them, formal considerations determine their work more than their identity as women or dykes. The book on one hand tried to dismantle essentialist notions of art made by lesbians and on the other was tied to the constraints of identity politics in its very conception. I suppose it resembles the way I deal with being Protestant. I reference and renounce it at the same time.

Your poems were published throughout the 1990s from the VIRAGO NEW POETS *(1992) to the poems in* NORTHERN NARRATIVES: WRITING ULSTER *(1999). Have the central concerns of the poetry shifted over the last ten or twelve years?*
I think I must have mined seams of my childhood thoroughly and then another early memory surfaces, inviting another poem. Dorothy Porter's *Akhenaten* encouraged me to use the first person narrator for other personae more. An interest in Buddhism and haiku is finding its way into later work.

Do you have a particular way of writing poems or does the process alter each time? 'Eating Periwinkles' takes culinary risks in an ' experimental zeal/which led to the edge of manners and taste/where only the game could follow.'
Lined paper. A well-sharpened pencil. Silence. It's akin to a meditative state and I don't make enough time for it to visit me. The first stage is hallowed. The following stages involve reading aloud over and over and over. I try not to tamper with its mystery. As Marguerite Duras says, 'Writing is trying to know beforehand what one would write if one wrote, which one never knows until afterward; that is the most dangerous question one could ever ask.'

Does style embody a tension between dressing up and the 'sheer enterprise of walking naked'?
I've always been one for paring down, as I put it in 'In Check', slitting to the hilt. There's so much dressing up in fiction that I often can't wade through it, or I edit as I read.

The back-cover blurb of your debut poetry collection relates the poems to the 'northern lyric'. You're in a poetic, lyric, tradition from the North of Ireland?

You can take the girl out of "Norn Iron", but you can't take "Norn Iron" out of the girl. There's a flintiness in my work that I see in other Northern Irish poets, but also in Scottish poets. Being thran, with a happy melancholy seem typical too. When I read the Scottish writer Jackie Kay's *Trumpet*, I was reminded how close the colloquialisms and rhythms of speech are between the Northern Irish coast and Scotland. There is also a restlessness in my work, the longing for home, and the love of the beauty of the coastal landscape which made me feel rooted in the North. Living in a semi-rural environment forges a territorial, possessive and unalienable sense of belonging to the land and to Ireland, even though my parents carried British passports. The respect for direct "plain speaking" and the rhythms and simplicity of Presbyterian hymns also find their way into my writing. I wouldn't feel the same honour if I were included in the tradition of the "English lyric".

How does the vernacular get into poems? 'Coming Home' hovers between TVAM's 'Mag-here-a' and 'Magherafelt' to reveal that those 'sticky place names of the North/get caught in an English throat...'
The boundary between "English" and "Irish-English" was policed. If your use of the vernacular is corrected and undermined you use it less, secretly or with irony. It is a sign of "badness" in my work. A thranness and sometimes it's just for the pleasure of the sound and rhythm the word or accent confers. Before Heaney, I'd never seen any of these words written. The vernacular is part of my oral and aural memory and its getting tellingly outdated. Someone from Lurgan said to me the other day, 'He's nothin' but a fat tube.' I hadn't heard that word since the '70s. A walking gullet. Mighty.

How do you see the relation between music (rhythm or rhyme) and poetic form? Is music from outside the literary tradition ever an influence within it for you?
'The Love I Lost' by Harold Melvin and the Bluenotes. 'In the Bleak Mid Winter' by Christina Rossetti and Gustav Holst. 'Lay Lady Lay' by Bob Dylan. 'Suzanne' by Leonard Cohen. Much of Van Morrison, Marvin Gaye, Joni Mitchell. Soul, soul, soul. Gregorian chants. Thomas Tallis. Early Sinead O'Connor. Bach.

Does this music chime in poems, though, as echo, cadence or reverberating phrase? Suzanne brings tea and oranges; Christina brings a colder earth and 'water like a stone'.
Maybe the rhythms of melancholy and seduction are similar in this music and in my work. I like simplicity and repetition. I like emotional frankness. To be honest though, I find myself more likely to write a poem after reading another poet than listening to music. It tugs at me more without the accompaniment of instruments and melody.

Is there a relationship between the dramatic and poetic for you? I'm thinking of the way poems deal with phone calls and meetings between people?
Yes. It has a performative element to it. I like the way spoken language can turn in a tight corner. I've referred to Beckett and Pinter. I've written a short play and I'd like to explore that genre further.

In DAMN FINE ART you mention Modernist and post-modernist strategies or narratives in relation to visual art? How would you define the difference between these strategies? Do these theories or strategies come into play in the making of your poems?
I see post-modern work as being allusive, fragmented, parodic, intertextual. To set out with post-modern strategies in mind when I write a poem would kill it dead on the first line. It's much more a process of infiltration.

Do the politics of left and right matter to you as a poet? In the poem 'The Big House' you leave the 'cosy grunts of port-soaked pleasures' for a pre-dawn garden which is 'marvellous and mine'.
If you are too aware of any ideology, the work risks becoming didactic. I wouldn't say that left and right matter but that my vision of the world is constructed around ideas of equality not elitism, towards balance rather than excess. Those views are reflected in the poets I usually read. In 'The Big House' I imagined myself as a maid in a large country house, whose chance for possession is rare and stolen.

In 'Area of Detail' you describe being 'politicised by feminism, peace activism and lesbianism' in the '80s – coming to realise that ' it is important to occupy a post-Protestant nationalist position…' This position might be critiqued as English/American centred: reliant on nationality as connective tissue between communities superceding its function as marker of acute, internal, difference in Northern Ireland or suppressing the existence of a post-Nationalist-Catholic-, Dublin, stance, where the inter- or multi- national come into play. To what extent should political positions implicitly or explicitly enter poems?
I wanted to claim the Protestant tradition of Nationalist struggle — Wolfe Tone, Robert Emmet, etc, while also distancing myself from the Unionist position. Afro-Caribbean poets, in general, are more politically explicit in England because they experience oppression daily. They experience their blackness differently than they would have had they lived in the Caribbean. I experience my Irishness in a way I didn't living in the North. As long as the Irish experience oppression under the British, in whatever form, there will be a political voice in Irish poetry. It's not a question of 'should', it's a question of addressing injustice in the powerful, packed punch of form.

'Packed punch' echoes Sartre's 'What is Literature?' where form is not merely

autonomy (a bourgeois notion) but also political engagement — the pen doesn't rest 'snug as a gun' but it's a fully 'loaded pistol' pointed at political targets. Sartre was a big influence on my formative thinking. The existentialist notions of 'Mauvaise foi' and engagement cut through the Christian tradition of the objective, detached, apolitical poet and atheist nihilism. I must go back and read that essay again.

'Area of Detail' sees Protestantism as something you take 'flight from', which you 'claim in order to dismantle' and yet those 'Presbyterian hymns... find their way into my writing.' You've mentioned Les Murray's 'Poetry and Religion'. Poems are the site of faith in language and site of rejection of religious belief? It's a bit like being a secular Jew. If I was English, didn't go to church, and said I didn't believe in a Christian God, I would be classed as an atheist. As a northern Prod, even if I say these things, I remain a Prod. It's a cultural belonging that I cannot reject even if I am an atheist supporter of a united Ireland. Poetry, like religion, is a way of understanding death. As Hélène Cixous suggests, 'Writing: a way of leaving no space for death, of pushing back forgetfulness, of never letting oneself be surprised by the abyss.' There have been times when I felt I could not be Irish enough because I was Protestant and then not Protestant enough because I was a lesbian. I gained legitimacy for my own Irish and Protestant identity through my writing. Many Ulster emigrants disappear in their new country, their assimilation made easier in the Protestant New World and in England. Without the need to write I may have disappeared.

You've written essays and catalogue introductions on visual art and the closing poem in WHEN THE LIGHTS GO UP *connects the 'smoothed round of basalt/hot with inward heat' with the title of a 1990 sculpture by Eilis O'Connell. 'Area of Detail' states: 'The complex cluster of simultaneous realities occurs in many of my poems'; that reminds me of Dermot Seymour's canvases where the super- and surreal are simultaneously possible.* DAMN FINE ART *quotes Sherrie Levine: 'A picture is a tissue of quotations drawn from innumerable centres.' Do you connect the processes of your poetry with those of visual artists you admire?* The cunning retreats and returns that every artist encounters when about to start a new piece of creative work are very similar. The point of knowing when to stop and set down the pencil or paintbrush requires the same fine tuning of sensibility and caution. I find the rigour and diversity of Irish visual art very sustaining — much closer to what I'm trying to do than say Irish music or film. The writing around the visual arts also influences, creating a provocative context for the astonishing ways new identities and aesthetics are being defined by Irish art.

I admire the work of Ciaran Lennon, for instance, which aspires to a state of being, rather than a didactic statement. I get an equally humming, satisfied pleasure from a good painting as I do from a good poem. Dermot Seymour's work unsettles me and makes me laugh. I don't have that surreal edge in my work but I can see how canny it can be in trying to understand the anomalies of the North. I also enjoy the wit and conceptual integrity of Dorothy Cross. Rita Duffy uses the trope of childhood in some of the same ways as I do. I like the bizarre, dark, exaggeration in her recent work. Fionnuala Ni Chiosain has a delicious lyricism and lightness of touch which is more calligraphic than figurative and, again, she is challenging traditional form using sumi ink on paper. Blaise Drummond is also developing his own unique way of pushing the boundaries of landscape painting which is exciting. Ronnie Hughes has an extraordinary palette. Alice Maher's 'Berry Dress' and 'Bee Dress' are genius. The tender yet robust way she handles the pain, eroticism and vulnerability of female subjectivity is inspirational. I know you'd like me to talk about paint versus words. If I could I would paint. I find it a deeply relaxing thing to do. Sometimes I imagine being free of the warp and weft of words and letting myself speak through paint. I often think of an emotional state and a natural landscape and wonder how I can paint them in words. How to get the specifics of shade and tone and hue exact. It would be amazing to be able to bring those visual nuances to language and deliver the emotional particulars in paint. If I painted it would be abstract — much more abstract than I can reach in poetry. There are two quotes by two artists I like to keep in mind: 'In art there is only one thing that counts; the thing you can't explain.' That's Georges Braque. 'A woman has no place as an artist unless she proves again and again that she won't be eliminated.' Louise Bourgeois.

Your last poem in the first collection, 'The End of July' concludes with 'all division illusory'. Are you aligning poetry with peace or with faith in 'basalt, hot with inward heat'?
I'm wishing for non-duality, a place where the divisions that have motivated murder no longer will. It's also a quest for oneness, with my country, my father, myself. The poem stores the best of the afternoon and a small hopefulness for the future.

> He hands me a smoothed round
> of basalt, hot with inward heat
> drawn from a sun behind thin cloud.
> It stays warm until we reach the car.
> I know it will become his worry stone,
> and hope it stores the best of this afternoon:
> the seeping milky light, water and sky as one,
> all division illusory.

MARTIN MOONEY

You were born in Belfast in 1964. Your grandparents appear in one poem, 'A Connswater Elegy', and in THRESHOLD *(No. 38, Winter 1986/87) you quote John Hewitt's contention that, 'It is from grandparents that tradition comes.' Your mother came from this east Belfast, Protestant background and your father from a Catholic family in Newtownards. How would you describe the influence of your family background in your formation?*

The whole 'mixed marriage' thing? I'm hesitant to describe my background as programmatically as that; you'll know what I mean from Paul Muldoon's poem 'Mules'. Neither of my parents were believers. They carried their independence lightly and I'm eternally grateful for that. It was, in many ways, an innocent family. My maternal grandparents, though both had a puritan streak which I've probably inherited, weren't churchgoers when I knew them, and my maternal grandmother has only recently returned to Mass-going after an argument with the local clergy. So, at least in a religious sense, I was brought up in a healthy vacuum.

Nor was it a particularly bookish family, in the sense of formal education and systematic reading. But my maternal grandfather was a voracious consumer of westerns, thrillers, that sort of thing and a regular user of the public library. In my own immediate family we used the library a lot too — my mother had worked as a librarian before her marriage — and I read everything from history books to comics to the back of the cereal packet.

You grew up in east and west Belfast before the family moved to Newtownards on the outbreak of the "Troubles" in 1969 and you went to Londonderry Primary School there. There are poems like 'A Protestant School' and 'Singing Together'. How did the language and values of school, home, and the street differ?

Watching my own kids playing I'm not sure if the phrase "grew up" quite catches how or where you become conscious. I was conscious of disruption or interruption as the family moved from a maisonette in Moyard in west Belfast to Newtownards. In 1969 these moves were hurried. My father's friend brought a builder's lorry from Ards, and we loaded our belongings and drove off. I suppose we were displaced persons, refugees, part of that huge population shift as the city formalised its sectarian geography.

So I remember bits and pieces, fragments that may be constructions out of memories or may be family hearsay. But I trace a sense of continuous consciousness back to Newtownards. The Glen Estate there was just being built as we moved in and there were huge slopes of un-landscaped waste ground, full of rocks and gorse, which never became more than big windy slopes. I remember wondering if this half-built place was really ready to live in.

Shifting between different registers you learned the hard way. My dad is from a generation of cinema-goers and a lot of hard-man or wise-guy language would find its way into play. But I remember using a playground swearword instead of the Cagneyesque 'rat' during a mock shoot-out with him, only to find myself promptly landed flat out on my back. That was an early lesson in vocabulary and decorum. Later, trying to write, you become aware of those eighteenth century values of decorum, of tone and manner — which I admire — but we're now at a point, possibly similar to America of two hundred years ago, where we can synthesize a new kind of English that's not just a matter of restricting yourself to fine feelings in fine words. All kinds of registers, languages and different discourses are floating around us. Internet jargon, Ulster-Scots and Irish. Whatever else I think about the way Tom Paulin writes I admire his readiness to welcome these different registers.

And of course, moving between a pretty disciplined but secular home-life, a pretty ferocious and religious school system, and a wild and unsupervised streetlife as a kid, you had to be able to navigate between them or you were open to all kinds of dangers of humiliation, of punishment, of violence.

World War II is recalled in poems like '1941';'The General' filters the war through movies like THE DAMBUSTERS *and a gas mask becomes a sex aid in 1990s London in* GRUB. *Surely the war was dead and buried for someone born in the 1960s?*
Why? The Second World War went on until at least 1989. In the '60s we were all still playing soldiers. Any attempt at truth to childhood needs to deal with the paraphernalia of the war. My son's Action Man figure is nowadays a creature of science-fiction and fantasy, but the Action Man I played with as a boy came uniformed in World War II outfits. Right through the '60s and '70s boys read those little Commando war comics, completely fixated with the war. Why? Well we still knew people who had been through it. The market was saturated with reminders. And perhaps it was a way of managing the violence that had erupted in our own community though I don't remember knowing a great deal about that.

In the poem '1941' I'm fascinated by the distinguished looking, silver haired man who was my grandfather. A photograph of him in his forties, in full RAF uniform, hung above my granny's side-board and rumour had it that he had fought at the Dardanelles (although he would have been fourteen then) and the poem's image of the key tied to the letterbox was an image of connectedness: the war I read about and re-enacted with toy soldiers had been a reality for these two old people, which made it a kind of imaginative reality for me.

You were a pupil at Regent House Grammar School in Newtownards (1975-83). 'Dimitri Gregorievich Rasputin' imagines pupils in a school photograph as 'the spit' of Rasputin's son Dimitri (shoplifters, cider- drinkers and truants found in 'fish and chip shop mirrors'); 'Recorder Music' recalls a mix of para-military gear and the tartan outfits of the Bay City Rollers. How would you describe those secondary school years?

The poems you mention actually refer to my primary school years. At secondary school I wanted to be either a scientist or a visual artist. It's more absent in the poems. I'd work hard at maths or science and the amount of effort I put into representational drawings of things like a pair of boots far outweighed the effort I put into English essays. Primary school friends with great potential had put more intellectual effort into failing the eleven plus exam than I put into passing it. In primary seven it was rumoured that Movilla School had a hard initiation ceremony — many of the lads wanted to go there to prove themselves — while Regent House was reputed to be a "snob school". Which in many ways it was, an environment driven by the need for public prestige and social success.

Poems like 'A Protestant School' look like they recall a transition, starting a new school after leaving west Belfast. What was growing up in Newtownards like?

As I said, we came from west Belfast "in a hurry", to use a euphemism. A mixed family weren't particularly welcome in an estate increasingly defining itself as Catholic and Nationalist and my father would have been too stroppy an individualist to join in with the vigilante patrols and so on. I've a hazy memory of being four or five and answering a knock on the door and someone asking if my mother or father were in and — when I said no — they left an ultimatum telling us to leave or be burned out. I don't consciously recall that period as traumatic, but perhaps a kind of trauma surfaces in the poems. 'A Protestant School' recalls the terrifying first day at Londonderry Primary School. My mother recalls that she was equally terrified after the upheaval, the move to a town she didn't know. Here was a young woman, who had moved to a new estate with what little possessions she had, facing an entrance form in a state school which asked questions about my religion for which there was no family answer. I'm down on the official files as a Presbyterian only because it was the first safe label that sprang to her mind.

Newtownards is a Plantation market town. Just outside Belfast, it escaped much of the "Troubles". So growing up there, though you were conscious of the sectarian divide, you were also living a life that had a lot in common with teenagers in Glasgow or London or Dublin. That shared popular culture, the ambiguities of its infestation by sectarian strife and the rumours of communal violence, is actually the subject of the poems you mention. The BCR meant more than the UDA or the IRA, and I'd be untruthful if I wrote as if the established ideological map of the North really reflected my own experience. Though the relationship between the experience and the imposed map is an important subject.

Schooling in the '70s and '80s in Northern Ireland often introduced the English tradition in poetry anthologies like A CHOICE OF POETS *or through a certain solid or stolid critical approach to Milton or Shakespeare. Was there an Irish poetry tradition at school? Which poems or poets struck you early on or lasted?*
God knows. Sometimes it feels as if I was hardly conscious of literature then. I might have missed it altogether. Concentrating on those years when I was more interested in science or the visual arts I can recall poems from the *Touchstones* anthologies that still feel important: 'Naming of Parts', 'Mr Bleaney'. Then late in secondary school I came across those animal or plant poems by D.H. Lawrence in *A Choice of Poets* and they impressed me. I was a young, miserable, weird adolescent taking lonely walks in quarries and abandoned cement works, and the simplicity of those outbursts seemed to offer a way of making some kind of expressive move. I remember writing early poems modelled on Lawrence but I haven't read his work in years. Other poems and poets from that anthology that mattered then and now are Eliot, of course, (though that's very much an introduction to the work, with 'Prufrock' and other short pieces) and Wordsworth. Was Dylan Thomas in there?

As for an Irish tradition, once I'd begun to dabble in writing, and to love reading poetry, I began to piece together fragments of an Irish poetic tradition, from the schoolbooks used in my friends' or relative's Catholic schools, or from anthologies I'd pick up in second-hand bookshops. I started looking into contemporaries like Fiacc and Mahon, who still mean a lot to me. Heaney we'd actually glanced at in primary school, those easy-to-teach early poems that offered us a frisson of local recognition, but little else.

You studied English Literature and Philosophy at Queen's University in Belfast (1982-86) and undertook postgraduate research in contemporary Irish poetry in the following three years when Medbh McGuckian and James Simmons were writers-in-residence there. You interviewed Simmons in an early RHINOCEROS *and wrote about Medbh McGuckian in* GOWN LITERARY SUPPLEMENT. *Were they influences you assimilated as a writer?*
I'm deeply fond of Medbh. But Medbh's poetry is Medbh's, and unassim-

ilable. Talking to her at Queen's I became aware of her sheer dedication to the craft of writing. She's deeply conscientious and informed about the mechanics of sentences — the grammar, structure and syntax. Perhaps she was more model than an "influence", someone who imparted a great sense of what it meant to have the aspiration to be a writer.

I met Jimmy at Queen's although I'd stolen his *Selected Poems* from the school library in sixth form. I think that Jimmy has the Augustan virtues, and vices, and a healthy scepticism of romantic ideas of the poet's role. Jimmy is always keenly aware of the need to entertain, to occupy an audience. Here's a poet who uses traditional forms and ordinary demotic language without subjecting them to undue strain or pressure. Poetry doesn't always have to say the fine thing — Jimmy Simmons reminded you of that and, yet, he was also a link to a tradition from which most people from my background felt separated. He tells a story about how he met T.S. Eliot, when he won a prize, and borrowed a couple of quid on the strength of that from the older poet.

I suppose Jimmy and Medbh cleared space for younger writers at Queen's. Jimmy in particular, gave me room to write and not worry about writing the great poem.

He also reminded T.S. Eliot that 'No Land is Waste'. How do you see Eliot?
Eliot — the Eliot of 'Prufrock' and *The Waste Land*, and the early essays — still is important to me as a writer. His cultural authority deserves scepticism and deconstruction, but the poetic authority of those poems is unquestionable. I think Jimmy mixes the two things up, but however reactionary the cultural ideas, even the aesthetics, it's a mark of the imaginative power of Eliot's poetry that *The Waste Land* could be a liberating experience for a working class youth, a field for recognition at least as immediate as Heaney's and far more challenging to the accepted order of things.

There were writing groups at Queen's and new poetry magazines like GOWN LITERARY SUPPLEMENT *(which you co-edited when it evolved into* THE BIG SPOON *in 1993) and* RHINOCEROS *(which you co-founded in 1988) in Belfast in the '80s. How would you describe the poetry scene and your own writing then?*
At the time the poetry scene felt alive, at the cutting edge, but looking back I feel there was a certain implicit obligation to write, to be part of a next generation of northern poets, part of a new wave of writing that would come out of Queen's. Very few of the writers who emerged in the 1980s went on to produce or publish substantial first and second volumes. Perhaps the whole scene was too heavily concentrated around academia; in the English scene of that time poets went out and performed in pubs and clubs. Maybe too many models were available, too much of the jigsaw already in place; maybe it was too easy or expected — harder to sustain.

Partly my own poetry was a matter of trying out rhetorics, trying to fit my own experience and images into the available rhetoric and fill in the gaps.

In the '80s your poems appeared in journals and magazines and a selection was published in TRIO *5 by Blackstaff (1987). Which influences were you assimilating?*
With hindsight (and even though Muldoon seemed to the few people who read the stuff to be an important or over-important influence) I think I was heavily impressed by Mahon and was struggling for a poetry that, like his, would offer room for thought, flexible public and private rhetoric.

Poetry and philosophy were both studied by poets like Paul Muldoon, John Hughes and yourself. One might suggest this produces a deep scepticism about literature, about language itself as a medium?
I guess there's a potential distrust of the simple statement which appears to say exactly what it means. At Queen's there was scholastic philosophy, which poets like John Hughes and Damian Smyth read, and it looked back to Aquinas; and there was "straight" philosophy — empiricist, pragmatic, Anglo-Saxon, analytical — that looked to A.J. Ayer, Wittgenstein or Bertrand Russell — which I studied, along with English, for four years. The philosophy was probably more influential in writing the poems. The scepticism it produced wasn't about literature or language per se, but about mystical or pseudo-religious approaches to those things.

Is there a relationship between writing from the North before the '70s and the poetry that emerged in the '80s? In MAP MAKERS COLOURS: NEW POETS OF NORTHERN IRELAND *(1988) you co-edited a selection of '80s northern poets; Michael Keneally's preface mentions a 'detached, almost philosophical manner'. Gerald Dawe's subsequent* THE NEW YOUNGER IRISH POETS *(1991) stressed the individualism of each writer but also noted the northerners' 'self-deprecating wit' and 'keen tactics of evasion.' John Goodby in* THE IRISH REVIEW *(no 11, Winter 1991/92) stated: 'The Ulster brat pack born since 1960 — Eliot, Smith, McDonald, Ramsey, Mooney and Kelly — is an impressive one, far more a "school" than their co-evals in the Republic. Irony in their work, as in Muldoon's is of an intertextual rather than obviously political kind; it is a function of style first and foremost.' Was, is, there such there such a thing as "northern writing"?*
On the most pragmatic level, of course there is northern writing: there's a degree of self-sufficiency (or incest) and a critical environment that has a character all of its own (newspapers that don't review, magazines that prefer bitchiness and backstabbing to intelligent and informed discussion). And of course many of the northern poets share elements of an outlook — ironic, stylish, suspicious of obvious "sincerity". Peter Sirr from

Dublin once hazarded the opinion that northerners were a little more syntactically scrupulous (or over-scruplous?) and there might be something in that. Derek Mahon's *The Sphere Book of Modern Irish Poetry* stated that: 'Whatever we mean by "the Irish situation", the shipyards of Belfast are no less part of it than a country town in the Gaeltacht.' Perhaps in the '60s the northern poets defined the Irish situation disproportionately. Absolute definitions, though, can make for good journalism — Thomas Kinsella called northern writing a 'journalistic entity' because once you go for certain themes that move along neat tracks then people can be brought in to fit — and the picture is more complicated than that. Many writers from the North have left and continued to write so that the place where someone is from is hardly the over-riding determinant of all of the themes or how good the poetry is.

There are as many things that separate individuals as unite them, and I think relations between the literary micro-climates within these islands are healthier than ever before.

In the '80s you reviewed new volumes by Roy McFadden, Padraic Fiacc (the 'elder statesmen') and James Simmons in the IRISH REVIEW *(No 2, 1987). Hewitt, for Simmons 'the daddy of us all', appears as a more grandfatherly figure in your article in* THRESHOLD. *Did these writers mean anything to you as a writer?*

I read Hewitt in the '80s. Here was a man writing in Northern Ireland at a time when the very notion of doing that appeared virtually ludicrous and so, for that reason alone, he is a hero. I'd read Seamus Heaney at primary school — before I was aware of a whole tradition of writing in the light of trying to develop as a writer myself — but I found that the more I read Hewitt's work the less I liked the clenched craft. There's a certain classic Ulster Protestant clumsiness about Hewitt as a versifier, a certain insistence on nineteenth century poetic diction.

Surely poems like 'Because I Paced My Thought' — 'I stake my future/on birds flying in and out of the schoolroom window, /...the picture carried with singing into the temple' — are liberated from clumsiness?

Well, that poem is a major achievement in the cultural wasteland of '50s Northern Ireland even though the cracks in that culture were appearing. But isn't there something dogged and willed about that poem too, something over-earnest? I think we love it for its opposition to sectarian or labourist dogma, but what on earth does it mean to stake one's future on picture-worship? Isn't the urban/rural contrast overworked? And when will we get the weather to allow the sunburnt comrades to hold their outdoors' soviet? As so often, in our desire to outgrow our philistine reputation, we mistake the will for the deed, the music for the meaning.

You worked in London (1989-91) as a barman and bar manager and returned to the North in 1992. GRUB *(1993) is bi-focal, it moves between Belfast and London literally, and the radio in 'Aubade' speaks of 'murder in Belfast, drowning in the Thames'. Did Belfast offer perspectives on London and London offer perspectives on Belfast?*

London exists in *Grub* as a kind of encrustation of the culture, not just British culture but a kind of Western humanist civilisation that I can't deny allegiance to but which I have deeply ambivalent feelings about. There's no question that Thatcherite London was a vicious and nasty place, yet the presence of progressive politics there made a huge contrast with an even nastier Belfast. And much that we think of as an Irish identity is forged by emigrés, and I wanted to look a little at the role of northern emigrés in that process.

In GRUB *there is a cast of recurrent characters adrift in '90s London living in desperate social circumstances amidst squats and the poll tax; there's the whole social scene — porn-shops, rent-boys, home-made tattoos, body-piercing, clothes with multi-zips, punk and desperation. Images of animal predation, diseased bodies or death run through the book. The novel (Dickens,* RIPLEY BOGLE*), the non-naturalistic play (Brecht) or the long journalistic poem (*AUTUMN JOURNAL*) come to mind reading* GRUB *because narrative, morality and public life seem to be key concerns. Did you have literary models in mind in writing this book?*

Grub is a narration. *Autumn Journal* was certainly in my head when I was writing it as was *The Rough Field* and Heaney's *Station Island* had just come out. In *Grub* you meet ghosts and go on a pilgrimage — not to Lough Derg but to certain places in London. London, particularly for many Irish immigrants, can be a kind of pilgrimage where you escape certain elements of your past life, go for renewal or re-invention and it can be a tour around certain stations where you cannot avoid a kind of tragicomic — as opposed to spiritually uplifting — pilgrimage, where you walk smack-bang into history. There's a lot of seventeenth and eighteenth century "stuff" hanging around in the shadows of *Grub* — Defoe, Fielding, the 'Dunciad', and that's a bedrock I've valued for a long time.

The juncture between politics and poetry is often fraught, fought over. Marx, Brecht and Trotsky appear in GRUB *and the blurb mentions 'political hypocrisy' exposed in 'hard-edged satirical parables'. In one poem, 'The Works', the narrator finds himself 'drunk on politics and spleen/and bashing Thatcher with rolled-up copies/of his Class War, my Socialist Worker.' Is there a relationship between your poetry and politics? Is this link different than it might have if you had been born in England?*

Impossible to answer. In the North we have no living Labourite or reformist tradition, so progressive politics struggle to find a home. The kind of exploration involved in politics on the left here is close to how one uses poems to explore and try out perspectives, voices, experiences. I don't mean that as a dilettante thing, though in my time in the Socialist Workers' Party I was a terrible activist, embarrassed on paper sales and demos. But British poets I'm friendly with have the same difficult relationship with the political culture within which they grew up, and poetry is often a way of negotiating that terrain, that distance between ethics and environment.

In GRUB *there are painters: Munch, Breughel, Grosz, Botticelli and da Vinci. There are poems titled after visual art: 'Madonna and Child' (a homeless woman encountering a young drunk); 'Pieta' (someone drunk returning to a squat); 'Odalisque' (set in a porn-shop); 'Nude Descending A Stair' (where 'portraits and landscapes' which 'hug their alarms' in a locked gallery are left for a council block, a 'graffitied lair') and 'Ready-Mades' (depicting a rent-boy and Tory). In your latest volume a poem is written 'after Picasso' and bonfires are constructed as 'Dada/haystacks'. In 'Salting the Brae', looking at a power-plant, you ask : 'Light and work, are they opposites?' What is the link for you between poetry and visual art?*

At 'A' Level I studied English, History and succeeded in getting Art History on to the syllabus, so I came into contact with art. We had a great art teacher in Billy Bogle; he showed me poems by Louis Aragon like 'Red Front'. I came across visual art by Duchamp and André Breton and French surrealism and German Expressionism stuck. I like Duchamp's a 'Bride Stripped Bare by Her Batchelors'. I confess to liking much contemporary British art where the conceptual seems to have so much to do with the single poetic image, the comic existentialism. Damien Hirst's shark in formaldehyde incarnates in a single image of life and death, the kind of image a good poem uncovers in passing. I like Tracey Emin's recent work. So much of northern poetry in the last thirty years has been in a bind in which the border figures or there's a political focus behind all the personal 'field work' and I'm as guilty as anyone else of that. Maybe what could be learned from contemporary British art and some of the art produced here in the North is how to sidestep some of the political ideas and constrictingly predictable forms you inherit here.

'The Pastor's Sunday Morning' notes how daybreak in east Belfast 'bristles with scripture" among the tabernacles although 'Angels' notes that 'the children we don't have... are already immune to religion.' How immune to religion and its language is your poetry?

It's wishful thinking to think you are immune to religion. My son is a natural for religion, temperamentally, and he's taught it at school so part of your family life is devoted to theological debate. No one learning to read or write in this country is immune to religion and its function is inscribed in language. I've never attended church as a worshipper — merely once or twice as a tourist — but it comes at you daily in primary and secondary school in the state sector and I imagine that compulsory religious education is even more intensive in the maintained sector. The echoes and rhetoric of the King James Bible or Wesleyan hymns are inescapably around you here in the tones, manners and the way people speak. You also can't read seriously or deeply without coming across the Authorized Version. I suppose I'm on the lookout for those tones or echoes these days. I once discussed this with James Simmons. He admires the Bible as literature but I don't any more: it's role is simply too important to treat it just as a book; its psychological, political and theological impact as belief means you cannot overlook all the corny rubbish of what it says by simply seeing it as telling lovely stories in beautiful language. I no longer have a copy of the King James Bible at home and I don't think I'm missing anything but, either consciously or unconsciously, I'm sure there are a lot of echoes of it in *Grub*.

There are also the ghettoblasters, karaoke and punk music of the '80s and '90s in that book and they are outpacing the showbands, fleadhs and recorders, the 'Gypsy Rover' or songs of a '60s schooling. 'Decline and Fall' features Elvis and dictionaries. How do you see the relationship between music and poetry?
In *Grub* music is probably used more as image than as subject matter. I'm not a hugely knowledgeable music enthusiast but I do have a record collection. Music is unavoidably part of the world and it's part of the book because the poetry I try to write does not close the door against popular culture in any form. Perhaps I use music in poems to set mood or location as a cinema director might.

The whole "sounds" behind the poems in GRUB *are a shift forward in time from, say, Longley's jazz or Simmons's blues. I hear The Sex Pistols — 'God Save the Queen' — as one background track. You have favourite records?*
That's probably far too embarrassing to leave on record. A couple of years ago I worked as a writer-in-residence with an orchestra so there was a steep learning curve in terms of classical music which occupied me then. The Sex Pistols' 'Never Mind the Bollocks' was an epoch-making album and for a whole generation it brought down the shutters by asking the Spike Milligan sort of question: 'What are we going to do now?' I guess *Grub* does have soundtracks: The Pistols, The Clash, Sinead O'Connor, The Pogues. I was listening to a lot of that stuff as a barman in London in the late '80s.

In a review of DEDALUS IRISH POETS *in the* HONEST ULSTERMAN *(no. 94, 1992) you write of Austin Clarke as a 'master of native linguistic textures' and you commend the volume for providing 'down-to-earth, intelligent accounts of how the poet works'. What way do you work in constructing a poem?*

I've gone back to notebooks, taking observations, but this does not take you beyond the starting line into areas which seem promising or interesting. I'm not a great believer in inspiration. The moment when the circuit connects is something I'm not sure about in terms of knowing how to prompt. I know, from past experience, that most of the poems that really work need some kind of formal hurdle or obstacle course or framework, something to work at, but this may have disappeared by the time the poem finally reaches the page so I'm not a consistent formalist either. There are specific forms I love like the sonnet, a real home. Robert Lowell's *Notebook* with those big loose fourteen liners is the kind of poetry book I would take to my desert island. It has amazing form. Terza rima — three-line interconnecting stanza patterns and variations of this — fascinates me so there's a group of poems in the new collection, *Rasputin and his Children*, which work something like that, as well as a whole group of sonnets. Those big solid stanzas of Yeats's (intricately rhymed with around ten or so syllables in each line and somewhere between eight and twelve lines in each verse) are good at making certain kinds of semi-public, rhetorical statements. There's also slender things or free verse — a couple of poems in the new book occupy that lightness of space — but you sometimes have to resist the poem as just a visual apparition on the page. Sometimes you are torn between poetry as a delicate instrument and poetry that has the force, solidity and muscle of certain forms.

Can form obstruct message?

No, that's not how it works. Form reveals meaning, meaning inheres in form. But like anything else it can be handled badly.

In RASPUTIN AND HIS CHILDREN *(2000) poems like 'Blowfish' recount an 'accent like a shower of anthracite,/the same good barbarian Ulster-Scots' and the Scotsman James Watt hears a 'common tongue' when he stays in Antrim. The Preface quotation is from MacDiarmid and one poem against nuclear dumping talks directly to Burns in Ulster Scots. It could be argued that poems entirely in Ulster Scots are synthetic or artificial, reducing the language to something 'couthy' or 'quaint'. Critics of Ulster Scots would say it's alive in selective, wonderful words and sporadic spoken phrases which survive within a framework governed by post-plantation English?*

Undoubtedly I'm synthentically constructing a voice, making an artefact from linguistic material, but that's what happens when you make any poem in any language. There's a whole cultural-political angle on the promotion of Ulster Scots but there's a difference between making a poem by using synthetic language as a literary instrument and synthesising a linguistic community for cultural-political reasons. Having said all that, I've no problem with the notion that Ulster Scots exists and is still spoken by many like my Catholic granny. Scots is a language, Ulster Scots a dialect of that language. To say that these things operate within a framework of post-plantation English implies a Anglocentric perspective. There's a great deal that we hear as English which might be described as language shared with Scots and that closeness is very hard to disentangle so that anyone who claims to be fluent in pure Ulster Scots is also being disingenuous. Its role in our social lives is neither wide enough nor established enough for that claim to have meaning. I've constructed poems that sound like Ulster Scots in *Rasputin* because it simply felt like an entertaining and constructive use of my time. The reader, of course, will judge.

You relate to Burns and MacDiarmid?

Burns was around the home, in expurgated, heavily selective editions. He's pretty much a fixture in our local culture or at least he was, good for recitals. Like Robert Service he's become the poet of the "turn", the last resort for those of us with no singing voice. I suppose Burns also has a heroic stature in that hard-drinking, anti-authoritarian image, which doesn't stand up to much scrutiny but which no amount of scholarly examination can quite eradicate from the popular mind, or my own for that matter. He's both a model and a stereotype of the poetic life.

There's much in MacDiarmid's work that you can be attracted to. The politics were initially important to me but, the more I read, I came across the crankyness in essays like the one where he argues for a brand of a Scottish Fascism which even the most avid supporter would need to keep under wraps. I read Heaney's essay on MacDiarmid — although it's modified in a poem — as noticing MacDiarmid's poetry as a sheer act of will, the construction of a tool kit from language, poetry made from as many disparate vocabularies as possible. MacDiarmid has the sheer bloody-minded insistence of a lunatic lexicographer. I can't read 'Hymn to Lenin' though without wishing he'd shut up for a while. He uses rhythms, vocabularies and tones that don't belong to something called "Poetry" when it's placed in inverted commas or capitalised, so I like his sheer openness to language, which is exemplary. But perhaps it's all easier to admire in principle than in the reading. Linguistic courage and inventiveness, though, are always to be cherished. In that respect, it reminds me of someone like Tom Paulin.

You were critical, though, of IRELAND AND THE ENGLISH CRISIS *in the* HONEST ULSTERMAN *(No 80, Spring 1986) where you wrote of 'deferrals' of class politics and proper democracy on behalf of the ' "national question" (to which he allows only one answer)'. Is the question of Nationalism/Unionism defunct, outmoded? Your poem 'Carrick Revisited' humorously opens: 'William of Orange is a rastafarian dwarf/The wallpaper shop in Irish Street is having a border sale.'*

Paulin's political-cultural conclusions seem to me wrong headed in that book. The Academy of Hiberno-English begs too many questions in one statement. It looks like a legalistic device, which cannot compensate for creativity nor can you advocate reform like that from the top down. It looks like a Liberal bourgeois ideal or one sprung from the French Revolution or 1798. It won't work in 2001 here.

The whole sectarian binary opposition isn't defunct — clearly, too many people have internalised it, and our new political system has it built into voting mechanisms and so on — but it is not a natural phenomenon, not a necessity, and can be challenged. It describes so little of our lives, even here, and deserves to be mocked, as do the religions upon which it claims to be based.

Two shipping disasters (the loss of life as the whaler Juan Peron was being built in Belfast in the '50s and the sinking of the Marchioness in the Thames in the '90s) feel like focal poems in GRUB. *Recent poems in the new collection recall the scuttling or loss of ships in Cairnryan or the Irish Sea. Why so many shipping disasters?*

I'm only really conscious of this in answering this question, with hindsight, but in writing those two poems in *Grub* there was some sense of a relationship. 'Operation Sandcastle' in the new book looks like part of that theme too and I've been involved recently in discussions of plans for a theatre piece in Belfast on the Russian Kursk submarine disaster. I'm not sure where the exact psychological resonances come from although I'm aware of the academic cliché, the analogy between ships and the ship of state. The Juan Peron disaster is set in a time when the Northern Irish state and Protestant culture were in turmoil, in the grip of Cold War paranoia and its sectarian version, and on the verge of the challenges thrown up by the '60s. The Titanic as an emblematic moment in Ulster? Perhaps we have a propensity to invest great emotional and cultural weight in disasters such as this; the Somme too comes to mind. Our puritan side (and both religions have one) needs the flagellation.

Surely poems on the Titanic or shipping disasters also turn on the idea of man-made technology being pitted against something called nature or God?

In my poems about shipping disasters that's not important. These aren't acts of hubris, but of criminal negligence. In each case the disasters are man-made, acts of incompetence and — in contemporary jargon which

I'm not using flippantly — these are health and safety issues related to money. Events like these don't go away. They resurface at inquests, not just as powerful visions of 'death by water', because they have burrowed deep into the psyche. I first heard of the Juan Peron disaster in a pub. I'd been on a Thames cruise the week before the Marchioness sank. And the Irish Sea arms' dumping issue was not only in the press, it was actually washing up on a beach a few yards from my front door. So as well as for large thematic reasons (and deep archetypal or psychological reasons) and for the choice of subject matter, it's also part of a sense that poetry has a journalistic conscience too, an idea of the poem as eye witness or bystander.

In 'Fleadh' a barmaid has two keep-sakes, a black eye from Willy Yeats and Kavanagh's pickled 'lung' — poets often cited as assimilated influences for writers here. Are they important for you?
Yeats is so massive. To talk of him as important for myself as a poet writing to-day would be just plain silly, hubris. Heaney, I think, is one of the few poets who can talk about the relationship with Yeats sensibly and not sound megalomaniac. But I look to Yeats as very much a public poet, his work always a private rhetoric designed for a public context. He's more than just a lyric poet, an exemplar of the private form.

Kavanagh? I love Kavanagh's 'The Great Hunger' as the first really Irish long poem in English, and I think it was a mistake on his part to reject it. I never got on with the satires, which seem like clunky constructions or left-hand exercises, and Kavanagh held many opinions which I simply don't like. I love, though, the post-illness poems, the canal bank sonnets.

Between 1993 and 1996 you taught M.A. classes in contemporary Irish poetry in the Poets' House in Portmuck with James Simmons and Janice Fitzpatrick-Simmons. You currently still live on the Antrim coast looking towards Scotland. Does geography matter in the poems?
Many of the poems are set within specific landscapes, but the current of opinion which states that Irish poetry is inextricably linked to landscapes, often then assumes that there are certain landscapes which are particularly poetic. The bare, rugged or picturesque landscapes, the west. But this must be mystical nonsense, an aesthetic lapse: sheer failure of imagination. You once mentioned the influence of Caspar David Friedrich's landscape painting on Beckett's *Godot*. The Nietzschean romantic landscape type of thing. I simply like landscapes on a human scale. I'm a County Down boy. Wherever you are if your eyes and ears are open and you're doing the job properly then surely you must take part in the landscape and inform or be informed by it?

You once talked to me about teaching American students Irish writers like MacNeice and there's your critique of Michael Donaghy's ERRATA in the HONEST ULSTERMAN (No 96, Autumn 1993) as 're-cycling' rhymes in 'a sub-MacNeicean game'. Was — is — MacNeice an important writer for you either as a poet or teacher?

MacNeice is a great teaching aid. He allows you to teach technique because he's a remarkable formalist. His is a degree of sophistication that few writers accomplish but he talks too of poetry as not simply a detached, formal activity. In *Modern Poetry* he makes the anti-modernist argument about poetry as alive to the forces in and around the life of the writer, poetry open to journalism, and he would have the poet fond of the opposite sex and fond of a drink. Beyond his own specifically male perspective I think he's stating an act of faith in a poetry that is not detached and that's important to me. There's so much to love, to get lost in, in MacNeice. *Autumn Journal* contains some terrific love poetry, intelligent political meditations, landscape poetry, dream visions. As Frank Ormsby points out in *Rage for Order* there are so many northern writers since MacNeice who have argued with him, or started where he left off, that sometimes you have to see MacNeice and *Autumn Journal* in particular as a "source poem" for almost everything that comes after.

There has been an acceleration of change in the North of the '90s: the re-mapped docklands of Belfast, the Good Friday Agreement, inchoate devolution and the threatened break-downs of Nationalism and Unionism. What is emerging looks like a strange mix of international capital and some of Hewitt's regional-democratic structures. Is that how you see the North that's emerged recently?

I have never thought that Regionalism held water. As with Paulin's political ideals I see a writer's metaphor telling you more about their own imagination than about serious prescriptions for social or political change. Regionalism emerged from '30s thinking. It's an interesting idea from Hewitt at a particular time but it sits uneasily within the whole of his Socialist-leftist thinking and I think it has little to do what has emerged here in the 90s...

Surely a near or locally elected government is infinitely better than a 'remote and ignorant one' to paraphrase Norman MacCaig?

Yes. As a Socialist you would argue that this type of government is more easily overthrown. But devolution and the driving forces behind political developments here have also opened Northern Ireland to international capitalism. I'm not a political pundit but I think that the '90s and current developments have emerged from two different pressures: the pressure from ordinary folk who took the brunt of thirty years of shite, who simply had enough; the pressure (from the top down) to open up the local market place to international business and global capitalism. For these forces the shipyards might be viewed as having a highly educated, skilled, labour force at the best affordable price outside of the Third World. It would be foolish and churlish to say that the shakey Good Friday Agreement is not a step forward but I think we also need to be aware of the complex social strands and pressures that are making for change. I think that Hewitt's Regionalism did not take account of all these complexities either.

Why the interest in Rasputin in your latest collection? Photography seems to interest you a lot in the poems. Is it a different inspiration from painting?
The interest in Rasputin was sparked by a family photograph of Rasputin and his children. It's a remarkable image, a nexus of the domestic and the macro-political, the vast historical landscape. The collection tries to chart how one leads into the other, sometimes in bizarre or strange ways. I was once asked what it means to be a Marxist poet. I'm not sure exactly what that means but there is a commitment to realism which does link with photography. At one level photography addresses realism like no other art-form. There's the very direct relationship between viewer, technology and what is out there. I know photography is used in hoaxing representations and attacking our expectations of it as a medium — there are fascinating photographs of fairies or UFOs — but as the youngest artform, little over a hundred years old or so, it has revolutionised our relationship with the past and with the way we perceive the lived texture of our recent past. For a writer, photography provides all kinds of new evidence and checks about accuracy, authenticity and anachronisms which were unavailable until recently. Naturalism became more important with photography and writing that breaks the boundaries of naturalism — which it's entitled to do — allows photography to throw back at us questions of authenticity and accuracy. The whole human interest in history, the documentary form or family holiday photographs often allow the distinction between art and documentary to become blurred. Photography can operate as a craft, an artisanal activity in the sense that a Magnum news photograph can be both as artistically willed and constructed as a poem and yet still maintain its primary function of telling you what happened on Friday. It's real art and artisanal activity.

A poem, 'Operation Spanner,' in RASPUTIN AND HIS CHILDREN *seems to look askance at any poem written easily about the "Troubles" or victims of the "Troubles" — the 'recording it all for posterity' mechanism. Surely good poems have been written about victims?*
I've never consciously connected 'Operation Spanner' with the "Troubles". It was about the arrest of a group of gay men who engaged,

with their own consent, in sado-masochistic sexual activity and then, curiously, faced charges of aiding and abetting assaults on themselves. The body — damaged or physically injured — lies at the core of this poem, at the core of many poems in both *Grub* and *Rasputin*. Often in writing about the "Troubles" you try to avoid your own glib politics getting in the way of the poem but, maybe, what can happen is that the "Troubles", as a subject, enters into the poems without your being conscious that this has happened.

'Carrick Revisited' and 'Homage to Vauban' images your children born before (but growing up after) the last '90s ceasefire, building and destroying a fortified sandcastle. Are you suggesting a place where 'hope and history rhyme' or a time when the little children of the future will wonder what we were talking about?

There is no description of the good place or a recipe for social salvation in the poems. I don't think those recipes exist and, if I did, writers would probably be the last people to ask about them. In some ways these are anti-political poems. I'm trying to say that for all the talking by rational people in comfortable surroundings you ignore the grass roots, the warriors and the machinery of warfare at your peril. Rational people discussing things in comfortable surroundings do not solve those kind of problems. These poems are meditations from a place located at the edge of European wars. They are not "Troubles' poems" per se but they deal with the type of mind-set that looks to militarism for solutions although that may mean, at some level, they argue against some of the militaristic foundations upon which we live here now.

Which poems are you happiest with in RASPUTIN AND HIS CHILDREN.

'Salting the Brae' means a lot to me because I think it's one of the best made poems in the book (which maybe doesn't say much). I knew what I was going for; after hard work on the formal structure of the poem, I think I got there. The poem's companion piece is 'Decline and Fall', the Elvis poem, which has also a strict formal set-up, although the two are not thematically related. The poem is based on an anecdote from a biography of Elvis. He arrives in Graceland and tells his entourage, who are all hanging around bored, with more money than sense, that they should learn a new word from the dictionary everyday. Although it's a formal poem, in Sapphic stanzas, I'm still not sure what its ending means: ' "Ass," he said again, "Is."' So those two, two variants of control versus mystery, still excite me.

CONOR O'CALLAGHAN

Birth: a cause for celebration (Seamus Heaney's 'The Cot' recalls a time 'When the whole world was a farm that eked and/crowed'); a parallel for writing (Michael Longley's font and fontanelle); a locus of fear (Louis MacNeice's shadowy nursery or 'Prayer Before Birth') or a subject for speculation (Paul Muldoon's conception of his conception that 'leaves' us 'in the dark')? How do you see the 'where' or 'when' of your own birth in the border town of Newry in 1968?

I was born in Newry because Dundalk hospital did not have a maternity wing at that time. Now that the one it built has just closed down, another generation from Dundalk will be born again in either Newry or Drogheda. My paternal grandfather and all his people were from Newry. But my immediate family moved house before I was born, so I grew up in Dundalk. There's a sense of a displacement between my present life now and my birthplace, a sense of remove, of being born elsewhere. I travel to Newry once or twice a week but it feels like a foreign place. My birthplace then is not so much a place I go home to, as a place I go away to.

If your birthplace is 'elsewhere', does ancestry register? In poems there are 1940s photographs recalling an aunt, with her 'university scarf' by a greenhouse, a grandfather 'in plus-fours', a granduncle and your 'parents' also appear in poems?

Do they though? We shouldn't get away from the whole idea of poetry as fiction or fairy-stories, making up pasts or past lives for yourself. As a poet you have to be allowed that latitude and freedom because you're largely using these narratives as metaphors rather than as a means of examining your own family's past. I mentioned my parents in my first book but some of the references are true and some simply are not. 'Pigeons', for instance, suggests my father was a welder. In truth, he was an insurance broker who turned van-driver for a fruit importer. I gave him a different profession because I liked the image of a failing industrial landscape and felt I couldn't do much, poetically, with his real profession in that poem. The descriptions of my mother's side of the family in the book are probably, coincidentally, more factually true. My mother's family were from rural Co. Monaghan and the title poem is based on an aerial photograph taken of my mother's home during the Second World War. Even here, though, the factual reality of the past is manipulated through the lens of poetry to suit the formal needs of the poem. Overall, the connections between poems and the family life are tenuous, muddy. I'm not sure that I ever could, let alone should, entirely understand these things. If I'd actually said or done or thought half the things that are in the second collection, *Seatown*, I'd have probably had my collar felt a long time ago.

Were you aware of poetry, of writing or a sense of the imagination, either at home or growing up in Dundalk?
Dundalk is, was, a very non-literary, town. Growing up there, like many of my peers or contemporaries, I looked up to footballers or snooker players. I'd prefer to think that a literary bent doesn't come from anywhere. I'm suspicious of the idea that you can look back and detect this in terms of ancestry or family, that a poetic gift is a matter of mere pedigree! Possibly my paternal grandmother had something to do with it. She was one of the first women to get a degree from University College Dublin. She taught French and English until she married my grandfather, a rather obnoxious insurance broker, who made it clear that the frivolities of literature were going to play no part in their life in the depression years. After my grandfather died I'd take turns, with my brothers, to visit her house and we'd stay overnight to keep her company. I remember distinctly, at the age of twelve, reading Tennyson's 'In Memoriam' to her from her favourite book, *The Poetical Works of Tennyson*, which I inherited from her. I also remember visiting her in the nursing home in Newry shortly before her death. She was in her early eighties, and her bedside reading was a life of Voltaire. She'd say that literature was furniture for the mind.

Did you encounter northern poets at secondary school in the 1980s with the Christian Brothers in Dundalk?
Dundalk is a very northern town, closer to the North than the South of Ireland. I think that's a fact and not just my own preference speaking. Vona, my wife, recently edited an issue of the American magazine *Verse* featuring Irish women poets, and many poets who submitted work from Dublin sent international reply coupons. Some people, at least, from the Republic must assume that Dundalk isn't based in the same state as their own. Dundalk has probably more contact with Belfast than Dublin of the sort that feeds into your everyday life. Primarily, though, it's neither a question of affiliation to region nor nationality, of thinking to yourself, 'I want to be a northern poet'. You want, first and foremost, to be a good poet. And it just so happened that the vast majority of good contemporary poets who were published at the time when I started out writing came from the North of Ireland — from above, rather than below, Dundalk in terms of geography.

Was this a case of the poetic voice colliding with the voices of popular culture? In PREOCCUPATIONS: SELECTED PROSE 1968-1978 *(1980) Seamus Heaney refers to 'finding a voice' which 'began when my roots were crossed by my reading', as northern accent, home, place and early rhymes met the sprung rhythm and the 'heavily accented consonantal noise of Hopkins's poetic voice'. Did you come across poetic voices that mattered in that way?*

Absolutely. There's the moment that you start believing in yourself as a poet after having being aware of that huge canyon between your family background, the domestic culture, and the voice of poetic culture, the English tradition. In the early '80s I started reading poets like Seamus Heaney and Derek Mahon. Paul Muldoon's *Quoof* came out in 1983. There you recognised accents that sounded more like your own and voices which, at the same time, brought the English lyric closer and made it more available. Until then my own writing of poems had largely been a process of mimicry, as if you spoke one accent at home and then, in writing poems, spoke another as though you were on stage. Actually, up until my late teens, I used to recite my own very bad poems in a BBC accent! I was conscious that the poetic voice I was trying to create just wasn't quite mine. Those poets represented accents, a set of references and a vocabulary, that I recognised and which seemed to bring the poetic tradition closer, to make it more available.

What criteria are you using to define these poets as 'good'?
I simply liked this work a lot but there's also formal criteria which makes some poetry good and other poetry less good. The poets from the North not only had a vocabulary or accent that I recognised but there was a strong formal control and an original adventurousness in the work that is the hallmark of poetry of the first order. Surely everyone knows that poets like Muldoon are good and that anybody suggesting otherwise is simply not likely to know a serious amount about poetry? It's also a question of time, the belief in a given piece of poetry to survive beyond the modes and criteria of its own historical moment.

Edna Longley's recent book POETRY AND POSTERITY *suggests that northern '60s poetry drew on the Americans — Wallace Stevens, Hart Crane, Lowell and Frost. Frost has also been repeatedly linked with poets like Muldoon.*
Yes. The value in having poets from the North, that good and close-by, in the early '80s was that they mediated other traditions like the American tradition or that particular strand of the English lyric which, up to then, had only been available through Browning, Hardy, Larkin or the Movement poets who sounded slightly foreign. Northern poets acted as a bridge to that particular tradition or strain of influence and it also meant you could be influenced by poets like Frost indirectly. I'd read Frost. There was also Frost-through-Muldoon.

Your poem 'East' suggests an orientation where there is a degree of fun to be had at the expense of Irish poetic and geographic landscapes; you refuse to 'play Gaelic' with the western seaboard facing America and its 'elemental Atlantic guff' turning to an eastern seaboard town where 'the moon and stars are lost in the lights of the greyhound track', where 'exile' in England is as likely as in America.
The Irish comedian Tommy Tiernan points out that when you leave Ireland the first question people often ask is whether you are from the North or the South and when you reply that you are from the west this confuses people. Neither east nor west are supposed to exist. The affiliation with the east is largely tongue-in-cheek but it was a way of removing oneself and the work from the whole North-South axis that exists politically, socially and in terms of the poetic tradition. In the '80s the idea of a 'Dublin syndrome' surfaced in the *Honest Ulsterman* as a caricature that was largely true in terms of portraying two literary communities where you were either affiliated to the North (and published work permeated by "foreign"influences) or you published out of Dublin (and were suspicious of good poetry). I came into writing in the '80s and '90s with the sense of polarised writing communities. Writing a poem like 'East' was a way of trying to step outside that. I wouldn't like to think, though, that 'give me a dreary eastern town' is a phrase they'll inscribe on my tombstone. That relationship between Irish and American poetry has often been rooted in Nationalism when American poetry is seen to represent a way of breaking out of the neat stanzaic structures of the English tradition. Thomas Kinsella virtually admits as much in John Haffenden's *Viewpoints: Poets in Conversation*. He realised that, up to the late '60s, he was mimicking Auden and, therefore, in some way obedient or subservient to that lyric tradition. He then kicked this asunder and came under the influence of American poetry — its freedom or formal open-endedness — which in Kinsella becomes the formal embodiment of Nationalism. I mean this only as an observation, and certainly not as criticism. A similar observation (although with different emphasis) could be made about the work of someone like Eavan Boland. Irish poetry, in the last twenty years, has often consciously looked to America to escape the rigid constraints of its relationship with England.

You would distinguish between the free, high, spirits of Ginsberg and more formal adventures by poets like Frost or Lowell in terms of American influences on your own work?
I like neat stanzas, small music and whole lines so the whole English thing and the eastward look seems inherently attractive. The less formally structured, free, adventures of Ginsberg and American, or some Australian, poetry seem less attractive the older I get. Maybe I'm kidding myself, though, in thinking that susceptibility to forms is now a less politicised issue than it would have been for poets of a previous generation.

You have three-line forms, couplets, and chunky, squatter shapes in poems like 'Landscape with a Canal' or 'Sublet'. How do form and content relate?
The choice is largely intuitive. There's a lot of guff talked about what informs these choices that I'm not sure I understand or really need to understand. Occasionally working with forms which John Ashberry called 'resistant', like sestinas, you're working with forms that pre-impose themselves but decisions about form happen almost always at an intuitive level.

The two titles poems in SEATOWN, *ferried across three-line stanzas, look like forms evolved towards specific purposes?*
I once heard John McGahern remark that the easiest thing to do after finishing a novel was to write a sequel, since everything had been set in place and the mould was there. The 'Seatown' poems were an occasion where I acceded to that. I'm not sure now that it's such a good idea. Randall Jarrell once remarked that a poem is a process that destroys its own method of making. A formula, having a mould set in place that you can re-set using different images, simply seemed attractive at the time. It is, however, something all writers have to resist. As Miroslav Holub says in one of his very last poems, 'The essence of art/ is that we aren't very good at it.' I think now that the first 'Seatown' is more successful than the second, so that's probably a salutary lesson to learn about form.

The first poem moves out into the tidal estuary; the second turns in on the industrial town, ending with a near-Beckett state where 'I could go on'.
Yes. The first poem looks at possibilities of escape and freedom but the second ends with a more terminal admission where 'I could go on', suggestive of the idea that I could but won't. I wanted both poems to seem to cover the cycle of a full year.

You did 'go on' from Dundalk to University College, Dublin, in 1985 but then you dropped out after a year. Why?
I started at U.C.D. at the age of sixteen, when I was too young and immature to handle the experience of finding myself in lecture theatres full of five hundred other students. I'd yet to acquire the skill of moving away from home and didn't find that I was a natural academic. Recently I've reflected on that period, which seems more interesting in retrospect, in a poem with the working title 'Nineteen Eighty Five', set a year after Orwell's *Nineteen Eighty Four*. The poem refers to 'the first of several bids for freedom' and the U.C.D. adventure was a failed bid. At the risk of narcissism I'll mention an article that I wrote — as one of the hundreds of Irish writers interested in cricket! — in a book called *Playing the Field* that is just as much an anatomisation of life in those eight years between leaving UCD and the first volume as it is about cricket. That was a transition

period where someone who left college with aspirations to write poetry became somebody who thought of himself as a poet without embarrassment.

Before the first book, THE HISTORY OF RAIN, *was published in 1993 'Two Poems, After Montale' appeared in the* HONEST ULSTERMAN *in 1989. Why the interest in Montale?*
I came home to the editor's, Robert Johnstone's, acceptance letter for those poems in 1988 as the Irish football team were losing a match to Spain in the Bernabéu Stadium. Steven Staunton, from Dundalk, had a terrible debut. I was jumping around the house, delighted with Montale, while my younger brother looked absolutely disgusted with Ireland in dire straits. Of course, in the late '80s, the world and his wife were obsessed with European poetry. Of all those European voices in translation Montale's struck me most. I'd first come across Montale in Robert Lowell's *Imitations*. I didn't like whole poems but some images were so blindingly striking that I tried to track down more photographic translations — George Kay's in *Penguin Modern Poets* and other glosses of the poems. In the poems I tried to take Montale away from Lowell, to restructure — not translate — his poems as composite versions; it was a way of trying to teach myself how to write poetry, to work with a logic of imagery as opposed to fact. I'd hardly stand entirely by those poems now but their success — in terms of being printed then — I took as indicating that I was somehow on the right track.

One of the Montale poems, 'Saturday Night, Sunday Morning', concludes that 'Even a feather duster, murdered, / Can visualize the long arms at the window'. You were responding to a dark moodiness in Montale?
Phrases like that, 'a feather duster, murdered', now make me wince. In those gestation poems from late adolescence I had phrases trying too hard to sound like poetry, as if terrified of being either totally understood or capable of saying something simple well. Those poems? Ancient history. I was attracted though, and still am, to the images of strong sunlight and colour in Montale, to those dark shadows that strong sunlight casts. Someone pointed out that the first book, *The History of Rain*, has all that Mediterranean sunlight which you would hardly associate with living and writing in Dundalk.

I'm reminded that MacNeice — you once mentioned to me that you used his 'Cushendun' model for your poem 'The Good Room' — is also a poet of 'sunlight'.
I'd not discovered MacNeice at that stage though. Paul Durcan had suggested that I read MacNeice's work and, around 1986, I bought his *Collected Poems* in the old paperback centre in Suffolk Street in Dublin. But I didn't really absorb them or read them until much later.

Your poems in 12 BAR BLUES: RAVEN INTRODUCTIONS 6 *(1990), 'from Five Iconic Love Songs' and 'Californian Villanelles', have 'dreams' that 'bled' and the crack of a distant shotgun. You went to Eavan Boland's poetry workshops at Trinity College in the previous year and I'm reminded that her* WAR HORSE *looks like a fearsome, partly northern, beast that breaks into the southern suburbs 'like a rumour of war'.*

Well, despite the title, only three 'Iconic Love songs' actually existed and the other two were never written. Different influences were beginning to infiltrate the work by that stage but many of those poems now look like pure pastiche. Geoffrey Hill was an influence on those. I discovered his collection *Tenebrae*, became interested in poems like 'Hymns to Our Lady of Chartres'. I'm still very interested in the tension between rhetoric and contemporary diction. That should be obvious in the 'Seatown' poems, although in a less obvious or ham-fisted way. Those early, sunny, 'Villanelles' are re-works of REM songs set in California where I'd never been at that stage: 'early summer... your mouth... your yellowing dress'. I did four readings there last year and didn't dare read those poems although, to use Hill's vocabulary, I atoned for having written them by completing a long poem, 'Timezones', when I came home.

From REM to the Rosary. One of those 'Iconic Love Songs' has the supplication 'Pray for us'; another wishes for 'the strength to run' having 'jeered the mere consolation of belief.' In 20TH CENTURY STUDIES *(November 1970) Derek Mahon notes 'an assumption of faith in Heaney's work and an assumption of ecclesiastical formality in Longley's attitude to birth, marriage and death...'; Edna Longley's* POETRY & POSTERITY *(2000) notes the redemptive or apocalyptic in Mahon and the transcendence in Heaney. In what way does religion or its vocabulary feature in your work?*

Those invocations or incantations, 'Pray for us', are a nineteen year old poet playing with rhetoric. It's not just a juvenile preoccupation because that conflict between 'high' and 'low' styles never goes away. Recently Hugo Williams, in the *TLS*, recalled a conversation with Michael Hofmann where he expressed a desire to abandon a 'low' style (with which they are both associated) for a 'high' one to the dismay of the Anglo-German poet. Williams's view has a lot of truth in it though: you only write in a 'low' style as a substitute for a 'high' style, an indirect way of recognising that this style is neither tenable nor acceptable in 2001. But the subconscious wish or aspiration that poems are written to be read in a cathedral still remains. I start every poem with that aspiration buried far back in my head, hoping it won't have to be compromised. It's like Donald Davie's famous phrase about the Movement's 'lowered sights and patiently diminished expectations'. It's just that I think that description applies to almost all poetry. It seems to be that experimental poetry is born of a refusal to lower its sights. The vast majority of it is seriously rhetorical.

You've never started to consciously retain or rework the language of religion — the rosary as a semi-pagan prayer, as in John Montague's 'Hillmother'?
No. Dundalk, where I grew up, is a highly secular town. Perhaps the ways in which the "Troubles" meant that one's religion often seemed to define political allegiance as well as a spiritual self-definition in the North were less acutely felt here. My parents were churchgoers by rote but I didn't hear the rosary at home and when I abandoned mass at thirteen there was little said at home. If my family had read those references to the rosary in 'Iconic Love Songs' they'd have thought I was either rebelling towards religion or mixing with a bad lot.

The title poem in THE HISTORY OF RAIN *is dedicated to Johnny McCabe and set in 1940. Why did you call this poem, this volume,* THE HISTORY OF RAIN *?*
I liked the title at that time and it tied in with a lot of confluences in the poems where rain appeared a lot and there's a concern with the metaphorical dimensions of the weather. I almost used a sentence from Mandelstam's *Notebooks* as an epigraph for the book: 'The storm in nature acts as a prototype for the historical event'. The title now looks overly poetic and, I suppose, I've that uneasy relationship that many poets have with their first book. Recently I listened sympathetically to a poet on the radio describing his fantasy of creating an art installation by burying every copy of his first volume. The only poem, apart from 'Mengele's House', that I read on any regular basis in public is 'The Last Cage House in Drogheda': it nicks the form of Derek Mahon's 'Disused Garage in County Cork'; it has strong, Mahon-type, rifts in it; it fits with the whole notion of the weather as a catalyst for social change or national independence that's in the book.

'National independence' raises the question of poetry and politics. There's the noise of border surveillance posts, 'tundral outposts', foreshortened to become 'deafening' in poems like 'Blood' in SEATOWN. *I'm not sure, though, if the ambiguous 'states' (emotional or political) of that book indicate whether politics is a central or peripheral concern in the poetry?*
The relationship is pretty tenuous but it's there. As in other poetry the vocabulary and phrases are steeped in meanings which far outweigh their immediate surface sense. 'Swanns Cross' is probably the most obviously politicised poem in *Seatown* and it describes my grandfather's arrest during the War of Independence for his part in a famous shoot-out on the platform of Clones Railway Station in 1921 with the A Specials. He was arrested two days after that shoot-out and taken to Crumlin Road prison

in Belfast from which he escaped dressed up as a woman. 'Swann's Cross' treats those facts as poetic subject matter. My own personal political allegiances might be described loosely as Republican in an ambiguous, confused, kind of way. (I play cricket, for Christ's sake!) And yet the second I start describing myself like that I'll start questioning what I've become. I don't think of poetry, though, as a way of making political or simple moral points. I think of poetry primarily as a spatial form that's essentially amoral. Obviously poetry feeds out into other larger debates about language and power but the individual poem should never pander to political slogans or beliefs or party lines. When people start to suggest that it has to I'll run an Irish mile in the other direction. Poetry and politics? No. In poetry, politics is the last resort of the truly talentless.

This might suggest that your poetry is primarily concerned with time as opposed to history — poetry as disinterested philosophy or contemplation as opposed to historical commitment? 'Nothing important changes', one poem says; others seem to screw up linearity with 'the digital clock's ellipsis' or the appearance of someone who is both 'anticipated and sudden'. Could we substitute the word "time" for history in the poems?
I like the idea of poetry as describing a time or a moment where political beliefs or certainties become blurred but, I guess, you might substitute place for time in the work. Poetry is the moment when historical or political certainties disappear, as opposed to the moment when these things are confirmed.

Sometimes the narrator, as in 'Slips', disappears too? Why?
There's a line in Shakespeare: 'I am conqueror of myself'. I went to such lengths in many poems to elide the 'I', the first person singular. It's a process of depersonalising the poems, the 'I' disappearing between gaps in the images or narrative, a compromise between the lyric impulse and the desire to break form down.

This dispersal of the self, Paul Muldoon's digression within the digression within the digression that he mentions in TO IRELAND, I — *does this lead to the narrator's repeated reappearance in other guises that speak 'me', multiple ventriloquism?*
I prefer the disappearance of the 'me' or the 'I' because it's the most difficult letter to assert in poems. You're cautious about using 'I' or 'me' in poems because it can make them sit up, like Ronald MacDonald, and say, 'look at me, I'm here' until you almost hear the reader groan: 'Oh my God, not you again!' The urge of certain film makers, Jean Luc Godard for instance, to turn the camera on themselves is a kind of last resort. It's as if they're saying, 'I'm making this, lest we forget'. A recent poem,

'This', talks the reader through the process of writing (or of not writing or failing to write) but it's quite tongue-in-cheek. There's the danger of becoming narcissistic in that sort of poem so I wouldn't recommend it as a long term strategy. Dropping the 'I' in poems is a way of not making the reader too conscious of the making of the poem or its making by 'me'.

You have used 'you' to straddle both narrator and the voice of 'the other' who is encountered in that strange poem, 'Landscape with a Canal'.
Yes. The 'you' is a slightly more impersonal or demotic substitute for the 'I', a way of setting up a smokescreen or frosted glass between the reader and myself. It is a strange poem, probably the quickest I've ever written. It was prompted by looking at a dark, black, landscape painting in the Museum of Modern Art in Oslo, where you just about see the silver slick of a canal. I'd have liked that painting on the front cover of *Seatown* but I couldn't quite source it. It was a very beautiful, dark, evocative, landscape, a psychological landscape.

THE HISTORY OF RAIN *has a 1970s David Hockney print activated by 'a restlessness to break out/ from paper pools'. Is there a relationship between visual art and poetry for you?*
There is, but that's not to say I know a great deal about it. The process of writing poems about paintings is a dodgy business. There is a book combining poetry and visual images by the Ulster Museum to which I've contributed but I'm slightly queasy about the whole process since there's a facility when you have the images already in place. A painting that's worth its bacon doesn't need a poem to versify or illustrate it. The word 'cinematic' has been used in relation to the work and I like that because I hope that the poetry itself creates strong, evocative, visual images like cinema.

And yet you've upbraided the Australian, experimental, poet John Kinsella in the TIMES LITERARY SUPPLEMENT *(Aug 18, 2000) in quoting his own lines against him: 'poetry will not tolerate/ a mix of concept and the visual'?*
His use of the visual I've no problems with; his use of the concept or the conceptual in relation to the visual image I do have problems with. Visual images have meanings and nuances beyond language that are already there or apparent. To articulate or nail those meanings of the visual down to one particular meaning or set of meanings is reductive. Why paraphrase, in language, the meaning of a non-linguistic medium? You don't either, by and large, try to paraphrase a poem in a visual image because, when you do, it adds nothing to the poem and will inevitably be limiting — the kind of thing that happens when some documentary-maker reduces the lines of a good poem by Heaney about water, say, to some bloody awful images of one particular stream or another.

You seem attracted to the industrial as a visual image — those spilled coals become 'windfalls' and the Hillman Hunter ends up in the fields.
It's the romance of the post-industrial. It's very English. A poet like Jamie McKendrick is also smitten with those sort of rusty images of nuts and bolts that are redolent of something past and there's a lot of pure nostalgia in it all. That landscape is pure Dundalk. Even though the town appears in many poems I don't really have any further poetic ambitions for this landscape as poetic subject matter. It's my hometown but I'm not a poetic tourist. The poetry is not necessarily tied directly into the realities of the place that I live in. To be honest, both Vona and myself would happily up sticks, but so far have allowed ourselves to be tied to the town by the daft property market in Ireland at the moment. I'd even go so far as to say that a large part of me has grown to hate the place. I thought of prefacing *Seatown* with Hugh O'Neill's quotation about Dundalk but I probably wouldn't have got away with it: 'I loved it more than any town in Ireland, but I would burn it.'

Sport recurrently enters the poetry. Is it a metaphor or analogy for poetry?
I've always been genuinely interested in sport but I'd be slow to give it any grand metaphorical status it doesn't need. There's the old notion of the soul of man being fought over by the sciences, arts and religions. In truth the soul of man has long been won over by organised sport. Anybody who thinks otherwise is kidding himself. Most of the heroes in my life have been sporting heroes and they feed into the work. My brothers and myself idolised the snooker player Alex Higgins. He was Irish and from the North. He was a free spirit and, as my grandmother put it, a Belfast 'gurrier'. He was the original flawed genius. Statistically, he could never be considered among the all-time greats. But he did things on the green baize that no one else would dream of attempting. I liked the sporting analogy Heaney used, after he won an *Irish Times* Prize. He was asked about being the best, winning the most awards. He said that it wasn't a question of being the best, but about what you could do with the ball. It's a good thing to say in that it's both gracious and correct. I know I'll never come close to the poets of that generation. So why do I keep going? Because I hope that every once in a blue moon, like Alex, I'll do something with it that no one else would dream of attempting.

You've mentioned northern poets in general but is there a northern poet whose influence you have particularly assimilated?
Derek Mahon is the poet most often mentioned in relation to the work. I think the influence is less these days. In the early '90s, when myself and Vona lived in Dublin, we'd see him around Baggot Street. We'd totter curiously around after him, not from any sinister or prurient motives but

just out of awe. A poet and friend, Justin Quinn, said he felt the same about Mahon when he'd spot him as writer-in-residence at Trinity in the library. Either literally or metaphorically, we were following Mahon. The work seemed so stylish, so European, with that ironic twinkle in its eye. It wore its whole learning and breadth of reference at such a rakish angle.

In Mahon, too, you sometimes have the narrator's disappearance or dispersal — as in your 'Sublet' where you're only traceable in objects left about the house — in poems where we're put in our place by 'the mute satire bandied about by inanimate objects'. What is it in Mahon's work you warm to?
I'm interested in that whole disappearance of self, of people vanishing: it's a social phenomenon in Ireland and around eighteen hundred people disappear here every year; it's largely the men who never show up again and they seem to, inexplicably, vanish from the centre of their lives or leave their lives behind them. I also think it's one of the most common human fantasies, to lose everything and find oneself without home or family or friends. You'll remember Mahon's 'The Last of the firekings':

> I want to be
> Like the man who descends
> At two milk churns
>
> With a bulging
> String bag and vanishes
> Where the lane turns,
>
> Or the man
> Who drops at night
> From a moving train
>
> And strikes out over the fields
> Where fireflies glow
> Not knowing a word of the language.

That's beautiful. The interest in that image fed into, or rather fed out from, the poems. The poem 'Anon' in *Seatown* is pitched as an existential riddle: 'What's my name? What am I? / Call it an old-fashioned riddle, / a snapshot of the perfect family/with a blind spot in the middle.'

Muldoon too postulates poetry as one of the alternative 'roads' and he's said that, 'One of the ways in which we are most ourselves is that we imagine ourselves to be going somewhere else.'
Yes. In Muldoon you have that dispersal, or split, which keeps coming back to the same point to possibly start all over again. I totally admire the

work but it's not something I can do in my own poems. The alternative is Heaney's great rootedness in accent and time and locale, a belief in eternal verities, and here the 'I' is central to a place and time and it makes the figure of the poet somehow tenable. These are things of great value but I don't feel that I can express them in poems because I don't particularly feel rooted in a place like Dundalk. You buy a house and get tied in commercially to a place for which you feel both affection and frustration but with little sense of roots.

You seem interested in renovating cliché.
Yes, definitely. Phrases within the language are often inherently poetic in a way that supercedes the usual grammatical logic and you use these phrases continually, trying to polish them down or to restore their poetic potential. In the first collection in 'Mengele's House', for instance, the pretty commonplace, colloquial, phrase about 'darkening one's door' is used in place of 'visiting one's house'. Mengele never had the neighbours past his gate and 'never even once/ darkened their doors'. I'm trying to restore the overlooked visual impact of that colloquial phrase to suggest evil without saying evil. You can learn a lot about that sort of thing from Muldoon.

In the last poem in THE HISTORY OF RAIN, *'Silver Birches', the dark underside or two-tone leaves of these trees near the concentration camp at Birkenau carry the ambivalent hope that 'the shadows from a story will survive like this.' Is this a metaphor for the function of poetry?*
Well, I think that poetry has that dual function of saying what it says and saying what it doesn't say. The darkened underside of what is not in a poem is often as important as what is in a poem. Eavan Boland once praised Northern Irish poets for the way they'd mastered the whole process of what is included and excluded in poems.

Inclusions and exclusions are often considerations in writing poems about love and sex where private and public worlds are sometimes on the line. You've written poems about love and sex and you claim, in METRE 3 *(August 1997), that in Jamie McKendrick's* THE MARBLE FLY *'His love poems are always sensual, but could never be described as horny.'*
These poems can be a source of confusion. When you write a poem like 'Nobody You'd Know' in the voice of a man whose wife is having an affair some people can assume that it's just pure autobiography. It isn't. I remember Derek Mahon's review of Frank Ormsby's *The Long Embrace*, an anthology of love poems written in Ireland down the centuries. Mahon pointed out that there was nothing for the voyeur. If you did a similar anthology of American or British poetry there would be a lot of sex poems. The whole notion of love as a pledge of decency, companionship and honesty is

slightly dull or safe. I like erotic poetry; I'd like to do a lot more of it. There are poems like 'The Oral Tradition' or 'Green Baize Couplets' but it can be hard to read these to middle-aged Irish couples in public.

You have favourite Irish love poems?
I really like John Montague's famous poem 'All Legendary Obstacles'. It's a great poem. There's Heaney's 'Act of Union' where the intimate or private world of birth, sex and impregnation doubles as a political metaphor for colonisation and that is an inherent part of the Irish tradition. Medbh McGuckian has written some wonderful love poetry. Vona Groarke has written the best love poems of my generation. But I would say that, given that she's my wife and they were written for me!

SEATOWN *was published in 1999. Is it fin de siècle or a pointer towards the twenty first century?*
I think there's more of a fin de siècle in the book and its sense of nostalgia doesn't easily pave the way for a sequel. There are also many stylistic ticks in *Seatown* that I fear will come to seem too much of its age. After I published the first book I wanted to do something more exact which I did, to some extent, but it's important to always move on, to learn to hate your previous work. Right now I hope the third book will be, somehow, larger and freer, noisier, jauntier, more shambolic and through-other, and have more nonsense poetry. This urge for a mutable voice in new poems will have to negotiate with the other voice that tells you that you can't escape the urge for an even quieter or more elegant voice than the one you've already tried to create.

To what extent is this whole process of talking of poems in retrospect, different from that of making a poem?
I did a talk in Trinity College recently on the practise of writing, describing my own methods of composition. I started it off by talking about a documentary I once saw about Matisse that included footage of the artist at work. The close-ups showed the extraordinary fast instinctive movement of his hand. It seems that after Matisse was shown that footage, he became too self-conscious of his own working process and was unable to paint for months. I think, fundamentally, we have to hang on to the notion of poetry as defying paraphrase because if we lose that we've lost everything. Talking about work after it's done can be interesting; it runs the risk of being masturbatory but it's infinitely preferable to talking about work before it gets done and it can be instructive to read about what other poets think about work they have made. I'd certainly be more superstitious or suspicious of talking about work before it gets done. In Dublin you sometimes hear people blathering in the pub about poems/novels/films

they're going to write but I'm superstitious about that as a substitute for getting down to making the actual work. I've the sense that in Belfast more people kept their heads down and produced the work. Only when I've a poem four-fifths completed will I show it to Vona for criticism. So there's a certain amount of healthy secrecy around what will be made. Also, when someone comes to you with their idea for a new poem, it's obvious they haven't a clue how an actual poem happens. Above all else, we have to hold fast to the conviction that poetry is not merely a process of versifying images around a pre-existing "idea" or "meaning". It is a process of creating a whole new 'meaning' which didn't exist before that poem, and which can't subsequently be paraphrased away.

COLETTE BRYCE

You were born in Derry in 1970 and grew up in the Bogside area. The sense of haunted poverty in this Derry landscape is evoked in Seamus Deane's READING IN THE DARK; *the Derry hinterland appears in your poems. How do you see the circumstances, the place or time, you were born into?*

I was born into the current phase of the "Troubles" so I grew up as the war grew up and it was a big part of my life. The "Troubles" were taking place on our doorsteps, literally. There was a constant army presence in our area and houses could be raided at any time. I have memories of raids in the early hours where my mother would make the soldiers stack their rifles under the hall table before going through the house full of sleeping children. Barricades, rioting, burning vehicles, shootings and burnt out buildings were all part of the landscape. But this was normality, it didn't seem strange at the time. I love the town and I grew up in a very close community. There was a lot of unemployment and hardship so emigration still seemed a very real option. Being on the border, I felt equally linked with the South as with the rest of the North. My father has a great love of the countryside so we travelled over the border regularly, and spent a lot of time in Donegal.

'Father, in the face' and 'Emigrant' are poems which refer to parents. How would you describe your family background? Did it influence you in terms of becoming a poet or as a subject in poems?

I'm from a large family, seven sisters and a brother. My mother was a teacher and had a strong belief in education, seeing it as a passport out of unemployment. Poetry wasn't a central thing but song and prayer were. The prayers are stamped forever into my mind, 'to thee do we cry, poor banished children of Eve, to thee do we send up our sighs, mourning and weeping in this vale of tears…', my first awareness of poetry, its rhythms and its power. The 'Desiderata' hung by the front door, its advice to 'Go placidly amid the noise and haste' proving more useful on the way in than out. Hymns, also, and traditional songs. I read for pleasure from an early age and there were always plenty of books around. Becoming a poet was never an option. Being a teacher, or anything with a secure salary, was the ultimate goal. One way my family background has affected my writing is through a sense of collective experience, being constantly surrounded by siblings. Memories of the early years are unconsciously plural: *we* did this, *we* felt that, something happened to us. It took a long time to be able to sort out my individual experience from the group. I'm not sure I've succeeded yet.

What kind of books were around?

My earliest memories of books are of Grimm's and Andersen's Fairy Tales, *Tikki Tikki Tembo* by Arlene Mosel and Enid Blyton stories (we must have got through a ton of them). Having seven older sisters meant an accumulation of children's books by the time I started to read and, later, a build-up of set texts for English, *Classic Irish Drama*, the Brontes, Hardy, Lawrence, Orwell, Harper Lee, various Penguin Shakespeare plays. I still have an old copy of *Dubliners* underlined and annotated in red, blue, black and pencil by four different hands. And an early edition of *Door into the Dark*, complete with doodles and crayon marks. Added to these were heaps of popular fiction, comics, annuals, Agatha Christies, detective and horror stories. *True Irish Ghost Stories* ('Startling accounts of unexplained happenings supplied by people all over Ireland following an appeal made in the national press for evidence of paranormal experiences!') was a favourite. The main family bookshelf included the Illustrated Gospels, the Bible, Webster's Dictionary, a set of *Encyclopaedia Britannica*, The Book of Saints and the collected novels of Dickens.

*Seamus Heaney in 'The Sense of Place' (*PREOCCUPATIONS*) refers to two ways of knowing a place: 'One is lived, illiterate and unconscious, the other learned, literate and conscious.' Educated at St. Eugene's Primary School in the 1970s, you evoke primary school in the poem 'Chapter Eight of A Child's Companion'. How — in what way — did you 'live' and 'learn' Derry back then?*

I lived and learned the strange mix of the religious, the historical and political, and the day to day. Easter is a good example of this mix, preceded by the dark penitence of Lent, then a celebration of the risen Christ, the pagan ritual of Easter eggs, and a march to commemorate the Easter Rising. The symbols of darkness and light were prevalent, the flame being passed from candle to candle in a dark cathedral at the Easter vigil blends with later memories of candlelight protest against conditions in the women's prison. It was all woven together.

At secondary school in Thornhill College, Derry, (1981-88) did you encounter poetry or poets who lasted? Was poetry important at school?

Yes, we studied poetry. I was attracted to the Metaphysical poets, especially Donne through the sheer drama of his address in the poems we read, his grand imperatives, 'Death be not proud', 'Batter my heart, three-personed

God', enough to awaken the laziest student. I also recall studying R.S. Thomas, a poet whose work I've returned to time and again. Many people remember being put off Shakespeare at school, but I had a good experience of the plays (through good teachers) and have retained a love and curiosity about them. We staged a dramatisation from Longfellow's *Song of Hiawatha* where I played the vital role of a robin: 'Do not shoot us, Hiawatha!' was my one line. We drew from an anthology, *Gallery: Poets Past and Present*, starting with Wyatt in the sixteenth century and ending with Heaney, then a young poet. I was appalled when I found it a few years ago and realised that, in five centuries, not one woman poet was included. This communicated a very clear message about poetry to a class full of girls. It seemed that poetry was written by (usually dead) men so there was never a feeling that it was something I could participate in. It was for analysing. Poems were approached as riddles that would reveal an 'answer' if you stared at them and underlined 'key words' for long enough.

In poems like 'Break' (the narrator with the 'Miraculous Medal' and the soldier with the 'bullet proof vest') and 'Hit Shite and It Flies High' the fissures of the "Troubles" seem to appear. Did the "Troubles" affect your life as a teenager in Derry? In what way do the "Troubles" register in the poems?
'Break' comes from a real, remembered incident, the only difference being that the woman in the poem becomes my adult self. It's hard to say how the "Troubles" register in the poems, but they must do and they're bound to. They are part of my landscape. I don't have a conscious wish to avoid them or to comment on them through my work, but if they turn up in a poem I'll let them in. Poems chart their own waters; I find it difficult to sit down and intentionally approach a "subject" in poetry. They just grow, if it's going well, and hopefully, surprise you. Poems that relate to political issues can be hard to handle because the language of politics is so prosaic and manipulative. The challenge is, if they must be written, to find a new way, new language. What comes into poems depends a lot on where you're at in life; I believe there's a time for everything and I don't think I've engaged with that subject matter very much to date.

Were you politically active as a teenager in Derry? Is your poetry political in terms of engaging with the politics of the North or Ireland?
Poetry is political because the people who write it are. I think it was Yehuda Amichai who said that even to live in an ivory tower is a political statement. Political activism was a big part of life in Derry, it was all around me and I was part of it. My remembered experience was of Thatcherism, the Hunger Strikes, memorials, protests and funerals. A lot of it was about remembering and grieving, some of it was about seeking change. I'll never forget the billboard clocking up the days of hunger strikes, the

black armbands, the collective anger. The tension in the air was palpable. This is all part of what I lived and learned, and everything I write is coloured by who I am. I wouldn't say that I attempt to engage with Irish politics through my work, it's not what I'm after. If I wish to engage with politics there are far more direct and effective avenues. However, it's impossible to separate the political from the historical, the social and the moral, and these are things I must engage with in my work.

Other northern poets and writers have been associated with Derry: Robert Greacen, James Simmons, Seamus Deane, Seamus Heaney and, Sean O'Reilly's recent CURFEW AND OTHER STORIES *(2000) draws on Derry as a location. Do you still feel a sense of affinity with writers from Derry or with the place?*
Yes, I do, I seek out writing from and about Derry. A sense of affinity is laced with a sense of distance — perhaps something I need. Deane's novel affected me on a level beyond the beauty of the language and its compositional grace. His realisation of the place and people triggered my own memories of those streets and the stories from my mother's youth, and recognition of the layers of silences and mysteries.

In 1988 you moved to England to study English Literature and Sociology at St. Mary's College, Twickenham (1988-91). Did college confirm your course as a poet? Did you read writers or poets who mattered at college?
I didn't start writing until after university, so I had no course to be confirmed, just a strong interest in and response to poetry. Poets and writers that mattered to me at the time included Blake, Browning, Beckett and Orwell. Larkin and Plath were important and led me forward in my own reading, and eventually into writing. An odder couple would be hard to find, but I was equally drawn to Larkin's rational process and Plath's exploration of the psyche, and to the perfect marriage of voice and craft in both. Larkin's use of the vernacular and his refusal to resort to the myth kitty was also refreshing at that point in my reading. Apart from Plath, women poets didn't really feature, but I did have the opportunity to study twentieth century women writers (fiction mainly) later on, which I took. What we are all looking for in poetry is a sense of our own lives and minds. Writers whose work inspires a sense of recognition are most important to us, and by this I don't mean locality or circumstances but the difficult business of living our lives. For this reason, finding women writers as points of reference was essential for me but this happened more after college. Irish poetry is short of women role models so I had to look elsewhere.

Jesus, Colette: Beckett and Browning — can you eat ice cubes and fruit cake together?
You certainly can, John, but the jury's still out on the long-term side-effects.

Poets are often associated with other disciplines. Heaney has been linked with archaeology and Mahon with anthropology. Did studying sociology matter in terms of writing poems?

Well, I suppose it went towards making me who I am, so it comes into my writing indirectly. At times, this course seemed far more interesting and relevant to me than the literature we were studying. The sociology of race and ethnicity had a big effect on me. At that time, my only experience was of the sectarian divide in Northern Ireland, I had no awareness of what was going on in the world, the wider context. The sociology of language is also something I'm very glad to have studied. The role of language in perpetrating prejudice and oppression, especially around race and gender, was a revelation to me at nineteen and awareness of it was something that I was able to apply to my own life. In terms of writing poems, studying sociology contributed to the development of my social conscience, which in turn has an effect on my writing.

What is the relationship between the North and northern poetry and your work? How would you place the influence of northern poetry in relation to potential influences from other places — Ireland in general, England, America?

I would give it an important place now, but within Irish poetry. To be honest, the border doesn't mean much to me as a reader and writers south of it have been equally influential to me. When I started writing I had no sense of fitting into a northern tradition. It's an almost exclusively male tradition. I've mentioned before the need to find women poets and many of these were contemporary Americans: Elizabeth Bishop, Muriel Rukeyser, Audre Lorde, Sharon Olds as well as Plath; and the Russians, Akhmatova and Tzvetaeva. It wasn't, for me, a question of finding one poet of special significance, rather of learning from the wide range of voices available to me.

Throughout my education, poetry seemed a finite, completed thing. I had no sense of it as living, changing today. Reading younger contemporary poets changed this for me, some of them seemed to be pushing open doors and admitting a good deal of fresh air. I found the work of Carol Ann Duffy, Simon Armitage and Selima Hill inspiring and I could see my own world reflected in their work. I do think there is a right time to read certain poets; some writers failed to reach me as a young graduate yet when I come back to them now I'm able to engage more fully with their work. Ten years down the line I'm sure I'll have different responses. The biennial Poetry International Festival at London's South Bank introduced me to the work of European and international poets I may not have discovered otherwise.

Twelve of your poems appeared in Anvil New Poets 2 *(1995) edited by Carol Ann Duffy; her introduction links your work with the 'dramatic monologue'. Is your work intentionally dramatic and, if so, in what sense?*
The dramatic speaker is a useful device. Poems are not always true, and I have no qualms about using the first person when they're not: it's the voice of the poem rather than a confession from the writer. Each poem finds it's own voice, sometimes it's a part of myself, sometimes an imagined or known character — not always announced to the reader, but they are always fuelled by personal experience. Using other voices in my work can be liberating.

Some of these twelve poems were edited or dropped in your first collection. Why?
All part of the process.

Are there narrative stances — the first person singular or 'we' — which you favour in writing poems?
Probably, on the whole, the first person singular.

Your work has been associated with song. Does this mean you are a lyric poet?
I'm attracted to the lyric, but also to narrative. With only one book behind me it's difficult to say what kind of poet I am, if any. It's hard to know where my work will take me in the future.

Does music from outside the literary tradition — one poem plays Patsy Cline and in another, 'Wish You Were', the 'evenings fall / like discs in a jukebox' — influence what you attempt as a poet?
I don't think so. I grew up listening to my older sisters' records — The Beatles, The Sex Pistols, Fleetwood Mac, Deep Purple, David Bowie. Later on I fell in love with certain voices — Nina Simone singing just about anything has the power to move me in a way that poetry can't. The issue of whether song lyrics are poetry or not has been debated a lot recently, and I'd be on the side of 'not'. They just don't read well.

In one poem, 'Form', you link shape and hunger. How does form or shape emerge in your work? Are there certain forms you favour?
That poem came out of an interest in hunger. I'd been reading around the subject for some time and it continues to interest me. Physical, emotional and spiritual hunger. I was particularly interested in the tradition of hunger artists and fasting saints, eating as a metaphor for interaction with the world. Poems discover their own forms, to communicate their own music. Sound and rhythm dictate them. I can't say I favour any one traditional form over another, I love the possibilities — Muldoon's experimentation with form, for example, never ceases to amaze me. Music is my

central preoccupation when writing; I don't consider any poem to be without form. Successful poems adhere to inner music, inner forms. Formally, I write for the ear more than for the eye. Some is learned, some is instinct.

In 1997 you spent a year in Madrid teaching English at the British Council Institute. Padraic Fiacc answers 'oui' and 'si' to the influence of French and Spanish poetry in his work. Does the appearance of Nevers *(France) and Spain imply that Spanish or French poetry is an assimilated influence in your poetry?*
Non and no. But the Spanish culture and landscape have always attracted me, the visual art more than the poetry. I became interested in Lorca, though, through a love of Andalucia and have translated some poems for pleasure, as the translations that I had access to weren't enough. I've read French poetry in translation over the years but with no noticeable side-effects. I've spent more time reading the Russians and other eastern and central European poets. Reading poetry in translation is always problematic; someone described it well as being like listening to music through a wall.

In 1998 you returned to London and your first collection, THE HEEL OF BERNADETTE, *was published by Picador in 2000. Are there recurring thematic threads in this collection or do you see it as one of individual poems?*
Both, really. Images of lines move through many of the poems, whether visual or of lineage, division and connection. These wouldn't have made a very memorable title though, but they may have prevented people from calling me Bernadette at readings. My experience of writing my first collection was a slow, accumulative process, involving constant rejection of poems. You end up with what you consider to be the strongest poems to date, and hopefully those that are really yours, in terms of moving past your influences.

Ciaran Carson writes in SHAMROCK TEA *of 'icons and other holy images' as 'portals to the trans-temporal world' so that, in writing, 'It is efficacious to choose an appropriate saint's feast day for one's jumping-off point.' How does religion figure in your life and work? There's that wonderful image of the Pope's blessing like the raised arms of a 'cork-screw'; another poem reminds us, a bit like Paul Durcan, that 'Jesus lives / deep in the ditch of my mother's ear.' Is your attitude to religion satirical or serious?*
I don't set out to satirise religion but there are many aspects of the Catholic Church that I find it impossible to respect. The poem 'Itch' is both satirical and serious, about how the judgemental stance encouraged by organised religion can be the cause of a lot of distance between people and a lot of pain. These judgements are usually made about women, around the issue of sexual freedom. But I have also seen some people, my

mother's generation, derive a great deal of solace from religion, from its rituals and promises. These days, I could only call myself 'roughly Christian', in that I believe that basic Christian teaching is a good moral code to live by. I'm interested in morality and I believe in good. I have a sense of God in my life that isn't something I could articulate. I'm Catholic, though, in the same essential way that I'm Irish, having lived and learned it. It's not something that I could change even if I wished to. It's all there.

'The Pieces' seems to read like a list of nouns musically arranged. I'm reminded of Michael Longley's procedure in some poems. What were you after in this poem?
There are some poems that you have doubts about publishing, and that was one — in that I wasn't sure if it admitted the reader. It grew from the pieces of thirty years of photographs, destroyed in distress by someone close to me, that I was trying to piece together again. It's a very visual list. I suppose that I was hoping that the objects or fragments of scenes conveyed something of a life, and that the form itself conveyed something of the irreparable breakdown that had occurred. That's what I was after.

To what extent are love and desire important themes in your work? Are there love poems or poets that you admire?
I worked as a bookseller for a long time. While sales of contemporary poetry were depressingly slow, the market for love poems never diminished — especially for small anthologies, ideally with red covers and "love" clearly visible on the front. Perhaps all poets should try red covers and stick "love" in the title, sales might improve dramatically. Love and desire are important themes for me, but broadly speaking. Love, or the lack of it, affects just about everything. The American poet Sharon Olds writes about love and sex in a singular way, and her love poems to her children are very powerful.

To what extent are Blake's themes of the tension between innocence and experience a central concern in THE HEEL OF BERNADETTE?
To a large extent, in that this tension is a central concern in the part of the mind from which poems come, that meeting of memory, learning and instinct. I think that this tension is central to poetry, all poetry. Blake's songs are important to me. I come back to them every so often and they always elicit a new response.

'Phone' imagines language as linked transference — 'a harness between us, in all fairness, / you in my hereness, me in your thereness.' — and in the last poem in the volume language reaches the 'Nevers of the mind'. Do you have a way of looking at the way poetry or language works or functions?

I find it useful to remember that poetry is essentially about communication, a bridging from one's own experience to that of the reader. Another important factor for me is the ear, harnessing the music of the poem through all of the devices available.

'The Praying Poplars, Easter Saturday' which are 'domino-felled' somehow reminds me of Hopkins and his poplars. Is Hopkins a poet you relate to?
I admire Hopkins' work, but relating to it is a different thing. I find it difficult and brilliant. I've engaged more with Hopkins' work since writing my first book than I was able to before.

You don't appear to mention visual artists or painters in poems. Is visual art or the links between poetry and visual art something that holds little interest for you?
I have a strong interest in visual art and try to keep up with contemporary art as much as I can. Visual art, for me, feeds into certain images or trains of thought rather than inspiring poems about the piece. Sometimes, with conceptual installation work, it is the concept that inspires — if only in terms of a single image. A small lyric 'Wish You Were' has an image — 'these rooms protect / their space with outstretched walls, / and wait'. At the time, I was interested in the work of Rachel Whiteread and had been to see her ghostly sculpture 'House' — a casting of the space inside a terraced house in East London, around which the building had been demolished. Her work made me perceive the spaces we inhabit in a new way. Other contemporary artists I admire are the sculptor Rebecca Horn and the video-artist Tacita Dean, whose recent work 'Fernsehturm' is breathtaking, and poetic. I think all the arts can feed into your creative energy; theatre and world cinema also play a part for me.

Do you think there's a difference in the language or making of visual art and the spoken/written language of poems?
I think there is. Very generally — there is more precision involved in poetry, more responsibility for meaning (over effect), and less acceptance of abstraction.

Does gender matter in relation to the poet's voice or the subject matter of the poems?
That big question. Gender seems to matter far more in how poetry is criticised. Publishing has opened up, thankfully, but criticism seems to find change harder. Male poets are usually criticised in relation to the canon whereas women poets are often discussed as though working in a vacuum. Gender matters in subject matter in the same way as it matters in society. The constraints are external and communicated to women from childhood on, overtly and subtly, and so internalised. A writer, male or female,

has to work against his/her own inner censor, and that's not always easy. I've mentioned the dearth of role models for Irish women poets before, but there are women poets today that will undoubtedly have a positive influence on future generations. I'd like to believe that it gets easier for women with each generation but I think it's a very slow process. The fact that it's still necessary to publish anthologies of 'women poets' is sad.

Paul·Muldoon's 'Author's Note' to his new collection POEMS 1968-1998 *(2001) states that he hasn't revised the poems: 'The person through whom a poem was written is no more entitled to make revisions than any other reader'. Has he been reading those wee black volumes by Frenchmen that have no pictures on the cover and decided to kill himself as a revising author? Does language speak us, speak through us, 'like a holy ghost'?*

It's an interesting question — some believe that Auden should have left well alone in the poems he revised. Leaving out perceived quality, the temptation to reconcile early work with later religious or political beliefs is understandable. It could be argued that, once poems are published in a collection, the author does in some way relinquish ownership, in the way a visual artist can't demand a work back from collectors to change it. If you look at the evolution of Muldoon's work, the poet of *Why Brownlee Left* is a very different person to the author of *Hay*. That's part of the beauty of it, and the author of *The Annals of Chile* should no more be let loose on *New Weather* than vice versa. Poems are of their time and the author of the time. The poems remain while time and the author batter on.

You currently work and live in London as a freelance writer; in the 1990s you seem to have spent as much time there as in the North of Ireland. Does London bring Derry into focus and vice-versa? In what way does living in England shape or influence your voice or alter the co-ordinates with which you perceive Ireland or "home"?

I left Ireland at eighteen, as that was the thing to do at the time. I've lived in Spain for a year but mainly in London. I think living elsewhere has shaped my consciousness, and changed my co-ordinates. I was formed in Derry but continued to grow away from there, and I think the process of really becoming myself took place after leaving Derry. The Derry that comes into poems is definitely of the past, of memory, perceived by my self of that time. That said, I consider Derry home and probably always will. If I had stayed, I might be a very different writer, or exactly the same, or not be writing at all. I'll never know.

As the new century opens do you feel that the North of Ireland and England — London — are converging or diverging in terms of landscapes you inhabit as you move between Heathrow and Derry airport?

I come hurtling into Derry as often as I can — Ryan Air speciality; one steward insisted the planes are fine but that there's always a pocket of turbulence over Derry. Derry has changed a lot since I left in 1988, for the better. Every visit home seemed to reveal new buildings and the city has healed a lot, visibly and psychologically, since I lived there. There's a good atmosphere there, and for me it still feels like a safe place. I can't see the two landscapes converging at all, thanks be to God.

SELECT BIBLIOGRAPHY

ROBERT GREACEN B.1920

POETRY COLLECTIONS:
One Recent Evening (Favil Press, 1944)
The Undying Day (Falcon Press, 1948)
A Garland For Captain Fox (Gallery Press, 1975)
I, Brother Stephen (Profile Poetry, 1978)
Young Mr Gibbon (Profile Poetry, 1979)
A Bright Mask: New & Selected Poems (Dedalus Press, 1985)
Carnival at the River (Dedalus Press, 1990)
Collected Poems 1944-1994 (Lagan Press, 1995)
Protestant Without a Horse (Lagan Press, 1997)

PROSE/CRITICISM:
Brief Encounters: Literary Dublin & Belfast in the 1940's (Cathiar Books, 1991)
Even Without Irene (Dolmen, 1969; re-issued, Lagan Press, 1995)
The Art Of Noel Coward (The Hand and Flower Press, 1953)
The World of C.P. Snow (Scorpion Press, 1962)
The Sash My Father Wore (Mainstream, 1997)
Rooted in Ulster: Nine Ulster Lives (Lagan Press, 2000)

AS EDITOR:
Poems From Ulster (Erskine Mayne, 1942)
Northern Harvest: An Anthology of Ulster Writing (Derrick MacCord, 1944)
Irish Harvest: An Anthology of Poetry & Prose (New Frontiers Press, 1946)

AS CO-EDITOR:
Lyra (The Grey Walls Press, 1942; Co-edited with Alec Comfort.)
The Faber Book of Contemporary Verse (Faber, 1949; Co-edited with Valentin Iremonger.)

ROY MCFADDEN 1921 - 1999

POETRY COLLECTIONS:
Swords and Plough Shares (Routledge, 1943)
Flowers for a Lady (Routledge, 1945)
The Hearts Townland (Routledge, 1947)
The Garryowen (Chatto and Windus, 1971)
Verifications (Blackstaff Press, 1977)

A Watching Brief (Blackstaff Press, 1979)
The Selected Roy McFadden (Blackstaff Press, 1983)
Letters to the Hinterland (Dedalus Press, 1986)
After Seymours Funeral (Blackstaff Press, 1990)
Collected Poems, 1943-1995 (Lagan Press, 1996)

AS CO-EDITOR:
Ulster Voices (1943) Co-edited with Robert Greacen.
Irish Voices (1943) Co-edited with Robert Greacen.
Rann (1948-1953) Co-edited with Barbara Hunter.

PADRAIC FIACC B.1924

POETRY COLLECTIONS:
By the Black Stream (Dolmen, 1969)
Odour of Blood (Goldsmith Press, 1973)
Nights in a Bad Place (Blackstaff Press, 1977)
The Selected Padraic Fiacc (Blackstaff Press, 1979)
Missa Terrablis (Blackstaff Press, 1986)
Ruined Pages: Selected Poems (Blackstaff Press, 1994)
Red Earth (Lagan Press, 1996)
Semper Vacare (Lagan Press, 1999)

AS EDITOR:
The Wearing of the Black (Blackstaff Press, 1974)

JOHN MONTAGUE B.1929

POETRY COLLECTIONS:
Poisoned Lands (MacGibbon and Kee, 1961; revised edition, Dolmen Press, 1977)
A Chosen Light (MacGibbon and Kee, 1967)
Tides (Dolmen Press, 1970)
The Rough Field (Dolmen Press/Blackstaff Press, 1972; Bloodaxe Books, 1989)
A Slow Dance (Dolmen Press, 1970)
The Great Cloak (Dolmen Press, 1978)
Selected Poems (Dolmen Press, 1982)
The Dead Kingdom (Dolmen Press/ Blackstaff Press, 1984)
Mount Eagle Gallery Press, 1988)
New Selected Poems (Gallery Press, 1989)
About Love (Sheep Meadow Press, 1993)
Time in Armagh (Gallery Press, 1993)
Collected Poems: John Montague (Gallery Press, 1995)
Chain Letter (Poetry Society, 1997)
Smashing the Piano (Gallery Press, 2000)
Selected Poems (Penguin, 2001)

PROSE/ CRITICISM:

The Lost Notebook (Mercier Press, 1987)

The Figure in the Cave and Other Essays (Lilliput Press, 1989, edited by Antoinette Quinn)

Company (Gerald Duckworth, 2001)

AS EDITOR:

The Faber Book of Irish Verse (Faber, 1974)

Bitter Harvest (Scribner's, 1989)

SHORT STORIES:

Death of a Chieftain (MacGibbon and Kee, 1964; Poolbeg Press, 1978)

An Occassion of Sin (White Pine Press, 1992, edited by B Callaghan & B. Lampe)

A Love Present and Other Stories (Wolfhound Press, 1997)

TRANSLATIONS:

Selected Poems by Francis Ponge, translated by Margaret Guiton, John Montague & C.K. Williams (Faber & Faber, 1998)

Carnac by Guillevic, translated by John Montague (Bloodaxe Books, 1999)

James Simmons 1933 - 2001

POETRY COLLECTIONS:

Late but in Earnest (Bodley Head, 1967)

In the Wilderness and Other Poems (Bodley Head, 1969)

Energy to Burn (Bodley Head, 1971)

No Land is Waste, Dr Eliot (Keepsake Press, 1972)

The Long Summer Still to Come Press (Blackstaff Press, 1973)

West Strand Visions (Blackstaff Press, 1974)

Judy Garland and the Cold War (Blackstaff Press, 1976)

The Selected James Simmons (Blackstaff Press, 1978)

Constantly Singing (Blackstaff Press, 1980)

From the Irish (Blackstaff Press, 1985)

Poems 1956-1986 (Gallery Press/Bloodaxe Books, 1986)

Mainstream (Salmon Publishing, 1994)

Elegies (Sotto Voice Press, 1995)

The Company of Children (Salmon Publishing, 1999)

PROSE/CRITICISM:

Sean O'Casey (Macmillan, 1983)

AS EDITOR:

Honest Ulsterman (Ulsterman Publications, 1968: issues 1-19)

Ten Irish Poets (Carcanet Press, 1974)

RECORDINGS/SONG COLLECTIONS:

City and Eastern

Love in the Post

The Rostrevor Sessions

Latest Songs

SEAMUS HEANEY B. 1939

POETRY COLLECTIONS:
Death of a Naturalist (Faber & Faber, 1966)
Door into the Dark (Faber & Faber, 1969)
Wintering Out (Faber & Faber, 1972)
North (Faber & Faber 1975)
Field Work (Faber & Faber, 1979)
Selected Poems 1965-1975 (Faber & Faber, 1980)
Sweeney Astray: A Version from the Irish (Field Day/ Faber & Faber, 1983)
Station Island (Faber & Faber, 1984)
The Haw Lantern (Faber & Faber, 1987)
New Selected Poems 1966-1987 (Faber & Faber, 1990)
Seeing Things (Faber & Faber, 1991)
Sweeney's Flight (with photographs by Rachel Giese)
Hailstones (Gallery Press, 1984)
The Spirit Level (Faber & Faber, 1996)
Opened Ground: Poems 1966-1996 (Faber & Faber, 1998)
Electric Light (Faber & Faber, 2001)

PROSE/CRITICISM:
Homage to Robert Frost, with Joseph Brodsky and Derek Walcott (1977)
Preoccupations: Selected Prose 1968-1978 (Faber & Faber, 1980)
The Government of the Tongue (Faber & Faber, 1988)
The Redress of Poetry: Oxford Lectures (Faber & Faber, 1995)
The Place of Writing: Richard Ellman lectures at Emory University (Scholars Press, 1989)
Crediting Poetry (Gallery Press, 1996)

PLAYS:
The Cure at Troy, a version of Sophocles' Philoctetus (Faber & Faber, 1990)

AS EDITOR/CO-EDITOR:
Soundings: An Anthology of New Irish Poetry (Blackstaff Press, 1972)
The Rattle Bag: An Anthology of Poetry, selected by Seamus Heaney and Ted Hughes (Faber & Faber, 1982)
The School Bag, ed. Seamus Heaney & Ted Hughes (Faber & Faber, 1997)

TRANSLATIONS:
Beowulf (Faber & Faber, 1999)
The Midnight Verdict (Gallery Press, 1993; re-issued 2000)
Laments by Jan Kochanowski, with Stanislav Baranczak (Faber & Faber, 1995)

MICHAEL LONGLEY B.1939

POETRY COLLECTIONS:
No Continuing City (Macmillan, 1969)
An Exploded View (Gollanz, 1973)

Man Lying on a Wall (Gollanz, 1976)
The Echo Gate (Secker and Warburg, 1979)
Selected Poems 1963-1980 (Wakeforest University Press, 1981)
Poems 1963-1983 (Secker and Warburg, 1991)
Gorse Fires (Secker and Warburg, 1991)
The Ghost Orchid (Jonathan Cape, 1995)
Broken Dishes (Abbey Press, 1998)
The Weather in Japan (Jonathan Cape, 2000)

PROSE/CRITICISM/AUTOBIOGRAPHY:
Tuppeny Stung: Autobiographical Chapters (Lagan Press, 1994)

AS EDITOR:
Causeway: The Arts In Ulster (The Arts Council of Northern Ireland, 1971)
Over the Moon, Under the Stars (The Arts Council of Northern Ireland, 1971)
Louis MacNeice: Selected Poems (Faber and Faber, 1988)
Poems: W.R. Rodgers (Gallery Press, 1993)

SEAMUS DEANE B. 1940

POETRY COLLECTIONS:
Gradual Wars (Irish University Press, 1972)
Rumours (DolmenPress, 1977)
History Lessons (Gallery Press, 1983)
Selected Poems (Gallery Press, 1988)

PROSE/CRITICISM:
Celtic Revivals: Essays in Modern Irish Literature (Faber, 1985)
A Short History of Irish Literature (Hutchinson, 1986)
The French Enlightenment & Revolution in England 1789-1832
    (Harvard University Press, 1988)
Strange Country: Modernity and Nationhood in Irish Writing Since 1790
    (Claredon Press Oxford, 1997)

AS EDITOR:
Field Day Anthology of Irish Writing, c. 550 — 1990, 3 vols (Faber, 1991)

AS CO-EDITOR:
Atlantis
Crane Bag, Vol III, no 1 & 2, 1979 (Wolfhound Press, Crane Bag Vols. 1 &2, 1982)

PROSE FICTION:
Reading in the Dark (Jonathan Cape, 1996)

DEREK MAHON B.1941

POETRY COLLECTIONS:
Night-Crossing (Oxford University Press, 1968)
Lives (Oxford University Press, 1972)
The Snow Party (Oxford University Press, 1975)
Poems 1962-1978 (Oxford University Press, 1979)
Courtyards in Delft (Gallery Press, 1981)
The Hunt By Night (Oxford University Press, 1982)
Antartica (Gallery Press, 1985)
Selected Poems (Viking/Gallery, 1991)
The Hudson Letter (Gallery Press, 1995)
The Yellow Book (Gallery Press, 1997)
Collected Poems (Gallery Press, 1999)

PROSE/CRITICISM:
Journalism, edited by Terence Brown (Gallery Press, 1996)

AS EDITOR/CO-EDITOR:
The Sphere Book of Modern Irish Poetry (Sphere Books, 1972)
The Penguin Book of Irish Poetry, with Peter Fallon (Penguin Books, 1990)

TRANSLATIONS/POETRY:
Phlleppe Jacottet, Selected Poems (Penguin 1988)
Words in the Air: A selection of poems by Philippe Jacottet (Gallery Press, 1998)

TRANSLATIONS/PLAYS:
The Chimeras, a version of Les Chimeras by Gérard de Nerval (Gallery Press, 1982)
High Time, a version of Moliere's L'Ecole des Maris (Gallery Press, 1985)
The School for Wives, a version of Moliere's L'ecole des Femmes (Gallery Press, 1986)
The Bacchae (Gallery Press, 1991)
Phaedra, a version of Racine (Gallery Press, 1996)

FRANK ORMSBY B. 1947

POETRY COLLECTIONS:
A Store of Candles (Oxford University Press, 1977; re-issued by Gallery Press, 1986.)
A Northern Spring (Gallery Press/Secker & Warburg, 1986)
The Ghost Train (Gallery Press, 1995)

AS EDITOR:
Poets from the North of Ireland (Blackstaff Press, 1979; re-issued Blackstaff Press, 1990)
Northern Windows: An Anthology of Ulster Autobiography (Blackstaff Press, 1987)
The Long Embrace: Twentieth-century Irish Love Poems (Blackstaff Press, 1987)
Thine in Storm & Calm: An Amanda McKittrick Ross Reader (Blackstaff Press, 1988)
The Collected Poems of John Hewitt (Blackstaff Press, 1991)
A Rage For Order: Poetry of the Northern Ireland Troubles (Blackstaff Press, 1992)
The Hip Flask (Blackstaff Press, 2000)

AS EDITOR/ CO-EDITOR:

Honest Ulsterman (1969-1989, Ulsterman Publications, co-edited with Michael Foley, 1969-72, & Robert Johnstone, 1972-89).

CIARAN CARSON B. 1948

POETRY COLLECTIONS:

The New Estate (Blackstaff Press, 1976)
The Irish for No (Gallery Press, 1987)
The New Estate & Other Poems (Gallery Press, 1988)
Belfast Confetti (Gallery Press/Bloodaxe Books, 1989)
First Langauge (Gallery Press, 1993)
Letters From the Alphabet (Gallery Press, 1995)
Opera Et Cetera (Gallery Press, 1996)
The Twelfth of Never (Gallery Press, 1998)
The Alexandrine Plan (Gallery Press, 1998)
The Ballad of HMS Belfast (Gallery Press, 1999)

PROSE/CRITICISM:

The Pocket Guide to Irish Traditional Music (Appletree Press, 1986)
Last Night's Fun: A Book about Traditional Music (Jonathan Cape, 1996)
The Star Factory (Granta Publications, 1997)
Fishing for Amber (Granta Publications, 1999)
Shamrock Tea (Granta Publications, 2001)

TOM PAULIN B. 1949

POETRY COLLECTIONS:

A State of Justice (Faber & Faber, 1977)
The Strange Museum (Faber & Faber, 1980)
Liberty Tree (Faber & Faber, 1983)
Fivemiletown (Faber & Faber, 1987)
Selected Poems, 1972-1990 (Faber & Faber, 1993)
Walking A Line (Faber & Faber, 1994)
The Wind Dog (Faber & Faber, 1999)

PROSE / CRITICISM:

Thomas Hardy: The Poetry of Perception (Macmillan, 1975)
Ireland & The English Crisis (Bloodaxe Books, 1984)
Minotaur: Poetry & the Nation State (Faber, 1992)
Writing to the Moment: Selected Criticial Essays (Faber & Faber, 1996)
The Day-Star of Liberty: William Hazlitt's Radical Style (Faber & Faber, 1998)

AS EDITOR:

The Faber Book of Political Verse (Faber & Faber, 1986)
The Faber Book of Vernacular Verse (Faber & Faber, 1990)

ADAPTATIONS:
The Riot Act: A Version of Sophocles' Antigone (Faber & Faber, 1985)
Seize the Fire: A Version of Aeschylus' Prometheus Bound (Faber & Faber, 1990)

PLAY:
The Hillsborough Script: A Dramatic Satire (Faber & Faber, 1987)

MEDBH MCGUCKIAN B. 1950

POETRY COLLECTIONS:
The Flower Master (Oxford University Press, 1982; Gallery Press, 1993)
Venus and the Rain (Oxford University Press, 1984; Gallery Press, 1994)
On Ballycastle Beach (Oxford University Press, 1988; Gallery Press, 1995)
Two Women, Two Shores, with Nuala Archer (Salmon Publishing & New Poets
   Series, Baltimore, Maryland, 1989)
Marconi's Cottage (Gallery Press, 1991)
Captain Lavender (Gallery Press, 1994)
Selected Poems:1978-1994 (Gallery Press, 1997)
Shelmalier (Gallery Press, 1998)
Drawing Bellerinas (Gallery Press, 2001)

PROSE/CRITICISM:
Horsepower Pass By (Cranagh Press, 1999)

AS EDITOR:
The Big Striped Golfing Umbrella: An Anthology of Children's Poetry from Northern Ireland
   (Arts Council of Northern Ireland, 1982)

PAUL MULDOON B. 1951

POETRY COLLECTIONS:
New Weather (Faber & Faber, 1973)
Mules (Faber & Faber; Wake Forest University Press, 1977)
Why Brownlee Left (Faber & Faber; Wake Forest University Press, 1980)
Quoof (Faber & Faber; Wake Forest University Press, 1983)
The Wishbone (Gallery Press, 1995)
Mules and Early Poems (Wake Forest University Press, 1987)
Selected Poems 1968-1983 (Faber & Faber, 1986)
Meeting the British (Faber & Faber; Wake Forest University Press, 1987)
Selected Poems 1968-1986 (Ecco Press, 1987)
Madoc — A Mystery (Faber & Faber; Farrar, Straus & Giroux, 1994)
The Prince of the Quotidian (Gallery Press; Wake Forest University Press, 1994)
The Annals of Chile (Faber & Faber; Farrar, Straus & Giroux, 1994)
New Selected Poems 1968-1993 (Faber & Faber, 1996)
Kerry Slides, with photographs by Bill Doyle (Gallery Press, 1996)

Hopewell Haiku (Warwick Press, 1997)
Hay (Faber & Faber; Farrar, Straus & Giroux, 1998)
Poems 1968-1998(Faber & Faber 2001)

PROSE/CRITICISM:
To Ireland, I (OUP, 2000)

PLAYS:
Monkeys (BBC, 1989)
Six Honest Serving Men (Gallery Press, 1995)

AS EDITOR:
The Scrake of Dawn: Poems by Young People from Northern Ireland (Blackstaff Press, 1979)
The Faber Book of Contemporary Irish Poetry (Faber & Faber, 1986)
The Essential Byron (Ecco Press, 1989)
The Faber Book of Beasts (Faber & Faber, 1997)

TRANSLATION:
The Astrakan Cloak: Poems in Irish by Nuala Ni Dhomnaill with translations into English by Paul Muldoon (Gallery Press, 1992)
The Birds, after Aristophanes (Faber & Faber, 1997)

BOOKS FOR CHILDREN:
The O-O's Party, New Year's Eve (Gallery Press, 1980)
The Last Thesaurus (Faber & Faber, 1995)
The Noctuary of Narcissus Batt (Faber & Faber, 1997)

LIBRETTI:
Shining Brow (Faber & Faber, 1993)
Bandana (Faber & Faber, 1999)
Vera of Las Vegas (Gallery Press, 2001)

GERALD DAWE B. 1952

POETRY COLLECTIONS:
Sheltering Places (Blackstaff Press, 1978)
The Lundys Letter (Gallery Press, 1985)
Sunday School (Gallery Press, 1991)
Heart of Hearts (Gallery Press, 1995)
The Morning Train (Gallery Press, 1999)

PROSE/CRITICISM:
How's the Poetry Going? (Lagan Press, 1991)
A Real Life Elsewhere; Literary Irelands (Lagan Press, 1993)
False Faces: Poetry, Politics and Place (Lagan Press, 1994)
Against Piety: Essays in Irish Poetry (Lagan Press, 1995)
The Rest is History (Abbey Press, 1998)
Stray Dogs and Dark Horses: selected essays on Irish writing and criticism (Abbey Press, 2000)

AS EDITOR:
The Younger Irish Poets (Blackstaff Press, 1982; revised edition, 1991)
Yeats: the poems, a new selection (Anna Livia Press, 1991)

AS CO-EDITOR:
Across a Roaring Hill: The Protestant Imagination in Modern Ireland (Blackstaff Press, 1985)
The Poet's Place: Essays on Ulster Literature & Society in Honour of John Hewitt,
　　with John Wilson Foster (Institute of Irish Studies, 1991)
Ruined Pages: Selected Poems of Padraic Fiacc, with Aodán MacPoilin (Blackstaff
　　Press, 1994)
Krino: 1986-1996, an anthology of modern Irish writing, with Jonathan Williams
　　(Gill & MacMillan, 1996)

JEAN BLEAKNEY B. 1956

POETRY COLLECTIONS:
The Ripple Tank Experiment (Lagan Press, 1999)

MOYRA DONALDSON B. 1956

POETRY COLLECTION:
Snakeskin Stilettos (Lagan Press, 1998)
Beneath the Ice (Lagan Press, 2001)

CATHAL Ó SEARCAIGH B. 1956

POETRY COLLECTIONS:
Miontragóid Chathrach (Cló Uî Chuirreáin, 1975)
Tuirlingt (Clódhanna Teoranta, 1978)
Suilé Shuibhne (Coiscéim, 1987)
An Bealach 'na Bhaile (Cló Iar-Chonnachta, 1991)
Homecoming/An Bealach 'na Bhaile (Cló Iar-Chonnachta, 1996)
Out in the Open (Cló Iar-Chonnachta, 1997)
Eagathóir An Chéad (Cló Iar-Chonnachta, 1997)
Ag Tnúth leis an tSolas (Cló Iar-Chonnachta, 2000)

PROSE/CRITICISM:
Tulach Beag Laoich: Inné agus Innui / Tulach Begley: Past & Present
　　(Glór nGael an Fháilcharraigh, 1994)

CHERRY SMYTH B. 1960

POETRY COLLECTIONS:
When the Lights Go Up (Lagan Press, 2001)

PROSE/CRITICISM:
Queer Notions (Scarlet Press, 1992)
Damn Fine Art by Lesbian Artists (Cassell, 1996)

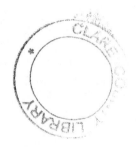

MARTIN MOONEY B. 1964

POETRY COLLECTIONS:
Grub (Blackstaff Press, 1993)
Rasputin & His Children (Blackwater Press, 2000)

AS CO-EDITOR:
Mapmakers' Colours: New Poets of Northern Ireland (Nu-Age Editions, 1988)

CONOR O'CALLAGHAN B. 1968

POETRY COLLECTIONS:
The History of Rain (Gallery Press, 1993)
Seatown (Gallery Press, 1999)

COLETTE BRYCE B. 1970

POETRY COLLECTIONS:
The Heel of Bernadette (Picador, 2000)